BUSINESS AND
GENERAL
REFERENCE
BOOK SERIES
FROM IDG

The GRE® For Dummies®, 2nd E...

W9-BZD-860

Sheet

Success on the Verbal Section

General tips

- Use roots, prefixes, and suffixes to determine the gist of an unfamiliar word.
- Guess quickly at questions that have unfamiliar answer choices.
- Choose positive or neutral answers, not negative ones.

Antonym tips

- Create an approximate definition of the word in your mind.
- Predict the obvious opposite.
- Remember that words have more than one meaning.

Reading Comprehension tips

- The questions are usually arranged in the same order as the information in the passage.
- Guess on Roman numerals or negative/exception questions and then return to them if you have extra time.
- Don't choose an answer simply because it's true; make certain that it answers the question correctly.

Steps for Completing Analogy questions

1. Make up a sentence that uses both words (one that describes the relationship between the two words).
2. Use that sentence on each answer choice.
3. If two answer choices have the same relationship, eliminate them; they can't both be right.
4. Watch out for answers that have the reverse relationship of the question word (part to whole, not whole to part for example).

Steps for Figuring Out Sentence Completion questions

1. Read the whole sentence to get its gist before you look at the individual blanks.
2. Look for key connector words, such as *but, however, despite:* they change the meaning of the sentence.
3. Decide whether the blanks need positive or negative words.
4. Remember that easy questions come first in the test and usually have easy answers.

This test is rated PG — Proctor Guarded.

Proctors have been genetically altered to have eyes in the backs of their heads; they'll catch you if you peek at this cheat sheet during the GRE. Learn it, and then burn it.

BUSINESS AND GENERAL REFERENCE BOOK SERIES FROM IDG

The GRE® For Dummies®, 2nd Edition

Cheat Sheet

Tips for Success on the Math Section

General tips

- ✔ Lose the calculator, scratch paper, and testing aids. You can't use them on the test.
- ✔ The GRE tests algebra, geometry, and arithmetic, not calculus or trig.
- ✔ Memorize formulas before you take the test. The GRE doesn't provide them.

Quantitative Comparison tips

- ✔ Do these problems first, but triple-check answers. They're easy but full of traps.
- ✔ Remember that the answer choices are the same for every question. Choose A if Column A is greater than Column B; B, if Column B is greater; C, if the two columns are equal; and D, if insufficient information is given. Don't choose E.
- ✔ If the columns seem to be equal, do the calculations required to prove that they are.
- ✔ Play the what-if game by plugging in 1, then 2, 0, −1, −2, and ½. If the answer depends on what you plug in for the variable, choose D.

Problem-Solving tips

- ✔ Circle what the question specifically asks for: perimeter, area, length, degree, fraction, percentage, and so on.
- ✔ Before you begin working on the problem, read the answer choices. You may be able to estimate and answer without working out the solution.
- ✔ When you guess at an answer, make a mark in the margin and come back to the problem if you have extra time.
- ✔ Plug answer choices into the question to see which one works. Do the easy choices first; you may not have to do the hard ones.

Tips for Success on the Analytical Ability Section*

Logical Reasoning tips

- ✔ Do these questions before you do the Analytical Reasoning questions.
- ✔ Determine the style of the questions (strengthens/weakens, draws conclusion, parallel reasons, and so on) and complete the ones you do best first.

Analytical Reasoning tips

- ✔ In the margin, jot down a list of the people or items involved in the question.
- ✔ Complete the *always/never* questions first.
- ✔ Be prepared to make more than one diagram when new information is introduced.
- ✔ Don't use information given in one question as you answer another question.

*Some schools don't use the Analytical Ability section score.

Tips for GRE Success*

- ✔ Half right is average. You don't have to get every question correct.
- ✔ The questions go from easier to harder; most people don't get the last few questions correct.
- ✔ Guess when you don't know the correct answer; the GRE doesn't subtract points for wrong answers.
- ✔ Mark your answers on the grid *and* in the booklet — in case you get on the wrong line in the grid and so that you can double-check your work.

*These tips do not apply to the CAT version of the GRE. On the CAT, you can't return to questions, so be careful to get the correct answers the first time.

IDG BOOKS WORLDWIDE

...For Dummies™ : Best-Selling Book Series for Beginners

THE GRE®
FOR
DUMMIES™

2ND EDITION

THE GRE® FOR DUMMIES™

2ND EDITION

by Suzee Vlk

IDG BOOKS WORLDWIDE

IDG Books Worldwide, Inc.
An International Data Group Company

Foster City, CA ♦ Chicago, IL ♦ Indianapolis, IN ♦ Dallas, TX

The GRE® For Dummies™, 2nd Edition

Published by
IDG Books Worldwide, Inc.
An International Data Group Company
919 E. Hillsdale Blvd.
Suite 400
Foster City, CA 94404

Library of Congress Catalog Card No.: 96-76365

ISBN: 1-56884-399-2

Printed in the United States of America

10 9 8 7 6 5 4 3 2 1

2M/RY/QW/ZW/IN

Distributed in the United States by IDG Books Worldwide, Inc.

Distributed by Macmillan Canada for Canada; by Contemporanea de Ediciones for Venezuela; by Distribuidora Cuspide for Argentina; by CITEC for Brazil; by Ediciones ZETA S.C.R. Ltda. for Peru; by Editorial Limusa SA for Mexico; by Transworld Publishers Limited in the United Kingdom and Europe; by Academic Bookshop for Egypt; by Levant Distributors S.A.R.L. for Lebanon; by Al Jassim for Saudi Arabia; by Simron Pty. Ltd. for South Africa; by Pustak Mahal for India; by The Computer Bookshop for India; by Toppan Company Ltd. for Japan; by Addison Wesley Publishing Company for Korea; by Longman Singapore Publishers Ltd. for Singapore, Malaysia, Thailand, and Indonesia; by Unalis Corporation for Taiwan; by WS Computer Publishing Company, Inc. for the Philippines; by WoodsLane Pty. Ltd. for Australia; by WoodsLane Enterprises Ltd. for New Zealand. Authorized Sales Agent: Anthony Rudkin Associates for the Middle East and North Africa.

For information on where to purchase IDG Books Worldwide's books outside the U.S., contact IDG Books Worldwide's International Sales department at 415-655-3078 or fax 415-655-3281.

For information on foreign language translations, contact IDG Books Worldwide's Foreign & Subsidiary Rights department at 415-655-3018 or fax 415-655-3281.

For sales inquiries and special prices for bulk quantities, contact IDG Books Worldwide's Sales department at 415-655-3200 or write to the address above.

For information on using IDG Books Worldwide's books in the classroom or for ordering examination copies, contact IDG Books Worldwide's Educational Sales department at 800-434-2086 or fax 817-251-8174.

is a trademark under exclusive license to IDG Books Worldwide, Inc., from International Data Group, Inc.

5/22/96

About the Author

Suzee Vlk

Although more likely to admit to being a mortician, used-car salesperson, or guinea pig for Army experiments, Suzee Vlk has been a test prep specialist since 1975, working her way through graduate business school and law school teaching courses in GRE, GMAT, LSAT, SAT, and ACT preparation. She found the paranoia and take-no-prisoners mind-set required for doing well on the GRE a big help in developing cutthroat tactics to use in the boardroom or courtroom.

Today Suzee is president of Suzee Vlk Test Prep (no ego involved in *that* company name!) and has taught thousands of students in dozens of courses at universities and private corporations, including "mature" adults who have been out of school for a decade (or two or three) and international students from countries all over the world. (All victims have, so far, survived.) She has written material used in GRE and SAT preparation software and videos (starring in one set of videos when she was younger and blonder). Her prep books for the GRE and other standardized exams have been published worldwide.

Suzee currently specializes in one-on-one tutorials and teaches GRE prep tricks and traps to all levels of students, from those who are struggling to remember the basics ("Let's see. A triangle has three sides, or is it four?") to whiz kids who will probably be her boss one day. Her students have not only been accepted at graduate business programs in colleges and universities nationwide, including such dream schools as Harvard and Stanford, but have done well enough on their GREs to be awarded scholarships (to the unbounded joy of their parents, who can now spend what's left of their kids' education funds on sailboats, flashy sports cars, and other midlife crises toys).

ABOUT IDG BOOKS WORLDWIDE

VIII
WINNER
Eighth Annual
Computer Press
Awards 1992

IX
WINNER
Ninth Annual
Computer Press
Awards 1993

Welcome to the world of IDG Books Worldwide.

IDG Books Worldwide, Inc., is a subsidiary of International Data Group, the world's largest publisher of computer-related information and the leading global provider of information services on information technology. IDG was founded more than 25 years ago and now employs more than 7,700 people worldwide. IDG publishes more than 250 computer publications in 67 countries (see listing below). More than 70 million people read one or more IDG publications each month.

Launched in 1990, IDG Books Worldwide is today the #1 publisher of best-selling computer books in the United States. We are proud to have received 8 awards from the Computer Press Association in recognition of editorial excellence and three from Computer Currents' First Annual Readers' Choice Awards, and our best-selling ...*For Dummies*® series has more than 19 million copies in print with translations in 28 languages. IDG Books Worldwide, through a joint venture with IDG's Hi-Tech Beijing, became the first U.S. publisher to publish a computer book in the People's Republic of China. In record time, IDG Books Worldwide has become the first choice for millions of readers around the world who want to learn how to better manage their businesses.

Our mission is simple: Every one of our books is designed to bring extra value and skill-building instructions to the reader. Our books are written by experts who understand and care about our readers. The knowledge base of our editorial staff comes from years of experience in publishing, education, and journalism — experience which we use to produce books for the '90s. In short, we care about books, so we attract the best people. We devote special attention to details such as audience, interior design, use of icons, and illustrations. And because we use an efficient process of authoring, editing, and desktop publishing our books electronically, we can spend more time ensuring superior content and spend less time on the technicalities of making books.

You can count on our commitment to deliver high-quality books at competitive prices on topics you want to read about. At IDG Books Worldwide, we continue in the IDG tradition of delivering quality for more than 25 years. You'll find no better book on a subject than one from IDG Books Worldwide.

John J. Kilcullen

John Kilcullen
President and CEO
IDG Books Worldwide, Inc.

IDG Books Worldwide, Inc., is a subsidiary of International Data Group, the world's largest publisher of computer-related information and the leading global provider of information services on information technology. International Data Group publishes over 250 computer publications in 67 countries. Seventy million people read one or more International Data Group publications each month. International Data Group's publications include: **ARGENTINA:** Computerworld Argentina, GamePro, Infoworld, PC World Argentina; **AUSTRALIA:** Australian Macworld, Client/Server Journal, Computer Living, Computerworld, Digital News, Network World, PC World, Publishing Essentials, Reseller; **AUSTRIA:** Computerwelt, PC TEST; **BELARUS:** PC World Belarus; **BELGIUM:** Data News; **BRAZIL:** Annuário de Informática, Computerworld Brazil, Connections, Super Game Power, Macworld, PC World Brazil, Publish Brazil, SUPERGAME; **BULGARIA:** Computerworld Bulgaria, Networkworld/Bulgaria, PC & MacWorld Bulgaria; **CANADA:** CIO Canada, ComputerWorld Canada, InfoCanada, Network World Canada, Reseller World; **CHILE:** Computerworld Chile, GamePro, PC World Chile; **COLUMBIA:** Computerworld Colombia, GamePro, PC World Colombia; **COSTA RICA:** PC World Costa Rica/Nicaragua; **THE CZECH AND SLOVAK REPUBLICS:** Computerworld Czechoslovakia, Elektronika Czechoslovakia, PC World Czechoslovakia; **DENMARK:** Communications World, Computerworld Danmark, Macworld Danmark, PC World Danmark, PC World Danmark Supplements, TECH World; **DOMINICAN REPUBLIC:** PC World Republica Dominicana; **ECUADOR:** PC World Ecuador, GamePro; **EGYPT:** Computerworld Middle East, PC World Middle East; **EL SALVADOR:** PC World Centro America; **FINLAND:** MikroPC, Tietoverkko, Tietoviikko; **FRANCE:** Distributique, Golden, Info PC, Le Guide du Monde Informatique, Le Monde Informatique, Reseaux & Telecoms; **GERMANY:** Computer Business, Computerwoche, Computerwoche Extra, Computerwoche Focus, Electronic Entertainment, GamePro, I/M Information Management, Macwelt, PC Welt; **GREECE:** GamePro, Macworld & Publish; **GUATEMALA:** PC World Centro America; **HONDURAS:** PC World Centro America; **HONG KONG:** Computerworld Hong Kong, PCWorld Hong Kong, Publish in Asia; **HUNGARY:** ABCD CD-ROM, Computerworld Szamitastechnika, PC & Mac World Hungary, PC-X Magazine; **INDIA:** Computerworld India, PC World India, Publish in Asia; **INDONESIA:** InfoKomputer PC World, Komputek Computerworld, Publish in Asia; **IRELAND:** ComputerScope, PC Live!; **ISRAEL:** PC World 32 BIT, People & Computers; **ITALY:** Computerworld Italia, Computerworld Italia Special Editions, Lotus Italia, Macworld Italia, Networking Italia, PC Shopping, PC World Italia, PC World/Walt Disney; **JAPAN:** Macworld Japan, Nikkei Personal Computing, SunWorld Japan, Windows World Japan; **KENYA:** East African Computer News; **KOREA:** Hi-Tech Information/Computerworld, Macworld Korea, PC World Korea; **MACEDONIA:** PC World Macedonia; **MALAYSIA:** Computerworld Malaysia, PC World Malaysia, Publish in Asia; **MEXICO:** Computerworld Mexico, GamePro, Macworld, PC World Mexico; **MYANMAR:** PC World Myanmar; **NETHERLANDS:** Computable, Computer! Totaal, LAN Magazine, Macworld, Net Magazine; **NEW ZEALAND:** Computer Buyer, Computerworld New Zealand, MTB, Network World, PC World New Zealand; **NICARAGUA:** PC World Costa Rica/Nicaragua; **NIGERIA:** PC World Africa; **NORWAY:** Computerworld Norge, Computerworld Privat, CW Rapport Klient/Tjener, CW Rapport Nettverk & Telecom, CW Rapport Offentlig Sektor, IDG's KURSGUIDE, Macworld Norge, Multimedia World, PC World Ekspress, PC World Nettverk, PC World Norge, PC World's Produktguide, Windows Spesial; **PAKISTAN:** Computerworld Pakistan, PC World Pakistan; **PANAMA:** GamePro, PC World Panama; **PARAGUAY:** PC World Paraguay; **P. R. OF CHINA:** China Computerworld, China Infoworld, Computer & Communication, Electronic Product World, Electronics Today, Game Camp, PC World China, Popular Computer Week, Software World, Telecom Product World; **PERU:** Computerworld Peru, GamePro, PC World Profesional Peru, PC World Peru; **POLAND:** Computerworld Poland, Computerworld Special Report, Macworld, Networld, PC World Komputer; **PHILIPPINES:** Computerworld Philippines, PC Digest, Publish in Asia; **PORTUGAL:** Cerebro/PC World, Correio Informático/Computerworld, Mac•In/PC•In Portugal; **PUERTO RICO:** PC World Puerto Rico; **ROMANIA:** Computerworld Romania, PC World Romania, Telecom Romania; **RUSSIA:** Computerworld Rossiya, Network World Russia, PC World Russia; **SINGAPORE:** Computerworld Singapore, PC World Singapore, Publish in Asia; **SLOVENIA:** MONITOR; **SOUTH AFRICA:** Computing S.A., Network World S.A., Software World; **SPAIN:** Computerworld España, COMUNICACIONES WORLD, Dealer World, Macworld España, PC World España; **SWEDEN:** CAP&Design, Computer Sweden, Corporate Computing, MacWorld, Maxi Data, MikroDatorn, Nätverk & Kommunikation, PC/Aktiv, PC World, Windows World; **SWITZERLAND:** Computerworld Schweiz, Macworld Schweiz, PCtip; **TAIWAN:** Computerworld Taiwan, Macworld Taiwan, PC World Taiwan, Publish Taiwan, Windows World; **THAILAND:** Thai Computerworld, Publish in Asia; **TURKEY:** Computerworld Monitör, MACWORLD Turkiye, PC WORLD Turkiye; **UKRAINE:** Computerworld Kiev, Computers & Software Magazine, PC World Ukraine; **UNITED KINGDOM:** Acorn User, Amiga Action, Amiga Computing, Amiga, Appletalk, CD Powerplay, CD-ROM Now, Computing, Connexion, GamePro, Lotus Magazine, Macaction, Macworld, Open Computing, Parents and Computers, PC Home, PC Works, The WEB; **UNITED STATES:** Cable in the Classroom, CD Review, CIO Magazine, Computerworld, Computerworld Client/Server Journal, Digital Video Magazine, DOS World, Electronic, InfoWorld, I-Way, Macworld, Maximize, MULTIMEDIA WORLD, Network World, PC World, PUBLISH, SWATPro Magazine, Video Event, WebMaster; **URUGUAY:** PC World Uruguay; **VENEZUELA:** Computerworld Venezuela, GamePro, PC World Venezuela; and **VIETNAM:** PC World Vietnam   10/17/95a

Dedication

This book is dedicated to Dr. Regis Weiss, my oncologist, who will be in my thank-you prayers every night for the rest of my long, long, loooooonnng life.

Acknowledgments

After years of having California students groan at my puns, make rude hand gestures in response to my scintillatingly clever quips, and threaten to storm out of the classroom if I tell my geometry jokes one more time, it's wonderful to get the chance to inflict my dysfunctional sense of humor on a worldwide, unsuspecting audience. The decline of civilization begins here.

Thanks to my agent Bill Gladstone of Waterside Productions in Cardiff, California, for getting me this opportunity. A panegyric and paean for my project editor, Colleen Rainsberger, not only for her erudition but also for her effervescence and ebullience that didn't flag even under deadlines. Special thanks to Barb Terry for the iron fist in a velvet glove (and for laughing at most of my jokes). Many thanks also go to Kristin Cocks, Michael Simsic, and Jennifer Wallis, as well as Allan Swett and Flora Valentine.

Thanks to independent college counselor Jill Q. Porter of La Jolla, California, for her up-to-the minute insights about what college and university programs seek.

And thanks as always to my students over the years, those wonderful young and not-so-young adults who have had enough faith in me to use my tricks and tips and enough kindness to let me share their joy in the good scores that result. You all keep this fun.

Publisher's Acknowledgments

We're proud of this book; please send us your comments about it by using the Reader Response Card at the back of the book or by e-mailing us at feedback/dummies@idgbooks.com. Some of the people who helped bring this book to market include the following:

Acquisitions, Development, & Editorial

Project Editors: Colleen Rainsberger, Barb Terry

Acquisitions Editor: Kathleen A. Welton

Assistant Acquisitions Editor: Gareth Hancock

Product Development Manager: Mary Bednarek

Permissions Editor: Joyce Pepple

Technical Reviewer: Michael D. Knox

General Reviewer: Dr. Cary Wintz

Editorial Manager: Kristin A. Cocks

Editorial Assistants: Chris H. Collins, Ann Miller

Production

Project Coordinator: Regina Snyder

Layout and Graphics: Brett Black, Dominique DeFelice, Maridee V. Ennis, Jane Martin, Michael Sullivan, Angela F. Hunckler, Gina Scott

Proofreaders: Christine Beck, Dwight Ramsey, Nancy Price, Carl Saff, Rob Springer, Karen York

Indexer: Richard S. Shrout

General & Administrative

IDG Books Worldwide, Inc.: John Kilcullen, President & CEO; Steven Berkowitz, COO & Publisher

Dummies, Inc.: Milissa Koloski, Executive Vice President & Publisher

Dummies Technology Press & Dummies Editorial: Diane Graves Steele, Associate Publisher; Judith A. Taylor, Brand Manager; Myra Immell, Editorial Director

Dummies Trade Press: Kathleen A. Welton, Vice President & Publisher; Stacy S. Collins, Brand Manager

IDG Books Production for Dummies Press: Beth Jenkins, Production Director; Cindy L. Phipps, Supervisor of Project Coordination; Kathie S. Schnorr, Supervisor of Page Layout; Shelley Lea, Supervisor of Graphics and Design

Dummies Packaging & Book Design: Erin McDermitt, Packaging Coordinator; Kavish+Kavish, Cover Design

◆

The publisher would like to give special thanks to Patrick J. McGovern, without whom this book would not have been possible.

◆

Contents at a Glance

Cartoons at a Glance

By Rich Tennant • Fax: 508-546-7747 • E-mail: the5wave@tiac.net

page 159

page 17

page 5

page 73

page 341

page 133

page 175

Table of Contents

Introduction

Welcome to *The GRE For Dummies*, 2nd Edition. Don't take the title personally. You're no dummy; you're just normal. Unfortunately, the GRE is anything *but* normal. As I've learned in more than two decades of fighting the GRE wars, the GRE has no connection to the Real World. When you were given the dire news that you had to take the GRE to get into graduate school, you probably flashed back to the SAT (lovingly known as Sadists Against Teenagers) that you had to take to get into college. While there are some similarities (both exams are the leading causes of ulcers, migraines, and decisions to become a Bora Bora beachcomber), there are even more dissimilarities.

The primary dissimilarity has to do with how familiar you are with the material. In high school, instructors often "teach to the test." They know that their students are going to take the SAT, know the kids themselves, and teach them what will be on the test and how to take the exam. In college, you're on your own. Your professors may not have any idea who you are ("The kid in the *I'm only here for the beer* T-shirt who sits in the upper row of the lecture hall? In my mind I call him Bud, but I don't know him at all."), and they almost certainly are not going to take time away from class to discuss the tricks and traps on the GRE. In addition, you have spent the last few years of college working on the courses specific to your major: invertebrate biology, lifestyles of the upper Botswana natives, sociological and psychological implications of domestic dissonance. It's been a long, long time since you've taken basic algebra, geometry, and arithmetic (found in the math portions of the exam), or English and logic (found in the verbal and analytical portions of the exam). And what about those of you who are no longer in college? I, for one, entered college in the days of parchment and quills but didn't get around to taking the GRE until the era of laptops and battery packs. No doubt about it; you need some help. And the skills you need are best provided by a specialist. Think of this book as a SWAT team you can call in when the situation gets desperate.

Like a SWAT team, this book aims to deal with the crisis efficiently, do the job, save the day, and get you out as quickly as possible. I know that you have a life you'd like to get back to. The goal of this book is to help you to learn what you need and can use on the GRE — period. No extra garbage is thrown in to impress you with esoteric facts; no filler is added to make this book the fattest one on the market. If you need a doorstop, go pick up the New York City telephone directory. If you need a quick 'n easy guide to surviving the GRE, you're in the right place.

Why You Need This Book

It's Us versus Them. Who are They? The creators of the GRE, those gnomes in green eyeshades. The next time you're trying to get away from a *soporific dolt* (sleep-inducing dummy) at a party, answer the question, "So, what do you do for a living?" with the response, "I create questions for the GRE." That conversation stopper is guaranteed to send that sweetheart *manqué* (would-be sweetie) running screaming into the night.

In *The GRE For Dummies,* 2nd Edition, I show you how to approach each type of question, recognize the traps that are built into the questions, and master the tricks that help you to avoid those traps. The book is full of Gotchas! that I (a test prep tutor since the Dawn of Time) have seen students fall for repeatedly. In this book, you learn to think the GRE way (don't worry; it's not permanent), to identify the point behind the various styles and types of questions and what each is trying to test. This book also gives you a review of the basics (math formulas and common roots, prefixes, and suffixes useful for improving your vocabulary) along with a laugh or two to make learning the material as painless as possible.

Note to nontraditional students: As I mentioned before, I'm aware of the fact that some of you are not 21-year-old college seniors taking this exam to go into graduate school right after college. You may have been out of college so long that your *children* are 21-year-old seniors! Maybe you've just decided to go back to grad school after a long career or after raising a family, and you need help getting back into math and verbal stuff that you had in what seems like another lifetime. I sympathize with you; it's tough to deal with nonagons, quadratic equations, and analogies again. Don't despair; you can get outside help, especially in math, which is one of the first things to go for most people when they get away from school. Call a community college (or even a high school; the math on this exam doesn't exceed what is taught in upper-division high school math classes, depressing as that may seem to you as you're sweating through it). Ask for help in finding a tutor or for suggestions on finding a quick review course in your area. You also can call your local library for assistance.

How to Get Your Money's Worth Out of This Book

If you use this book just to prop open a window or as a booster seat for a toddler, you won't get the best out of it. I suggest two alternatives:

- ✔ *Fine-tune your skills.* Turn to specific sections for specific information and help. The organization of the book makes it very easy to find the type of math question you always have trouble with, suggestions for answering reading questions without having finished the passage, and tricks for guessing. If you are in college classes or in a career in which you use this jazz every day (maybe you're a math major at school or teach high school English classes) and need just a nudge in one or two areas, you can work through those sections only.

- ✔ *Start from scratch.* Read through the whole book. Actually, this is what I'd like you to do. No matter how well you do on a section, you can improve. It's a common mistake to believe that you should work on your weakest sections only. The 50 points you gain in your mediocre section by skimming through the suggestions in this book are just as worthwhile as the 50 points you get by grunting and groaning and sweating through the most difficult portions. If you have the time, do yourself a favor and read the book from cover to cover. Besides, you don't want to miss any of my jokes, now do you?

The GRE For Dummies, 2nd Edition, is simple and straightforward enough for first-time GRE victims, er, students that they can understand the entire exam and do well right out of the starting gate. But it's also detailed and sophisticated enough that veterans — those of you who have taken the exam once or twice before but aren't resting on your laurels (sounds painful, anyway) — can learn the more complicated information you need to get those truly excellent scores.

To help you to get through this book more quickly, I include some icons that flag the particularly important stuff. If you need to work on your vocabulary, for example, flip through the book to find the Vocabulary icons and then make a list of the accompanying words and their meanings. The icons look like this.

This icon points out the big words (useless in the Real World and therefore almost inevitably tested on the GRE) that you may not know. (Let's face it: Some of the vocab words on the GRE are so tough that you practically have to be constipated to pronounce them!) Learning those words and their definitions is sure to help you on the GRE. The words themselves are in a special typeface — *like this* — and their meanings appear next to them. (You'll fix these words even more in your memory if you try to use them in your real life. Call your roommate or your children *indolent*, *lethargic*, and *listless* when they don't jump up to do the dishes right after dinner; promise your professor you will be *diligent*, *meticulous*, and *painstaking* in your lab assignment.)

This icon marks sample problems that appear in the lectures.

This icon directs you to tips that should make taking the GRE go much more smoothly. These tips alone are worth the price of this book. Trust me.

The test makers throw in some nasty traps that may get you if you don't think about the questions carefully. Learn the tricks marked by this icon, and you'll be amazed at how easily you can outsmart the GRE.

Be wary of the important stuff that this icon points out to you. If you skip these sections, I claim no responsibility for what may happen to you.

This icon points out information pertaining to international students and suggestions that can make life easier for those of you for whom English is a second or third language (which questions are worth doing and which to "guess and go" on, for example). International students, please see welcoming comments to you in Chapter 1.

Pardon Me for Having a Life: Who Has Time for This?

You have school or work, sports or other hobbies, family responsibilities and, oh yes, a social life. How on earth are you going to fit in studying for the GRE?

Time required to go through the GRE lectures

Buying this book was brilliant. (Okay, so your roommate, your spouse, or some significant other bought it and tossed it at you with the snide comment, "Hey, you can sure use all the help you can get." Whatever.) How much time should you take to go through this book? I suggest 31 hours.

Each subject (antonyms, analogies, sentence completions, reading comprehension, quantitative comparisons, problem solving, analytical reasoning, logical reasoning, and analysis of explanations) includes a chapter on the format, approach, and tricks and traps for that particular type of question. A quiz chapter featuring a sampling of questions that test what you learned in the lecture follows each lecture. The detailed answer explanations point out the traps you may have fallen for and the tips that you should have used to avoid the traps. You learn which questions to skip (as either too hard or too time-consuming) and which to double-check. You should spend about two hours per lecture, including the quiz. The book also includes a three-part math review; each section (geometry, algebra, and arithmetic) should take roughly one hour, for a total of three hours.

Time required to go through the practice GREs

At the end of the book are two full-length GREs. Each exam takes three hours to complete (not including the two ten-minute breaks you can give yourself) and about another hour to an hour and a half to review. My thinking that you should take an hour and a half to review the exam does not reflect a lack of confidence in your *erudition* and *sagacity* (knowledge and wisdom). I'm not saying that you're so *inept* and *bungling* (unskilled) that you're going to miss a *plethora* (abundance) of questions. My suggestion is that you review all the answer explanations, even for the questions you answer correctly. You'll learn some good stuff there; you'll review formulas, find shortcuts, and see more tricks and traps. I'll exaggerate and say that the whole test and review should take you five hours. The following table gives you what I think is a reasonable timetable.

Activity	Time
9 lectures at 2 hours per lecture	18 hours
2 exams at 5 hours per exam (including review)	10 hours
3 math review chapters at 1 hour per chapter	3 hours
Time spent laughing hysterically at author's jokes	5 minutes
Time spent composing letter complaining about author's crummy jokes	5 minutes
TOTAL	**31 hours, 10 minutes**

No one expects you to read this book for 31 hours straight. Each unit is self-contained. The answer explanations may remind you of things from other units because repetition aids learning and memorizing, but you can read through each unit separately.

Are you ready? Stupid question. Are you resigned? Have you accepted your fate that you're going to take the GRE no matter what and you may as well have fun studying for it? Take a deep breath, turn the page, and go for it. Here's hoping that, for you, GRE comes to stand for Genius Rocks Exam!

Part I

An Aerial View: Putting the GRE into Perspective

The 5th Wave   By Rich Tennant

SHERLOCK HOLMES TAKES THE GRE

In this part . . .

1 know, I know — the only aerial view you'd like to have of the GRE is the one you see from 10,000 feet up as a jet takes you far, far away from this exam. Use the info in this book correctly and you can ace the GRE, go to a top grad school, get a great job — and then buy your own private jet and buzz the office of that college guidance counselor who told you your best chance at a good life would be to marry rich. Hey, it's something to aim for (the goal, not the college counselor!).

You're probably eager to get right into studying for the GRE (or maybe not), but take a few minutes to go through this introductory material. It's good strategy to find out everything you can about your enemy before going into battle.

Chapter 1

Know Your Enemy: What the GRE Looks Like

. . . .

In This Chapter

▶ Understanding the format: Number and types of questions

▶ Timing it right

▶ Doing the Backpack Boogie: What to take with you to the test

▶ Dealing with unusual circumstances

▶ Scoring the exam

▶ Serial guessing

▶ Taking the CAT (Computer Adaptive Test)

▶ Repeating the test

. . . .

Up in the air over the GRE? Table 1-1 provides a quick overview of what the GRE is all about, how many questions it has, and how much time you have. The sections of the test may be arranged in any order.

Table 1-1	GRE Breakdown by Section	
Section	*Number of Questions*	*Time Allotted*
Verbal	38	30 minutes
Math	30	30 minutes
Analytical	25	30 minutes
Verbal	38	30 minutes
Math	30	30 minutes
Analytical	25	30 minutes
Unscored	25 to 38	30 minutes

Table 1-2 shows another way to look at the GRE: by the number of each type of question.

Table 1-2	GRE Breakdown by Question Style (Not Including the Unscored Section)
Type of Question	*Number of Questions*
Antonyms	22
Analogies	18
Sentence Completions	14
Reading Comprehension	22
Quantitative Comparisons	30
Problem Solving	30
Analytical Reasoning	26
Logical Reasoning	12
Analysis of Explanations	12

Want it spelled out? You have two verbal sections, two math sections, two analytical sections . . . and one uncounted, experimental section. Each section on the exam is 30 minutes. Sections can be arranged in any order. Murphy's Law definitely applies: If you think math questions are a waste of paper and trees (Question: If a tree falls in the forest, who notifies the next of kindling?) and absolutely hate getting up early in the morning, your exam will begin with two math sections — while you're still half asleep. You can count on it.

Why does the GRE feature one 30-minute section that doesn't count? The test makers are using you as guinea pigs, trying out new questions on you, double-checking that current questions are fair. You are an unwilling — and unwitting — participant. You're obviously unwilling — who would want to prolong this agony? You're unwitting because you don't know which section is experimental. The experimental or uncounted section can be verbal, math, or analytical. You will have absolutely no idea which section is uncounted. Well, you know that if you have three verbal sections, one of them will be the experimental section — but which one? Don't try to outsmart the test makers. The GRE has rooms full of men and women whose only task in life is to create these mind-warping questions. You, as a normal person, don't stand a chance of outsmarting them; why even try? Just do your best on every section.

Add it all up, and you'll find that the test itself takes three and a half hours (not including the Bladder Breaks discussed in the next section). Keep in mind, though, that you'll probably be at the test site for at least four hours, including the time before the test when the proctors give out the papers and go through directions. In other words, kiss the whole morning good-bye.

Gimme a Break! The GRE Intermission

Yes, you do get at least one break during the GRE, usually two. Depending on whether your bladder is the size of Rhode Island or Texas, you may or may not spend most of your break in the bathroom. Do yourself a favor: Don't drink more than a mouthful or eat much during the break. There's nothing worse than sitting there crossing and uncrossing your legs during the test, slowly feeling your eyeballs turn yellow.

You may want to take some munchies to eat at the breaks, but make sure that they're light and nutritious. Sugar makes you high for a few minutes, and then brings you way down. You don't need to crash right in the middle of a quadratic equation ("Twinkies Trauma: Film at 11:00 . . ."). Take a handful of peanuts, some trail mix, or anything light that won't send all the blood from your brain down to your stomach for digestion. Life's hard enough without trying to figure out how to find the interior angles of a nonagon by using your stomach instead of your brain.

The Computer Adaptive Test

Good news: You have a choice. No, there's no choice whether to take the GRE or not (sorry if I got your hopes up only to dash them cruelly); there's a choice whether to take the pencil-and-paper GRE or the new Computer Adaptive Test (the GRE on computer).

Since 1992, testers have had two ways to take the GRE. The former is the old-fashioned way, with a pencil and paper in a test room with a proctor. The latter is the new high-tech way: with a computer. In the Computer Adaptive Test — fondly referred to as CAT, much to the delight of those *ribald* (coarse, lewd) types who now refer to testing sites as CAT houses— the level of questions is tailored to your own abilities. You have a *bespoke* (custom-tailored) exam. The exam begins with questions of average difficulty. Then the computer figures out where you're coming from and changes the level of the questions. If you got all the average questions right, you get a harder test. If you got the average questions wrong, you get an easy test.

The CAT consists of three scored sections: one 30-minute verbal, one 45-minute quantitative (math) and one 60-minute analytical. Typically, you are given 30 verbal questions, 28 quantitative questions, and 35 analytical questions, with the number of each question type (such as Analogies, Quantitative Comparisons, or Logical Reasoning) proportional to what appears on the pencil-and-paper version of the test.

You are given more time per question on the CAT than on the pencil-and-paper test. Be sure to use this time wisely. Because you cannot go back and change your answers, you must be as accurate as possible on the first several questions of average difficulty to ensure that you *will* be given harder questions for the rest of the exam! Sound bizarre? Strange but true. You *want* harder questions because your score is determined by the level you reach. If you slip up and miss one early question, you can still reel off a series of correct answers, show that your mistake was a fluke, and get to the harder questions. However, if you miss a handful of early questions, the computer determines that these questions are too difficult for you and gives you easy questions. You may answer all these easy questions correctly, but your test will be over by the time the computer raises the difficulty level to the high-score range.

You do not need to answer every question in the section to get a score. The CAT usually requires that you answer only 24 verbal questions, 23 quantitative questions, and 28 analytical questions to receive a score. The numbers may vary a bit, but you will know at the beginning of a section how many questions you need to answer.

Once you reach this number, do not answer the question on the computer screen unless you are sure of the answer. You can receive an 800 just by correctly answering the minimum number of questions. Of course, answering questions beyond the minimum number could help your score because you probably will not be at 800, but an incorrect answer could hurt your score more than a correct one would help it. Once again, do not answer a question once you hit the minimum unless you *know* your answer is correct.

While taking your time at the beginning is important, be sure that you answer the minimum number of questions. You can't skip a question; you must mark an answer to go on to the next question. So, if you are completely stuck, don't agonize and waste time. Guess quickly and move on.

Like the pencil-and-paper test, the CAT gives you an experimental section which is indistinguishable from the scored sections. However, the CAT sometimes gives an identified experimental section, which you do not even need to take, at the end of the test. If you feel like playing with the computer and helping out ETS (Educational Testing Service), go ahead and take it, but you have no obligation to do so.

When you are finished, you have the option of seeing your score or canceling it. You *cannot*, however, decide to cancel the score once you have seen it, so think carefully about how you feel you've done. Finding out your score at the end of the testing session is one of the many advantages of taking the CAT. Another advantage is that the schools will receive the scores within 15 days, much less time than it takes to get the pencil-and-paper test scores out. If you're trying to beat an application deadline and you are comfortable using a computer, the CAT may be the way for you to go. Other benefits of the CAT include being able to sign up just a few days before, flexible scheduling (great if you're not worth much on a Saturday morning), and a quieter testing environment.

While taking the CAT version has many advantages, though, it does have some disadvantages. The greatest one for many test takers is that you can't do scratch work on the computer screen the way you can in the test booklet during the pencil-and-paper test. You are given blank scrap paper for scratch work during the CAT, but some students have difficulty focusing when they have to go back and forth between the screen and the scrap paper. Also, the lack of a test booklet makes reading comprehension and analytical reasoning (logic games) particularly annoying for some stressed-out students because they have to scroll through the passage or game as they read it and then answer the questions.

Beat the Clock: Timing Tips

So now you know that each section takes 30 minutes. As you read the chapters in this book that teach you how to approach each question style (on your knees humbly and submissively, acknowledging the awesome power of the GRE), you'll learn how much time to allot to each style of question. In general, questions go from easier to harder. The last two or three questions in each section are incredibly difficult — so hard that only those testers with brains oozing out their ears get them right. If you're an oozer, go for it. But if you're like most people, you may want to skip those super-hard ones at the end. Doing so frees up more time for the easy-and medium-level questions in the rest of the section. In other words, don't worry about getting to every single question. You can get a very good GRE score without having solved every problem or answered every question.

The GRE (unlike the SAT and GMAT, for those of you with experience in those tests) has *no penalty* for a wrong answer. It is to your advantage to fill in every blank. Try to save one minute at the end of the test to fill in an answer for each question you didn't get to. (Scoring is discussed in more detail in the section, "Everyone Wants to Score.")

What to Take to the GRE

Take your brain down from the shelf, dust it off, and take it to the exam with you. In addition, you'll want to tote along a few more items.

 ✔ **Admission ticket:** This should come in the mail a week or two before the actual exam. If you haven't received it ten days before the test, call ETS (Educational Testing Service, home to the sadists responsible for putting you through all this anguish) at 609-771-7670 (Princeton, New Jersey) or 510-654-1200 (Bay Area, California). Face it: There's no way that you're going to get out of taking the test. They've got your number (and now you have theirs).

✔ **Map or directions:** Be sure that you know how to get to the test center. Drive to the test site a few days in advance and check out how long the drive takes you, where to park (if you are not currently going to college, you may be shocked at how far the parking lots are from the classrooms in many of the universities today), and so on. The last thing you need the morning of the test is more stress.

✔ **Photo file record:** Your photo file record contains a recent photo of you THAT LOOKS LIKE YOU DO THE DAY YOU TAKE THE TEST. If you shaved your beard or grew a beard, get a new photo of you with the appropriate visage. If you cut your hair, grew a third eye in the middle of your forehead, whatever, change your photo to match your current state. The photo must be 2 × 2 inches (you can often get these shots in those three for a buck photo booths found in malls) and must be glued or taped to the photo file record (do NOT staple it). Your photo file record — and you — will be kicked out of the test room if your photo

is stapled to the record,

is computer generated,

is laminated, or

is a photocopy of a photo.

You will learn how to obtain a photo file record when you apply to take the GRE.

✔ **Photo ID:** *In addition to* the photo file record, you need two forms of photo ID. One piece must have your recent photo and signature, the second must have a signature and either a photo or a physical description. For example, you may take a driver's license (if it has a photo), passport, or employee ID card. A social security card, student ID, credit card, or library card won't cut it. *Note:* There are very, very specific procedures you have to go through if you don't have two forms of photo ID. If you need all that info, get the GRE Registration and Information Bulletin (free from ETS; call the number given above) and go through all the details. I refuse to be so *soporific* (sleep-inducing) as to induce *ennui* (boredom) by making the rest of you plod through such *picayune* matters. (Picayune means minor, trivial, insignificant. I bet you've said *picayune* — pronounced "pick-a-you-n" — a bunch of times but maybe have never seen it in print before. Don't be surprised if it's a vocabulary word on your test.)

✔ **Pencils:** Take two, three, or a dozen sharpened number two pencils with you. Take a small pencil sharpener and a good eraser as well (for the *remote* chance that you're not perfect after all).

✔ **Clothes:** You signed up for the special Nude GRE you say? Well, everyone else should remember to take a few extra layers. Classrooms are notorious for being either freezing cold or boiling hot. It's the pits to sit in a room for three hours either shivering because you're so cold or sweating all over your answer grid from the heat.

What Not to Take to the GRE

Besides your dreams, hopes, goals, and aspirations, leave these things at the door of the GRE testing room:

✔ **Books and notes:** Forget about last-minute studying. You aren't allowed to take books or notes into the room. If you don't know the material by then, you never will. (I had one student who asked me whether he could take in a dictionary. You gotta give the guy credit for hope, but somehow I think he missed the point of the verbal questions. . . .)

✔ **Scratch paper:** You are not allowed to bring scratch paper. *Note:* If you are taking the CAT, the computerized GRE, you *are* allowed to take scratch paper. For the rest of us, the good news is that the exam has plenty of empty space on which to do calculations and scribbling. I understand, however, that ETS owns the copyright to all Last Will and Testaments written during the test. . . .

✔ **Calculator:** You are not allowed to use a calculator on the exam. Those of you who grew up before calculators were common and learned your times tables have a definite advantage here over those young whippersnappers who can't add 2 + 2 without dragging out the calculator.

✔ **Testing aids:** ETS defines testing aids pretty broadly. You cannot take in highlighters (which may be useful in the Reading Comprehension passages), rulers, or any sort of noisy device, including a portable stereo (Walkman, in other words) or a watch with an alarm. Careful! Proctors have been known to confiscate watches that have beepers or alarms. There's nothing more nerve-wracking than having your watch taken away when you're used to glancing at it every few seconds. If your watch is so complicated that you don't know how to turn off the beeper (welcome to the High-Tech generation), borrow a simpler watch from a friend.

Isn't That Special? Unusual Circumstances

Dare to be different. If you have a special circumstance, you can have a slight change in your GRE. For example, if you have a learning disability (no, that doesn't include being bored and frustrated), you may be able to get additional testing time. Following is a brief list of special circumstances and what to do about them.

✔ **Learning disabilities:** These can range from attention deficit disorder to dyslexia and all sorts of other things. To find out whether you qualify for a disabilities waiver of any sort, contact the Test Administration Services For Disabled Test Takers at 609-921-9000 or fax 609-520-1092.

✔ **Physical disabilities:** Pay attention: I'm about to say something nice about ETS here, a once-in-a-googolplex occurrence for me. The ETS tries very hard to accommodate everyone. People can get Braille or large print exams, can have test readers or recorders, can work with interpreters, and so on. You can get the information about what are considered disabilities and how they can change your taking the GRE in the GRE Information and Registration Bulletin.

✔ **Financial difficulties:** Until you ace the GRE, get into a top-notch graduate school and come out with a smokin' brain ready to make your first million before your 30th (40th? 50th?) birthday, you may have a rough time paying the GRE fees. Fee waivers are available. Note that this waiver applies only to the actual GRE fee, not to miscellaneous fees, such as those for test disclosure service, hand-grading service, and so on. Your college counselor can help you to obtain and fill out the appropriate request forms. (If you're not currently in college, a counselor or financial aid specialist at the closest college or university may still be glad to help you. Just call for an appointment.) The GRE is inflicted upon rich and poor alike.

✔ **Religious obligations:** If your religion prevents your taking the test on a Saturday, you may be able to take the test on a Monday. Monday testing is NOT offered for every administration; check the bulletin to see whether your particular exam date offers this alternative arrangement. The registration form makes clear to you how to register for Monday testing. You need a letter of explanation signed by your cleric (rabbi and so on) saying that you are associated with a religion that celebrates the Sabbath on a Saturday. No, claiming a religious holiday by having your friend forge a signature on stationery you swiped from the "HolyDay" Inn isn't going to do it. . . .

The watch game: Using your watch to simplify the test

Here's the deal. The proctor — whom you're pretty sure you saw on "America's Most Wanted" last week — tells you at 8:47 that you may begin. You have 38 questions. The time is now 9:09, and you're on question 17. How are you doing for time? Can you relax and slow down, or are you entering Panic City?

Who needs this kind of stress? It's like adding on another whole math problem. Don't strain your brain; make

life easier by resetting your watch. What's your lucky number? Three? Then use three o'clock as your ending time. When the proctor tells you to begin and the time allotted is 30 minutes, set your watch for 2:30. That way, you're counting down the minutes to your lucky number. A glance at your watch tells you how many minutes you have left. Who cares what the time is outside in the Real World? You want to use your watch as a stopwatch for the exam, not as a timepiece.

Everyone Wants to Score

You don't have the Ferrari yet (if you do, and you are a single, eligible male, please write to me care of the publisher . . .). You don't have the six-digit paycheck yet (if you do, please see parenthetical comment supra). It's rough being 21 (or 25 or 30). You need something to boast about. How about your GRE scores? GRE scores are to would-be graduate students what salaries are to people in the Real World. Students brag about them, exaggerate them, or try to impress others with them. How are your scores determined?

How scores are determined

The GRE are three separate scores: verbal, math, and analytical, not one "combined" score. That is, you won't be boasting to your buddies, "Yeah, I got an 1800 on my GRE." Every score is separate (unlike, for instance, the SAT of your youth, in which people added their verbal and math scores and spoke of one combined score).

✔ **The Verbal Score:** The verbal score (called verbal ability or sometimes qualitative ability) ranges from 200 to 800. You get 200 points just for signing your name. Good news! You can get a perfect score without being perfect. There are 76 verbal questions. You can get 74 and sometimes lower and still get an 800. Who says there's no such thing as a free lunch anymore?

✔ **The Math Score:** The math score also ranges from 200 to 800. Sometimes you can get as low as 57 out of 60 questions and still get the "perfect" score of 800.

✔ **The Analytical Score:** Take a wild guess . . . you got it. The analytical score ranges from 200 to 800 as well. You can get as low as 48 out of 50 questions and still get the perfect 800.

Not every graduate school looks at every score. My experience has been that one of the three scores counts much more than the other two, depending on the program to which you are applying. For example, if you are applying to engineering graduate school, your math score is more closely scrutinized than are your verbal and analytical scores. Students going to grad school in journalism can expect their verbal score to be the most important. *Many schools don't obsess over the analytical scores.* Before you go through this book, *before* you begin sweating out the lectures, *before* you spend the time and destroy brain cells learning the three types of analytical questions, find out from the grad schools in which you are interested whether they even care about the analytical score. And get that information in writing. You want an official letter on letterhead stationery telling you that analytical scores aren't considered.

On the GRE, you DO NOT lose points for wrong answers. That's right, the GRE has <u>no</u> penalty points (unlike penalties assessed on the SAT and GMAT). Therefore, you obviously should *fill in every answer.* Do not leave any ovals blank. Be sure to leave yourself a minute or two at the end of each section to fill in all the ovals in a last-minute desperate bid for a few more points. That is, set your watch to show that you have only 28 minutes per section instead of 30. If your "time is up" when you are on question 32 out of 38 questions, you have 2 minutes to fill in ovals for the rest of the questions. Which ovals should you fill in? Any. There is no truth to the *scurrilous* (obscenely abusive) rumors that the exam has more *A*s or more *B*s or more whatevers. Every answer has the same probability.

All the questions you answer correctly are added together, a magic wand is waved, three virgins are sacrificed, and somehow the score is *transmogrified* (changed) into that 200–800 scale. Isn't modern science wonderful?

What is a good score?

On a recent GRE, the averages (that is, half the students taking the exam were above these scores, half were below these scores) were as follows: verbal 480, math 570, analytical 550. Averages change according to the administration. Your individual goals should depend on which grad schools you are applying to and what GPA (grade point average) you have. There is no such thing as a passing or failing score — only what you need to get accepted at the college you have your heart set on.

Number of correct answers needed for specific scores

Here are rough estimates of how many questions you must answer correctly to get certain scores on each section. Keep in mind that these numbers change from exam to exam.

Verbal scores
To get a 400, you need 36 out of 76 questions correct (about 47 percent).
To get a 500, you need 46 out of 76 questions correct (about 60 percent).
To get a 600, you need 56 out of 76 questions correct (about 73 percent).
To get a 700, you need 64 out of 76 questions correct (about 84 percent).

Math scores
To get a 400, you need 23 out of 60 questions correct (about 38 percent).
To get a 500, you need 31 out of 60 questions correct (51 percent).
To get a 600, you need 40 out of 60 questions correct (about 66 percent).
To get a 700, you need 49 out of 60 questions correct (81 percent).

Analytical scores
To get a 400, you need 20 out of 50 questions correct (about 40 percent).
To get a 500, you need 26 out of 50 questions correct (about 52 percent).
To get a 600, you need 33 out of 50 questions correct (66 percent).
To get a 700, you need 41 out of 50 questions correct (82 percent).

Déjà Vu All Over Again: Repeating the Test

Should you repeat the test? Before you make that decision, ask yourself the following questions:

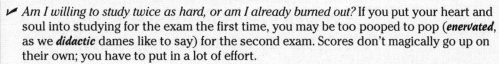

✔ *Am I repeating the test to get a certain minimum qualifying score or just to satisfy my ego?* If you have your heart set on a particular graduate school that requires a minimum GRE score, you may want to take the test again and again and again until you get that score. If you're taking the test only because your ego was demolished by your not scoring as well as your friends, you should probably think twice before putting yourself through all that trauma again.

✔ *Am I willing to study twice as hard, or am I already burned out?* If you put your heart and soul into studying for the exam the first time, you may be too pooped to pop (*enervated*, as we *didactic* dames like to say) for the second exam. Scores don't magically go up on their own; you have to put in a lot of effort.

✔ *What types of mistakes did I make on the first test?* If you made mistakes because of a lack of familiarity with either the test format (you didn't understand what to do when faced with a Quantitative Comparison question) or substance (you didn't know the vocabulary words or were baffled by the geometry problems) you're a good candidate for repeating the test. If you know what you did wrong, you can fix it and improve your score.

However, if your mistakes were due to carelessness or a lack of concentration, you are very likely to make those same types of mistakes again. If you truly, honestly, sincerely, without *dissembling* (lying) feel that you can sit in the test room and stay focused this time and not make the same stupid mistakes, go for it. But chances are, if you're the type who either always makes a lot of careless mistakes or rarely makes them, you're not going to change your whole test-taking style overnight.

✔ *Were there extenuating circumstances beyond my control?* Maybe your nerves were acting up on the first exam, you were feeling ill, or you didn't get enough sleep the night before. In that case, by all means, repeat the exam. You're bound to feel better the next time.

✔ *Did I leave answers blank?* If for some reason you left a lot of answers blank, take the test again and fill in everything. You're going to get some points just by the luck of the draw.

Can repeating the exam hurt you? Not really. Most schools look only at your highest score. Find out from the individual schools you are interested in whether this is their policy; not all schools do so. If you are borderline or several students are vying for one spot, sometimes having taken the exam repeatedly can hurt you (especially if your most recent score took a nosedive). On the other hand, an admissions counselor who sees several exams with ascending scores may be impressed that you stuck to it and kept trying, even if your score went up only a little bit. In general, if you're willing to take the time to study and take the repeat seriously, go for it.

GRE score reporting is cumulative; that is, all the scores you obtain for five years are sent to the schools you designate. You cannot, I repeat, CANNOT send scores from only one exam date. For example, if you do great in October, take the exam again in April and blow it big time, you cannot tell ETS to ignore the April *debacle* (a sudden collapse, a rout) and send just the October scores. All scores are part of your permanent record.

Can You Use Older Scores?

What if you took the GRE years and years ago when you thought you were going to go to grad school and then elected to take a job or start a family instead? Between October 1, 1974, and September 30, 1985, ETS had promised students that scores would be valid for 20 years. Never one to go back on its word, ETS (noted for its *veracity*, or truthfulness) agrees to send those scores out if you so desire . . . but will do so with a note to the schools to be extra careful in looking at such old scores. But the good news is, if you liked your scores from as long ago as two decades, you may be able to get away with sending those and not taking the exam again at all. If that's so and you're waving me good-bye at this point, adios and good luck to you. For the rest of you who can't escape my company so quickly, read on.

I wish it were all Greek to me: A welcome to international students

Students the world over take the GRE in order to attend American graduate schools. I've taught GRE prep courses that had students from Brazil, Taiwan, the Ivory Coast, Egypt, Japan, all over the globe. When I got my own graduate degree, my courses were enriched by the contributions of students from Korea, Hong Kong, Saudi Arabia, the Netherlands, and Mexico. To all of you readers from other nations, welcome!

As international students, you have strengths and weaknesses that are different from those of American students; therefore, the focus of your study should be different as well. Here are my suggestions to help you to get the most out of this book and to help you do your best on the actual GRE:

1. **Concentrate on the questions that test vocabulary, Antonyms and Analogies.** You probably have an advantage over American students in this section, believe it or not — especially if your native tongue is a Romance language, such as Spanish or French. Romance languages are Latin-based and commonly use words that are uncommon in English. Take, for example, *bibliophile.* A Spanish speaker knows biblio means book (bibliotéca means library) and can figure out this "hard" word pretty easily. (A bibliophile is a book-lover.)

   One more thing: Because you've studied English, you're used to memorizing vocabulary tests (unlike American students who haven't taken vocabulary tests since junior high). Although you probably can't dramatically change your basic reading comprehension level in a few hours, you *can* dramatically add to your vocabulary. You, more than American students, need to keep and learn the vocabulary lists suggested throughout.

2. **Forget about Reading Comprehension.** The GRE's reading passages are long, hard, and booooring. They are difficult enough to understand for people who grew up speaking and reading English, and are totally demoralizing for people who didn't. My suggestion is that you not take reading comp too seriously. Take your time, read one of the passages (there are two in a section) very slowly and carefully, and try to answer the questions regarding just that passage. Doing fewer questions and getting them right, is better than trying to do all the questions and missing them. Remember, however, to fill in something, anything, for all the questions because the GRE does *not* count off for wrong answers.

3. **Concentrate on the math, especially geometry.** While you do get separate verbal and math scores, some colleges concentrate on your overall or combined score. Doing extremely well on math can compensate for weaker verbal skills. I suggest that you pay particular attention to the geometry problems. They rarely are "word problems," — questions that require a lot of reading. Geometry problems usually feature figures that you can easily understand and use to answer the questions even if English is not your strong suit.

4. **Guess, Guess, Guess!** I've said it before and I'll say it again: The GRE does *not* subtract points for wrong answers. Be sure to fill in an answer for every question, even if you're just making a wild guess. If you want to skip a question and come back to it later to rethink it, fill in the oval *anyway.* That way you'll at least have a shot at the points, even if you run out of time and don't get back to the question.

Part II
A Word to the Wise: Verbal Questions

The 5th Wave — By Rich Tennant

"EXCUSE ME – DOES ANYONE KNOW WHAT 'SOPORIFIC' MEANS?"

In this part . . .

Two of the six scored sections on the GRE are verbal. Altogether, there are 74 to 76 (the number varies) verbal questions in four styles: Antonyms (finding words that are opposites), Analogies (far and away the easiest for most people), Sentence Completions (good ol' fill-in-the-blanks, the same stuff you've been doing since kindergarten), and Reading Comprehension (dull and deadly). Each question style has a chapter of its own in this part. You learn the format of the question (what it looks like), an approach to the question (where to begin, an organized plan of attack), and the various tricks and traps built into the questions (with, of course, suggestions for recognizing and avoiding such traps). Vocabulary-building material features roots, prefixes, and suffixes. Following each lecture chapter is a chapter that includes particularly wicked practice questions followed by detailed answer explanations that show you what you should have done, how to make the best use of your time, and what you should have guessed at randomly. (**Remember:** No points are subtracted for wrong answers on the GRE; you should never leave any bubbles blank.)

Chapter 2

Starting with the Easy Stuff: Analogies

• •

In This Chapter
▶ Understanding the format of an analogy
▶ Building your vocabulary with prefixes and suffixes
▶ Answering an analogy question with the correct two-step approach
▶ Recognizing the nasty and vile traps built into analogies
▶ Learning to recognize and avoid dumb (trap) answers

• •

The answer: The shiny red bike you got for your tenth birthday. Your first kiss from someone who wasn't related to you. Analogies.

The question: Name three of the best gifts you've ever received.

Analogies are a gift. Manna from heaven. Freebies. For most students, analogies are the place to scarf up the points big time. The GRE has 18 analogies, nine in each of the two scored verbal sections.

The great thing about analogies is that they are doable. Some Reading Comprehension passages are so hard that you're not sure whether they're printed in your native language. Some of the Sentence Completion questions are so long that you may be tempted to take a snooze in the middle of them. But analogies are great. You read 12 words, apply a few tricks, and you're outta there. Here's how it's done.

If Only All Relationships Were This Easy: The Format

Some people look at analogies and wonder, "Where's the question?" Even though analogies are quite simple (with practice), the format is bizarre. Here's an example of what you see:

PIG : STY ::

 (A) teenager : rubble

 (B) roommate : bathroom

 (C) bird : nest

 (D) swine : bathtub

 (E) barnacle : barn

You see two words in uppercase letters. The five answer choices consist of two words in lowercase letters. Not a lot of reading here. When you get good at analogies, you can zoom through them faster than you can finish a pint of Haagen-Dazs. And remember: Every minute you save in the analogies is another minute you can use for the Reading Comprehension (where you need all the time you can get).

Your job is to identify the *relationship* between the question words and then choose a pair of answer words that expresses the *same* relationship.

Approaching Perfection

When you see an Analogy question, you should take this very straightforward two-step approach:

1. **Use both words in a *descriptive* sentence.**

   Make a sentence using the words. Avoid something vague and useless such as "has." For example, do *not* say, "A pig *has* a sty." That tells me nothing. From the sentence, I have no idea what the relationship between a pig and a sty is. Pretend that I'm a Bulgarian exchange student. I come up to you and say, "Excuse me, please. What is this pig : sty?" If you tell me that a pig *has* a sty, I may go away thinking that a sty is a curly tail, a snout, or a big stink. But if you say to me, "A pig *lives in* a sty," I now understand the relationship. A good sentence paints a mental picture; you can actually see the scene in your mind.

2. **Apply the *exact* same sentence to each answer choice.**

   Go through each of the answer choices using your sentence.

   (A) *A teenager lives in rubble.*

   Maybe you flash back to your teenage years and recall having to wade through the *detritus* (trash, rubble) of your bedroom to get to the door, but this is the GRE. The test makers assume that all of you were sweet little kids who obeyed your parents, respected traffic signals, and didn't ever use the middle finger of your hand for pointing or otherwise gesticulating. By the way, *rubble* is the ruined remains of a building, such as knocked-down bricks and junk. If you forget this word, think of Barney Rubble from the Flintstones. He's short, like a knocked-down pile.

   (B) *A roommate lives in the bathroom.*

   It may seem like it sometimes, but it ain't so. Any answer that is funny, witty, or charming is almost certainly the wrong answer. (The GRE has nooooooo sense of humor; count on it.) If you think that the answer is funny — or desperately *trying* to be funny — you can be sure that it's wrong.

   (C) *A bird lives in a nest.*

   Sounds pretty good, but you have to go through all the answer choices, just in case. Just like not marrying the first person you kiss, don't immediately choose the first answer that looks good. There may be something later that makes you happier.

   (D) *A swine lives in a bathtub.*

   If you choose this answer, remind me not to come to your house! The trap here is that a pig (from the question) and a swine are much the same. Be careful: Just because words are connected in *meaning* does not mean that the answer is right. The *relationship* between the words is being tested. For example, the question may be about perfume, and the correct answer may involve sweat socks. No connection.

   (E) *A barnacle lives in a barn.*

   If you don't know what a barnacle is, you may be tempted to choose E, but C is the right answer. A *barnacle* is a creature that lives in the water (not in a barn) and often attaches itself to the bottoms of ships. You scrape the barnacles off the ship periodically to clean the ship's hull. *Correct Answer:* C.

Just Because You're Paranoid Doesn't Mean They're Not Out to Get You: Traps, Tricks, and Tips

Face it — this is why you really bought this book. You want to know those little traps that are built into the questions, sitting there waiting to pounce on unsuspecting victims. What time bombs have the test makers created, ready to go off in your face? Here are a few, with suggestions for how to deal with them.

Turn a verb into an infinitive

No, an infinitive is not the latest Japanese import car. An infinitive is the "to" form of any verb: to drink, to burp, to party. When an analogy features a verb, turn it into an infinitive and the sentence practically writes itself.

GIGGLE : LAUGH ::

To giggle is *to laugh* a little bit.

YELL : TALK ::

To yell is *to talk* loudly.

RUN : WALK ::

To run is *to walk* rapidly.

Notice that I'm adding another word on the end, usually an adverb to answer the "How?" question. How do you laugh when you giggle? A little bit. How do you talk when you yell? Loudly. How do you walk when you run? Rapidly. It's not enough to say, "To giggle is to laugh." You want to fine-tune the sentence, tweak it a little bit to clarify the relationship between the words. Remember: That Bulgarian exchange student is counting on you.

Identify the part of speech of the question word

Sometimes your sentence is easier to write if you know which part of speech — noun, verb, or adjective — a difficult word is. You find out by looking at its counterparts in the answer choices. That is, if you want to know which part of speech the first word in the question is, look at the first words in the answers. If you want to know which part of speech the second word in the question is, look at the second word in the answer choices.

DASHIKI : TAILOR ::

(A) shovel : professor

(B) table : singer

(C) garment : jock

(D) cake : baker

(E) book : poseur

Don't know what the word *dashiki* means? You're not alone; it's a pretty hard word. Not to worry. You know by looking at the first words in the answer choices — shovel, table, garment, cake, and book — that *dashiki* must be a noun and is a thing. (Remember that nouns are persons, places, or things.) Your very simple sentence should be: "A dashiki is a thing of a tailor." That's all you can do for now. Go through each answer choice.

(A) shovel : professor — Although it can get deep in the classroom sometimes, a shovel is not standard equipment for a professor.

(B) table : singer — A singer may stretch herself out on a table during a Las Vegas lounge act, doing a sexy, sultry number, but a table is not normally associated with a singer.

(C) garment : jock — This is a trap answer. You may be tempted to choose it because a tailor (from the question) deals with garments. However, you've already learned that the meanings of the question words are not necessarily related to the answer; the *relationship* between the pairs of words is important. Had the question said GARMENT : SEAMSTRESS or even GARMENT : MODEL, it would have been a good choice. But a garment is not necessarily a thing of a jock.

(D) cake : baker — A cake is a thing of a baker. Yeah, this answer sounds pretty good. There is a logical connection. Try the next one to be sure, but D is probably right.

(E) book : poseur — This answer is put here to trap students who immediately assume that the hardest word in a question or any word they themselves don't know must be the correct answer. A *poseur* is someone with an attitude, a person who adopts an affected style. People who go around using words like *poseur* are often poseurs themselves.

The right answer is D. A *dashiki*, by the way, is a type of shirt, and a tailor creates a dashiki just as a baker creates a cake. You can get the question right without knowing what the word means. *Correct Answer:* D.

Look for the salient features of a word

The *salient feature* is what makes something stand out. The salient feature of a basketball player is his or her height. The salient feature of a genius is his or her intelligence.

MINNOW : FISH ::

(A) elephant : animal

(B) recluse : shy

(C) gnat : insect

(D) giraffe : quadruped

(E) votary : peremptory

The salient feature of a minnow is that it is a *small* fish. While most of the answers are or may be synonyms (an elephant *is* an animal; a recluse *may be* shy), only C gives the salient or outstanding feature. A *gnat* is a *small* insect. Choice E features antonyms. A *votary* is a devoted follower (think of a votary as an elegant, grown-up groupie!). *Peremptory* means absolute, imperative, allowing no disagreement. The boss may be peremptory; the votary would more likely be *docile* (easily swayed). *Correct Answer:* C.

Backing into it

QUESTION: Is it okay to make the sentence by using the words backward?

ANSWER: Sure, as long as you remember to use the answer choices backward as well. That is, don't say, "A tailor makes a dashiki," and then say, "A cake makes a baker."

Identify common relationships

Certain standard relationships are often found in the analogies. There is a *plethora* (a lot) of them; here are ten of the most useful ones.

1. **Opposites**

   BIG : LITTLE
   PULCHRITUDINOUS : UGLY

2. **Synonyms**

   HAPPY : GLAD
   PUSILLANIMOUS : COWARDLY

3. **Cause and effect**

   TICKLE : LAUGHTER
   OSSIFY : BONE

4. **Part to whole**

   TOES : FOOT
   TALON : EAGLE

5. **Position**

   FRAME : PICTURE (a frame goes *around* a picture)
   SHOULDER : ROAD (a shoulder is to *the side of* a road).

6. **Greater to lesser**

   OVERJOYED : HAPPY
   CATACLYSMIC : UNFORTUNATE

7. **Location**

   PIG : STY
   WARREN : RABBIT

8. **Purpose or function**

   PILOT : FLY
   PUGILIST : BOX

9. **Characteristic**

   BLEAT : SHEEP (a bleat is the sound a sheep makes)
   POD : WHALES (a pod is a group of whales)

10. **Member to group (or specific to general)**

    FORK : UTENSIL
    ISLANDS : ARCHIPELAGO (an archipelago is *a group* of islands)

Use roots, prefixes, and suffixes

My three favorite words. Other women like "I love you," but I live for "roots, prefixes, and suffixes." These three words can bump up your score significantly. If you know just a few basic roots, prefixes, and suffixes, you can write magnificent analogy sentences and avoid falling into traps.

Suppose that the question is

IMPECUNIOUS : MONEY ::

If you don't know *impecunious*, you may be tempted to make the words synonyms and simply say, "Impecunious *is* money." A tempting and logical answer may be, for example, reservoir : water. Alas, once again you pay the price for giving in to temptation.

If you know that *-ous* means full of and *im-* means not, you can make a good sentence: "*Impecunious* is *not full of* money." That changes the whole picture. Now the right answer may be, for example, vacuum : air. A *vacuum* is *not full of* air. Note that a *reservoir* in fact *is* full of water; this is just the opposite of what you want to say.

Although you can learn hundreds of prefixes and suffixes, I realize that you have a limited number of brain cells you are willing to devote to this subject. Therefore, here is a list of ten of the most commonly used prefixes and eight of the most commonly used suffixes, with examples of each. Memorize them. Burn them in your brain. I'll get to some of the most common roots later on in Chapter 6. I don't want you to get overexcited by this stuff all at once.

Prefixes

1. **a- = not or without:** Someone *amoral* is without any morals, like the sadist who designed this test. Someone *atypical* is not typical, like the students who wear pocket protectors and love to take tests. Someone *apathetic* is without feeling, uncaring, like most students by the time they have finished the test and are leaving the exam room. ("The world is going to end tomorrow? Fine; that means I can get some sleep tonight.")

2. **an- = not or without:** An *anaerobic* environment is without oxygen (like the test room feels when a killer question leaves you gasping for air). *Anarchy* is without rule or government (like a classroom when a substitute teacher is in for the day).

3. **eu- = good:** A *eulogy* is a good speech, usually given for the dearly departed at a funeral. A *euphemism* is a good way of saying something or a polite expression, like saying that someone has passed away instead of calling him worm meat.

4. **ben-/bon- = good:** A *benefit* is something that has a good result, an advantage. Someone *benevolent* is good and kind; a benevolent father lets you take his new car on a date rather than your old junker. *Bon voyage* means have a good voyage; a *bon vivant* is a person who lives the good life.

5. **caco- = bad:** Something *cacophonous* is bad-sounding, such as nails on a chalkboard.

6. **ne-/mal- = bad:** Something *negative* is bad, like a negative attitude. Someone *nefarious* is "full of bad," or wicked and evil, like a nefarious wizard in a science fiction novel. Something *malicious* also is "full of bad," or wicked and harmful, like a malicious rumor that you are really a 30-year old narc in disguise.

7. **im- = not:** Something *impossible* is not possible. Someone *immortal* is not going to die but will live forever. Someone *implacable* is not able to be calmed down, stubborn. Notice that *im-* can also mean inside (*immerse* means to put into), but that meaning is not as common on the GRE. First, think of *im-* as meaning not; if that doesn't seem appropriate, switch to Plan B and see whether the *im-* can mean inside in the context of the question.

8. **in- = not:** Something *inappropriate* is not appropriate, such as the language people may use in front of small children when studying for the GRE. Someone *inept* is not adept, not skillful. Can you sue an inept surgeon who amputates the wrong leg? Nah, you wouldn't have a leg to stand on! Someone *insolvent* has no money, is bankrupt, like most students after four years of college. *In-* can also mean inside (*innate* means something born inside of you) or beginning (the *initial* letters of your name are the beginning letters). However, its most common meaning is not. Think of that one first; if it doesn't seem to work, try the others.

9. **ante- = before:** When the clock tells you that it's 5 a.m., the a.m. stands for *ante meridian*, which means before the middle, or the first half of the day. *Antebellum* means before the war. Tara in *Gone with the Wind* was an antebellum mansion, built before the Civil War. *Antediluvian* literally means before the flood, before Noah's deluge. Figuratively, it means very old; if you call your mother antediluvian, you mean that she's been around since before the flood. It's a great word to use as an insult because almost no one knows what it means and you can get away with it.

10. **post- = after:** When the clock tells you that it's 5 p.m., the p.m. stands for *post meridian*. It means after the middle, or the second half of the day. Something *postmortem* occurs after death. A postmortem exam is an autopsy.

Suffixes

1. **-ette = little:** A *cigarette* is a little cigar. A *dinette* table is a little dining table. A *coquette* is a little flirt (literally, a little chicken).

2. **-illo = little:** An *armadillo* is a little armored animal. A *peccadillo* is a little sin. (Do you speak Spanish? *Pecar* is to sin.)

3. **-ous = full of (very):** Someone *joyous* is full of joy. Someone *amorous* is full of *amour,* or love; very loving. Someone *pulchritudinous* is full of beauty, beautiful.

4. **-ist = a person:** A *typist* is a person who types. A *pugilist* is a person who fights (*pug-* means war or fight), a boxer. A *pacifist* is a person who believes in peace, a noncombatant (*pac-* means peace or calm).

5. **-ify (-efy) = to make:** To *beautify* is to make beautiful. To *ossify* is to make bone. (If you break your wrist, it takes weeks to ossify again, or for the bone to regenerate.) To *deify* is to make into a deity, a god.

6. **-ize = to make:** To *alphabetize* is to make alphabetical. To *immunize* is to make immune. To *ostracize* is to make separate from the group, to shun.

7. **-ate = to make:** To *duplicate* is to make double. To *renovate* is to make new again (*nov-* means new). To *placate* is to make peaceful or calm (*plac-* means peace or calm).

8. **-ity = noun suffix that doesn't actually mean anything; it just turns a word into a noun:** *Jollity* is the noun form of jolly. *Serenity* is the noun form of serene. *Timidity* is the noun form of timid.

Flash your friends: How to use flashcards

Go out and buy the largest index cards you can find. Get them in white and two other colors. Put all the roots, prefixes, and suffixes you learn that have negative connotations on cards of one color. For example, *ne-* means bad or not; put it on a brown card. *ben-* means good; put it on a pink card. *-ous* means full of. It doesn't "feel" good or bad; it's neutral. Put it on a white card.

When you get to the exam, you may encounter the word *nefarious.* You know you've seen it before, but you can't for the life of you remember what it means. Then a little picture unfolds in front of your eyes: You see *ne-* on a brown card. Aha! If it's on a brown card, it must be something negative. Just knowing that much often helps you to get the right answer.

Say the analogy is NEFARIOUS : SAINT. Normally, you assume that the words are synonyms and say, "A saint *is* nefarious." However, remembering that *ne-* is on a brown card, which means that it is negative, makes you change the sentence to "A saint is *not* nefarious,"

because saints are generally considered pretty good. (I make no comments about the New Orleans Saints football team, strong though the temptation is.)

There is no right or wrong way to classify the roots. If you think that a root is positive, fine, it's positive. If you think that a root is negative, fine, it's negative. The whole purpose of flashcards is to help you associate the words. Go with whatever works for *you.*

Bonus! When you come across a word that incorporates the root, put that word on the card as an example. That way, you learn both the root and the vocabulary word: two for the price of one. If you're reading a newspaper article about a program that will have a *salubrious* effect on the economy, you should note that *sal-* means health (I cover that root later) and *-ous* means full of. You know immediately that the word means healthful. Put it on both the *sal-* card and the *-ous* card. You'll learn the vocabulary without realizing it.

The Terminator: Eliminating Dumb Answers

The first answer to eliminate is the one that is backward. As you'll see, putting answers in reverse order is a common trap. If the question goes from greater to lesser (OVERJOYED : CONTENT), there is almost certainly a trap answer that goes from lesser to greater (displeased : furious). Look for it.

Another good answer to eliminate is one that duplicates the *meaning* rather than the relationship between the words. The question may be PROFESSOR : EDUCATED. The words are synonyms. A good answer to eliminate is teacher : moronic. Even though a professor is a teacher and those words have the same meaning, the *relationship* between the trap answer words is antonymous, not synonymous.

Finally, forget about humor. Anything funny or trying to be funny is outta here. Correct answers are almost always dull and boring.

Déjà Vu Review

Before going on to the practice questions, review what you've learned about analogies. There is a simple two-step approach to answering an analogy question:

1. **Use both words in a *descriptive* sentence.**

2. **Use the *exact* same sentence on each answer choice.**

Even if you don't have a clue what the words in an analogy mean, you can often get the correct answer by using the following five tips. These tips help you to identify the relationship between the words well enough to make a reasonable guess. If you are feeling particularly unreasonable (downright *sanguinary* — bloodthirsty — in fact), go ahead and guess. You lose no points for wrong answers on the GRE.

✔ Turn a verb into an infinitive.

✔ Identify which part of speech — noun, verb, or adjective — the question word is.

✔ Use roots, prefixes, and suffixes.

✔ Look for the *salient features* of a word.

✔ Identify common relationships.

Ten words that Cindy Crawford never hears				
obese	flaccid	unkempt	fleshy	frowzy
corpulent	drab	rotund	homely	slovenly

Chapter 3

The Dirty Dozen:
Analogy Practice Questions

• •

*R*eady to practice what I've been preaching? Here are The Dirty Dozen Analogy practice questions to get you into the swing of things. This chapter is loaded with good vocabulary words. Don't forget to pay extra-careful attention to the words that are in this font: *vocabulary word*.

Q 1. PEANUT : SHELL ::

    (A) atom : proton

    (B) clock : dial

    (C) corn : husk

    (D) emollient : solid

    (E) enamel : tooth

Make a simple sentence defining the relationship between the words : "A peanut is surrounded by a shell." Corn is surrounded by a husk. Choice D, emollient, is much too hard of a word for the first question. Questions go from easy to hard. A word you can't define would probably not be the correct answer in the first half of the exam but may very well be the best choice in the second half. An *emollient* is something that makes the skin smooth and soft, like a hand lotion. It wouldn't be "surrounded by a solid." *Correct Answer:* C.

Choice E is backward. The enamel is not surrounded by the tooth but vice versa. Keep your eyes open for a backward answer among the answer choices; one is frequently put there to getcha.

Q 2. HYMN : SONG ::

    (A) screech : whisper

    (B) waltz : dance

    (C) misnomer : correction

    (D) discussion : altercation

    (E) smile : reproof

A simple test sentence is "A hymn is a type of song." A waltz is a type of dance. A *screech* is a loud noise, just the opposite of a whisper. Your tires screech when you take the corner wide in your rush to get to the GRE, having overslept that morning. (I know. I shouldn't even joke about such a thing!) In choice C, a *misnomer* is the wrong name, calling someone Tracy instead of Stacy, for example. It therefore is not a correction but a mistake. An *altercation* is a disagreement. While it may be a discussion, the answer is not as close to being synonymous as is choice B. In choice E, a *reproof* is a condemnation, a criticism. Words like altercation and reproof are probably too difficult to be the correct answers this close to the beginning. *Correct Answer:* B.

Easy questions usually have easy answers; hard questions often have hard answers.

3. CHUCKLE : MERRIMENT ::

    (A) goosebumps : denial

    (B) blush : glee

    (C) scowl : perfidy

    (D) wince : discomfort

    (E) shout : fury

Make your sentence : "A chuckle indicates merriment" or "A chuckle is the result of merri-ment." *Merriment* is just what it looks like, happiness. The suffix *-ment* doesn't mean anything; it just turns a word into a noun, such as content and contentment, or argue and argument. A *wince* (an involuntary shrinking back or flinching) indicates discomfort. You wince when your Dearly Beloved says to you, "We *have* to talk. . . ." In choice A, *goosebumps* indicate cold or fright, not denial. Choice B could trap a careless reader who thinks that because *glee* means happiness or merriment, this answer fits. In choice C, *perfidy* means disloyalty and is too hard of a word for this close to the beginning of the test. Choice E is a "mebbe so, mebbe not" answer. A shout may indicate fury (you shout at the ATM when it gobbles up and shreds your bank card), but it does not necessarily do so. Always look for the salient or outstanding feature of the word. *Correct Answer:* D.

Remember: You are to choose an answer based on the *relationships* between the words, not on the meanings of the words. The question can be about houses and the answer about canta-loupes; they don't have to have any connection whatsoever.

4. COW : TERRIFY ::

    (A) praise : disparage

    (B) interest : fascinate

    (C) invigorate : exhaust

    (D) soothe : agitate

    (E) diminish : lessen

Okay, suppose that you have no idea what the word *cow* as a verb means. You can still get this question right by the process of elimination. Choices A, C, and D all have the relationship of antonyms. Because they can't all be correct, they must all be wrong. You now know that *cow* and *intimidate* are not antonyms. As quickly as that, you've narrowed the answers down to two, but can you narrow the answers down even further? The relationship between the words in choice B is lesser to greater; that is, interesting someone is less intense than fascinating that person. Because *terrify*, in the question, is such a strong word, it's unlikely that the first word, *cow*, is something even stronger. Just so you'll know, to *cow* means to intimidate, to browbeat. *Correct Answer:* B.

Words have more than one meaning. A test question may key into this fact. If your first response seems to make no sense in the context of the question ("Why would a cow terrify anyone?") try to think of alternate meanings of the word.

5. XENOPHOBIC : STRANGERS ::

    (A) claustrophobic : Christmas

    (B) hydrophobic : fires

    (C) agoraphobic : open spaces

    (D) pyromaniac : animals

    (E) romantic : love

You may not know the word *xenophobic*, but you can deduce that *phobic* means fearful of because you know such relatively easy words as *hydrophobia* (fear of water) and *claustrophobia* (fear of closed spaces). Therefore, make the sentence: "*Xenophobic* is fearful of strangers." *Agoraphobic* means fearful of open spaces. An agoraphobe is often afraid to leave the house at all. When it's your turn to shovel the snow off the front walk, you may suddenly turn into an agoraphobe.

Choice A is a lame attempt at humor (and won't be found on the actual GRE, which has no humor at all, lame or otherwise). *Claustrophobic* does not mean fearing Santa Claus and Christmas. *Hydrophobic* means fearing water, not fires. Someone who is a *pyromaniac* has a love of fire. Someone romantic has a love of love, not a fear of love. *Correct Answer:* C.

6. ELEGIAC : JOY ::

  (A) innocuous : harmful

  (B) phlegmatic : peace

  (C) implacable : tranquillity

  (D) dynamic : energy

  (E) disparaging : insults

Something elegiac is not full of joy. An *elegy* is a sad or mournful poem. Something *innocuous* is not full of harm. (Figure this out using the roots: *In-* usually means not; *noc* means harm; *-ous* means full of, not full of harm.)

Often if you don't know a word, you make the "is" sentence: Elegiac is joy. But in this case, just to make you miss the question and therefore help you to remember the word *elegiac* (sad or mournful), I've made it the opposite. But you should still have gotten this question correct because choice D, *dynamic*, does mean full of energy, and choice E, *disparaging*, does mean full of insults. Because two answers can't both be correct, they must both be wrong. Knowing that should send you back to the drawing board to change from an "is" to an "is not" sentence.

Choice B, *phlegmatic*, means calm, composed. Now that you know this word, you can remain phlegmatic when you encounter it on the GRE and not panic. Choice C, *implacable*, means unchangeable, stubborn. An implacable toddler yells "NO!" no matter what the harassed parents suggest. (Do you see the roots? *im-* means not; *plac* means peace or calm; *-able* is able to be. Someone implacable is "unable to be calmed down," or just plain stubborn.) *Correct Answer:* A.

7. PECCADILLO : TRANSGRESSION ::

  (A) felony : crime

  (B) nibble : bite

  (C) alias : name

  (D) cacophony : noise

  (E) eructation : hill

You know the suffix *-illo* means small or little. Make the sentence : "A peccadillo is a small transgression." You don't even have to know what the words mean to get a good sentence. (A *peccadillo* is a small wrong or fault. A *transgression* is a trespass or sin, a wrong.) A nibble is a small bite. In choice C, an *alias* is a different name, not a small name. In D, *cacophony* is a bad or harsh sound, like my singing voice or the sounds of an orchestra warming up. The roots help you to define this word; *caco* means bad, *phon* means sound : bad sound. Choice E is my gift to you, a little comic relief. An *eructation* is a belch. While a volcano may eructate, an eructation itself is not a hill or a volcano. *Correct Answer:* B.

8. PROGNOSTICATION : SOOTHSAYER ::

(A) tumult : arbitrator

(B) duplicity : idiot

(C) fanaticism : zealot

(D) adulation : adult

(E) retrospection : prophet

Whoa! Suddenly these words have gotten terribly hard. Try saying: "Prognostication *is* sooth-sayer." Therefore, you are looking for two answer words that are synonyms or at least mean *nearly* the same thing.

Fanaticism is the state of being a *fanatic* (did you know that the word *fan*, like a rock star's groupie, comes from the word *fanatic*?), being really into something. *Zealous* also means very into something, enthusiastic, involved. The words are synonyms. A *zealot* is one who is zealous.

You may have known the words for choice C but not for the other answers. Let's review them quickly. You may be familiar with *tumult* in another form, *tumultuous*. It means wild, chaotic, disorganized. An *arbitrator* is a mediator, a go-between in a fight or controversy. An arbitrator's job would be to stop the tumult, to calm things down and bring about a rational discussion. The words are closer to antonyms than synonyms.

By the way, a favorite ETS trick is to give you a common word in an uncommon form, just to confuse you and make your life miserable. For example, do you know this word?

RUTH

Seeing it all by itself like that, you may swear that you'd never seen the word before. But you probably know it in another form:

RUTHLESS

Ah, you know that *ruthless* means cruel, without pity or compassion. Work backwards. If ruthless means *without* pity, ruth must mean *with* pity. *Ruth* is pity or compassion, kindness, mercy. Ruth used to be a very popular girl's name.

The moral of the story is, when you see a word that looks slightly familiar, knock it around a little bit. Change its form to see whether you can discover its meaning more easily. *Tumult* is just the noun form of the more common word, tumultuous.

In B, *duplicity* is the quality of being *dup,* or double, as in double-dealing, double-crossing, double-talking. Benedict Arnold was noted for his duplicity. It has nothing to do with being an idiot. However, there is a trick here. A *dupe*, or a person who has been double-crossed or swindled, is in fact rather idiotic. This would be an easy trap to fall for.

Choice D is silly. *Adulation* has nothing to do with being an adult. Adulation is hero worship, extreme admiration. You would have adulation for a war hero or for the person who discovers the cure for cancer.

Choice E is also closer to antonyms than to synonyms. *Retrospection* is a look back, a review. At my sixteenth birthday party, my parents showed home movies of my baby pictures: me naked in the bathtub at six months, me crawling around on a rug at seven months, and so on. They called it the Suzee Retrospective. I called it Death By Embarrassment. Come to think of it, I wanted to *fustigate* everyone involved with that *retrospective*. A prophet is supposed to *prophesy* or predict the future, not look back at the past. *Correct Answer:* C.

9. EXCULPATE : BLAME ::

    (A) demean : average

    (B) compromise : peril

    (C) proliferate : abundance

    (D) perturb : exasperation

    (E) exonerate : guilt

Just to keep you on your toes, I put in a question in which the right answer actually did have the same meaning as the question words. This situation is rare, but I always want to emphasize to you that my suggestions are tips, not rules. Never shut off your own brain in favor of mine. To *exculpate* is to remove the blame. Think of the roots: *ex-* means out of or away from; *culp* means guilt or blame; *-ate* means to make: To make away from the guilt or blame. When your roommate comes in breathing fire because someone has borrowed his car and put a big dent in it, you thank your lucky stars that you went to class with friends in their car that day and have witnesses to exculpate you. To *exonerate* is the same thing, to remove the guilt or blame. A defense attorney sends his or her investigators out looking for evidence to exonerate the client.

To *compromise* means to imperil, to put into danger. For example, a young girl who stays out all night long with her date — even though they are just talking — compromises her reputation. A congressman who is seen fraternizing with lobbyists may be compromising his integrity, putting it into some question or doubt. As you learned with *cow* in question 4, words may have more than one meaning. The first definition most people provide for *compromise* is to come to terms by mutual concession, to meet in the middle and agree. As that meaning has no connection with peril, you need to wrack your brains for another, less-common meaning.

In choice C, to *proliferate* is to grow in number or size, to become more abundant. The most common meaning of *pro-* on the GRE is big or much; a *proliferation* is an abundance, very much. In choice D, to *perturb* is to *exasperate*, to annoy or harass. If you missed this question, you are probably perturbed and exasperated with yourself. *Correct Answer:* E.

10. DESICCATE : MOISTURE ::

    (A) sanction : restrictions

    (B) enervate : energy

    (C) swindle : chicanery

    (D) attenuate : attention

    (E) derogate : epithets

Don't be disheartened if you don't know any of the words in the answer choices. That's normal for this close to the end of an exam. But because there is no penalty on the GRE for guessing, guess and go. Make a quick guess and go on.

To *desiccate* is to dry out, to remove moisture. (Ever hear of desiccated liver tablets? Some health food stores sell them for people who don't want to eat liver and would prefer to ingest it in dehydrated or pill form.) You could figure this relationship out by knowing that *de-* means out of or away from: A desiccant moves moisture out of or away from something. To *enervate* is to devitalize, to remove the energy from, to weaken.

Choice A, to *sanction* is to prohibit. You have probably heard of economic sanctions, in which our government prohibits businesses from working with companies in other countries. To sanction, therefore, would be to add restrictions rather than to take them away. In choice C, to *swindle* is to cheat or trick, as in swindling someone out of his money. *Chicanery* is trickery in matters of law. To swindle is not to take away chicanery but to add to it. In choice D, to *attenuate* is not to take away attention (you didn't fall for such a cheesy trick, did you?) but to make slender, thin, or diluted. An emaciated person looks attenuated. In choice E, to *derogate* is to denounce or be critical of. An *epithet* is a descriptive term, often one used derogatorily or critically. *Correct Answer:* B.

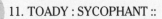

11. TOADY : SYCOPHANT ::

   (A) recluse : pedant

   (B) heretic : leader

   (C) malingerer : prodigy

   (D) bluestocking : gymnast

   (E) miser : pennypincher

If you don't know the words in the question, you're not alone. They are very difficult words, put there in the hopes that you would remember what to do when you don't have a clue: First, try making the words synonyms. Make the simple sentence: A toady is a sycophant. As it turns out, that's correct. Both a *toady* and a *sycophant* are over-flatterers, kiss-ups, yes-men. A groupie to a rock star is a toady and a sycophant. A student trying to get the professor to turn a borderline A-/B+ into the A is a toady and a sycophant. In the correct answer, E, a *miser* (a cheapskate, someone stingy) is in fact a pennypincher. A *pennypincher* is just what it looks like, a person who pinches pennies, holding them securely, not letting them go or spending them.

Here are the definitions for the other words. A *recluse* is a hermit, a solitary person. You may have heard this word in another form, reclusive. A *pedant* is a teacher, especially one who is overly precise and didactic. A *heretic* is a rebel, particularly one who doesn't agree with the orthodox religion. Joan of Arc was burned at the stake as a heretic. A *malingerer* is one who pretends to be sick in order to get out of work. All of us have been malingerers on the morning of a big exam at school, swearing to a variety of symptoms that would kill an ox. A *prodigy* is a highly talented person (Mozart was a child prodigy). A *bluestocking* is a learned woman, especially one in literary circles. She has nothing to do with gymnastics. *Correct Answer:* E.

12. PUGILIST : BELLICOSE ::

   (A) benefactor : beguiling

   (B) chatterbox : taciturn

   (C) narcissist : charismatic

   (D) scholar : erudite

   (E) imbecile : obsequious

A *pugilist* is a boxer, one who fights (the root *pug* means war or fight and *-ist* is a person). *Bellicose* is like belligerent: hostile, argumentative, fighting. The test sentence is: "A pugilist is bellicose." If you don't know the words and assume they are synonyms, you are right. A scholar is in fact *erudite*, which means well-educated or scholarly. In choice A, a *benefactor* is a person who does good, one who brings *benefits* (to use a more common form of the word). He or she probably would not be *beguiling*, which means tricking or confusing. In choice B, a *chatterbox* is just what it looks like, one who chatters or talks a lot. *Taciturn* means not talkative, of few words. A chatterbox is not taciturn.

TIP

Have you heard of a *tacit* agreement? It's an unspoken agreement. Try to think of more common or familiar forms of the word. If you can remember how you've used those in context, you can often get a "good enough" definition for the more difficult word.

In choice C, a *narcissist* is a person overflowing with self-love, someone who thinks he or she is just the most wonderful thing around. While the narcissist may think he or she is *charismatic* (inspiring loyalty), 'tain't necessarily so. In choice E, an *imbecile* is a feebleminded person, a fool (what most of us feel like when we don't know all these words). An imbecile may or may not be *obsequious*, which means excessively flattering. Remember the toady and sycophant from a previous question? Now *they* would be obsequious. *Correct Answer:* D.

Chapter 4

If Opposites Attract, Why Are Antonyms So Repulsive?

• •

In This Chapter

▶ Is that all there is? The format of an Antonym question

▶ Let's get this over with fast: The approach

▶ What to do when you ain't got a clue

▶ Bad things come in small packages: Tricks, traps, and tips

• •

Think of the antonyms as the Terrible Twos of the vocabulary world. Just like a *cantankerous* (grumpy) kid who answers your "Good morning!" with "No, it's not; it's a bad morning!" Antonym questions are looking to contradict everything.

Is That All There Is? The Format

Antonyms are a fish out of water, a word out of context (a cliché out of a Dummy). An Antonym question features one word in capital letters followed by five lowercase answer choices. The prima donna antonym stands alone. You have no context to help you to define the vocabulary. It's you against the word. For example:

LOQUACIOUS:

  (A) quotidian

  (B) taciturn

  (C) contentious

  (D) guileless

  (E) perfunctory

I'm looking forward to this	
harbinger	auguries
prescient	portent
presage	prognosticate
prognosis	bode

You have to keep your sense of humor

levity	ribald
jocose	puckish
wag	jocular
risible	badinage
japing	jollity
twit	mirth

Your task is to define the question word and then choose the answer with the meaning most nearly opposite. The good news is that doing so takes almost no time. These questions are over with faster than your last relationship. You can build up a good reservoir of time here that you can use (and will probably need) on the Reading Comprehension questions later. The bad news is that some of this vocabulary is so difficult you may think you've wandered into the Greek GRE by mistake.

Let's Get This Over with Fast: The Approach

The antonyms are the least complicated portion of the GRE. Take a simple two-step approach:

1. **Define the question word.**

2. **Choose the opposite.**

Sounds simple, right? It is . . . _if_ you know what the question word means. If the question word is _happy,_ choose _sad._ If the question word is _tall,_ choose _short._ So far, so good. But what happens when you _don't_ know what the question word means?

It's a sad day if you don't know your vocabulary

Weltschmerz	lachrymose
jeremiad	dour
doleful	lugubrious
maudlin	saturnine
contrite	bereft

What to Do When You Ain't Got a Clue

Suppose that you look at a word and think it looks more like an ink blot test than like any vocabulary word you've ever seen. The word may be *cadging*. Not a clue, right? (And no, it's not a typo or a misspelling of "cage.") What do you do next? You have one of three options.

1. **Dissect and define the term using roots, prefixes, and suffixes.**

   As you learned in the analogies chapter, roots, prefixes, and suffixes are the real key to vocabulary on the GRE. Unfortunately, **cadging** has no root, prefix, or suffix that you have learned. Proceed to option 2.

2. **Eliminate answer choices that are synonyms of each other.**

   Suppose that choice A is *bubbly* and choice D is *effervescent*. Both words mean exuberant, joyful. Because two answer choices cannot both be correct, they must both be wrong. You've narrowed the answer choices down to three. Should you guess?

   Absolutely! (Stupid question.) In case you've forgotten, the GRE does not subtract points for a wrong answer. Go for it.

3. **Bail out! Choose an answer and leave the scene as quickly as possible.**

   Suppose that you have no idea what the word means. It has no identifiable root, prefix, or suffix. No two answer choices mean the same thing. There's no way to narrow the answers down. What happens now? Guess and go. Choose something, anything, and go on to the next question.

The biggest mistake you can make on an Antonym question is to waste time. The longer you sit there, stare at the word, scratch your head, and wait for heavenly revelation, the more the test makers in their dark cubbyholes chortle with glee at your struggling in the *quagmire* (bog) they designed for you. Get through an Antonym question quickly: You either know it, or you don't know it, and then you're outta there. Think of an Antonym question as a blind date. You can tell in the first few minutes whether something's happening or not. (P.S. *Cadging* means begging or scrounging. GRE students often cadge notes from friends for classes.)

That's easy for you to say

declaim	exhort
stentorian	philippic
persiflage	pontificate
raconteur	prolix
voluble	tergiversate

Bad Things Come in Small Packages: Tricks, Traps, and Tips

How, you wonder, can there be tricks and traps on a one-word question? Read 'em and weep.

Ignore the synonym

You may be lucky enough to encounter a very difficult word that you just happen to remember. Suppose that the question word is *pulchritudinous*. If you have already gone through the analogies portion of this book, you remember that pulchritudinous means beautiful. Choice A is "Beautiful." You are so pleased with yourself for remembering this hard word that you choose A ("ah, there it is!") and go your merry way. It isn't until you're boasting to your friend later that afternoon about having remembered *pulchritudinous* that your mistake dawns on you: You were supposed to choose the *antonym,* not the synonym. In short: If you see a word in the answer choices that means the same, or nearly the same as the question, ignore it. It's put there just to ruin your day.

Use roots, prefixes, and suffixes

As I have mentioned throughout this material, roots, prefixes, and suffixes (RPS) can save you when you have to wade through this polysyllabic pit. If you have not yet learned the roots, prefixes, and suffixes given to you in the analogies chapter, I strongly suggest you do so now. You can analyze even the most difficult word using roots. Even if you can't get the exact definition, you can get a general idea of the word well enough to choose it or lose it.

Suppose that the question word is *abjure*. You don't know what it means, but you recall that the prefix *ab-* means away from. A queen abdicates a throne, or goes away from a throne. One of the answer choices is *embrace*. To embrace something is to take it as your own, to accept it, as in embracing the principles of democracy. If you trust your roots-sense and choose this, you'll get a hard question correct in just a few seconds. (To *abjure* is to renounce or reject.)

Memorize connotation cards

I talk in Chapter 2 about creating flash cards for the roots, prefixes, and suffixes. You should have those cards completed by now and be ready to move on to a more sophisticated type of flashing: *connotation cards.*

Just how boring *is* this vocabulary?

ennui	trite
platitude	hackneyed
prosaic	vapid
listless	soporific
bromide	tedious
somniferous	

It takes a lot of guts to know these words

audacity	intrepid
doughty	redoubtable
undaunted	effrontery
impudent	uncowed

You'll notice I'm not wasting your time or mine by giving you a list of a thousand words. It would be useless for you to sit down and try to memorize so many. You'd get to a point where each new word would *supplant* (displace, push out) a previous word. So how *can* you cram the most vocabulary into the least brain space? Memorize groups of words by their connotation.

A *connotation* is an association or idea, an implication. It is what the word means to you, how you remember it. Use index cards for clustering words by their connotations. For example, on one side of a card, write *fat,* and on the other side, write *thin*. Every time you encounter a word that has one of these meanings, put it on the card. On the fat side, you might have: *corpulent*, *fleshy*, *rotund*, and *obese*. On the thin side, you might have: *emaciated*, *attenuated*, *svelte*, and *lanky*.

Suppose you get to the exam and you see the word *svelte* but can't for the life of you remember what it means. In your mind's eye, you see the word on the *fat/thin* card. Voilà! Or on second thought: Ooops! Wait a minute: Does *svelte* mean fat, or does it mean thin?

Write words with positive meanings in red ink and words with negative meanings in black ink. For example, most people would consider being thin better than being fat. Write all the *thin* words in bright red magic marker to make them stand out. Write all the *fat* words in black magic marker. During the exam, you can remember that *svelte* is a red word on the *fat/thin* card. That means it must mean thin. You'll be surprised how many questions you can get correct without knowing precise definitions, just hazy general concepts.

Hip, hip, hooray! Words of praise

laud	extol
paean	accolade
eulogy	plaudits
encomium	sycophant
kudos	toady
panegyric	obsequious

Don't anticipate and misread

The GRE often features some pretty bizarre-looking words. My favorite is *froward* (stubborn). At least once a year, some student will call me, overjoyed at having "conquered" the GRE: "Suzee, you won't believe it. The GRE had a typo. One of the antonyms said *froward* instead of *forward*. However, the answer choice 'backward' was there, so I had no trouble figuring it out." No, no, a thousand times, no! The GRE has no typos. The GRE has no spelling errors. The GRE has no heart. It's very easy to see what you want to see rather than to read what's actually printed on the page. Double-check that you have read the word correctly, not rewritten the test to match your preconceptions.

If you are nearing the end of the antonyms where the questions are supposed to be very difficult and you think a word is wonderfully easy, you may have confused that word with another.

Peroration (A Summing Up)

An Antonym question requires a simple two-step approach:

1. **Define the word.**

2. **Choose the opposite.**

Antonyms are small but deadly. Remembering the following can help you to get through these questions efficiently:

✔ Use roots, prefixes, and suffixes.

✔ Eliminate answer choices that are synonyms of each other.

✔ Look for and avoid the answer choice that is a synonym of the question word.

✔ Learn vocabulary words in clusters using connotation cards.

✔ Don't anticipate and misread unusual words (like *froward*).

✔ Guess and go: Because the GRE has no penalty for wrong answers, choose an answer quickly and move on.

Are you sick to death of vocabulary?

dirge	morbid
demise	obsequies
valetudinarian	noxious
elegy	insalubrious
cadaver	wan

Chapter 5

Unattractive Opposites: Antonym Practice Questions

You say you've been using a dictionary for a pillow for the last six weeks, believing some of the words and their definitions would penetrate your skull by osmosis? Here's a chance to test your theory.

Q 1. CHANGING

(A) lightweight

(B) cautious

(C) immutable

(D) delicious

(E) soft

You can get this question correct by the process of elimination. The opposite of changing is not changing, unchanging. You know that lightweight, cautious, delicious, and soft do not mean "not changing," which narrows the answers down quickly to the correct one. Use your roots to define *immutable*. *Im-* means not; *mut* means change. ***Im-mut-able*** literally means not changeable, unchanging. *Correct Answer:* C.

Q 2. RECUPERATE

(A) sicken

(B) invent

(C) operate

(D) elongate

(E) balance

To *recuperate* is to regain your health. The opposite is to sicken. Choice C has a small trap in it. A person recuperating may have been operated on, but just because an answer choice seems connected to the question word (both *recuperate* and *operate* have to do with health) does not mean the choice is correct.

Did you use your common sense to eliminate choice B? What word could possibly be the opposite of *invent*? As far as I know, there is not word meaning "uninvent." If you can't think of a logical opposite for a word, then it probably is not an antonym of the question. *Correct Answer:* A.

3. OPAQUE

    (A) old-fashioned

    (B) angry

    (C) improper

    (D) outdated

    (E) transparent

Something *opaque* is not clear, not see-through. It blocks the light (*op* means block or against). Something *transparent* is clear, does not block the light. Did you notice that you could eliminate choices A and D because they were synonyms of each other? If two words mean the same (or nearly the same), they can't both be correct and therefore must both be wrong. *Correct Answer:* E.

4. LOQUACIOUS

    (A) elegant

    (B) quiet

    (C) overweight

    (D) excited

    (E) incapable

If you know your roots, this question is easy. If not, you may as well make a wild guess (remember that the GRE has no penalty for wrong answers, so guessing can only help, not hurt, you). *Loq* means speech or talk; *-ous* means full of or very. Someone *loquacious* is full of talk, very talkative. The opposite is quiet. *Correct Answer:* B.

Most of my students are quite loquacious in telling me that their biggest problem is vocabulary. They just plain can't remember pages and pages and pages of words. My suggestion is always the same: Concentrate on learning roots, prefixes, and suffixes, which can expand your vocabulary exponentially. In this book, lists of roots, prefixes, and suffixes can be found in Chapters 2 and 6.

5. SKEPTICAL

    (A) fast-acting

    (B) punctual

    (C) depressed

    (D) credulous

    (E) effervescent

If you are *skeptical*, you are dubious or doubtful. You are looking for a word that means not doubtful. Eliminate the words you do know, choices A, B, and C. *Credulous* can be defined using the roots: *cred* means trust or belief; *-ous* means full of or very. Someone *credulous* is full of trust, naive, gullible — just the opposite of skeptical. *Effervescent* means bubbly. When an <u>Effer</u>dent (a denture-cleaning tablet) is put into a glass of water, it bubbles. *Correct Answer:* D.

6. VIABLE

    (A) solid

    (B) moribund

    (C) vital

    (D) integral

    (E) irreplaceable

If you chose C, you fell for the trap. *Vital* means essential, critical. Just because it has a *vi* like the question word does not mean vital is the right answer (and anyway, you are looking for antonyms, not synonyms). Choices C, D, and E are similar enough in meaning that selecting one over the others would be hard. You can't have three right answers, so eliminate them all.

Viable means capable of working or developing adequately, livable. A plan for learning several new roots like *vi* (meaning life) daily is viable (it can be done). *Moribund* means near death or extinction. A company that is bankrupt and firing employees may be described as moribund. *Correct Answer:* B.

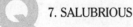

7. SALUBRIOUS

(A) unhealthy

(B) serendipitous

(C) dour

(D) rapid

(E) monumental

Salubrious means healthful, wholesome, salutary (*sal* means health, *-ous* means full of). Unhealthful is as logical an opposite as you're ever going to find. Choice B, *serendipitous,* means fortuitous, a happy, lucky occurrence. It would be serendipitous to walk out your front door and find a hundred dollar bill on your doorstep. Choice C, *dour,* means gloomy. Finding out that the hundred dollar bill you so serendipitously found on the sidewalk featured a picture not of Ben Franklin but of Alfred E. Newman will leave you dour. *Correct Answer:* A.

8. IRASCIBLE

(A) mendacious

(B) serpentine

(C) phlegmatic

(D) fatigued

(E) tepid

Irascible means hot-tempered, easily angered. Choice C, *phlegmatic,* means slow, having a solid temperament, not easily excited to action. Choice A, *mendacious,* means lying, dishonest, untruthful. Don't confuse the adjective mendacious, meaning dishonest, with the noun *mendicant,* a beggar. A mendicant may be mendacious when he tells you how he's going to spend the quarter you just gave him. Choice B, *serpentine,* means like a snake, twisting or turning. The road to Pike's Peak is a serpentine road. Choice E, *tepid,* means lukewarm. A tepid response to a marriage proposal should send you to your lawyer's office to get a prenuptial agreement. *Correct Answer:* C.

9. FRANGIBLE

(A) refulgent

(B) histrionic

(C) unbreakable

(D) unfriendly

(E) masculine

Frangible means breakable. The opposite, amazingly enough, is unbreakable. Choice A, *refulgent,* means shining, radiant, gleaming. Choice B, *histrionic,* means theatrical, hysterical, dramatic. *Correct Answer:* C.

10. PALLIATE

    (A) laud

    (B) appraise

    (C) exacerbate

    (D) befriend

    (E) mitigate

To *palliate* is to soften, lessen, or assuage. You can palliate an insult by smiling to take the sting out. Choice C, *exacerbate,* is to make more severe, to aggravate. You exacerbate a fight when you slam the door in your opponent's face. Choice A, to *laud,* is to praise. (Think of ap<u>laud</u>.) Choice D, to *befriend,* is to make a friend of. (*Be* is a prefix meaning completely; however, you can basically ignore this prefix. To befriend someone is simply to "friend" him.) Choice E, *mitigate,* is the same as palliate. To mitigate is to lessen or decrease, to make less severe. You may have heard of "mitigating circumstances." Hot wiring and stealing a car is a felony that can land you in prison; taking the car because your wife is in labor and you have to get to the hospital pronto is a mitigating circumstance (but if you take <u>my</u> car, you have *unmitigated* gall!). *Correct Answer:* C.

 11. CONDIGN

    (A) incapable

    (B) inevitable

    (C) inconsistent

    (D) unremitting

    (E) undeserved

Condign means deserved or appropriate. A condign punishment for those of you who do not laugh at my jokes is to spend eternity listening to your parent's old record albums. The opposite (logically enough) is *undeserved. Correct Answer:* E.

12. SALACIOUS

    (A) wholesome

    (B) rustic

    (C) noxious

    (D) merry

    (E) puissant

Salacious means lustful, lecherous, lewd — the opposite of wholesome. Choice B, *rustic,* means rural, appropriate for the country. A rustic outfit would be plus fours and a shooting stick. Choice E, *puissant,* means strong, influential, powerful. *Correct Answer:* A.

 Did you fall for the trap answer, C? *Sal-* means health; *-ous* means full of. No one can fault you if you thought salacious meant "full of health." However, the word for that is *salubrious.* Choice C, *noxious,* means poisonous. It is a good antonym for salubrious but not for salacious. Remember the last question in a section is usually very hard or very tricky or both.

 No, no, don't panic. Of course, this section is hard for you. But I have news for you: It's just as hard for native English speakers. It's true! Your average American has no more idea of the meanings of *prolix* (verbose and long-winded) and *salubrious* than you do. We're all equal when it comes to needing to learn roots, prefixes, and suffixes.

Chapter 6

Finish What You Start: Sentence Completions

- -

In This Chapter

▶ Drawing a blank: what Sentence Completion questions look like

▶ Cutting away the deadwood: dissecting and simplifying the sentences

▶ Sweeping away the trash: eliminating wrong answers

- -

Sentence Completion questions are the blind dates of the GRE. What you see is not necessarily what you get . . . or what you want. Looks can be deceiving. Don't judge a book by its cover. Beauty is only skin deep. Let's see, have I left out any other trite, banal, hackneyed clichés? The point of all this babbling is that Sentence Completion questions can be sneaky, tricky, duplicitous, and worse than they look. Fortunately, there are ways to beat the questions at their own game.

What Sentence Completion Questions Look Like

A Sentence Completion question consists of one sentence with one or two blanks. Your job, should you choose to accept it, is to fill in the blanks. Usually only one word goes in each blank; occasionally, however, the blank requires a few words or a short phrase instead. Here is an example:

Disgusted at having to spend the entire weekend studying for the GRE instead of going hang gliding, Faye - - - - her book across the room with such - - - - that it soared high into the sky, causing three of her neighbors to call the UFO hot line.

   (A) tossed .. gentleness

   (B) hurled .. ferocity

   (C) pitched .. glee

   (D) carried .. gloom

   (E) conveyed .. reluctance

The key word in this example is "disgusted," indicating strong, negative emotions. Only choice B offers two words that match the tone of "disgusted." *Correct Answer:* B.

Looking at the Sentence and Drawing a Blank

Do you look at Sentence Completion questions and draw a blank? (Sorry, I couldn't resist.) Knowing where to start is a great confidence builder and time-saver. Try the following steps.

1. **Read the entire sentence for its gist.**
2. **If possible, predict words to fit the blanks.**
3. **Insert the answer choices.**

The following sections explain these steps.

Read the entire sentence

Although this may seem obvious, many people read until they get to the first blank and then head for the answers. The problem is that the sentence may change in midstream, messing everything up. Note, for example, the big difference between

> Having been coerced by her mother into accepting a blind date, Mitzi was ---- *because* Marty turned out to be ----.

> — and —

> Having been coerced by her mother into accepting a blind date, Mitzi was ---- *although* Marty turned out to be ----.

In the first example, you may want to say something like this:

> Having been coerced by her mother into accepting a blind date, Mitzi was *ecstatic* because Marty turned out to be *gorgeous*.

In the second example, you could say the following:

> Having been coerced by her mother into accepting a blind date, Mitzi was *content* although Marty turned out to be *mediocre*.

How you fill in the blanks depends on the middle term — in this case the conjunction *because* or *although*.

Keep in mind that the purpose of Sentence Completion questions is to measure your ability to recognize words and phrases that logically and stylistically complete the meaning of the sentences.

Predict words to fit the blanks

Notice the careful hedge, "if possible." You can't *always* predict words. But it's amazing how often you can get close. Consider the following example:

> Hal was ---- when his new computer arrived because he realized he'd have no excuses now for not finishing his homework.

You can predict that the word should be something negative, such as *depressed, sad,* or *unhappy.* (If your vocabulary is up to the task, you can also predict negative words such as *lachrymose, dolorous,* and *lugubrious.*)

Did you predict something positive, such as *happy* or *glad?* If you did, you probably headed for the answers before you read the entire sentence. What did I just tell you in the preceding section? Tsk, tsk.

Insert the answer choices

Don't try to save time by hurrying through Sentence Completion questions. You just need to plug and chug. Plug in every answer choice and chug through the whole darn sentence again. Occasionally, you can eliminate answers because you know the word *must* be positive, but that answer choice is negative. After you eliminate everything you can, you must insert the remaining answers into the blanks and read through the sentences that result. Try the following example:

As a public relations specialist, Susan realizes the importance of - - - - and - - - - when dealing with even the most exasperating tourists.

(A) dignity .. etiquette

(B) fantasy .. realism

(C) kindness .. patience

(D) courtesy .. compassion

(E) truth .. honesty

Because the two blanks are connected by *and,* the words in those blanks should be synonyms (or almost synonyms). They may not need to mean exactly the same thing, but they certainly should not be opposites. They should be on the same wavelength. That means you can eliminate choice B because *fantasy* and *realism* are opposites. That's the only answer, however, that you can eliminate immediately. The others are all close enough in meaning to fit together.

This leaves you with no choice but to plug and chug. Insert every answer and see which one makes the most sense. The right answer here is choice C. Choice A looks pretty good, but you don't "treat someone with etiquette." *Etiquette* is a system of rules for manners. Choice D also looks pretty good, but treating with compassion someone who is *exasperating* is not as logical as treating the person with patience. Choice E is very tempting until you plug it into the sentence. *Truth* and *honesty* are synonyms, but they don't fit as well in the context of the sentence as do *kindness* and *patience. Correct Answer:* C.

Forget about taking a lot of shortcuts. After you eliminate the obviously incorrect answers, take your sweet time going back and inserting every remaining answer into the sentence. Sentence Completion answers aren't right or wrong so much as good, better, or best. Sometimes all the answers seem to "sorta fit"; your job is to choose the one that fits best.

TNT: Dynamite Traps 'n Tricks

Let me introduce you to the nasty little gremlins lurking in the Sentence Completion questions and give you some suggestions for dealing with them.

1. **Look for key connecting words that may change the meaning of the sentence.**

2. **Predict positive or negative words to fit in the blanks.**

3. **Don't waste time scratching your head over questions with vocabulary that is totally unfamiliar to you: Make a guess and go on to the next question.**

The following sections explain these steps.

Connections count

Changing an *and* to an *or* or a *because* to a *however* can change everything, as the following example shows:

> Buzz was content to - - - - *and* - - - - on his weekend, answering to no one but himself, doing exactly as he liked.

Perhaps you would fill the blanks with *rest..relax.* You know that the concepts are synonyms. Now check this out:

> Buzz was content to - - - - *or* - - - - on his weekend, answering to no one but himself, doing exactly as he liked.

The *or* changes everything. You may fill the blanks with *sleep..party* or perhaps *work..play.* You know that the concepts must be opposites here.

Here's a brief list of some of the most common connecting words:

although	however	or
despite	moreover	either/or
in spite of	but	because
nonetheless	therefore	and
but for		

Whenever you see the preceding words, your antennae should go up, putting you on the alert for a plot twist — a trap of some sort.

Use your crystal ball

Sometimes the sentences are so long and **convoluted** (twisting or turning) that you can't make heads or tails of them. In that case, dissect the sentence. (A sentence so confusing probably makes you bloodthirsty or **sanguinary** enough to want to dismember something right about about then. . . .) Isolate just a bit of the sentence around the blank and try to predict whether that blank requires a positive or negative word. Consider the following:

> "Blah blah blah blah blah blah blah blah blah blah blah," Frances cursed - - - -.

Because people rarely curse or swear nicely, you can predict that the blank must be filled with a negative word. Maybe Frances curses *harshly, rudely,* or *viciously* (or *stridently, stentorianly,* or *fulminatingly*). You can eliminate answer choices such as *sweetly, kindly,* or *courteously* (as well as *benignly, amiably,* or *decorously*).

Guess and go

Many times you can get the right answer in Sentence Completion questions by process of elimination. You may have a hazy idea what type of word (positive or negative) or words (antonyms or synonyms) go into the blank or blanks. But what happens if you can't eliminate any answers because you don't know what any of the words mean? Hit the road, Jack. Get outta there fast. Because the GRE does not penalize you for wrong answers, you always want to make a guess — but guess quickly and go on to the next problem. If you are making a wild guess anyway, why spend time deliberating over it? Guess and go!

A vocabulary helper bonus

You'll be delighted to know that roots, prefixes, and suffixes help you immensely on the Sentence Completion vocabulary, just as they do on the analogies. If you don't know what the words mean, use your RPS to figure them out (see Chapter 2 for more on RPS). For example, consider the following sentence:

> Jane refused to eulogize Donald, saying that she thought he was a - - - - fellow.

Obviously, the entire sentence depends on the meaning of *eulogize*. If it means something bad, Jane refused to bad-mouth Donald and thought that he was a swell fellow. If it means something good, Jane refused to say anything good about Donald, thinking he was a bad fellow. Which is it? As you may recall, *eu* (along with *ben* and *bon*) means

good. You also learned the suffix-*ize*, which means to make. And *log* means speech or talk. You can reason out that *to eulogize* means to make good speech or talk. If she refused "to make good speech or talk" about Donald, she didn't like him. Fill the blank with a bad word, such as *rotten, terrible*, or *disgusting*.

Try this one:

> Ashamed of his obvious trembling and - - - - when confronted by the farmer's wife, Blind Mickey told his two good friends, "I thought I was a man, but I'm just a mouse."

You need a word here that means fear. The right answer may be **trepidation.** You can figure out the word if you know that the root *trep* means fear.

Although she usually was of a cheerful nature, Putty was - - - - when she heard the history professor assign a paper that would be due the first day back after Spring Break.

    (A) ebullient

    (B) indolent

    (C) supercilious

    (D) enigmatic

    (E) lugubrious

Okay. You know that the blank needs to be filled with a word that means sad, gloomy, or glum. So far so good. But then you get to the answer choices, and life as you know it ceases to exist. You don't know *any* of those words. Because everything depends on vocabulary words you don't know, skip the question. You can't get this one right except by randomly guessing. Fill in something, anything, and zoom on to the next question. I suggest that you put a big arrow in the margin of the test booklet, pointing to the question. That way, if you have time left over at the end of the section, you can come back and *cogitate* over (think about) this question some more. But for right now, don't waste more than a few seconds on it.

Leaving you hanging on this sentence would be too vicious, even for me. After all, I'm only an *unofficial* test maker, a tyrant-in-training, as it were. The correct answer is E. **Lugubrious** means sad. As for the other words, **ebullient** means happy, overjoyed. **Indolent** means lazy, laid back. **Supercilious** means stuck-up, conceited. **Enigmatic** means mysterious, difficult to figure out. An *enigma* is a puzzle or a mystery, like the enigma of how you ever let yourself in for something as soul-leeching as this exam. *Correct Answer:* E.

Getting Back to Your Roots

Chapters 2 and 4 present basic prefixes and suffixes. It's time now to increase your vast storehouse of knowledge by adding some of the important roots. The following is just a short list, but it is representative of what can greatly help you to figure out GRE *sesquipedalian* (foot and a half long!) vocabulary words.

If English is not your first language, vocabulary may be the hardest part of the exam for you. Using roots, prefixes, and suffixes can help you greatly.

1. **som = sleep:** Take *Som*inex to get to sleep. If you have in*som*nia, you can't sleep. (The prefix *in-* means not.)

2. **sop = sleep:** A glass of warm milk is a *sop*orific. So is a boring professor.

3. **son = sound:** A *son*ic boom breaks the sound barrier. Dis*son*ance is clashing sounds. (My singing, quite frankly, is so bad that the governor declared my last opera a disaster aria!) A *son*orous voice has a good sound.

4. **phon = sound:** *Phon*ics helps you to sound out words. Caco*phon*y is bad sound; eu*phon*y is good sound. Homo*phon*es are words that sound the same, such as *red* and *read*.

5. **path = feeling:** Something *path*etic arouses feeling or pity. To sym*path*ize is to share the feelings (literally, to make the same feeling). Anti*path*y is a dislike — literally, a feeling against, as in: No matter how much the moron apologizes, you still may harbor *antipathy* toward the jerk who parked right behind you and blocked you in, making you late for a date and causing all sorts of unfortunate romantic repercussions.

6. **mut = change:** The Teenage *Mut*ant Ninja Turtles *mut*ated, or changed, from mild-mannered turtles to pizza-gobbling crime fighters. Something im*mut*able is not changeable but remains constant. Don't confuse *mut* (change) with *mute* (silent).

7. **meta = beyond, after:** A *meta*morphosis is a change of shape beyond the present shape.

8. **morph = shape:** Something a*morph*ous is without shape. *Morph*ology is the study of shape. ("Yes, of course, I take my studies seriously. I spend all weekend on *morph*ology at the beach. . . .")

9. **loq, log, loc, lix = speech or talk:** Someone *loq*uacious talks a lot. (That person is literally full of talk.) A dia*log*ue is talk or conversation between two people. E*loc*ution is proper speech. A pro*lix* person is very talkative. (Literally, he or she engages in big, or much, talk.)

10. **cred = trust or belief:** Something in*cred*ible is unbelievable, such as the excuse: "I would have picked you up on time, Sweetheart, but there was a 75-car pile-up on the freeway." If you are *cred*ulous, you are trusting and *naive* (literally, full of trust). In fact, if you're credulous, you probably actually feel sorry for me being stuck in traffic.

Be careful not to confuse the words *credible* and *credulous*. Something *credible* is trustable or believable. A credible excuse can get you out of trouble if you turn a paper in late. *Credulous*, on the other hand, means full of trust, naive, or gullible. The more credulous your professor is, the less credible that excuse needs to be.

11. **gyn = woman:** A *gyn*ecologist is a physician who treats women. A miso*gyn*ist is a person who hates women.

12. **andro = man:** Commander Data on *Star Trek II: The Next Generation* is an *andro*id; he's a robot shaped like a man. Someone *andro*gynous exhibits both male (*andro*) and female (*gyn*) characteristics (literally, he/she is full of man and woman) — for example, the character Pat on the TV show *Saturday Night Live* is androgynous.

13. **anthro = human or mankind:** *Anthro*pology is the study of humans (not just men and not just women but humans in general). A mis*anthro*pe hates humans (an equal-opportunity hater: he or she hates both men and women alike).

14. **pac = peace, calm:** Why do you give a baby a *pac*ifier? To calm him or her down. To get its name, the *Pac*ific Ocean must have appeared calm at the time it was discovered.

15. **plac = peace, calm:** To *plac*ate someone is to calm him or her down or to make peace with that person. You placate your irate sweetheart, for example, by sending a dozen roses (hint, hint). Someone im*plac*able is someone you are not able to calm down — or someone really stubborn. If those roses don't do the trick, for example, your sweetheart is too implacable to placate.

16. **pug = war, fight:** Someone *pug*nacious is ready to fight. A *pug*ilist is a person who likes to fight — such as a professional boxer. (Did you ever see those big sticks that Marines train with in hand-to-hand combat — the ones that look like Q-Tips with a thyroid condition? Those are called *pug*il sticks.)

17. **bellu, belli = war, fight:** If you're *belli*gerent, you're ready to fight — in fact, you're downright hostile. An ante*bellu*m mansion is one that was created before the Civil War. (Remember that *ante-* means *before*. You saw this word in the prefixes section.)

18. **pro = big, much:** *Pro*fuse apologies are big, much — in essence, a *lot* of apologies. A *pro*lific writer produces a great deal of written material.

Note: *Pro* has two additional meanings less commonly used on the GRE. It can mean *before,* as in "A *pro*logue comes before a play." Similarly, to *pro*gnosticate is to make knowledge before or to predict. A *pro*gnosticator is a fortune teller. *Pro* can also mean *for*. Someone who is *pro* freedom of speech is in favor of freedom of speech. Someone with a *pro*clivity toward a certain activity is for that activity or has a natural tendency toward it.

19. **gnos = knowledge:** A doctor shows his or her knowledge by making a dia*gnos*is (analysis of the situation) or a pro*gnos*is (prediction about the future of the illness). An a*gnos*tic is a person who doesn't know whether a god exists. Differentiate an *agnostic* from an *atheist*. An atheist is literally without God, a person who believes there is no god. An agnostic is without knowledge, believing a god may or may not exist.

20. **scien = knowledge:** A *scien*tist is a person with knowledge. Someone pre*scien*t has forethought or knowledge ahead of time — for example, a prognosticator (a fortune teller, remember?). After you learn these roots, you'll be closer to being omni*scien*t — all-knowing.

21. **de = down from, away from (to put down):** To *de*scend or *de*part is to go down from or away from. To *de*nounce is to put down or to speak badly of, as in *de*nouncing those hogs who chow down all the pizza before you get to the party.

Many unknown words on the GRE that start with *de* mean to put down in the sense of to criticize or bad-mouth. Here are just a few: **demean**, **denounce**, **denigrate**, **derogate**, **deprecate**, **decry**.

22. **ex = out of, away from:** An *ex*it is literally out of or away from it — *ex*-it. (This is probably one of the most logical words around.) To *ex*tricate is to get out of something. You can extricate yourself from an argument by pretending to faint, basking in all the sympathy as you're carried away. To *ex*culpate is to get off the hook — literally to make away from guilt. *Culp* means guilt. When the president of the Hellenic Council wants to know who TP'ed the dean's house, you can claim that your sorority and your sisters are not *culp*able.

23. **greg = group, herd:** A con*greg*ation is a group or herd of people. A *greg*arious person likes to be part of a group — is sociable. To se*greg*ate is literally to make away from the group. *Se-* means apart or away from, as in *separate, sever, sequester,* and *seclusion.*

24. **luc, lum, lus = light, clear:** Something *lum*inous is shiny and full of light. Ask the teacher to e*luc*idate something you don't understand (literally, to make clear). *Lus*trous hair reflects the light and is sleek and glossy.

25. **ambu = walk, move:** In a hospital, patients are either **bedridden** (they can't move) or **ambulatory** (they can walk and move about). A somn*ambu*list is a sleepwalker. *Som-* means sleep; *-ist* is a person; *ambu* is to walk or move. A *somnambulist,* therefore, is a person who walks or moves in his or her sleep.

Enough for now. You'll find no *paucity* (lack or scarcity) of roots to learn, but these should provide you with a good foundation.

A Sense of Completion: Review

Before you go on to the practice questions in the following chapter, take some time to review the following approaches and tricks, as discussed earlier in this chapter.

Approaches

- Read the entire sentence for its gist.
- If possible, predict words to fit into the blanks.
- Insert *every* answer choice into the blanks and reread the sentence.

Tricks

- Look for key connecting words that may change the meaning of the sentence.
- Predict positive or negative words to fit in the blanks.
- Skip questions with answers that depend *entirely* on unknown vocabulary.

And, of course, you want to remember that using a few basic RPS (roots, prefixes, and suffixes) can help you to figure out the killer vocabulary.

A fun word: antepenultimate

Most of us know that *ultimate* means *the last,* just as *Z* is the ultimate letter of the alphabet. But which letter is the antepenultimate? Give up? It's *X.* The *ultimate* is the last; the *penultimate* is the second to last; the *antepenultimate* is the third to last (literally *before the second to last*). If you have three younger brothers, therefore, you can introduce them as your antepenultimate, penultimate, and ultimate siblings.

Chapter 7

Reality Check: Sentence Completion Practice Questions

• •

*I*t's that time again — when you use it or lose it. Answering the following questions should reinforce what you learned in the preceding chapter about Sentence Completion questions. I have made these sentences much more amusing than the deadly dull ones you'll see on the actual GRE, but the difficulty level and the vocabulary are the same.

Q 1. Although dismayed by the pejorative comments made about her inappropriate dress at the diplomatic function, Judy - - - - her tears and showed only the most calm and - - - - visage to her critics.

   (A) obviated .. agitated

   (B) suppressed .. placid

   (C) exacerbated .. unfazed

   (D) monitored .. incensed

   (E) curtailed .. articulate

TIP Look at the second blank first. Often the second blank is easier to predict than the first.

If Judy had a calm *and* (something) visage (a visage is a countenance, a facial expression), the (something) must go hand in hand with calm. While it doesn't have to be an exact synonym, it can't be an antonym, either. Look for a second word that means calm. *Placid* means calm, tranquil, as you know from the root *plac,* meaning calm. Check the rest of the second words. *Agitated* means upset or worried, just the opposite of what you're looking for. *Unfazed* may be good, as it means not bothered by. (Erudite types are unfazed by seeing how that word is spelled, knowing that *unphased* is a trap often found on grammar exams.) *Incensed* means upset, burning mad (think of burning incense). *Articulate* means well-spoken. Her visage, or facial expression, would not be well-spoken, although Judy herself may be. So, you've narrowed the answers down to B and C, based on the second words alone. Now check out the first words.

TRAPS & TRICKS To *exacerbate* is to make worse. Words as hard as this one can exacerbate your headache. But if you choose this answer, you let your insecurity complex get the better of you. It's normal for us all to think, "Oooh, big hard word; it must be the right answer." Wrong. In the beginning of the test, the correct answers are usually relatively simple words that you already know. That's not to say the question doesn't feature hard words, but they're usually the trap answers, not the correct answers. *Suppress* means to hold back and fits the sentence perfectly. *Correct Answer:* B.

Take a quick look at some of the other vocabulary. To *obviate* is to prevent, as in your learning these words now obviates your falling for traps by choosing them later. To *curtail* is to shorten (think of cutting off the tail of a word when you cur-tail it).

Did you note (or even circle) the word *although?* A key word like that can change the meaning of the entire sentence. If it weren't there, you may think that Judy in fact burst out crying from the criticism rather than holding back.

2. While there are those writers who carp and - - - - about the current depressed state of our economy, many people insist that such writers don't speak for the common man (or woman) who believes in the - - - - of the nation and the security of its future.

   (A) lampoon .. uniformity

   (B) grouse .. resilience

   (C) complain .. morbidity

   (D) laud .. strength

   (E) ridicule .. chaos

From Chapter 6, you should remember that you try to predict the words to fit into the blank or, failing that, predict the sense (positive or negative) of the words. You can predict here that the first word must be something bad (because the writers are carping or griping about a depressed economy) and that the second word must be something good (because the average man or woman believes in the future of the country). Eliminate all second words that are not good: *morbidity* (meaning gruesomeness) and *chaos* (meaning confusion and disorganization). Eliminate all first words that are not negative: *laud,* meaning to praise, as in to applaud. Now you've narrowed the choices down quickly to just two.

To *lampoon* is to ridicule (think of the satirical magazine, the *National Lampoon*). That may fit, but the second blank doesn't make much sense. Sure, it's good to believe in the *uniformity* or unity of a country, but that's not related to worrying about the depressed state of its economy. Choice B, *grouse*, is to complain or grumble. (The poet Dorothy Parker has a great stanza that says, "Cavil, quarrel, grumble, grouse/ I ponder on the narrow house/ I shudder at the thought of men/ I'm due to fall in love again!") And *resilience* is elasticity, the state of springing back. The average person thinks the economy will stage a comeback. *Correct Answer:* B.

3. The speaker, ironically, - - - - the very point he had stood up to make, and hurriedly sat down, hoping no one had caught his - - - -.

   (A) prognosticated .. summation

   (B) divulged .. information

   (C) refuted .. solecism

   (D) duplicated .. duplicity

   (E) ferreted out .. mistake

Predict that the second blank must be something negative, as the speaker hoped no one had noticed it. That eliminates answers A (a *summation* is just what it looks like, a summary, and is not necessarily bad) and B (*information* is also neutral). Now try the sentence with the remaining answer choices inserted.

To *refute* is to disprove or show to be false. It would be *ironic* (the opposite of what is expected) if the speaker were to disprove the very point he stood up to make. A *solecism* is an inconsistency, a mistake. *Correct Answer:* C.

Take a moment to go through the other words to increase your vocabulary. (As you are learning by now, many of the Sentence Completion questions can be narrowed down to just two or three answers based on the process of elimination, but to get the one right answer you have to know the words.) To *prognosticate* is to predict. You've had this word before in the analogies. *Pro* means before; *gnos* means knowledge; *-ate* means to make. To prognosticate is to "make knowledge before," to predict.

If you chose A, you probably fell for the trap of looking only at the answer choices and not reinserting them into the sentence. Yes, something ironic is the opposite of what is expected, and a prognostication is the opposite of a summation, but that answer doesn't fit when reinserted into the sentence. Be sure to take your time and go back to the sentence with each answer choice. The Sentence Completion section is not a place to try to save seconds.

In choice B, to *divulge* is to reveal. That first word works, but the second does not. It would not be ironic to divulge the very information you stand up to say; it would be normal.

In choice D, *duplicity* is a good word. The root *dup* means double, but duplicity is not "double-ness" in the sense of two of something. Duplicity is deception, being two-faced. A traitor is noted for his or her duplicity. And in choice E, to *ferret out* is to search diligently, as in a detective ferrets out clues to help his client. You ferret out the tips and traps scattered throughout these explanations to help you to remember them.

4. Although often writing of - - - - activities, Emily Dickinson possessed the faculty of creating an eclectic group of characters ranging from the reticent to the epitome of - - - -.

   (A) questionable .. taciturnity

   (B) mundane .. effrontery

   (C) egregious .. discretion

   (D) horrific .. stoicism

   (E) commensurate .. composure

This is the first question in the batch that you may have wanted to make a wild guess at. The entire question depends on vocabulary, and all the vocabulary is very difficult. If you encounter a question of this sort on the exam, don't waste too much time on it. Make a quick guess and go on to the next question.

If you know that *reticent* means shy and holding back, you can predict that the second blank must be the opposite of that, something bold and forward. *Effrontery* is shameless boldness and audacity. You have effrontery when you ask your boss for a raise right after she has chewed you out for bungling a project and costing the company money. Effrontery is the only second blank that fits. *Taciturnity* is the noun form of the word *taciturn*, meaning quiet, not talkative, not forward. *Stoicism* is not showing feelings or pain. Only a stoic can look at words like this without shrieking or ripping out her hair.

Let's look at the first blanks. *Mundane* means common, worldly. Mundane activities are the day-to-day tasks, nothing exciting like winning a lottery or visiting Antarctica. *Egregious* means terrible or flagrant. An egregious mistake is right out there for the world to see. *Commensurate* means equivalent to or proportionate. Your score on this section will be commensurate with your vocabulary. *Correct Answer:* B.

5. Dismayed by the - - - - evidence available to her, the defense attorney spent her own money (even though that would leave her nearly - - - -) to hire a private investigator to acquire additional evidence.

   (A) dearth of .. affluent

   (B) scanty .. insolvent

   (C) vestigial .. pecuniary

   (D) immense .. bankrupt

   (E) impartial .. penurious

Predict words to fit into the blanks. If the attorney were dismayed by evidence and hired an investigator to get *more* evidence, there must not have been much evidence to begin with. Predict the first word means not very much. *Scanty* means barely sufficient. A *dearth* of is a lack of. Those are the only two that fit for the first blank. *Vestigial* means not yet fully developed; for example, the tailbone of humans is a vestigial tail. *Immense* means large, just the opposite of what you want.

The words "even though" tell you that spending her own money to gather the extra evidence would have a negative effect on the attorney. She was nearly *insolvent*, or bankrupt. Choice A, *affluent,* means rich, wealthy, or — as a smart-aleck friend of mine says — financially oversupplied. That doesn't work, eliminating that choice.

In choice C, *pecuniary* means consisting of or pertaining to money matters. This could be a trick answer, as you know that the costs have to do with money as well. However, the first word definitely doesn't fit in this sentence. In choice E, *penurious* means poor, needy, destitute. It fits the second blank, but the first blank doesn't work with this answer. *Impartial* evidence is neutral, neither good nor bad. *Correct Answer:* B.

6. Unwilling to be labeled ----, Gwenette slowly and ---- double-checked each fact before expounding upon her theory to her colleagues at the convention.

    (A) precipitate .. meticulously

    (B) hasty .. swiftly

    (C) rash .. desultorily

    (D) efficacious .. haphazardly

    (E) painstaking .. heedlessly

The key here is pure vocabulary. You can probably predict what types of words you need, knowing that the first word must mean too fast and careless and the second word slow and careful. But if you don't have a clue what any of the words mean, don't waste time scratching your head over this one. Just guess and go.

Precipitate, hasty, and *rash* all mean overly quick, leaping before looking. Those would fit the first blank. *Efficacious* means efficient and effective, something Gwenette wants to be labeled. *Painstaking* means meticulous, careful and attentive to detail, another good thing to be. Dump choices D and E.

You know the second blank must be something good. *Meticulous* means careful with detail, paying careful attention. It is pretty much the opposite of *swiftly* (quickly), *desultorily* (aimlessly, not methodically), *haphazardly* (unsystematically, not methodically), and *heedlessly* (not paying attention). *Correct Answer:* A.

Even if you don't know the exact meanings of the words, you often have an idea whether they are positive or negative, whether they have good or bad connotations. If you sense that a word is bad when you need a good word, eliminate that answer choice. You'll be pleasantly surprised at how often your subconscious leads you to the correct answer.

If you didn't grow up in America, you may not be able to "sense" the meanings (good or bad) of words. In that case, it's even more important for you to make a *quick* guess and go on. Save your time to use on the Reading Comprehension passages and questions, where every extra second is needed.

Chapter 8

Readings That Can Affect Your Future: Blood Pressure, Astrology, and GRE

- -

In This Chapter

▶ Three commonly tested reading passages

▶ Last things first: reading the questions before the passages

▶ Questions you should always/never do

▶ Tricks to make life easier

- -

Feared by more students than Monday's mystery meat in the college cafeteria, Reading Comprehension questions comprise 22 out of 72–76 (the number varies) verbal questions, accounting for close to 30 percent of your verbal score. Each section has one relatively long passage (about one column of a page) followed by 7 or 8 questions pertaining to it, and one short passage (about a half a column) followed by 4 questions. If you're sitting at your desk scowling, thinking, "I never finish reading; there's just not enough time," you're not alone. The following lecture shows you how to use your time wisely and teaches you which questions after the passage you shouldn't take seriously.

Every question counts the same. A lengthy Reading Comprehension question that sends you back to the passage to search diligently (and sometimes futilely) for an answer or one that requires a lot of head scratching and deep thought counts only as much as another question that can be answered in a nanosecond. If you're not taking the CAT version of the GRE, do the hard, time-consuming questions last, *but* be careful not to get lost on the answer grid as you skip around. Mark the answers you skip and then fill in every space on your answer grid; that way, if you don't get back to check your wild guesses, you at least have a chance of getting an answer correct by luck. The GRE does not subtract points for wrong answers; you're in a win-win situation with guessing.

Why Do They Call It Reading Comprehension If I Don't Understand a Thing I've Read?

The origin of the *misnomer* (wrong name) "Reading Comprehension" is a great topic for a *deipnosophist*. (A *deipnosophist* is one who converses eruditely at the dinner table. Don't worry; you don't have to know the word for the GRE. I just threw it in so you could sound smart to your friends.) For now, you don't care so much what the section is called; you just want to get through it. The following information presents an overview of the types of passages you will encounter, the best approach to each distinct type of passage, and tips and traps for answering the questions based on those passages. Let's start by seeing what a Reading Comp question looks like.

Which of the following best describes the tone of the passage?

(A) sarcastic

(B) ebullient

(C) objective

(D) saddened

(E) mendacious

All questions can be answered from information stated or implied in the passage. You aren't expected to answer questions based on your own knowledge, and you don't need to know anything special about science or humanities to answer these questions.

The Three Commonly Tested Reading Passages

In their torture chambers over the years (would someone please call Amnesty International?), the test makers have decided to write passages based on biological or physical sciences, social sciences, and humanities. The following sections offer a preview of the passages to help you separate the devastating from the merely intolerable.

If you know that you are a slow reader who won't finish the section, pay special attention to the following material. In it, you will learn to identify the various types of passages and how well you do on each. Obviously, if you find that you always ace a biology passage but don't understand a word of an economics passage, you know where to focus your energies on the actual GRE.

Beam me up, Scotty! Biological and physical science passages

A science passage is straightforward, giving you information on how laser beams work, how to build a suspension bridge, how molecular theory applies, and so on. Although the passage itself may be very booooooooring to read (because it is full of just facts, facts, and more facts), this type of passage is often the best passage for people to tackle first because it has so few tricks and traps. In the practice exams that follow, I feature an inordinately large number of science passages. I do so because I think science passages give nearly all readers their best chance to do well, and because I want you to be completely comfortable doing this style of question.

Reading tip

Let's talk reality here: You're not going to remember — and maybe not even understand — what you read in a science passage. It's all just statistics and dry details. No matter how carefully and slowly you read through it the first time, you're almost certain to need to go back through the passage a second time to find specific facts. You end up reading the passage twice. Why waste time? Zip through the passage, just to get a general idea of what it's about and where the information is. (Paragraph one tells how molecules combine; paragraph two tells how scientists are working to split the atom; paragraph three tells. . . .) You may want to jot down a one- or two-word note in the margin next to each paragraph: Molecules. Atoms. Research. No need to waste time understanding every nuance if you can get the answer right by going back and finding the specific fact quickly. Because science passages can be done so quickly, work on them first.

Why do I say science passages are the best for slow readers when I tell you to read these passages quickly? I say so because you're not really *reading* the passages; you're skimming them. You don't have to understand what you read; just identify some key words.

Question tip

Science questions can often be answered directly from the facts provided in the passage itself. They are rarely the "inference" type that requires you to read between the lines and really think about what the author is saying, what point she is trying to make, how she feels about the subject, and so on. Here's an example:

The author states that spices were used

    I. to improve the taste of food

    II. for medicinal purposes

    III. to preserve food before refrigeration

    IV. as a substitute for cash

  (A) I and III only

  (B) I, II, and IV only

  (C) I, II, and III only

  (D) II and III only

  (E) I, II, III, and IV

To answer the question, return to the passage and look for the specific answers — which should be easy to locate if you made those handy little marginal notes during your first run-through (in this case, the notation may be *Purposes*).

It's not a disease: The social sciences passage

The GRE usually includes one social sciences passage. It may be about history, psychology, business, or a variety of other topics. The term "social sciences" is broad enough, in other words, to include whatever the test makers want it to include. The social sciences passage is often the most interesting of the passages you'll encounter. It may give you a perspective on history that you didn't know, or tell you insights into psychology or sociology that you can use to manipulate your friends. (Who says the GRE is useless?)

Reading tip

In many ways, social sciences passages are nearly the opposite of science passages. The questions here deal more with inferences and less with explicitly stated facts. You must read the passages slowly and carefully, therefore, trying to understand not only what is said, but also what is implied. Take your time. Underline key concepts. Circle important words. Think about what you are reading.

Question tip

The questions that follow social sciences passages may not be as straightforward as those for a biological or physical science passage. You may not be able to go back to a specific line and pick out a specific fact. Instead, you are asked to understand the big picture, to comprehend what the author meant but didn't come right out and say. You may be asked why an author included a particular example or explanation. In other words, you're expected to be a mind reader. Here's an example:

The author's primary motive in discussing Dr. Buttinski's theory was to

(A) impress the reader with Dr. Buttinski's importance.

(B) show that Dr. Buttinski overcame great odds to become a psychologist.

(C) ridicule Dr. Buttinski's adversaries, who disagreed with the theory.

(D) predict great things for Dr. Buttinski's future.

(E) evaluate the effect Dr. Buttinski's theory has had on our everyday lives.

Determining the author's motive involves as much reasoning as reading. No sentence specifically says: "Okay, listen up, troops. I'm going to tell you something, and my motive for doing so is blah, blah, blah." You need to read the passage slowly enough to develop an idea of why the author is telling you something and what exactly he wants you to take from this passage. Going back and rereading the passage doesn't do you much good; thinking about what you read does.

In the sample question provided here, every answer given probably would be true in the context of the passage itself. That is, the author probably thought Dr. Buttinski was important, probably believed that Dr. Buttinski had to overcome great odds to be a psychologist, and so on. Keep in mind, however, what the question is asking: *Why* did the author mention this specific thing? You must probe the author's mind.

Gimme a break, I'm only human: The humanities passages

Humanities passages may be about humans (well, duh!) or about art, music, philosophy, drama, or literature. The passages are usually positive, especially if they are talking about a person who was a pioneer in his or her field, such as the first African-American astronaut, or the first female doctor. Think about this logically: If the GRE bothers with writing about someone, that someone must have been pretty darn great or done something noteworthy. Keep this sense of admiration, even awe, in mind as you answer the questions related to the passage.

Reading tip

Have fun with the passage. This is the only passage you may actually enjoy reading. You don't need to zoom through it to finish before you fall asleep as you must with the science passages. You don't need to read it carefully for between-the-lines understanding as you must read the social sciences passages. You can read this passage normally. Pretend that you are reading an article in *People* magazine, for example.

Question tip

The questions following a humanities passage often require you to get into the mind of the author, to read between the lines and make inferences. While reading a passage about a particular person, for example, you are supposed to ascertain not just what the person accomplished but why he worked towards his goals and what mark he hoped to leave on the world. Here's an example:

It can be inferred from the passage that Ms. Whitecloud would be most likely to agree with which of the following statements?

(A) A good divorce attorney must take the broader view and in effect represent the marriage itself rather than either of the spouses.

(B) The job of a divorce attorney is similar to that of a psychologist, attempting to ascertain why the marriage failed and address that issue rather than just the legal issues.

(C) The most important function of a divorce attorney is to protect the interests of the children of the marriage.

(D) A divorce attorney's job is merely to represent the legal interests of his or her client and does not include becoming a "friend" to the spouses.

(E) A divorce attorney represents his or her success by how quickly the divorce is accomplished.

Last Things First: Reading the Questions before the Passages

Question: Should I read the questions before I read the passage?

Answer: I knew someone would ask this. Try working the passages both ways in the practice exam, one time reading the questions first and then a second time reading them after you read the passage. My anything-but-humble opinion, however, is that reading the questions first doesn't do you much good. You have sooooooo much information floating around in that brain of yours; are you really going to remember the questions while reading the passage? If you can do so, bully for you; go join the CIA! If you're normal, however, you just waste time reading the questions, reading the passage, reading the questions a second time, going back to the passage again to look for the answers. . . . You get the idea.

All or Nothing: Questions You Should Always Do; Questions You Should Never Do

Knowing how to approach the GRE Reading Comprehension passages is extremely important. Even more important than the passages themselves, however, are the questions following each passage. After all, the admissions officer at Harvard is not going to say to you, "Hey, tell me about that GRE passage you read about the curative properties of heavy metal music." The admissions officer is far more likely to ask, "How many questions did you answer correctly on the Reading Comprehension portion?" No matter how carefully you read the passage, no matter how well you understand it, you must be able to put that knowledge to work to answer the questions that follow those passages.

So just what kind of questions are you most likely to encounter in the Reading Comprehension portions of the test? The following sections describe the several basic question types you may face in the dark alleys of the GRE.

It's the attitude, Dude: The attitude or tone question

The author's attitude may be described as . . .

The tone of the passage is . . .

These two questions are variations on a single theme. What is the tone of the passage or the attitude of the author? Nothing in the passage answers this type of question directly. You can't find any one line reading: "In my opinion, which, by the way, is sardonic, the importance of. . . ." You simply must reason this one out.

Table 8-1 lists the tone or attitude likely found in each type of reading passage.

Table 8-1 Predominant Tones or Attitudes Found in GRE Reading Passages

Passage Type	Tone or Attitude	Explanation
Physical or biological sciences	Neutral or positive	A physical or biological science passage gives you just the facts. The author rarely evaluates the facts one way or the other and rarely expresses an opinion. After all, how opinionated can someone be about a color spectrum?
Social sciences	Positive or neutral	A social sciences passage may be about how some event unfolded or some theory was developed. For example, a passage may talk about history, presenting the good events and downplaying the bad ones. Think positive, or at the very worst, neutral.
Humanities	Positive or neutral	If the passage is about an individual, it is probably positive, saying good and respectful things about that person and his or her accomplishments. If it is about the other topics of humanities, such as art, music, philosophy, drama, and literature, it may be either positive or neutral. Only very rarely does a humanities passage have a negative tone.

Do you notice a pattern here? Everything is either neutral or positive, positive or neutral. Because so many of the tones or attitudes of the Reading Comprehension passages are positive or neutral, certain words are often good to choose as answers to attitude or tone questions. With neutral passages, the term *objective* (which means neutral, not taking one side or the other, not subjective or opinionated) is often a correct answer. Don't simply turn off your own brain and choose *objective* automatically, of course, but it's a good guess if you're stumped for an answer. Think of a passage as neutral until proven otherwise.

The following list offers several common positive words. Each word is followed by a more unfamiliar term that has the same meaning:

Common Positive-Attitude Word	More Difficult Word with the Same Meaning
Optimistic	Sanguine
Praising	Laudatory
Admiring	Reverential

You get the idea. Wrong answers — that is, negative answers — may include the words in the following list. Remember, these are words that you usually don't want to choose.

Common Negative-Attitude Word	More Difficult Word with the Same Meaning
Ridiculing	Lampooning
Sarcastic	Sardonic
Belittling	Denigrating

The answer choices to an attitude or tone question often use quite difficult vocabulary. If you knew from reading the passage that the author was delighted with something, which of the following would you choose to describe his attitude: *phlegmatic, dogmatic, ebullient, cantankerous, lethargic?* The right answer is *ebullient*, which means bubbling over with enthusiasm or excitement — but how many people know that word? I mean, it's not as if your best friend asks you, "So, how are you today?" and your immediate response is, "Well, I'm ebullient, thanks; and you?" If you don't know the vocabulary in the answer choices, *quickly* make a wild guess and go on. It can be very frustrating to do so, because you know what kind of word you are looking for, but when you can't define the answer choices, all you're doing is wasting time. Guess and go.

Will I rue it if I do it: Shall I even try?

An attitude or tone question is a good one to take a stab at even if you don't read the entire passage or if you read it but can't make heads or tails out of it. Because most correct answers to these questions are either neutral or positive, you can eliminate negative answer choices and at least make a pretty good guess.

What's the big idea: Main idea or best title

You can bet the farm (but, of course, only in states with legalized gambling) that you'll see a few main idea or best title questions; each Reading Comprehension passage usually has one. This type of question can assume any of the following forms:

> The main idea of the passage is . . .
>
> The primary purpose of the author is . . .
>
> The best title for the passage is . . .

The best place to find the main idea of the passage is in its topic sentence, which is usually the first or second sentence of the first paragraph. The topic sentence *may* be the last sentence of the passage, but such a structure is rare. Your game plan upon encountering one of these questions should be to head right back to the first sentence to locate a main idea.

Suppose that the passage begins as follows:

> The uses to which latex has been applied have exceeded the wildest fantasies of its creators.

What is the main idea of the passage: The uses of latex? The applications of latex? The many products made of latex?

After you've read the entire passage, all the darn answers in the main idea question may look pretty good. That's because they usually consist of facts stated in the passage. Just because something is true and just because it is discussed in the passage doesn't mean it's necessarily the main idea.

To do or not to do, that is the question

The main idea or best title question is pretty easy to answer if you remember to go back and reread the first few sentences. A main idea or best title question is one you should always answer. Even if you don't have time to read the entire passage — or even get started on it — you can nearly always hustle up an answer to this question by glancing at one sentence. It's worth a shot.

Because Reading Comprehension passages are almost always positive or neutral, the main idea/best title is almost always positive or neutral, too. Eliminate any negative answer choices right away.

The main idea of this passage is

(A) the submission and shame of the Native Americans.

(B) the unfair treatment of Native Americans.

(C) how Native Americans are taking charge of their own destinies.

(D) why native Americans fail.

(E) the causes behind Native American problems.

Because all the answers but C are negative, choose C. Humanities passages are often about people who have beaten the odds: inspirational pioneers and leaders. The passage is certain to be very admiring of those people. *Correct Answer:* C.

Don't pester me with details: The detail or fact question

One type of question very straightforwardly asks you about information explicitly stated in the passage. If a question begins with the phrase "According to the passage . . ." you've hit a detail or fact question — which is usually a very easy question to answer correctly. All you need to do is identify the key words in the question, return to the reading passage, and skim for those words. The answer is usually within a few sentences of those key words.

According to the passage, what two elements make up Drake's Elixir?

The key words are *Drake's Elixir.* Go back to the passage and find the exact answer.

According to the passage, why did Mr. Sanchez win a medal during the war?

The key words in this question are *Mr. Sanchez, medal,* and *war.* Go back to the passage and find the exact answer.

"According to the author" is not the same thing as "According to the passage." The two phrases may look the same, but author questions are often more difficult than passage questions and are not as straightforward. A question that asks you about the author may be more of a read-between-the-lines question than one about the passage — something you can answer only if you truly understand what you read. An "according to the passage" question, on the other hand, can often be answered even without reading the whole passage, by skimming for the key words.

Is answering a detail or fact question worth the effort? Absolutely. If you are running short on time and you know you won't finish all the questions, do this type of question. If you are not even going to read the passage, do this question. Because all you do is skim for a key word, your time investment is minimal.

The few to do: Mini review

You've learned so far about three common types of questions that *you should always answer.* You can answer these questions usually even if you haven't read the entire passage or read it and don't have a clue what just brushed past your brain.

- ✔ **Attitude or tone:** Knowing that the attitude or tone of a passage is usually neutral (*objective, unbiased*), you can eliminate negative answers (*sarcastic, dolorous*) and make a good guess.

- ✔ **Main idea or best title:** The main idea or best title is often found in the first sentence or two of the passage. It is usually positive or neutral, rarely negative.

✔ **Detail or fact:** This question asks for a specific detail or fact; it often begins with the words "according to the passage." Go back to the passage and skim for the answer.

None of these questions requires much effort. If you're running out of time, answer these questions first.

The power of positive thinking: Negative or exception questions

One type of GRE question is a trained killer and should be avoided: the negative or exception question. Here are a few ways this question may be worded:

Which of the following is *not* true?

Which of the following is *least* likely?

With which of the following would the author *disagree?*

All of the following are true *except* . . .

The questions are phrased in the negative, which makes them very tricky. You are actually looking for four correct answers and then by the process of elimination choosing the one that is not correct. It's easy to get confused and even easier to waste a lot of time. This is a good question to save for last or to guess at randomly.

Remember that questions go from easier to harder. If the negative question is only number two, it is probably easy; go ahead and give it a shot. But very often, the negative question is the last one of the batch. That makes it hard on its own and even harder because it's negative. With that double whammy, you may as well forget about it.

Toga! Toga! Toga! The Roman numeral question

A Roman numeral question looks like this:

The author mentions which of the following as support for her argument against unilateral intervention?

   I. economic considerations

  II. moral obligations

 III. popular opinion

(A) I only

(B) II only

(C) III only

(D) I and II only

(E) I, II, and III

Roman numeral questions are usually time-wasters. In effect, you have to go back and reread almost the whole passage to find whether I, II, or III was mentioned anywhere. A common trap is to have I and II mentioned close together . . . and then have III mentioned far down the passage. Most people will find I and II and then when III doesn't appear to be hanging around, choose I and II only, going down the tubes. (Hey, maybe the test makers get bonus points for every student they snare with a trick rather like a cop writing speeding tickets to meet his quota in a speed trap. Just a thought.) With a Roman numeral question, you have to make a commitment (did I just lose half my male readers?). You have to commit to rereading most of the passage just in case one of the concepts is floating around where you least expect it. If you are not willing (or able) to commit the time, forget about the question. Just make a random guess and go on.

The two to zoom through: Mini review

Two question types that are excellent to guess at quickly:

- ✔ **Negative or exception question:** This question is confusing in its wording and requires a lot of time to answer.
- ✔ **Roman numeral question:** This style is time-consuming and can be tricky if you don't reread enough of the passage.

The Swing Vote: Extending the Author's Reasoning

You've learned which questions you should always do and which questions you should usually guess at. The GRE has one more type of question that, while it has become increasingly rare lately, you need to be prepared to meet. This type of question asks you to extend the author's reasoning to another situation. The GRE may give a situation that is analogous, or similar to, the one described in the Reading Comprehension passage and then ask you to determine how the author's reasoning would or would not work in the new situation. The tone or attitude of this type of passage may be positive, neutral, or negative. Here's an example:

Which of the following would the author most likely feel would be a valid issue to appear on a referendum, based on his argument in the preceding passage?

(A) the right to die

(B) term limits for members of Congress

(C) expansion of the powers of the Judiciary

(D) increased student involvement in college application processes

(E) tax rate increases

This type of question may be ridiculously easy or annoyingly difficult. If you understand the passage well and understand the author's reasoning, this question is simple. Sometimes you can answer this question without understanding the entire passage, as long as you have some general idea of the author's purpose in writing the passage.

Don't immediately choose an answer just because it refers to the topic discussed in the passage. For example, the passage may be about education. The trap answer to the previous question would be choice D. However, you are asked to extend the author's reasoning to an *analogous* situation. The situation can be about the right to die or about congressional term limits or about anything else.

Something up My Sleeve: Tricks for Making Life a Little Easier

Now that you know about the types of passages and primary types of questions, it's time for the fun stuff: the tricks.

Reading passages you'll never see on the GRE

✔ **Biological Science:** Cannibalism and You: The Science of Pigging Out at a Barbecue

✔ **Social Science (Psychology):** The End of Political Correctness: An Analysis of Howard Stern and Rush Limbaugh

✔ **Social Science (Behaviorism):** An excerpt from *Confessions from the Funny Farm*, Chapter Two: How the GRE Pushed Me over the Edge

✔ **Humanities:** The Developer of the Prefrontal Lobotomy: "Inspiration struck while I was studying for the GRE," says Famous Surgeon

Be positive or neutral, not negative

I will say this over and over and over until you are exasperated enough to cut off my air supply. Because most of the passages are positive or neutral, most of the correct answers are positive or neutral. Because the test makers don't want to get sued for saying mean and vicious things about anyone, they will be sweet and charming (and probably go home, kick the dog, and evict a few widows and orphans just to get pent-up frustrations out of their systems after having to be so nice at work all day long). Be sweet and charming right back at 'em; choose positive, goody-goody answer choices.

Choose answers containing key words

The key words, often found in the topic sentence, are what the whole passage is about. The right answers usually feature those words. If the passage is about Chicano history, the right answer will often have the words *Chicano history* in it. Don't immediately choose an answer *only* because it has the key words in it, but if you can narrow the answers down to two, choose the one with the key words.

Be wishy-washy, not dramatic

The test makers realize that people have different points of view. They don't want to be *dogmatic* (narrow-minded), saying, "This is the right way, the only way. Zip your lip and don't argue." They want to hedge their bets, leave some space for personal interpretation. And, of course, they don't want to get sued. If you have two answers, choose the more moderate or wishy-washy of the two. Wimp out big time.

Let's suppose that you have narrowed the answer choices down to two:

(A) The author hates discrimination.

(B) The author is saddened by the discrimination and tries to understand its causes.

Choice B is the kinder, gentler, wimpier answer and would probably be correct.

Correct answers are usually a little above or a little below the key words or indicated line numbers

This can get nasty. The question will ask you about something and send you to a particular line number. When you go back there, either you won't find an answer, or you'll find the trap answer. Expand your horizons. Read a few sentences above and a few sentences below. The right answer will usually be found in the vicinity. If you just keep looking where they sent you, it'll be like looking for your car keys where they normally are and where you've searched a thousand times already, to no avail. You have to branch out.

Chapter 9

Practice What I Preach: Reading Comprehension Practice Questions

*T*his section features two reading passages and nine questions. For now, don't worry about timing yourself. Try to identify each selection as one of the types of reading passages described in Chapter 8 (science, humanities, and so on) and use the tips I gave you for reading that type of passage. As you answer the questions, try to identify whether each question is attitude/tone, main idea/best title, Roman numeral, and so on and then try to recall any traps inherent to that type of question.

Passage 1

Microbiological activity clearly affects the mechanical strength of leaves. Although it cannot be denied that with most species the loss of mechanical strength is the result of both
Line invertebrate feeding and microbiological breakdown, the example of *Fagus sylvatica* illustrates loss without any sign of invertebrate attack being evident. *Fagus* shows little sign of inverte-
(5) brate attack even after being exposed for eight months in either lake or stream environment, but results of the rolling fragmentation experiment show that loss of mechanical strength, even in this apparently resistant species, is considerable.

Most species appear to exhibit a higher rate of degradation in the stream environment than in the lake. This is perhaps most clearly shown in the case of *Alnus*. Examination of the
(10) type of destruction suggests that the cause for the greater loss of material in the stream-processed leaves is a combination of both biological and mechanical degradation. The leaves exhibit an angular fragmentation, which is characteristic of mechanical damage, rather than the rounded holes typical of the attack by large particle feeders or the skeletal vein pattern produced by microbial degradation and small particle feeders. As the leaves become less strong,
(15) the fluid forces acting on the stream nylon cages caused successively greater fragmentation.

Mechanical fragmentation, like biological breakdown, is to some extent influenced by leaf structure and form. In some leaves with a strong midrib, the lamina break up, but the pieces remain attached by means of the midrib. One type of leaf may break clean while another tears off and is easily destroyed once the tissues are weakened by microbial attack.

(20)   In most species, the mechanical breakdown will take the form of gradual attrition at the margins. If the energy of the environment is sufficiently high, brittle species may be broken across the midrib, something that rarely happens with more pliable leaves. The result of attrition is that, where the areas of the whole leaves follow a normal distribution, a bimodal distribution is produced, one peak composed mainly of the fragmented pieces, the other of the
(25) larger remains.

     To test the theory that a thin leaf has only half the chance of a thick one for entering the fossil record, all other things being equal, Ferguson (1971) cut discs of fresh leaves from 11 species of different leaf thicknesses and rotated them with sand and water in a revolving drum. Each run lasted 100 hours and was repeated three times, but even after this treatment, all
(30) species showed little sign of wear. It therefore seems unlikely that leaf thickness alone, without substantial microbial preconditioning, contributes much to the probability that a leaf will enter a depositional environment in a recognizable form. The results of experiments with whole fresh leaves show that they are more resistant to fragmentation than leaves exposed to microbiological attack. Unless the leaf is exceptionally large or small, leaf size and thickness
(35) are not likely to be as critical in determining the preservation potential of a leaf type as the rate of microbiological degradation.

1. Which of the following would be the best title for the passage?

   (A) Why Leaves Disintegrate

   (B) An Analysis of Leaf Structure and Composition

   (C) Comparing Lakes and Streams

   (D) The Purpose of Particle Feeders

   (E) How Leaves' Mechanical Strength Is Affected by Microbiological Activity

The main idea, main purpose, or best title is found in the topic sentence, which is usually the first sentence of the passage. The correct answer here is taken nearly word-for-word from the first sentence. Note that, because the passage is talking primarily about leaves, that word needs to be in the title, which eliminates choices C and D right off. Choice A is too broad; there may be other causes of disintegration that the passage doesn't mention. Choice B is too specific. The passage mentions leaf structure but doesn't make that topic its primary focus. *Correct Answer:* E.

2. Which of the following is mentioned as a reason for leaf degradation in streams?

   I. mechanical damage

   II. biological degradation

   III. large particle feeders

   (A) II only

   (B) I and II only

   (C) I and III only

   (D) II and III only

   (E) I, II, and III

Paragraph two of the passage tells you that ". . . loss of material in stream-processed leaves is a combination of biological and mechanical degradation." Statement III is incorrect because lines 12 and 13 specifically state that the pattern of holes is contrary to that of large particle feeders. *Correct Answer:* B.

Usually a Roman numeral question is difficult and time-consuming. So why was this question so simple? It's only the second question in the section. Questions go from easier to harder, remember. Even a tricky question is pretty easy if it's at the beginning.

3. The conclusion the author reached from Ferguson's revolving drum experiment was that

   (A) leaf thickness is only a contributing factor to leaf fragmentation.

   (B) leaves submersed in water degrade more rapidly than leaves deposited in mud or silt.

   (C) leaves with a strong midrib deteriorate less than leaves without such a midrib.

   (D) microbial attack is exacerbated by high temperatures.

   (E) bimodal distribution reduces leaf attrition.

Lines 30–32 tell you that it is unlikely that leaf thickness *alone* affects the final form of the leaf. You probably need to reread that sentence a few times to understand it, but this is the type of question you should definitely attempt to answer — a detail or fact question. Choice B introduces facts not discussed in the passage; there was no talk of leaves in mud or silt. Choice C is mentioned in the passage but not in Ferguson's experiments. Be careful to answer *only* what the question is asking; the mere fact that a statement is true or is mentioned in the passage means nothing if the question isn't asking about that point. Nothing appears in the passage about high temperatures, which eliminates choice D. (Did you know the word *exacerbated?* It means made worse — like this reading passage probably exacerbated your headache.) Choice E sounds pretentious and pompous — and nice and scientific — but again has nothing to do with Ferguson. To answer this question correctly, you need to return to the passage to look up Ferguson specifically, not merely rely on your memory of the passage as a whole. *Correct Answer:* A.

4. The tone of the passage is

   (A) mesmerizing.

   (B) biased.

   (C) objective.

   (D) argumentative.

   (E) dispariging.

You *had* to get this question correct. If you missed this question, please consider yourself totally humiliated. *Correct Answer:* C.

Most of the time, a science passage has a neutral, objective, unbiased tone. The author neither praises nor criticizes anything; he just gives the facts. *Biased* means prejudiced, having an opinion one way or the other, and is just the opposite of the correct answer. GRE passages are rarely argumentative, especially science passages. If you chose A or E, you let your insecurities get the better of you: "Oooh, big hard word. I don't know it. It must be the right answer!" *Mesmerizing* means hypnotic or captivating. You probably weren't held spellbound by this passage (if you were, hey, get a life!). By the way, do you know who Franz Mesmer was? He was called "the father of hypnotism." What we now know as hypnotism used to be called Mesmerism after Franz. (No extra charge for the fascinating facts.) In choice E, *disparaging* means in a degrading manner, speaking slightingly of. Disparaging is a negative answer, and as Chapter 8 says, GRE passages are rarely negative in tone.

5. The author most likely is addressing this passage to

   (A) gardeners.

   (B) botanists.

   (C) hikers.

   (D) mechanical engineers.

   (E) Adam and Eve.

The passage is talking about the microbiological activity affecting the strength of leaves. (You know this because you already answered a best title question on the topic — question number 1.) Although choosing D is tempting, given the topic of the passage, mechanical engineers are usually interested more in machines than in leaves. Botanists are the ones who would most likely read this passage. The advice is probably too technical for gardeners, choice A, and is waaaay too specific for hikers, choice C. Choice E was added for comic relief. (If anyone needed to know how and why leaves disintegrate, especially fig leaves, it would be Adam and Eve. . . .) *Correct Answer:* B.

Passage II

Multinational corporations frequently encounter impediments in their attempts to explain to politicians, human rights groups, and (perhaps most importantly) their consumer base why
Line they do business with, even seek closer business ties to, countries whose human rights records are considered heinous by United States standards. The CEOs propound that in the
(5) business trenches, the issue of human rights must effectively be detached from the wider spectrum of free trade. Discussion of the uneasy alliance between trade and human rights has trickled down from the boardrooms of large multinational corporations to the consumer on the street who, given the wide variety of products available to him, is eager to show support for human rights by boycotting the products of a company he feels does not do enough to help
(10) its overseas workers. International human rights organizations also are pressuring the multinationals to push for more humane working conditions in other countries and to in effect develop a code of business conduct that must be adhered to if the American company is to continue working with the overseas partner.

The president, in drawing up a plan for what he calls the "economic architecture of our
(15) times," wants economists, business leaders, and human rights groups to work together to develop a set of principles that the foreign partners of United States corporations will voluntarily embrace. Humans rights activists, incensed at the nebulous plans for implementing such rules, charge that their agenda is being given low priority by the State Department. The president vociferously denies their charges, arguing that each situation is approached on its
(20) merits without prejudice, and hopes that all the groups can work together to develop principles based on empirical research rather than political fiat, emphasizing that the businesses with experience in the field must initiate the process of developing such guidelines. Business leaders, while paying lip service to the concept of these principles, fight stealthily against their formal endorsement as they fear such "voluntary" concepts may someday be given the force of
(25) law. Few business leaders have forgotten the Sullivan Principles, in which a set of voluntary rules regarding business conduct with South Africa (giving benefits to workers and banning apartheid in the companies that worked with U.S. partners) became legislation.

6. Which of the following best states the central idea of the passage?

   (A) Politicians are quixotic in their assessment of the priorities of the State Department.

   (B) Multinational corporations have little if any influence on the domestic policies of their overseas partners.

   (C) Voluntary principles that are turned into law are unconstitutional.

   (D) Disagreement exists between the desires of human rights activists to improve the working conditions of overseas workers and the pragmatic approach taken by the corporations.

   (E) It is inappropriate to expect foreign corporations to adhere to American standards.

The main idea of the passage is usually stated in the first sentence or two. The first sentence of this passage discusses the difficulties that corporations have explaining their business ties to certain countries to politicians, human rights groups, and consumers. From this statement, you may infer that those groups disagree with the policies of the corporations. *Correct Answer:* D.

In choice A, do you know the word *quixotic*? It means idealistic, impractical (think of the fictional character Don Quixote tilting at windmills). While the president in this passage may not be realistic in his assessment of State Department policies, his belief was not the main idea of the passage.

Just because a statement is (or may be) true does not necessarily mean it is the correct answer to a question. The answer choices to a main idea question in particular often are correct or at least look plausible.

To answer a main idea question, I like to pretend that a friend of mine just came up behind me and said, "Hey, what 'cha reading there?" My first response is the main idea: "Oh, I read this passage about how corporations are getting grief from politicians and other groups because they do business with certain countries." *Before* you look at the answer choices, predict in your own words what the main idea is. You'll be pleasantly surprised how close your prediction is to the correct answer (and you won't be confused by all the other plausible-looking answer choices).

Choice E is a moral value, a judgment call. An answer that passes judgment, one that says something is morally right or morally wrong, is almost never the correct answer.

7. According to the passage, the president wants the voluntary principles to be initiated by businesses rather than by politicians or human rights activists because

    (A) businesses have empirical experience in the field and thus know what the conditions are and how they may/should be remedied

    (B) businesses make profits from the labor of the workers and thus have a moral obligation to improve their employees' working conditions

    (C) workers will not accept principles drawn up by politicians whom they distrust but may agree to principles created by the corporations that pay them

    (D) foreign nations are distrustful of U.S. political intervention and are more likely to accept suggestions from multinational corporations

    (E) political activist groups have concerns that are too dramatically different from those of the corporations for the groups to be able to work together

When a question begins with the words "according to the passage," you should go back to the passage and find the exact answer. In lines 21–22, you are told that ". . . businesses with experience in the field must initiate the process of developing such guidelines." Great— but what if you don't know the word *empirical*, which means based on experiment or experience rather than on theory? Keep on reading. The rest of the sentence divulges the right answer. Don't tune out as soon as you encounter a difficult word.

Choices B, C, D, and E are all judgment calls. You are assuming facts not in evidence, as the lawyers say. While you personally may believe the statements in these answer choices to be true, they don't answer the specific question. *Correct Answer:* A.

8. Which of the following best describes the reason the author mentions the boycott of a corporation's products by its customers?

    (A) to show the difficulties that arise when corporations attempt to become involved in politics

    (B) to predict the inevitability of failure of any plan that does not involve customer input

    (C) to disagree with the president's contention that big business is the best qualified to draw up the voluntary principles of workplace conduct

    (D) to indicate the pressures that are on the multinational corporations

    (E) to ridicule the consumers for believing that their small boycott would significantly affect the sales of a multinational corporation

This question is one of those mind-reading questions I warned you about. You are expected to get into the author's mind and understand why he said what he did. The concept of the consumer boycott follows closely the main idea of the passage, which is that the corporations have difficulty trying to explain themselves and their actions to all sorts of groups, including their customers. From this, you may infer that the point of the statement is to indicate the pressures placed on the corporations.

The next line in the passage states that human rights organizations *also* are pressuring multinational corporations, leading you to infer that the consumers are applying pressure. Remember that one of your tips was to expand your horizons. Read until you find what you think is the right answer . . . and then read a little further.

Choices C and E begin with negative words, *disagree* and *ridicule*. Negative answer choices are rarely correct. Be careful, however, not to take this tip as a hard and fast rule. If you'll go back to the correct answer to question number six, you'll see that you might interpret that answer as negative.

Choice B seems logical; common sense tells you that a company that ignores its customers will probably fail. However, a strong, dramatic word like *inevitably* is rarely correct. Few things in life are inevitable, as I've said before: just death, taxes, and the GRE. *Correct Answer:* D.

9. Which of the following statements about the Sullivan Principles can best be inferred from the passage?

   (A) They had a detrimental effect on the profits of those corporations doing business with South Africa.

   (B) They represented an improper alliance between political and business groups.

   (C) They placed the needs of the foreign workers over those of the domestic workers whose jobs would therefore be in jeopardy.

   (D) They will be used as a model to create future voluntary business guidelines.

   (E) They will have a chilling effect on future adoption of voluntary guidelines.

Choice A is the major trap here. Perhaps you assumed that because the companies seem to dislike the Sullivan Principles, they hurt company profits. However, nothing was said in the passage about profits. Maybe the companies still made good profits but objected to the Sullivan Principles, well, on principle. The companies just may not have wanted such governmental intervention even if profits weren't decreased. If you chose A, you read too much into the question and probably didn't read the rest of the answer choices.

In choice E, the words *chilling effect* mean negative effect, discouraging effect. Think of something with a chilling effect as leaving you cold. If your friend asks you to taste his soup, saying the dog loved it when he lapped up a few swallows, the statement about canine cuisine will have a chilling effect on your desire to taste the soup. Because few corporations have forgotten the Sullivan Principles, you may infer that these principles will discourage the companies from agreeing to voluntary principles in the future. *Correct Answer:* E.

In order to get this question correct, you really need to understand the whole passage. If you didn't know what was going on here, you would be better off to just guess and go. An inference question usually means you have to read between the lines; you can't just go back to one specific portion of the passage and get the answer quickly.

Part III
Two Years of Math in 58 Pages: The Dreaded Math Review

In this part . . .

No, no, please don't go get your pillow and PJs. I promise that this math review won't put you to sleep. I'm not going to start at 1 + 1 = 2 and take you through every math concept you've learned since kindergarten; I have more respect for you than that. This math review neither insults you nor wastes your time. Here, I keep the instruction down to what you really need for the GRE.

If you've been out of school for a while, don't despair. After you go through the math review, do as many of the math problems as you can. The answer explanations review the formulas and concepts again and again and again; some of them are bound to come back to you.

Chapter 10

More Figures Than a Beauty Pageant: Geometry Review

. . . .

In This Chapter

▶ Angles

▶ Triangles

▶ Similar figures

▶ Area problems

▶ Quadrilaterals and other polygons

▶ Shaded area problems

▶ Circles

. . . .

Here it is, that nightmare you thought you'd left behind years ago, Geometry.

You Gotta Have an Angle: Angles

Angles are a big part of the GRE geometry problems. Fortunately, understanding angles is easy once you memorize a few basic concepts. And keep in mind the best news: You don't have to do proofs. Finding an angle is usually a matter of simple addition or subtraction. These three rules generally apply to the GRE:

> ✔ There are *no negative angles.*
>
> ✔ There are *no zero angles.*
>
> ✔ It is extremely unlikely that you'll see any *fractional angles.* (For example, an angle won't measure $45\frac{1}{2}$ degrees or $32\frac{3}{4}$ degrees.)

Angles are whole numbers. If you're plugging in a number for an angle, plug in a whole number, such as 30, 45, or 90.

1. **Angles greater than zero but less than 90 degrees are called *acute.*** Think of an acute angle as being *a cute* little angle.

$45°$

Acute

2. **Angles equal to 90 degrees are called *right angles.*** They are formed by perpendicular lines and are indicated by a box in the corner of the two intersecting lines.

Right

A GRE trap is to have two lines appear to be perpendicular and look as if they form a right angle. Do not assume this to be true. An angle is a right angle *only* if (A) you're expressly told, "This is a right angle"; (B) you see the perpendicular symbol (⊥) indicating that the lines form a 90-degree angle; or (C) you see the box in the angle. Otherwise, you may be headed for a trap!

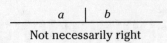

Not necessarily right

3. Angles that sum up to 90 degrees are called *complementary angles*.

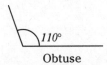

Complementary

Think of *C* for corner (the lines form a 90-degree corner angle) and *C* for complementary.

4. An angle that is greater than 90 degrees but less than 180 degrees is called *obtuse*. Think of obtuse as *obese*; an obese (or fat) angle is an obtuse angle.

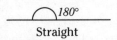

Obtuse

5. An angle that measures exactly 180 degrees is called a *straight angle*.

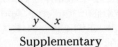

Straight

6. Angles that sum up to 180 degrees are called *supplementary angles*.

Supplementary

Think of *S* for straight angles and *S* for supplementary angles. Be careful not to confuse complementary angles (*C* for complementary; *C* for corner) with supplementary angles (*S* for supplementary; *S* for straight). If you're likely to get these confused, just think alphabetically. *C* comes before *S* in the alphabet; 90 comes before 180 when you count.

7. An angle that is greater than 180 degrees but less than 360 degrees is called a *reflex angle*.

Reflex angle

Think of a reflex angle as a reflection or mirror image of an acute angle. It makes up the rest of the angle when there's an acute angle.

Reflex angles are rarely tested on the GRE.

8. Angles around a point total 360 degrees.

360 degrees

9. Angles that are opposite each other have equal measures and are called *vertical angles*.
Note that vertical angles may actually be horizontal. Just remember that vertical angles are across from each other, whether they are up and down (vertical) or side by side (horizontal).

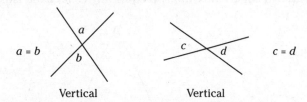

Vertical   Vertical

10. Angles in the same position (corresponding angles) around two parallel lines and a transversal have the same measures.

When you see two parallel lines and a transversal, number the angles. Start in the upper-right corner with 1 and go clockwise. For the second batch of angles, start in the upper-right corner with 5 and go clockwise:

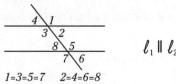

1=3=5=7   2=4=6=8

Note that all the odd-numbered angles are equal and all the even-numbered angles are equal.

Be careful not to zigzag back and forth when numbering, like this:

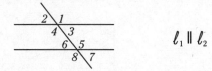

If you zig when you should have zagged, you can no longer use the tip that all even-numbered angles are equal to one another and all odd-numbered angles are equal to one another.

11. The exterior angles of any figure are supplementary to the interior angles and total 360 degrees.

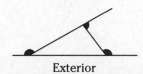

Exterior

Triangle Trauma: Triangles

1. A triangle with three equal sides and three equal angles is called *equilateral*.

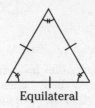

Equilateral

2. A triangle with two equal sides and two equal angles is called *isosceles*.

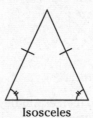

Isosceles

3. Angles opposite equal sides in an isosceles triangle are also equal.

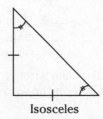

Isosceles

4. A triangle with no equal sides and no equal angles is called *scalene*.

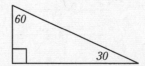

Scalene

5. In any triangle, the largest angle is opposite the longest side.

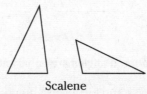

6. In any triangle, the sum of the lengths of two sides must be greater than the length of the third side. This is often written as $a + b > c$, where a, b, and c are the sides of the triangle.

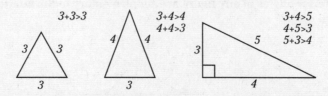

7. **In any type of triangle, the sum of the interior angles is 180 degrees.**

  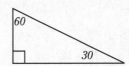

 Often a trap question wants you to assume that different-sized triangles have different angle measures. Wrong! A triangle can be seven stories high and have 180 degrees or be microscopic and have 180 degrees. The size of the triangle is irrelevant; every triangle's internal angles sum up to 180 degrees.

8. **One final concept: The measure of an exterior angle of a triangle is equal to the sum of the two remote interior angles.**

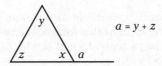

When you think about this rule logically, it makes sense. The sum of supplementary angles is 180. The sum of the angles in a triangle is 180. Therefore, angle $x = 180 - (y + z)$ or angle $x = 180 - a$. That must mean that $a = y + z$.

Similar figures

1. **The sides of similar figures are in proportion.** For example, if the heights of two similar triangles are in a ratio of 2:3, then the bases of those triangles are in a ratio of 2:3 as well.

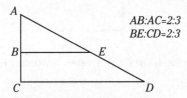

2. **The ratio of the areas of similar figures is equal to the square of the ratio of their sides.** For example, if each side of figure A is $^{1}/_{3}$ the length of each side of similar figure B, then the area of figure A is $^{1}/_{9}$ $[(^{1}/_{3})^{2}]$ the area of figure B.

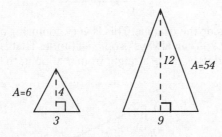

Two similar triangles have bases 5 and 25. Which of the following expresses the ratio of the areas of the two triangles?

(A) 1:5

(B) 1:15

(C) 1:25

(D) 2:15

(E) It cannot be determined from the information given.

The ratio of the sides is $^1/_5$. The ratio of the areas is the *square* of the ratio of the sides: $^1/_5 \times ^1/_5 = ^1/_{25}$. Note that answer E is a trap for the unwary. You can't figure out the exact area of either figure because you don't know the height (the area of a triangle is $^1/_2$ base × height). However, you aren't asked for an area, only for the ratio of the areas, which you can deduce from the formula discussed. *Correct Answer:* C.

Bonus: What do you suppose the ratio of the *volumes* of two similar figures is? Because volume is found in cubic units, **the ratio of the volumes of two similar figures is the *cube* of the ratio of their sides.** If figure A has a base of 5 and similar figure B has a base of 10, then the ratio of their volumes is 1:8 ([1:2³] which is $^1/_2 \times ^1/_2 \times ^1/_2 = ^1/_8$).

Don't assume that figures are similar; you must be told that they are.

Area

1. **The area of a triangle is $^1/_2$ *base* × *height*.** The height is always a line perpendicular to the base. The height may be a side of the triangle, as in a right triangle.

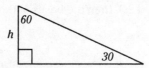

The height may be inside the triangle. It is often represented by a dashed line and a small 90-degree box.

The height may be outside the triangle. This is very confusing and can be found in trick questions. **Remember:** You can always drop an altitude. That is, put your pencil on the tallest point of the triangle and draw a line straight from that point to the base. The line can be outside the triangle.

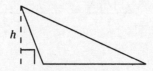

2. The perimeter of a triangle is the sum of the lengths of the sides.

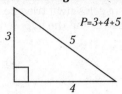

Pythagorean theorem

You have probably studied the Pythagorean theorem (known colloquially as PT). Keep in mind that it works only on *right* triangles. If a triangle doesn't have a right or 90-degree angle, you can't use any of the following information.

In any right triangle, you can find the lengths of the sides with the formula:

$$a^2 + b^2 = c^2$$

where a and b are the sides of the triangle and c is the hypotenuse. The hypotenuse is always opposite the 90-degree angle and is always the longest side of the triangle. Why? Because if one angle in a triangle is 90 degrees, no other angle can be more than 90 degrees. All the angles must total 180 degrees, and there are no negative or 0 angles. Because the longest side is opposite the largest angle, the hypotenuse is the longest side.

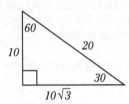

Pythagorean triples

It's a pain in the posterior to have to do the whole PT formula every time you want to find the length of a side. You'll find four very common PT ratios in triangles.

1. Ratio 3:4:5: In this ratio, if one side of the triangle is 3, the other side is 4, and the hypotenuse is 5.

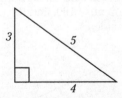

Because this is a ratio, the sides can be in any multiple of these numbers, such as 6:8:10 (twice 3:4:5), 9:12:15 (three times 3:4:5), or 27:36:45 (nine times 3:4:5).

2. Ratio 5:12:13: In this ratio, if one side of the triangle is 5, the other side is 12, and the hypotenuse is 13.

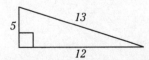

Because this is a ratio, the sides can be in any multiple of these numbers, such as 10:24:26 (twice 5:12:13), 15:36:39 (three times 5:12:13), or 50:120:130 (ten times 5:12:13).

3. **Ratio s:s:s√2:** where *s* stands for the side of the figure. Because two sides are the same, this formula applies to an isosceles right triangle, also known as a 45:45:90 triangle. If one side is 2, then the other side is also 2, and the hypotenuse is $2\sqrt{2}$.

This formula is great to know for squares. If a question tells you that the side of a square is 5 and wants to know the diagonal of the square, you know immediately that it is $5\sqrt{2}$. Why? A square's diagonal cuts the square into two isosceles right triangles (*isosceles* because all sides of the square are equal; *right* because all angles in a square are right angles). What is the diagonal of a square of side 64? $64\sqrt{2}$. What is the diagonal of a square of side 12,984? $12,984\sqrt{2}$.

There's another way to write this ratio. Instead of $s:s:s\sqrt{2}$, you can write it as $(^s/\sqrt{2}):(^s/\sqrt{2}):s$. *s* still stands for the side of the triangle, but now you've divided everything through by $\sqrt{2}$. Why do you need this complicated formula? Suppose that you're told that the diagonal of a square is 5. What is the area of the square? What is the perimeter of the square? Chances are good that one of the trap answers is "It cannot be determined from the information given." Chances are even better that you may fall for that trap answer.

However, if you know this formula, $(^s/\sqrt{2}):(^s/\sqrt{2}):s$, you know that *s* stands for the hypotenuse of the triangle, which is the same as the diagonal of the square. If *s* = 5, then the side of the square is $5/\sqrt{2}$, and you can figure out the area or the perimeter. Once you know the side of a square, you can figure out just about anything.

4. **Ratio s:s√3:2s:** This is a special formula for the sides of a 30:60:90 triangle.

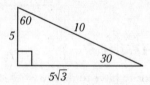

This type of triangle is a favorite of the test makers. The important thing to keep in mind here is that the hypotenuse is twice the length of the side opposite the 30-degree angle. If you get a word problem saying, "Given a 30:60:90 triangle of hypotenuse 20, find the area" or "Given a 30:60:90 triangle of hypotenuse 100, find the perimeter," you can do so because you can find the lengths of the other sides.

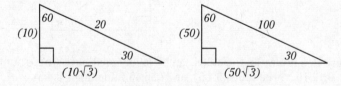

Thanks 4 Nothing: Quadrilaterals

1. Any four-sided figure is called a *quadrilateral*.

Quadrilateral

The interior angles of any quadrilateral total 360 degrees. Any quadrilateral can be cut into two 180-degree triangles.

2. A *square* is a quadrilateral with four equal sides and four right angles.

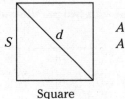

Square

The area of a square is side^2 (also called *base × height*), or $^1/_2$ diagonal^2.

3. A *rhombus* is a quadrilateral with four equal sides and four angles that are not necessarily right angles.

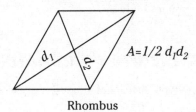

Rhombus

A rhombus often looks like a drunken square, tipsy on its side and wobbly. The area of a rhombus is $^1/_2 d_1 d_2$ ($^1/_2$ *diagonal 1 × diagonal 2*).

Any square is a rhombus, but not all rhombuses are squares.

4. A *rectangle* is a quadrilateral with two opposite and equal pairs of sides. That is, the top and bottom sides are equal, and the right and left sides are equal. All angles in a rectangle are right angles (*rectangle* means right angle).

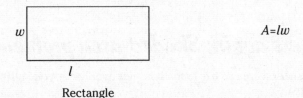

Rectangle

The area of a rectangle is *length × width* (which is the same as *base × height*).

5. A *parallelogram* is a quadrilateral with two opposite and equal pairs of sides. The top and bottom sides are equal, and the right and left sides are equal. Opposite angles are equal but not necessarily right (or 90 degrees).

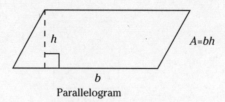

Parallelogram

The area of a parallelogram is *base × height*. Remember that the height always is a perpendicular line from the tallest point of the figure down to the base. Diagonals of a parallelogram bisect each other.

All rectangles are parallelograms, but not all parallelograms are rectangles.

6. A *trapezoid* is a quadrilateral with two parallel sides and two nonparallel sides.

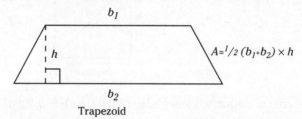

Trapezoid

The area of a trapezoid is $\frac{1}{2}$ (*base 1* + *base 2*) × *height*. It makes no difference which base you label *base 1* and which you label *base 2* because you're adding them together anyway. Just be sure to add them *before* you multiply by $\frac{1}{2}$.

Quaint quads: Bizarre quadrilaterals

Some quadrilaterals don't have nice, neat shapes or special names.

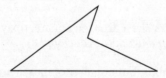

Don't immediately see a strange shape and say that you have no way to find the area of it. You may be able to divide the quadrilateral into two triangles and find the area of each triangle. You may also see a strange quadrilateral in a shaded-area problem; I'll tell you more about those in the next section.

Leftovers again: Shaded-area problems

Think of a shaded area as a *leftover*. It is "left over" after you subtract the unshaded area from the total area.

Shaded areas are often very unusual shapes. Your first reaction may be that you can't possibly find the area of that shape. Generally, you're right, but you don't have to find the area directly. Instead, be sly, devious, and sneaky; in other words, think the GRE way! Find the area of the total figure, find the area of the unshaded portion, and subtract.

1. s = 8
   Area of square = 64
2. r = 4
   Area of circle = 16π
3. Shaded area = $64-16\pi$

Missing Parrots and Other Polly-Gones: More Polygons

Triangles and quadrilaterals are probably the most common polygons tested on this exam. Here are a few other polygons you may see:

Number of Sides	Name
5	pentagon
6	hexagon (think of *x* in six and *x* in hex)
7	heptagon
8	octagon
9	nonagon
10	decagon

1. **A polygon with all equal sides and all equal angles is called *regular*.** For example, an equilateral triangle is a regular triangle, and a square is a regular quadrilateral.

   You usually will not be asked to find the areas of any polygons with more than four sides. You may be asked to find the *perimeter,* which is just the sum of the lengths of all the sides. You also may be asked to find the exterior angle measure, which is always 360.

2. **The exterior angle measure of *any* polygon is 360.**

Total interior angle measure

You may also have to find the interior angle measure. Use this formula:

$(n-2)\,180°$, where *n* stands for the number of sides

For example, the interior angles of the following polygons are

- **Triangle:** $(3 - 2)\,180 = 1 \times 180 = 180°$
- **Quadrilateral:** $(4 - 2)\,180 = 2 \times 180 = 360°$
- **Pentagon:** $(5 - 2)\,180 = 3 \times 180 = 540°$
- **Hexagon:** $(6 - 2)\,180 = 4 \times 180 = 720°$
- **Heptagon:** $(7 - 2)\,180 = 5 \times 180 = 900°$
- **Octagon:** $(8 - 2)\,180 = 6 \times 180 = 1{,}080°$
- **Nonagon:** $(9 - 2)\,180 = 7 \times 180 = 1{,}260°$
- **Decagon:** $(10 - 2)\,180 = 8 \times 180 = 1{,}440°$

Have you learned that proportional multiplication is a great timesaving trick? Numbers are in proportion, and you can fiddle with them to make multiplication easier. Suppose that you're going to multiply 5×180. Most people have to write down the problem and then work through it. But because the numbers are in proportion, you can double one and halve the other: Double 5 to make it 10. Halve 180 to make it 90. Now your problem is 10×90, which you can multiply to 900 in your head.

Try another one: $3 \times 180 = ?$ Double the first number: $3 \times 2 = 6$. Halve the second number: $^{180}/_2 = 90$. $6 \times 90 = 540$. You can do this shortcut multiplication in your head very quickly and impress your friends.

One interior angle

If you are asked to find the average measure of one angle in a figure, the formula is

$$\frac{(n - 2)\,180°}{n}$$

where n stands for the number of sides (which is the same as the number of angles).

Pentagon: $\dfrac{(5 - 2) \times 180}{5} = \dfrac{(3 \times 180)}{5} = \dfrac{540}{5} = 108$

Because all angles are equal in a regular polygon, the same formula applies to one angle in a regular polygon.

If you are given a polygon and are *not* told that it's regular, you can't solve for just one angle.

What's the measure of angle x? It cannot be determined. You can't assume that it is $\dfrac{(7-2)\,180}{7} = \dfrac{900}{7} = 128.57$.

Be sure to divide through by n, the number of sides (angles), not by $(n - 2)$. If you divide through by $(n - 2)$, you always get 180 ($^{900}/_5 = 180$). Knowing this, triple-check your work if you come up with 180 for an answer to this type of problem; you may have made this very typical but careless error.

Volume

1. **The volume of any polygon is** *(area of the base)* × *height.* If you remember this formula, you don't have to memorize any of the following more specific formulas.

2. **Volume of a cube:** e^3

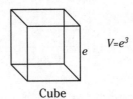

Cube

A cube is a three-dimensional square. Think of a die (one of a pair of dice). All of a cube's dimensions are the same; that is, *length = width = height.* In a cube, these dimensions are called *edges.* The volume of a cube is *edge × edge × edge = edge*^{3} = e^3.

3. **Volume of a rectangular solid:** $l \times w \times h$

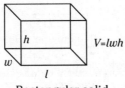

Rectangular solid

A rectangular solid is a box. The base of a box is a rectangle, which has an area of *length × width.* Multiply that by height to fit the original formula: Volume = *(area of base) × height,* or V = $l \times w \times h$.

4. **Volume of a cylinder:** (πr^2)**height**

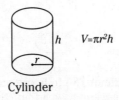

Cylinder

Think of a cylinder as a can of soup. The base of a cylinder is a circle. The area of a circle is πr^2. Multiply that by the height of the cylinder to get *(area of base) × height* = $(\pi r^2) \times height$. Note that the top and bottom of a cylinder are identical circles. If you know the radius of either the top base or the bottom base, you can find the area of the circle.

Total surface area (TSA)

1. **The total surface area, logically enough, is the sum of the areas of all the surfaces of the figure.**

2. **TSA of a cube: $6e^2$**

Cube

A cube has six identical faces, and each face is a square. The area of a square is $side^2$. Here, that is called $edge^2$. If one face is $edge^2$, then the total surface area is $6 \times edge^2$, or $6e^2$.

3. **TSA of a rectangular solid: $2(lw) + 2(hw) + 2(lh)$**

Rectangular solid

A rectangular solid is a box. You need to find the area of each of the six surfaces. The bottom and top have the area of $length \times width$. The area of the left side and right side is $width \times height$. The front side and the back side have the area of $height \times length$. Together, they total $2(lw) + 2(wh) + 2(hl)$ or $2(lw + wh + hl)$.

4. **TSA of a cylinder: $(circumference \times height) + 2(\pi r^2)$**

This is definitely the most difficult TSA to figure out. Think of it as pulling the label off the can, flattening it out, finding its area, and then adding that to the area of the top and bottom lids.

The label is a rectangle. Its length is the length of the circumference of the circle.

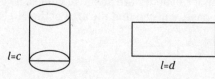

Its height is the height of the cylinder. Multiply *length* × *height* to find the area of the label.

You also need to find the area of the top and bottom of the cylinder. Because each is a circle, the TSA of the top and bottom is $2(\pi r^2)$. Add everything together.

I'm Too Much of a Klutz for Coordinate Geometry

The horizontal axis is the *x*-axis. The vertical axis is the *y*-axis. Points are labeled (*x,y*) with the first number in the parentheses indicating how far to the right or left of the vertical line the point is and the second number indicating how far above or below the horizontal line the point is.

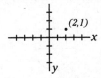

The intersection of the *x*- and *y*-axes is called the *point of origin,* and its coordinates are (0,0). A line connecting points whose *x*- and *y*-coordinates are the same forms a 45-degree angle.

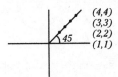

If you're asked to find the distance between two points, you can use the distance formula (which is based on the Pythagorean theorem):

$$\sqrt{(x_2 - x_1)^2 + (y_2 - y_1)^2}$$

Find the distance from (9,4) to (8,6).

$$9 = x_1$$
$$8 = x_2$$
$$4 = y_1$$
$$6 = y_2$$
$$(8 - 9)^2 = -1^2 = 1$$
$$(6 - 4)^2 = 2^2 = 4$$
$$1 + 4 = 5$$

$\sqrt{5}$ is the distance between the two points.

Running Around in Circles

Did you hear about the rube who pulled his son out of college, claiming that the school was filling his head with nonsense? As the rube said, "Joe Bob told me that he learned πr^2. But any fool knows that pie are round; *cornbread* are square!"

Circles are among the less-complicated geometry concepts. The most important things are to remember the vocabulary and to be able to distinguish an arc from a sector and an inscribed angle from an intercepted arc. Here's a quick review of the basics.

1. A radius goes from the center of a circle to its circumference (perimeter).

Radius

2. A circle is named by its center.

circle M

Center

3. A diameter connects two points on the circumference of the circle, going through the center and *is equal to two radii*.

Diameter

4. A chord connects any two points on a circle. The longest chord in a circle is the diameter.

Chords

Here's a lovely question you may see on the test. Choose

A if the quantity in Column A is greater.

B if the quantity in Column B is greater.

C if the two quantities are equal.

D if the relationship cannot be determined from the information given.

Column A	*Column B*
Area of a circle of radius 6	Area of a circle of longest chord 12

Many people choose D for this question. Although it's usually true that in QCs a geometry question with no figure is D because it *depends* on how you draw the picture, a circle is frequently an exception to this tip. A circle is a circle is a circle; it rarely depends on how you draw it. The key here is knowing that the *longest chord* is a fancy-schmancy way of saying the *diameter*. Because the diameter is twice the radius, a circle of diameter (or longest chord) 12 has a radius of 6. Two circles with radii of 6 have the same area (don't waste even a nanosecond figuring out what that area actually is; it's irrelevant to comparing the quantities in the two columns). *Correct Answer:* C.

Column A	*Column B*
Area of a circle of radius 10	Area of a circle of chord 20

If you chose C, you fell for the trap. A chord connects any two points on a circle. The *longest* chord is the diameter, but a chord can be any ol' thing. *Correct Answer:* D.

5. The perimeter of a circle is called the *circumference*. The formula for the length of a circumference is $2\pi r$ or πd (logical, because 2 radii = 1 diameter).

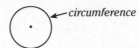

← *circumference*

Bonus: You may encounter a wheel question in which you're asked how much distance a wheel covers or how many times a wheel revolves. The key to solving this type of question is knowing that one rotation of a wheel equals one circumference of that wheel.

A child's wagon has a wheel of radius 6 inches. If the wagon wheel travels 100 revolutions, approximately how many feet has the wagon rolled?

(A) 325

(B) 314

(C) 255

(D) 201

(E) It cannot be determined from the information given.

One revolution is equal to one circumference: $C = 2\pi r = 2\pi 6 = 12\pi$ = approximately 37.68 inches. Multiply that by 100 = 3,768 inches = 314 feet. Choice E is definitely the worst guess you can make. If you have a radius, you can solve for nearly anything having to do with circles. Remember that there's a difference between "it cannot be determined" and "*I* cannot determine it." Just because you personally may not know what to do doesn't mean the problem is not "doable." If you're guessing, guess something else. *Correct Answer:* B.

6. The area of a circle is π radius^2.

$A = 16\pi$

7. A central angle has its endpoints on the circumference of the circle and its center at the center of the circle. The degree measure of a central angle is the same as the degree measure of its intercepted arc.

$\overarc{AC} = 90°$

8. An inscribed angle has both its endpoints and its center on the circumference of the circle. The degree measure of an inscribed angle is half the degree measure of its intercepted arc.

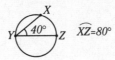

$\overarc{XZ} = 80°$

You may see a figure that looks like a string picture you made at summer camp, with all sorts of lines running every which way. Take the time to identify the endpoints of the angles and the center point. You may be surprised at how easy the question suddenly becomes.

In this figure, find the sum of the degree measures of angles $a + b + c + d + e$.

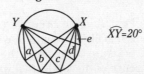

$\overarc{XY} = 20°$

<u>Note</u>: Figure not drawn to scale.

(A) 65

(B) 60

(C) 55

(D) 50

(E) 45

Each angle is an inscribed angle. That means it has half the degree measure of the central angle, or half the degree measure of its intercepted arc. If you look carefully at the endpoints of these angles, they're all the same: *XY*. Arc *XY* has a measure of 20°. Therefore, each angle is 10°, for a total of 50. *Correct Answer:* D.

9. **When a central angle and an inscribed angle have the same endpoints, the degree measure of the central angle is twice that of the inscribed angle.**

10. **The degree measure of a circle is 360.**

11. **An *arc* is a portion of the circumference of a circle. The degree measure of an arc is the same as its central angle and twice its inscribed angle.**

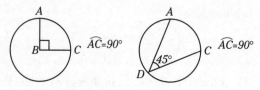

To find the length of an arc, follow these steps:

   1. **Find the circumference of the entire circle.**

   2. **Put the degree measure of the arc over 360 and then reduce the fraction.**

   3. **Multiply the circumference by the fraction.**

Find the length of arc *AC*.

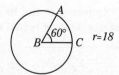

(A) 36π

(B) 27π

(C) 18π

(D) 12π

(E) 6π

Take the steps one at a time. First, find the circumference of the entire circle. C = 2πr = 36π. Don't multiply π out; problems usually leave it in that form. Next, put the degree measure of the arc over 360. The degree measure of the arc is the same as its central angle, 60°. $^{60}/_{360}$ = $^{1}/_{6}$. The arc is $^{1}/_{6}$ of the circumference of the circle. Multiply the circumference by the fraction: 36π × $^{1}/_{6}$ = 6π. *Correct Answer:* E.

Try another one. Once you get the hang of these, they're kinda fun.

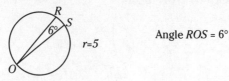

Angle *ROS* = 6°

Find the length of arc *RS* in this figure.

(A) ¹/₃π

(B) π

(C) 3π

(D) 4π

(E) 12

First, find the circumference of the entire circle. C = 2πr = 10π. Second, put the degree measure of the arc over 360. Here, the inscribed angle is 6°. Because an inscribed angle is ¹/₂ of the central angle and ¹/₂ of its intercepted arc, the arc is 12°. ¹²/₃₆₀ = ¹/₃₀. The arc is ¹/₃₀ of the circle. Finally, multiply the circumference by the fraction: 10π × ¹/₃₀ = ¹⁰/₃₀π = ¹/₃π. The length of the arc is ¹/₃π. *Correct Answer:* A.

Be very careful not to confuse the *degree measure* of the arc with the *length* of the arc. The length is always a portion of the circumference, always has a π in it, and always is in linear units. If you chose E in this example, you found the degree measure of the arc rather than its length.

12. **A *sector* is a portion of the area of a circle. The degree measure of a sector is the same as its central angle and twice its inscribed angle.**

To find the area of a sector, do the following:

  A. Find the area of the entire circle.

  B. Put the degree measure of the sector over 360 and then reduce the fraction.

  C. Multiply the area by the fraction.

Finding the area of a sector is very similar to finding the length of an arc. The only difference is in the first step. Whereas an arc is a part of the *circumference* of a circle, a sector is a part of the *area* of a circle. Try a few examples for sectors.

Find the area of sector *ABC*.

(A) 64π

(B) 36π

(C) 16π

(D) 12π

(E) 6π

First, find the area of the entire circle. *A* = πr² = 64π. Second, put the degree measure of the sector over 360. The sector is 90°, the same as its central angle: ⁹⁰/₃₆₀ = ¹/₄. Third, multiply the area by the fraction: 64π × ¹/₄ = 16π. *Correct Answer:* C.

Find the area of sector *XYZ* in this figure.

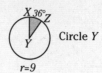

Circle *Y*

(A) 9.7π

(B) 8.1π

(C) 7.2π

(D) 6.3π

(E) 6π

First, find the area of the entire circle. $A = \pi r^2 = 81\pi$. Second, put the degree measure of the sector over 360. A sector has the same degree measure as its intercepted arc, here 36°: $^{36}/_{360} = ^1/_{10}$. Third, multiply the area by the fraction: $81\pi \times ^1/_{10} = 8.1\pi$. *Correct Answer:* B.

Chapter 11

Gotta Catch Some (Xs, Ys, and) Zs: Algebra and Other Sleeping Aids

In This Chapter

▶ Bases and exponents

▶ Ratios

▶ Symbolism

▶ Algebra basics and the FOIL method

▶ Roots and radicals

▶ Probability

Trivia Question: Where was algebra supposedly invented?

Answer: Algebra was invented in Zabid, Yemen, by Muslim scholars. See — you can't blame the Greeks for everything!

The Powers That Be: Bases and Exponents

Many GRE questions require you to know how to work with bases and exponents. The following sections explain some of the most important concepts.

1. **The *base* is the big number (or letter) on the bottom. The *exponent* is the little number (or letter) in the upper right corner.**

    In x^5, x is the base; 5 is the exponent.

    In 3^y, 3 is the base; y is the exponent.

2. **A base to the zero power equals one.**

    $x^0 = 1$

    $5^0 = 1$

    $129^0 = 1$

There is a long, *soporific* (sleep-causing) explanation as to why a number to the zero power equals one, but you don't really care, do you? For now, just memorize the rule.

3. A base to the second power is *base × base*.

This is pretty familiar stuff, right?

$$x^2 = x \times x$$

$$5^2 = 5 \times 5$$

$$129^2 = 129 \times 129$$

The same is true for bigger exponents. The exponent tells you how many times the number is repeated. For example, 5^6 means that you write down six 5s and then multiply them all together.

$$3^9 = 3 \times 3 \times 3 \times 3 \times 3 \times 3 \times 3 \times 3 \times 3$$

4. A base to a negative exponent is the reciprocal of something.

This one is a little more confusing. A *reciprocal* is the upside-down version of something. (Here's a **conundrum** [or riddle]: Is the North Pole the reciprocal of the South Pole?) When you have a negative exponent, just put the base and exponent under a 1 and make the exponent positive again.

$$x^{-4} = 1/(x^4)$$

$$5^{-3} = 1/(5^3)$$

$$129^{-1} = 1/(129^1)$$

The *number* is *not* negative. When you flip it, you get the reciprocal, and the negative just sort of fades away. *Don't* fall for the trap of saying that $5^{-3} = -(1/5)^3$ or $-1/125$.

When you take a base of 10 to some power, the number of the power equals the number of zeros in the number.

$$10^1 = 10 \text{ (one zero)}$$

$$10^4 = 10,000 \text{ (four zeros)}$$

$$10^0 = 1 \text{ (zero zeros)}$$

5. To multiply like bases, add the exponents.

You can multiply two bases that are the same; just add the exponents.

$$x^3 \times x^2 = x^{(3+2)} = x^5$$

$$5^4 \times 5^9 = 5^{(4+9)} = 5^{13}$$

$$129^3 \times 129^0 = 129^{(3+0)} = 129^3$$

You cannot multiply *unlike* bases. Think of it as trying to make dogs multiply with cats — it doesn't work. All you end up with is a miffed meower and a damaged dog.

$$x^2 \times y^3 = x^2 \times y^3 \text{ (no shortcuts)}$$

$$5^2 \times 129^3 = 5^2 \times 129^3 \text{ (you actually have to work it out)}$$

6. To divide like bases, subtract the exponents.

You can divide two bases that are the same by subtracting the exponents.

$$x^5 \div x^2 = x^{(5-2)} = x^3$$

$$5^9 \div 5^3 = 5^{(9-3)} = 5^6$$

$$129^4 \div 129^0 = 129^{(4-0)} = 129^4$$

(Did I getcha on that last one? It should make sense. Any base to the zero power is 1. Any number divided by 1 is itself.)

Did you look at the second example, $5^9 \div 5^3$, and think that it was 5^3? It's easy to fall into the trap of dividing instead of subtracting, especially when you see numbers that just beg to be divided, like 9 and 3. Keep your guard up.

7. Multiply the exponents of a base inside and outside the parentheses.

That's quite a mouthful. Here's what it means:

$$(x^2)^3 = x^{(2 \times 3)} = x^6$$

$$(5^3)^3 = 5^{(3 \times 3)} = 5^9$$

$$(129^0)^3 = 129^{(0 \times 3)} = 129^0$$

Try a few QC questions testing this concept.

The answer choices are

    A if the quantity in Column A is greater.

    B if the quantity in Column B is greater.

    C if the two quantities are equal.

    D if the relationship cannot be determined from the information given.

Column A	_Column B_
x^3	$\dfrac{x^7}{x^4}$

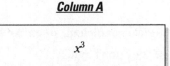
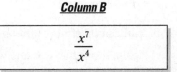

$x^{(7-4)} = x^3$, no matter what the value of x is. *Correct Answer:* C.

Column A	_Column B_
$(x^3)^4$	x^{12}

No matter what value x has, the two columns are the same: $x^{12} = x^{12}$. *Correct Answer:* C.

Column A	**Column B**
$(x^3)^4$	12

Everything *depends on* the value of x. Boy, this trap is really easy to fall for. You are so busy thinking of $3 \times 4 = 12$ that you may be tempted to choose C. But the automatic shut down valve in the back of your brain should alert you to the fact that *when two columns appear to be equal, it is usually a trap.* (See Chapter 13 for more information on this QC trick.) *Correct Answer:* D.

8. **To add or subtract like bases to like powers, add or subtract the numerical coefficient of the bases.**

The *numerical coefficient* (a great name for a rock band, don't you think?) is simply the number *in front of* the base. Notice that it is not the little exponent in the right-hand corner but the full-sized number to the left of the base.

In $31x^3$, 31 is the numerical coefficient.

In $-8y^2$, -8 is the numerical coefficient.

In x^3, the numerical coefficient is 1, because any number is itself times 1; the 1 is not always written out. Good trap.

In $37x^3 + 10x^3 = 47x^3$, just add the numerical coefficients: $37 + 10 = 47$.

In $15y^2 - 10y^2 = 5y^2$, just subtract the numerical coefficients: $15 - 10 = 5$.

You cannot add or subtract like bases with *different exponents*.

$13x^3 - 9x^2$ is *not* equal to $4x^3$ or $4x^2$ or $4x$. All it is equal to is $13x^3 - 9x^2$. The bases *and* exponents must be the same for you to add or subtract the terms.

Column A	**Column B**
$16x^4 - 4x^3$	$12x$

The answer depends on the value of x. If you chose C, you fell for the trap I just discussed. *Correct Answer:* D.

9. **You cannot simply add or subtract the numerical coefficients of unlike bases.**

Again, this is like working with cats and dogs. They don't mingle.

$$16x^2 - 4y^2 = 16x^2 - 4y^2$$

It is *not* $12x^2$ or $12y^2$ or $12xy^2$.

Column A	**Column B**
$10x^3 - 2y^3$	$8xy$

It depends on the values of x and y. C is the trap answer. *Correct Answer:* D.

Keep It in Proportion: Ratios

Once you know the tricks, ratios are some of the easiest problems to answer quickly. I call them "heartbeat" problems because you can solve them in a heartbeat. Of course, if someone drop-dead gorgeous sits next to you and makes your heart beat faster, it may take you two heartbeats to solve a ratio problem. So sue me.

1. **A ratio is written as $\frac{of}{to}$ or of:to.**

   The ratio *of* sunflowers *to* roses = sunflowers:roses.

   The ratio *of* umbrellas *to* heads = $\dfrac{umbrellas}{heads}$.

2. **A possible total is a multiple of the sum of the numbers in the ratio.**

   You may be given a problem like this: At a party, the ratio of blondes to redheads is $^4/_5$. Which of the following can be the total number of blondes and redheads at the party?

   Mega-easy. Add the numbers in the ratio: 4 + 5 = 9. The total must be a multiple of 9: 9, 18, 27, 36, and so on. If this "multiple of" stuff is confusing, think of it another way: The sum must divide evenly into the total. That is, the total must be divisible by 9. Can the total, for example, be 54? Yes, 9 goes evenly into 54. Can it be 64? No, 9 does not go evenly into 64.

After a rough hockey game, Bernie checks his body and finds that he has three bruises for every five cuts. Which of the following can be the total number of bruises and cuts on poor ol' Bernie's body?

   (A) 53

   (B) 45

   (C) 35

   (D) 33

   (E) 32

Add the numbers in the ratio: 3 + 5 = 8. The total must be a multiple of 8 (or, looking at it another way, the total must be evenly divisible by 8). Only E is a multiple of 8: $8 \times 4 = 32$. *Correct Answer:* E.

Did you notice the trap answers? 53 is a good trap because it features both 5 and 3, the numbers in the ratio. 45 is a trap. If you multiply $3 \times 5 = 15$, you may think that the total has to be a multiple of 15. No, the total is a multiple of the *sum,* not of the product. *Add* the numbers in the ratio; don't multiply them. 35 again has both terms of the ratio. 33 is a multiple of 3. Only 32 is a multiple of the *sum* of the terms in the ratio.

One more, because you should always get this type of problem correct.

Trying to get Willie to turn down his stereo, his downstairs neighbor pounds on the ceiling and shouts up to his bedroom. If she pounds 7 times for every 5 times she shouts, which of the following can be the total number of poundings and shouts?

   (A) 75

   (B) 57

   (C) 48

   (D) 35

   (E) 30

Add the numbers in the ratio: 7 + 5 = 12. The total must be a multiple of 12 (it must be evenly divisible by 12). Here, only 48 is evenly divisible by 12. Of course, 75 and 57 try to trick you by using the numbers 7 and 5 from the ratio. Choice D is the product of 7 × 5. *Correct Answer:* C.

Notice how carefully I have been asking which *can be* the *possible* total. The total can be *any* multiple of the sum. If a question asks you which of the following *is* the total, you have to answer, "It cannot be determined." You know only which *can be* true.

Column A	_Column B_

Ratio of CDs to tapes = 2:9

Total of CDs and tapes	11

You know the total must be a multiple of 11, but it can be an infinite number of terms: 11, 22, 33, 44, 55, and so on. This trap has destroyed a lot of overly confident students over the years. *Correct Answer:* D.

When given a ratio and a total and asked to find a specific term, do the following in order:

1. **Add the numbers in the ratio.**

2. **Divide that sum into the total.**

3. **Multiply that quotient by each term in the ratio.**

4. **Add the answers to double-check that they sum up to the total.**

Pretty confusing stuff. Take it one step at a time.

Yelling at the members of his team, which had just lost 21–0, the irate coach pointed his finger at each member of the squad, calling everyone either a wimp or a slacker. If there were 3 wimps for every 4 slackers and every member of the 28-man squad was either a wimp or a slacker, how many wimps were there?

1. **Add the numbers in the ratio: 3 + 4 = 7.**

2. **Divide that sum into the total: $^{28}/_7$ = 4.**

3. **Multiply that quotient by each term in the ratio: 4 × 3 = 12; 4 × 4 = 16.**

4. **Add to double-check that the numbers sum up to the total: 12 + 16 = 28.**

Now you have all the information you need to answer a variety of questions: How many wimps were there? Twelve. How many slackers were there? Sixteen. How many more slackers than wimps were there? Four. How many slackers would have to be kicked off the team for the number of wimps and slackers to be equal? Four. The GRE's Math Moguls can ask all sorts of things, but if you've got this information, you're ready for anything they throw at you.

Be sure that you actually do step 4, adding the terms to double-check that they sum up to the total again. Doing so will catch any careless mistakes you may have made. For example, suppose you divided 7 into 28 and got 3 instead of 4. Then you said that there were 3 × 3, or 9, wimps, and 3 × 4, or 12, slackers. That means that the total was 9 + 12 = 21 — *ooooops!* You know the total has to be 28, so you can go back and try again. You'll also catch a careless mistake in your multiplication. Suppose that you correctly divide 7 into 28 and get 4. But when you multiply 4 × 3, you get 43 instead of 12. (Hey, when the adrenaline's flowing during the exam, you'd be surprised at the kinds of mistakes you can make.) When you add the numbers, you get 43 + 16 = 59 instead of the 28 that you know is the total.

It takes longer to talk through these steps than it does to do them. After you learn this technique, it makes a lot of sense. Think of ratios as cliques. If there are 3 boys for every 5 girls, there are 8 kids in one clique. If there are 48 kids at a party, there must be 6 cliques (8 divided into 48 = 6). If there are 6 cliques at 3 girls per clique, there are $6 \times 3 = 18$ girls. If there are 6 cliques at 5 boys each, there are $6 \times 5 = 30$ boys.

Things Aren't What They Seem: Symbolism

You may encounter two basic types of symbolism problems. If so, do one of the following:

✔ Substitute the number given for the variable in the explanation.

✔ Talk through the explanation to see which constraint fits and then do the indicated operations.

1. **Substitute for the variable in the explanation.**

You see a problem with a strange symbol. It may be a variable inside a circle, a triangle, a star, or a tic-tac-toe sign. That symbol has no connection to the real world at all. Don't panic, thinking that your teachers forgot to teach you something. Symbols are made up for each problem.

The symbol is included in a short explanation. It may look like this:

$$a \# b \# c = \frac{(a + b)^c}{(b + c)}$$

$$x * y * z = {}^z/_x + \left(\frac{y}{z}\right)^x$$

$$m @ n @ o = mn + no - om$$

Again, the symbols don't have any meaning in the outside world; they mean only what the problem tells you they mean, and that meaning holds true only for this problem.

Below the explanation is the question itself:

$3 \# 2 \# 1 =$

$4 * 6 * 8 =$

$2 @ 5 @ 10 =$

Your job is one of substitution. Plug in a number for the variable in the equation. Which number do you plug in? The one that's in the same position as that variable. For example:

$$a \# b \# c = \frac{(a + b)^c}{(b + c)}$$

$$3 \# 2 \# 1 = \frac{(3 + 2)^1}{(2 + 1)} = {}^5/_3$$

Because *a* was in the first position and 3 was in the first position, substitute a 3 for an *a* throughout the equation. Because *b* was in the second position and 2 was in the second position, substitute a 2 for a *b* throughout the equation. Because *c* was in the third position and 1 was in the third position, substitute a 1 for a *c* throughout the equation.

Do the same for the other problems.

$$x * y * z = {}^z/x + \left({}^y/z\right)^x$$

$$4 * 6 * 8 = \left({}^8/4\right) + \left({}^6/8\right)^4 = 2 + \left({}^6/8\right)^4 = 2 + .316 = 2.316$$

$$m @ n @ o = mn + no - om$$

$$2 @ 5 @ 10 = (2 \times 5) + (5 \times 10) - (10 \times 2) = 10 + 50 - 20 = 40$$

This is the simpler of the two types of symbolism problems. Just substitute the number for the variable and work through the equation.

2. Talk through the explanation and do the operations.

This type of symbolism problem may seem more confusing until you've done a few. Then it becomes so easy that you wonder why you didn't see it before. Here are two possibilities.

$$\textcircled{x} = 3x \text{ if } x \text{ is odd.}$$

$$\textcircled{x} = \frac{x}{2} \text{ if } x \text{ is even.}$$

Solve for $\textcircled{5}$ + $\textcircled{8}$.

First, talk through the explanation. You have something in a circle. If that something in the circle is odd, you multiply it by 3. If that something in the circle is even, you divide it by 2.

In the question, there's a 5 in the circle. Because 5 is odd, you multiply it by 3 to get $5 \times 3 = 15$. In the second half of the question, there's an 8 in a circle. Because 8 is even, you divide it by 2. $^8/_2 = 4$. Now add: $15 + 4 = 19$.

Don't keep going. Do *not* say, "Well, 19 is odd, so I have to multiply it by 3, getting 57." You can bet that 57 is one of the trap multiple-choice answers.

You may still think of this second type of problem as a plug-in or substitution problem because you are plugging the number into the equation for x and working it through. However, you first have to figure out which equation to plug it into. That requires talking things through. You have to understand what you're doing in this type of problem. Try another:

$$\triangle{x} = 3x + {}^1/3x \text{ if } x \text{ is prime}$$

$$\triangle{x} = x^2 + \sqrt{x} \text{ if } x \text{ is composite}$$

$$\triangle{16} + \triangle{3} =$$

Aha! Now you have to know some math vocabulary. *Prime numbers* are numbers greater than 1, and cannot be divided other than by 1 and themselves. Examples are 2, 3, 5, 7, 11, and 13. *Composite numbers* are numbers that *can* be divided other than by just 1 and themselves, like 4, 6, 8, 9, 10, and 12. The first thing you do is decide whether the term in the triangle is a composite number or a prime number.

In $\triangle{16}$, because 16 is a composite number, use the second equation. Square 16: $16 \times 16 = 256$. Take the square root of 16: $\sqrt{16} = 4$. Add them together: $256 + 4 = 260$.

In $\triangle{3}$, because 3 is a prime number, use the first equation. $3^2 + {}^1/3(3) = 9 + 1 = 10$. Add the two solutions: $260 + 10 = 270$.

Sometimes, the solutions have symbols in them as well. Here's an example:

> $\bigcirc{x} = \frac{1}{2}x$ if x is composite
> $\bigcirc{x} = 2x$ if x is prime

Solve for $\bigcirc{5} \times \bigcirc{10}$.

(A) $\bigcirc{15}$

(B) $\bigcirc{25}$

(C) $\bigcirc{50}$

(D) $\bigcirc{100}$

(E) It cannot be determined from the information given.

First, you know to eliminate answer E. This is the sucker's answer, the one for people who have no idea what the cute little circle means and are clueless as to where to begin. You know by now that you *can* solve a symbolism problem — and pretty quickly, too.

Because 5 is prime, you multiply it by 2: $5 \times 2 = 10$.

Because 10 is composite, you multiply it by $\frac{1}{2}$: $10 \times \frac{1}{2} = 5$.

Multiply: $10 \times 5 = 50$.

Noooo! Don't choose answer C; that's the trap answer. Choice C doesn't say 50; it says $\bigcirc{50}$. That means that you have to solve the answer choice to see what it really is. Think of it as a choice in disguise with a false beard and glasses. Because 50 is even, you take half of it: $50 \div 2 = 25$. That's not the answer you want. Now go through the rest of the choices:

$\bigcirc{15}$: Because 15 is composite, multiply it by $\frac{1}{2}$: $15 \times \frac{1}{2} = 7.5$.

$\bigcirc{25}$: Because 25 is composite, multiply it by $\frac{1}{2}$: $25 \times \frac{1}{2} = 12.5$.

$\bigcirc{100}$: Because 100 is composite, multiply it by $\frac{1}{2}$: $100 \times \frac{1}{2} = 50$. You have a winner!

Whenever you see a symbol, get to work. That symbol may be in the question or in the answer choices. You still follow the explanation. But remember the trap I already discussed: Be super careful not to keep on going. That is, when you come up with 50 as your answer, don't say, "Well, 50 is composite, so I have to multiply it by $\frac{1}{2}$, getting 25." Stop when there are no more symbols. *Correct Answer:* D.

Have you studied functions? Maybe not in school, but if you've read the preceding material on symbolism, you have just studied functions. A function is very much like the symbolism you've just read about. You may see a problem like this:

$f(x) = (2x)^3$. Solve for $f(2)$.

The *f* stands for function. You do the same thing you did before: Talk through the problem. You say, "I have something in parentheses. My job is to multiply that something by two and then cube the whole disgusting mess." In other words, just plug in the 2 where you see an *x* in the explanation.

$f(2) = (2 \times 2)^3 = 4^3 = 64$

Try another one.

$f(x) = x + x^2 + x^3$. Solve for $f(10)$.

Just plug the 10 in for the x: $f(10) = 10 + 10^2 + 10^3 = 10 + 100 + 1,000 = 1,110$.

Now that you've acquired this skill, you can call yourself "fully functional."

Abracadabra: Algebra

You must be able to do three basic algebra concepts for the GRE.

✔ Solve for x in an equation.

✔ Use the FOIL method.

✔ Factor down a quadratic equation and take an algebraic expression from its final form back to its original form of two sets of parentheses.

To solve for x, follow these steps:

1. **Isolate the variable which means getting all the x's on one side and all the non-x's on the other side.**

2. **Add all the x's on one side; add all the non-x's on the other side.**

3. **Divide both sides of the equation by the number in front of the x.**

Now you try it: $3x + 7 = 9x - 5$

1. **Isolate the variable. Move the $3x$ to the right, *changing the sign* to make it $-3x$.**

   Forgetting to change the sign is one of the most common careless mistakes students make. The test makers realize that and often include trap answer choices to catch this mistake.

2. **Move the -5 to the left, *changing the sign* to make it $+5$. You now have $7 + 5 = 9x - 3x$.**

3. **Add the x's on one side; add the non-x's on the other side.**

   $12 = 6x$

4. **Divide both sides through by what is next to the x.**
   $$\frac{12}{6} = \frac{6x}{6}$$

   $2 = x$

If you're weak on algebra or know that you often make careless mistakes, plug the 2 back into the equation to make sure that it works.

$3(2) + 7 = 9(2) - 5$

$6 + 7 = 18 - 5$

$13 = 13$

If you absolutely hate algebra, see whether you can simply plug in the answer choices. If this were a Problem-Solving question with multiple-choice answers, you could plug 'n chug.

$3x + 7 = 9x - 5$. Solve for x.

  (A) 5

  (B) $3\frac{1}{2}$

  (C) 2

  (D) 0

  (E) –2

Don't ask for trouble. Keep life simple by starting with the simple answers first. That is, try plugging in 5. When it doesn't work, don't bother plugging in $3\frac{1}{2}$. That's too much work. Go right down to 2. If all the easy answers don't work, then you can go back to the hard answer of $3\frac{1}{2}$, but why fuss with it unless you absolutely have to? *Correct Answer:* C.

Curses! FOILed again

The second thing you need to know to do algebra is how to use the FOIL method. FOIL stands for *First, Outer, Inner, Last* and refers to the order in which you multiply the variables in parentheses. With the equation $(a + b)(a - b) =$

1. **Multiply the *First* variables: $a \times a = a^2$.**

2. **Multiply the *Outer* variables: $a \times -b = -ab$.**

3. **Multiply the *Inner* variables: $b \times a = ba$ (which is the same as ab).**

4. **Multiply the *Last* variables: $b \times -b = -b^2$.**

Add like terms: $-ab + ab = 0ab$. (Remember that you can multiply numbers forward or backward, such that $ab = ba$.) The positive and negative ab cancel each other out. You're left with only $a^2 - b^2$.

Try another one $(3a + b)(a - 2b) =$

1. **Multiply the *First* terms: $3a \times a = 3a^2$.**

2. **Multiply the *Outer* terms: $3a \times -2b = 6-ab$.**

3. **Multiply the *Inner* terms: $b \times a = ba$ (which is the same as ab).**

4. **Multiply the *Last* terms: $b \times -2b = -2b^2$.**

5. **Combine like terms: $-6ab + -ab = -5ab$. The final answer: $3a^2 - 5ab - 2b^2$.**

You should memorize the following three FOIL problems. Don't bother to work them out every time; know them by heart.

1. **$(a + b)^2 = a^2 + 2ab + b^2$**

    You can prove this equation by using FOIL: $(a + b)(a + b)$

    a. **Multiply the *First* terms: $a \times a = a^2$.**

    b. **Multiply the *Outer* terms: $a \times -b = -ab$.**

    c. **Multiply the *Inner* terms: $-b \times a = -ba$ (which is the same as $-ab$).**

    d. **Multiply the *Last* terms: $-b \times -b = =b^2$.**

    e. **Combine like terms: $-ab + -ab = -2ab$.**

    Final solution: $a^2 + 2ab - b^2$.

2. $(a - b)^2 = a^2 - 2ab + b^2$

You can prove this equation by using FOIL: $(a - b)(a - b)$.

a. **Multiply the *First* terms:** $a \times a = a^2$.

b. **Multiply the *Outer* terms:** $a \times -b = -ab$.

c. **Multiply the *Inner* terms:** $-b \times a = -ba$ (which is the same as $-ab$).

d. **Multiply the *Last* terms:** $-b \times -b = +b^2$.

e. **Combine like terms:** $-ab + -ab = -2ab$.

f. **Final solution:** $a^2 - 2ab + b^2$.

Be careful to note that the b^2 at the end is *positive*, not negative, because multiplying a negative times a negative gives a positive.

3. $(a - b)(a + b) = a^2 - b^2$

You can prove this equation by using FOIL: $(a - b)(a + b)$.

a. **Multiply the *First* terms:** $a \times a = a^2$.

b. **Multiply the *Outer* terms:** $a \times b = ab$.

c. **Multiply the *Inner* terms:** $-b \times a = -ba$ (which is the same as $-ab$).

d. **Multiply the *Last* terms:** $-b \times b = -b^2$.

e. **Combine like terms:** $ab + -ab = 0ab$.

Final solution: $a^2 - b^2$. Note that the middle term drops out because $+ab$ cancels out $-ab$.

Memorize these three equations. Doing so saves you time, careless mistakes, and acute misery on the actual exam.

Fact-or fiction: Factoring

Now you know how to do algebra forward; are you ready to do it backward? The third thing you need to know is how to factor down a quadratic equation and take an algebraic expression from its final form back to its original form of two sets of parentheses.

Given $x^2 + 13x + 42 = 0$, solve for x. Take this problem one step at a time.

1. **Draw two sets of parentheses.**

   $(\ \ )(\ \ ) = 0$.

2. **To get x^2, the *First* terms have to be x and x. Fill those in.**

   $(x\ \ )(x\ \ ) = 0$.

3. **Look now at the *Outer* terms.**

   You need two numbers that multiply together to be +42. Well, there are several possibilities: 42×1, 21×2, or 6×7. You can even have two negative numbers: -42×-1, -21×-2, or -6×-7. You aren't sure which one to choose yet. Go on to the next step.

4. **Look at the *Inner* terms.**

   You have to add two values to get +13. Now you know that you need *two positive* values to get the +13. What's the first thing that springs to mind? $6 + 7$, probably. Hey, that's one of the possibilities in the preceding step! Plug it in and try it.

$(x + 6)(x + 7) = x^2 + 7x + 6x + 42 = x^2 + 13x + 42.$

Great, but you're not finished yet. If the whole equation equals zero, then either $(x + 6) = 0$ or $(x + 7) = 0$. That's because the only way to make a product zero is to make one of the factors zero. Therefore, x can equal –6 or –7.

Again, if you have a multiple-choice problem, you can simply try the answer choices. Never start doing a lot of work until you absolutely have to.

Too Hip to Be Square: Roots and Radicals

To simplify working with square roots (or cube roots or any radicals), think of them as variables. You work the same way with $\sqrt{7}$ as you do with x, y, or z.

Addition and subtraction

1. **To add or subtract *like* radicals, add or subtract the number in front of the radical (your old friend, the numerical coefficient).**

   $2\sqrt{7} + 5\sqrt{7} = 7\sqrt{7}$ $2x + 5x = 7x$

   $9\sqrt{13} - 4\sqrt{13} = 5\sqrt{13}$ $9x - 4x = 5x$

2. **You *cannot* add or subtract unlike radicals (just as you cannot add or subtract unlike variables).**

   $6\sqrt{5} + 4\sqrt{3} = 6\sqrt{5} + 4\sqrt{3}$ (You cannot add the two and get $10\sqrt{8}$.)

   $6x + 4y = 6x + 4y$ (You cannot add the two and get $10xy$.)

Don't glance at a problem, see that the radicals are not the same, and immediately assume that you cannot add the two terms. You may be able to simplify one radical to make it match the radical in the other term.

$\sqrt{52} + \sqrt{13} = 2\sqrt{13} + \sqrt{13} = 3\sqrt{13}$

To simplify: Take out a perfect square from the term. $\sqrt{52} = \sqrt{4} \times \sqrt{13}$. Because $\sqrt{4} = 2$, $\sqrt{52} = 2\sqrt{13}$.

$\sqrt{20} + \sqrt{45} = (\sqrt{4} \times \sqrt{5}) + (\sqrt{9} \times \sqrt{5}) = 2\sqrt{5} + 3\sqrt{5} = 5\sqrt{5}$

Beware! You must simplify *first*. You can't say that $\sqrt{20} + \sqrt{45} = \sqrt{65} = 8.06$. When you work out the correct answer, $5\sqrt{5}$, you see that it's not 8.06, but 11.18.

Multiplication and division

1. **When you multiply or divide radicals, you just multiply or divide the numbers and then pop the radical sign back onto the finished product.**

   $\sqrt{5} \times \sqrt{6} = \sqrt{30}$

   $\sqrt{15} \div \sqrt{5} = \sqrt{3}$

2. **If you have a number in front of the radical, multiply it as well. Let everyone in on the fun.**

$6\sqrt{3} \times 4\sqrt{2} =$

$6 \times 4 = 24$

$\sqrt{3} \times \sqrt{2} = \sqrt{6}$

$24\sqrt{6}$

Try this example:

$37\sqrt{5} \times 3\sqrt{6} =$

(A) $40\sqrt{11}$

(B) $40\sqrt{30}$

(C) $111\sqrt{11}$

(D) $111\sqrt{30}$

(E) 1,221

$37 \times 3 = 111$ and $5 \times \sqrt{6} = \sqrt{30}$, so $111\sqrt{30}$. Straightforward multiplication. *Correct Answer:* D.

Inside out

When there is an operation under the radical, do it first and then take the square root.

$$\sqrt{\dfrac{x^2}{40} + \dfrac{x^2}{9}}$$

First, solve for $x^2/40 + x^2/9$. You get the common denominator of 360 (40×9) and then find the numerators: $9x^2 + 40x^2 = 49x^2/360$. *Now* take the square roots: $49x^2 = 7x$ (because $7x \times 7x = 49x^2$). $\sqrt{360} = 18.97$. Gotcha, I bet! Did you say that $\sqrt{360} = 6$? Wrong! $\sqrt{36} = 6$, but $\sqrt{360} =$ approx-imately 18.97. Beware of assuming too much; you can be led down the path to temptation.

Your final answer is $7x/18.97$. Of course, you can bet that the answer choices will include $7x/6$.

Probably Probability

Probability questions are usually word problems. They may look intimidating, with a lot of words that make you lose sight of where to begin. Two simple rules can solve nearly every probability problem tossed at you.

1. **Create a fraction.**

To find a probability, use this formula:

$$P = \dfrac{\text{Number of possible desired outcomes}}{\text{Number of total possible outcomes}}$$

Make a probability into a fraction. The denominator is the easier of the two parts to begin with. The denominator is the total possible number of outcomes. For example, when you're flipping a coin, there are two outcomes, giving you a denominator of 2. When you're tossing a die (one of a pair of dice), there are six outcomes, giving you a denominator of 6. When you're pulling a card out of a deck of cards, there are 52 outcomes (52 cards in a deck), giving you a denominator of 52. When 25 marbles are in a jar and you're going to pull out one of them, there are 25 possibilities, giving you a denominator of 25. Very simply, the *denominator* is the whole shebang — everything possible.

The *numerator* is the total possible number of the things you want. If you want to get a head when you toss a coin, there is exactly one head, giving you a numerator of 1. The chances of tossing a head, therefore, are $\frac{1}{2}$, one possible head, two possible outcomes altogether. If you want to get a 5 when you toss a die, there is exactly one 5 on the die, giving you a numerator of 1. Notice that your numerator is *not* 5. The number you want happens to be a 5, but there is only *one* 5 on the die. The probability of tossing a 5 is $\frac{1}{6}$: There are one 5 and six possible outcomes altogether.

If you want to draw a jack in a deck of cards, there are four jacks: hearts, diamonds, clubs, and spades. Therefore, the numerator is 4. The probability of drawing a jack out of a deck of cards is $\frac{4}{52}$ (which reduces to $\frac{1}{13}$). If you want to draw a jack of hearts, the probability is $\frac{1}{52}$ because there is only one jack of hearts.

A jar of marbles has 8 yellow marbles, 6 black marbles, and 12 white marbles. What is the probability of drawing out a black marble?

Use the formula. Begin with the denominator, which is all the possible outcomes: 8 + 6 + 12 = 26. The numerator is how many there are of what you want: 6 black marbles. The probability is $\frac{6}{26}$, which can be reduced or (as is more customary) changed to a percentage. What's the probability of drawing out a yellow marble? $\frac{8}{26}$. A white marble? $\frac{12}{26}$. *Correct Answer:* $\frac{6}{26}$ or $\frac{3}{13}$ or 23%.

A drawer has 5 pairs of white socks, 8 pairs of black socks, and 12 pairs of brown socks. In a hurry to get to school, Austin pulls out a pair at a time and tosses them on the floor if they are not the color he wants. Looking for a brown pair, Austin pulls out and discards a white pair, a black pair, a black pair, and a white pair. What is the probability that on his next reach into the drawer he will pull out a brown pair of socks?

This problem is slightly more complicated than the preceding one, although it uses the same formula. You began with 25 pairs of socks. However, Austin, that slob, has thrown 4 pairs on the floor. That means that there are only 21 pairs left. The probability of his pulling out a brown pair is $\frac{12}{21}$, or $\frac{4}{7}$, or about 57%. *Correct Answer:* 57%.

A cookie jar has chocolate, vanilla, and strawberry wafer cookies. There are 30 of each type. Bess reaches in, pulls out a chocolate and eats it, and then in quick succession pulls out and eats a vanilla, chocolate, strawberry, strawberry, chocolate, and vanilla. Assuming that she doesn't get sick or get caught, what is the probability that the next cookie she pulls out will be a chocolate one?

Originally, there were 90 cookies. Bess has scarfed down 7 of them, leaving 83. Careful! If you're about to put $\frac{30}{83}$, you're headed for a trap. There are no longer 30 chocolate cookies; there are only 27 because Bess has eaten 3. The probability is now $\frac{27}{83}$, or about 34%. *Correct Answer:* 34%.

Probability must always be between zero and one. You cannot have a negative probability and you cannot have a probability greater than 1, or 100%.

2. Multiply consecutive probabilities.

What is the probability that you'll get two heads when you toss a coin twice? You find each probability separately and then *multiply* the two. The chance of tossing a coin the first time and getting a head is $\frac{1}{2}$. The chance of tossing a coin the second time and getting a head is $\frac{1}{2}$. Multiply those consecutive probabilities: $\frac{1}{2} \times \frac{1}{2} = \frac{1}{4}$. The chances of getting two heads is one out of four.

What is the probability of tossing a die twice and getting a 5 on the first toss and a 6 on the second toss? Treat each toss separately. The probability of getting a 5 is $\frac{1}{6}$. The probability of getting a 6 is $\frac{1}{6}$. Multiply consecutive probabilities: $\frac{1}{6} \times \frac{1}{6} = \frac{1}{36}$.

Here's a good trick question.

<u>**Column A**</u>   <u>**Column B**</u>

A fair die is tossed twice.

Chances of getting a 5 on the first toss and a 2 on the second toss	Chances of getting a 6 on both tosses

If you chose A, you fell for the trap. You may think that it's harder to roll the same number twice, but the probability is the same as rolling two different numbers. Treat each roll separately. The probability of rolling a 5 is $\frac{1}{6}$. The probability of rolling a 2 is $\frac{1}{6}$. Multiply consecutive probabilities: $\frac{1}{6} \times \frac{1}{6} = \frac{1}{36}$. For Column B, treat each toss separately. The probability of rolling a 6 is $\frac{1}{6}$. The probability of rolling a second 6 is $\frac{1}{6}$. Multiply consecutive probabilities: $\frac{1}{6} \times \frac{1}{6} = \frac{1}{36}$. *Correct Answer:* C.

If you've had a course in statistics, you may have learned about independent events, mutually exclusive events, and interdependent events. Forget about them; they're not on the GRE. The material you just learned is about as complicated as probability gets.

Chapter 12

Miscellaneous Math You Probably Already Know

• •

In This Chapter

▶ Time, rate, and distance problems

▶ Averages

▶ Percentages

▶ Number sets and prime and composite numbers

▶ Mixture, interest, and work problems

▶ Absolute value

▶ Order of operations

▶ Units of measurement

▶ Decimals and fractions

▶ Statistics

▶ Graphs

• •

*Y*ou probably already know the material in this chapter, but a quick review can't hurt you. (The humor—now that's another story.)

DIRTy Math: Time, Rate, and Distance

D.I.R.T. Distance Is Rate × Time. $D = RT$. When you have a time, rate, and distance problem, use this formula. Make a chart with the formula across the top and fill in the spaces on the chart.

Jennifer drives 40 miles an hour for two and a half hours. Her friend Ashley goes the same distance but drives at one and a half times Jennifer's speed. How many *minutes* longer does Jennifer drive than Ashley?

Do *not* start making big, hairy formulas with *x*'s and *y*'s. Jennifer has no desire to be known as Madame *x*; Ashley refuses to know *y*. Make the DIRT chart.

Distance	=	*Rate*	×	*Time*

When you fill in the 40 mph and 2¹/₂ hours for Jennifer, you can calculate that she went 100 miles. Think of it this simple way: If she goes 40 mph for one hour, that's 40 miles. For a second hour, she goes another 40 miles. In a half hour, she goes ¹/₂ of 40, or 20 miles. (See? You don't have to write down 40 × 2¹/₂ and do all that pencil-pushing; use your brain, not your yellow #2.) Add them together: 40 + 40 + 20 = 100. Jennifer has gone 100 miles.

Distance	*Rate*	×	*Time*
100 (Jennifer)	40 mph		2¹/₂ hours

Because Ashley drives the same distance, fill in 100 under distance for her. She goes one and a half times as fast. Uh-uh, put down that pencil. Use your brain! 1×40 is 40; $\frac{1}{2} \times 40$ is 20. Add $40 + 20 = 60$. Ashley drives 60 mph. Now this gets really easy. If she drives at 60 mph, she drives one mile a minute. (60 minutes in an hour, 60 miles in an hour. You figure it out, Einstein.) Therefore, to go 100 miles takes her 100 minutes. Because your final answer is asked for in minutes, don't bother converting this to hours; leave it the way it is.

Distance	Rate	×	Time
100 (Ashley)	60 mph		100 minutes

Last step. Jennifer drives $2\frac{1}{2}$ hours. How many minutes is that? Do it the easy way, in your brain. One hour is 60 minutes. A second hour is another 60 minutes. A half hour is 30 minutes. Add them together: $60 + 60 + 30 = 150$ minutes. If Jennifer drives for 150 minutes and Ashley drives for 100 minutes, Jennifer drives 50 minutes more than Ashley. However, Ashley gets a speeding ticket, has her driving privileges taken away by an irate father, and doesn't get to go to this weekend's party. Jennifer goes and gets her pick of the hunks, ending up with Tyrone's ring and frat pin. The moral of the story: Slow . . . but steady!

Distance	Rate	×	Time
100 (Jennifer)	40 mph		150 minutes
100 (Ashley)	60 mph		100 minutes

Be careful to note whether the people are traveling in the *same* direction or *opposite* directions. Suppose that you're asked how far apart drivers are at the end of their trip. If you are told that Jordan travels 40 mph east for 2 hours and Connor travels 60 mph west for 3 hours, they are going in opposite directions. If they start from the same point at the same time, Jordan has gone 80 miles one way, and Connor has gone 180 miles the opposite way. They are 260 miles apart. The trap answer is 100, because careless people (not *you!*) simply subtract $180 - 80$.

It All Averages Out: Averages

You can always do averages the way Ms. Jones taught you when you were in third grade: Add all the terms, and then divide by the number of terms.

$$5 + 11 + 17 + 23 + 29 = 85$$

$$^{85}/_5 = 17$$

Or you can save wear-and-tear on the brain cells and know the following rule:

1. **The average of evenly spaced terms is the middle term.**

First, check that the terms are evenly spaced. That means that there is an equal number of units between each term. Here, the terms are six apart. Second, circle the middle term, which here is 17. Third, go home, make popcorn, and watch the late-night movie with all the time you've saved.

Try another one. Find the average of these numbers:

32, 41, 50, 59, 68, 77, 86, 95, 104

Don't reach for your pencil. You look and see that the terms are all nine units apart. Because they are evenly spaced, the middle term is the average: 68.

This is an easy trick to love, but don't march down the aisle with it yet. The tip works only for *evenly spaced* terms. If you have just any old batch of numbers, such as 4, 21, 97, 98, 199, you can't look at the middle term for the average. You have to find the average of those numbers the old-fashioned way.

Find the average of these numbers:

> 3, 10, 17, 24, 31, 38, 45, 52

First, double-check that they are evenly spaced. Here, the numbers are spaced by sevens. Next you look for the middle number . . . and there isn't one. You can, of course, find the two central terms, 24 and 31, and find the middle between them. That works, but what a pain. Not only that, but suppose that you have 38 numbers. It's very easy to make a mistake as to which terms are the central ones. If you're off just a little bit, you miss the question. Instead, use rule number two:

2. The average of evenly spaced terms is $^{(\text{first} + \text{last})}/_2$.

Just add the first and the last terms, which are obvious at a glance, and divide that sum by 2. Here, 3 + 52 = 55. $^{55}/_2$ = 27.5.

Note: Double-check using your common sense. Suppose that you made a silly mistake and got 45 for your answer. A glance at the numbers tells you that 45 is not in the middle and therefore cannot be the average.

This tip works for *all* evenly spaced terms. It doesn't matter whether there is a middle number, as in the first example, or no middle number, as in the second example. Go back to the first example.

> 32, 41, 50, 59, 68, 77, 86, 95, 104

Instead of finding the middle term, add the first and last terms and divide by 2, like this: 32 + 104 = 136. $^{136}/_2$ = 68. Either way works.

Missing term average problem

You are likely to find a problem like this:

A student takes seven exams. Her scores on the first six are 91, 89, 85, 92, 90, and 88. If her average on all *seven* exams is 90, what did she get on the seventh exam?

This is called a *missing term average problem* because you are given an average and asked to find a missing term. Duh.

1. You can do this the basic algebraic way.

$$\text{Average} = \frac{\text{Sum}}{\text{Number of terms}}$$

$$90 = \frac{\text{Sum}}{7}$$

Because you don't know the seventh term, call it x. Add the first six terms (and get 535) and x.

$$90 = \frac{(535 + x)}{7}$$. Cross-multiply: $90 \times 7 = 535 + x$

$$630 = 535 + x$$

$$95 = x$$

The seventh exam score was 95.

2. You can do these problems the commonsense way.

There is another quick way to do this problem. You've probably done it this way all your life without realizing what a genius you are.

Suppose that your dad tells you that if you average a 90 for the semester in advanced physics, he'll let you take that summer trip through Europe with your buddies that the two of you have been arguing about for months (he figures he's safe because there's no way you're going to get such a high grade in that incredibly difficult class). You take him at his word and begin working hard.

On the first exam, you get 91 and you're +1 point. That is, you're one point above the ultimate score you want, a 90. On the second exam, you get 89 and you're –1. On that test, you're one point below the ultimate score you want, a 90. On the third exam, you get an 85, which is –5. You're five points below the ultimate score you want, a 90.

Are you getting the hang of this? Here's how it looks.

$$91 = +1$$
$$89 = -1$$
$$85 = -5$$
$$92 = +2$$
$$90 = 0$$
$$88 = -2$$

The +1 and –1 cancel each other out, and the +2 and –2 cancel each other out. You're left with –5, meaning you're five points in the hole. You have to make up those five points on the last exam or get five points *above* what you want for your ultimate score. Because you want a 90, you need a 95 on the last test.

Try another, using the no-brainer method. A student takes seven exams. She gets an 88 average on all of them. Her first six scores are 89, 98, 90, 82, 88, and 87. What does she get on the seventh exam?

$$\text{Average} = 88$$
$$89 = +1$$
$$98 = +10$$
$$90 = +2$$
$$82 = -6$$
$$88 = 0$$
$$87 = -1$$

The +1 and –1 cancel. Then you have (10 + 2) = +12 and –6, for a total of +6. You are six points *above* what you need for the ultimate outcome. You can afford to lose six points on the final exam or to be six points *below* the average. That gives you an 82.

You may be given only five out of seven scores and asked for *the average of the missing two* terms. Do the same thing and then divide by 2.

Average of seven exams: 85

Scores of the first five exams: 86, 79, 82, 85, 84

Find: The average score of each of the remaining exams

Algebraic way: $85 = \dfrac{(86 + 79 + 82 + 85 + 84) + x + x}{7}$

Cross-multiply: $595 = 416 + 2x$

$595 - 416 = 2x$

$179 = 2x$

$89.5 = x$

Commonsense way:

Average = 85

86 = +1

79 = –6

82 = –3

85 = 0

84 = –1

The +1 and –1 cancel each other out. You are left with –9 for *two* exams or –4.5 per exam. If you are *down* four and a half points, you must *gain* those four and a half points on each of the two exams:

85 + 4.5 = 89.5

The shortcut, commonsense way is quick and easy, but don't forget to make the change at the end. That is, if you decide that you are *minus eight* points going into the final exam, you need to be *plus eight* points on that last exam to come out even. If you subtract eight points from the average rather than add them, you'll probably come up with one of the trap answers.

Weighted averages

In a *weighted average*, some scores count more than others.

Number of Students	Score
12	80
13	75
10	70

If you are asked to find the average score for the students in this class, you know that you can't simply add 80, 75, and 70 and divide by three because the scores weren't evenly distributed among the students. Because 12 students got an 80, multiply $12 \times 80 = 960$. Do the same with the other scores:

$$13 \times 75 = 975$$

$$10 \times 70 = 700$$

$$960 + 975 + 700 = 2{,}635$$

Divide *not by three* but by the total number of students: 35 (12 + 13 + 10)

$$\frac{2635}{35} = 75.29$$

You can often answer a Quantitative Comparison question on weighted averages without doing all the work, as demonstrated in the following. (See Chapter 13 for more information about QC questions and how to answer them.)

The answer choices are

A if the quantity in Column A is greater.

B if the quantity in Column B is greater.

C if the two quantities are equal.

D if the relationship cannot be determined from the information given.

| Column A | | | Column B |

Clothing	*Quantity*	*Cost per item*
Black T-shirts	5	$20
Denim shirts	8	$25
Blue jeans	20	$30

| Average cost per item of clothing | $25 |

You can work this whole problem out, finding the cost of all the T-shirts, denim shirts, and jeans and then dividing that cost by the number of items of clothing. When you do all that work, you get 27.27 (and a headache and a sore pencil-pushing finger). Or you can use your brain and common sense: 13 items are $25 or less, and 20 items are $30. Therefore, there are more items at above $25 than below $25. The average must be more than $25. Remember, because this is a QC problem, you don't need to solve it through for the final, precise solution; you need only enough information to compare the quantities in the two columns. *Correct Answer:* A.

Percentage Panic

The mere mention of the word *percent* may strike terror in your heart. There's no reason to panic over percentages; there are ways of getting around them.

1. **Ignore their very existence.** You can express a percentage as a decimal, which is a lot less intimidating. You do so by putting a decimal point two places to the left of the percentage and dropping the % sign.

   35% = .35   83% = .83   50% = .50   33.3% = .333   66.6% = .666

   If you have a choice of working with percentages rather than decimals, it's better to choose decimals.

2. **Another way to ignore a percentage is to convert it to a fraction.** The word *percent* means *per cent,* or *per hundred.* Every percentage is that number over 100.

   $50\% = {}^{50}/_{100}$ $33\% = {}^{33}/_{100}$ $75\% = {}^{75}/_{100}$

   If you can't ignore the percentage, remember that a percent is

   $$\frac{\text{Part}}{\text{Whole}} \times 100, \text{ or } \frac{is}{of} \times 100$$

   What percent *is* 45 *of* 90? Put the part, 45, over the whole, 90. Or put the *is,* 45, over the *of,* 90:

   $${}^{45}/_{90} = {}^{1}/_{2} \times 100 = {}^{100}/_{2} = 50\%$$

   42 *is* what percent *of* 126? Put the part, 42, over the whole, 126. Or put the *is,* 42, over the *of,* 126.

   $${}^{42}/_{126} = {}^{1}/_{3} \times 100 = {}^{100}/_{3} = 33\,{}^{1}/_{3}\%$$

   Here's a little harder one: What is 40% of 80? You may be tempted to put the *is,* 40, over the *of,* 80, and get ${}^{40}/_{80} = {}^{1}/_{2} \times 100 = {}^{100}/_{2} = 50\%$. However, when the problem is worded this way, you don't know the *is.* Your equation must be ${}^{x}/_{80} = {}^{40}/_{100}$. Cross-multiply: $3200 = 100x$. $x = 32$. There's an easier way to do it: *of* means times, or multiply. Because 40% = .40, multiply $.40 \times 80 = 32$.

Life has its ups and downs: Percent increase/decrease

You may see a problem asking you what percent increase or decrease occurred in the number of games a team won or the amount of commission a person earned. To find a percent increase or decrease, use this formula:

$$\text{percent increase or decrease} = \frac{\text{number increase or decrease}}{\text{original whole}}$$

In basic English, to find the percent by which something has increased or decreased, you take two simple steps:

1. **Find the *number* (amount) by which the thing has increased or decreased.** For example, if a team won 25 games last year and 30 games this year, the number increase was 5. If a salesperson earned $10,000 last year and $8,000 this year, the number decrease was 2,000. Make that the numerator of the fraction.

2. **Find the *original whole.*** This figure is what you started out with before you increased or decreased. If a team won 25 games last year and won 30 games this year, the original number was 25. If the salesperson earned $10,000 last year and $8,000 this year, the original number was 10,000. Make that the denominator.

You now have a fraction. Make it a decimal, and multiply by 100 to make it a percentage.

In 1992, Coach Jarchow won 30 prizes at the county fair by tossing a basketball into a bushel basket. In 1993, he won 35 prizes. What was his percent increase?

(A) 100

(B) 30

(C) $16^2/_3$

(D) 14.28

(E) $.1\overline{66}$

The number by which his prizes increased, from 30 to 35, is 5. That is the numerator. The original whole, or what he began with, is 30. That is the denominator. *Correct Answer:* C.

$$^5/_{30} = {}^1/_6 = 16^2/_3\%$$

If you chose E, I fooled you. The question asks what *percent* increase there was. If you say E, you're saying that there was a $.1\overline{66}$ percent increase. Not so. The $.1\overline{66}$ increase *as a percentage* is $16^2/_3\%$. If you chose D, you fell for another trap. You put the 5 increase over the 35 instead of over the 30.

Two years ago, Haylie scored 22 goals at soccer. This year, she scored 16 goals. What was her approximate percentage decrease?

(A) 72

(B) 37.5

(C) 27

(D) 16

(E) $.\overline{27}$

Find the number of the decrease: 22 − 16 = 6. That is the numerator. Find the original whole from which she is decreasing: 22. That is the denominator. $^6/_{22} \approx .\overline{27}$, or approximately 27 percent. *Correct Answer:* C.

If you chose A, you put 16 over 22 instead of putting the decrease over the original whole. If you chose E, again you forgot the difference between .27 and .27 *percent*. If you chose B, you put the decrease of 6 over the new amount, 16, rather than over the original whole. Note how easy these traps are to fall for. My suggestion: Write down the actual formula and then plug in the numbers. Writing down the formula may be boring, but doing so takes only a few seconds and may save you points.

Here's a tricky question that many people do in their heads (instead of writing down the formula and plugging in numbers) and blow big time.

Carissa has three quarters. Her father gives her three more. Carissa's wealth has increased by what percent?

(A) 50

(B) 100

(C) 200

(D) 300

(E) 500

Did you fall for the trap answer, C? Her wealth has doubled, to be sure, but the percent increase is only 100. You can prove that with the formula: The number increase is 75 (she has three more quarters, or 75 cents). Her original whole was 75. $^{75}/_{75}$ = 1 = 100%. *Correct Answer:* B.

When you double something, you increase by 100 percent because you have to subtract the original "one" you began with. When you triple something, you increase by 200 percent because you have to subtract the original you began with. For example, if you had three dollars and you now have nine dollars, you have tripled your money but increased by only 200 percent. Do the formula: number increase = 6 dollars. Original whole = 3 dollars. $^{6}/_{3}$ = 2 = 200 percent. Take a wild guess at what percent you increase when you quadruple your money? That's right, 300 percent. Just subtract the original 100 percent.

Ready, Sets, Go: Number Sets

There's no escaping vocabulary. Even on the math portion of the test, you need to know certain terms. How can you solve a problem that asks you to "state your answer in integral values only" if you don't know what integral values are? Here are the number sets with which you'll be working.

- **Counting numbers:** 1, 2, 3 . . . Note that 0 is *not* a counting number.

- **Whole numbers:** 0, 1, 2, 3 . . . Note that 0 *is* a whole number.

- **Integers:** . . . –3, –2, –1, 0, 1, 2, 3 . . . When a question asks for *integral values,* it wants the answer in integers only. For example, you can't give an answer like 4.3 because that's not an integer. You need to round down to 4.

- **Rational numbers:** Rational numbers can be expressed as $^{a}/_{b}$, where *a* and *b* are integers.

  Examples: 1 (because 1 = $^{1}/_{1}$ and 1 is an integer), $^{1}/_{2}$ (because 1 and 2 are integers), $^{9}/_{2}$ (because 9 and 2 are integers), and $-^{4}/_{2}$ (because –4 and 2 are integers).

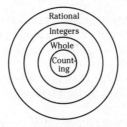

Notice that every number set so far has included the previous number sets. Whole numbers include counting numbers, integers include counting numbers and whole numbers, and rationals include counting numbers, whole numbers, and integers.

- **Irrational numbers:** The highly technical definition here is *anything not rational.* That is, an irrational number cannot be written as $^{a}/_{b}$, where *a* and *b* are integers. Numbers whose decimals do not terminate and do not repeat can't be written as a fraction and therefore are irrational.

  Examples: π cannot be written *exactly* as 3.14; it is nonterminating and nonrepeating. $\sqrt{2}$ is approximately 1.4142 but is nonterminating and nonrepeating.

  Irrational numbers *do not* include the previous number sets. That is, irrational numbers don't include counting numbers, whole numbers, integers or rational numbers.

✔ **Real numbers:** Briefly put, all of the preceding. Real numbers include counting numbers, whole numbers, integers, rationals, and irrationals. For all practical purposes, real numbers are everything you think of as numbers. When a question tells you to "express your answer in real numbers," don't sweat it. That's almost no constraint at all, because nearly everything you see is a real number.

There are such critters as *imaginary* numbers, which are *not* on the GRE. (Most of you probably stopped reading right there, figuring that you don't even want to hear about them if they're not going to be tested. I don't blame you.) Imaginary numbers are expressed with a lowercase *i* and are studied in upper-division math classes. I won't go into them here because, once again, *they are not tested on the GRE.* All numbers on the GRE are real numbers.

Prime and Composite Numbers

Prime numbers are positive integers which have exactly two positive integer factors; they cannot be divided by numbers other than 1 and themselves. Examples include 2, 3, 5, 7, and 11.

There are a few lovely tricks to prime numbers.

✔ Zero is *not* a prime number (by definition). Why? Because it is divisible by more than two factors. Zero can be divided by 1, 2, 3, and on to infinity. Although division by zero is undefined (and isn't tested on the GRE), you can divide zero by other numbers; the answer of course is always zero. $0 \div 1 = 0$; $0 \div 2 = 0$; $0 \div 412 = 0$.

✔ One is *not* a prime number (by definition). There are not two factors of 1. It cannot be divided only by 1 *and* itself. Confused? Don't worry about it. Just memorize the fact that 1 is not a prime number.

✔ Two is the *only* even prime. People tend to think that all prime numbers are odd. Well, almost. Two is prime because it has only two factors; it can be divided only by 1 and itself.

✔ Not all odd numbers are prime. Think of 9 or 15; those numbers are odd but not prime because they have more than two factors and can be divided by more than just 1 and themselves. $9 = (1 \times 9)$ *and* (3×3). $15 = (1 \times 15)$ *and* (3×5).

Composite numbers have more than two factors and can be divided by more than just 1 and themselves. Examples: 4, 6, 8, 9, 12, 14, and 15.

Note that composite numbers (called that because they are *composed* of more than two factors) can be even or odd.

Don't confuse *prime* and *composite* and *even* and *odd* with *positive* and *negative.* That's an easy mistake to make in the confusion of the exam. If a problem that you know should be easy is flustering you, stop and ask yourself whether you're making this common mistake.

I said that 0 and 1 are not prime. They are also not composite. What are they? Neither. You express this as "0 and 1 are neither prime nor composite." It's rather like wondering whether zero is positive or negative. You say, "Zero is neither positive nor negative." Why should you know this? Here's an example when the information can win you ten points (the approximate value of one correct math question).

The answer choices are

A if the quantity in Column A is greater.

B if the quantity in Column B is greater.

C if the two quantities are equal.

D if the relationship cannot be determined from the information given.

Column A	Column B
The number of prime numbers from 0 to 10 inclusive	The number of prime numbers from 11 to 20 inclusive

The prime numbers from 0 to 10 inclusive are 2, 3, 5, and 7. Note that 0 and 1 are *not* prime. If you count either or both as prime, you miss an otherwise very easy question. In Column B, the prime numbers from 11 to 20 inclusive are 11, 13, 17, and 19. Both columns have four prime numbers. *Correct Answer:* C.

I'm All Mixed Up: Mixture Problems

A mixture problem is a word problem that looks much more confusing than it actually is. There are two types of mixtures: those in which the items remain separate (when you mix peanuts and raisins, you still have peanuts and raisins, not pearains or raispeans) and those in which the two elements blend (these are usually chemicals, like water and alcohol). Check out the separate mixture first.

Marshall wants to mix 40 pounds of beads selling for 30 cents a pound with a quantity of sequins selling for 80 cents a pound. He wants to pay 40 cents per pound for the final mix. How many pounds of sequins should he use?

The hardest part for most students is knowing where to begin. Make a chart.

	Pounds	**Price**	**Total**
Beads	40	$.30	$12.00
Sequins	x	$.80	$.80x$
Mixture	$40 + x$	$.40	$.40(40 + x)$

Reason it out. In pennies, the cost of the beads (1200) plus the cost of the sequins ($80x$) must equal the cost of the mixture ($1600 + 40x$). Note that you dump the decimal point (officially, you multiply by 100 to get rid of the decimal point, but really, you dump it). Now you have a workable equation:

$$1200 + 80x = 1600 + 40x$$

$$80x - 40x = 1600 - 1200$$

$$40x = 400$$

$$x = 10$$

Careful! Keep in mind what x stands for. It represents the number of pounds of sequins, what the question asks for.

Go back and double-check by plugging this value into the equation. You already know that Marshall spent $12 on beads. If he buys 10 pounds of sequins for 80 cents, he spends $8, for a total of $20. He spends that $20 on 50 pounds: 2000 ÷ 50 = 40. How about that, it works!

Greed Is Great: Interest Problems

This is a pretty problem: PRTI, to be exact. P = Principal, the amount of money you begin with, or the amount you invest. R = Rate, the interest rate you're earning on the money. T = Time, the amount of time you leave the money in the interest-bearing account. I = Interest, the amount of interest you earn on the investment. A problem usually asks you how much interest someone earned on his or her investment.

The formula is $PRT = I$. Principal × Rate × Time = Interest.

Janet invested $1,000 at 5 percent annual interest for one year. How much interest did she earn?

This is the simplest type of problem. Plug the numbers into the formula.

$PRT = I$

$1,000 × .05 × 1 = 50$. She earned $50 interest.

The answer choices may try to trap you with variations on a decimal place, making the answers 5, 50, 500, and so on. You know that 5% = $5/100$ = .05; be careful how you multiply.

These problems are not intentionally vicious (unlike 99 percent of the rest of the GRE, right?). You won't see something that gets crazy on interest rates, like "5 percent annual interest compounded quarterly for 3 months and 6 percent quarterly interest compounded daily," blah, blah, blah.

(Useless but fascinating trivia: In Bulgarian, the word for *thank you* is pronounced *blah-go-dah-ree-uh*. But a shortened form, like *thanks,* is simply *blah*. If your mother takes you to task for being a smart aleck and going "blah, blah, blah" when she talks, you can innocently claim that you're practicing your Bulgarian and are just thanking her for her wisdom.)

All Work and No Play: Work Problems

The formula most commonly used in a work problem is

$$\text{Work} = \frac{\text{Time put in}}{\text{Capacity (time to do the whole job)}}$$

Find each person's contribution. The denominator is the easy part; it represents how many hours (minutes, days, weeks, and so on) it would take the person to do the whole job, working alone. The numerator is how long the person has already worked. For example, if Janie can paint a house in four days and has been working for one day, she has done $1/4$ of the work. If Evelyn can paint a house in nine days and has been working for five, she has done $5/9$ of the project.

So far, so good. The problem comes when more than one person works at the task. What happens when Janie and Evelyn work together?

Janie working alone can paint a house in six days. Evelyn working alone can paint it in eight days. Working together, how long will it take them to paint the house?

Find Janie's work: $x/6$. Find Evelyn's work: $x/8$. Together, the two fractions must add up to 1, the entire job.

$$x/6 + x/8 = 1$$

Multiply by the common denominator, 48, to eliminate the fractions.

$$48x/6 + 48x/8 = 48$$

$$8x + 6x = 48$$
$$14x = 48$$
$$x = \text{approximately } 3.43.$$

It would take the two women working together about 3.43 days to paint the house.

Double-check by using your common sense. If you get an answer of 10, for example, you know that you must have made a mistake because the two women working together should be able to do the job *more quickly* than either one working alone.

Reading between the Lines: Absolute Value

The absolute value is the magnitude of a number. So much for the official definition. The *Dummies* definition (that is, the easy way to think about it) of *absolute value* is the positive form of a number. Absolute value is indicated by two vertical parallel lines (like this: | |).

Any number within those lines is read as "The absolute value of that number." For example, | 3 | = 3 is read as "The absolute value of three equals three." That seems straightforward enough, but what if the number inside the straight lines is negative? Its absolute value is still positive: | –3 | = 3. Here's a tricky problem you're likely to see on the exam.

$$– | –3 | = –3$$

The answer may seem contrary to common sense. Isn't a negative times a negative a positive? True, but you have to work from the inside out. The absolute value of negative three is three. Then you multiple three by the negative to get negative three. Here's another example that's even a little harder. *Correct Answer:* –3

$$–| – | –5 | | =$$

Here's the official way to work the problem (**Hint:** The word *official* is a clue that in a minute I'm going to give you an unofficial, much easier way to solve this.) Work from the inside out. Say it to yourself as you go along: "The absolute value of negative five is 5. Then the negative of that is negative 5. But the absolute value of negative 5 is 5. And finally, the negative of that is –5." *Correct Answer:* –5.

Do you see the super-shortcut for the above example? You actually don't have to work the problem out at all! Anything and everything inside the absolute value signs is going to be positive. Then the one negative sign outside changes the whole problem to negative. You don't, in other words, have to go through the intermediate steps. With an absolute value, look to see whether a negative sign is outside the first absolute value symbol. If it is, the number is negative. If it's not, the number is positive. Simple as that.

Smooth Operator: Order of Operations

When you have several operations (addition, subtraction, multiplication, division, squaring, and so on) in one problem, there is a definite order in which you must perform the operations:

1. **Parentheses.** Do what's inside the parentheses first.

2. **Power.** Do the squaring or the cubing, whatever the exponent is.

3. **Multiply or divide.** Do these left to right. If multiplication is to the left of division, multiply first. If division is to the left of multiplication, divide first.

4. **Add or subtract.** Do these left to right. If addition is to the left of subtraction, add first. If subtraction is to the left of addition, subtract first.

An easy *mnemonic* (memory) device for remembering these is *Please Praise My Daughter And Son* (PPMDAS): Parentheses, Power, Multiply, Divide, Add, Subtract.

$$10(3 - 5)^2 + (^{30}/_5)^0 =$$

First, do what's inside the parentheses: $3 - 5 = -2$. $^{30}/_5 = 6$. Next, do the power: $-2^2 = 4$. $6^0 = 1$. (Did you remember that any number to the zero power equals one?) Next, multiply: $10 \times 4 = 40$. Finally, add: $40 + 1 = 41$. *Correct Answer:* 41. Try another.

$$3 + (9 - 6)^2 - 5(^8/_2)^{-2} =$$

First, do what's inside the parentheses: $9 - 6 = 3$. $^8/_2 = 4$. Second, do the powers: $3^2 = 9$. $4^{-2} = ^1/_{(4^2)}$ $= ^1/_{16}$. Multiply: $5 \times ^1/_{16} = ^5/_{16}$. Finally, add and subtract left to right. $3 + 9 = 12$. Then $12 - ^5/_{16} = 11^{11}/_{16}$. *Correct Answer:* $11^{11}/_{16}$.

Measuring Up: Units of Measurement

Occasionally, you may be expected to know a unit of measurement that the test makers deem obvious but which you have forgotten. Take a few minutes to review this brief list.

International students, in particular, need to memorize these as you may not have grown up using some of the same units of measurement as those used in the United States (and on the GRE).

1. **Quantities**

   16 ounces = 1 pound

   2,000 pounds = 1 ton

   2 cups = 1 pint

   2 pints = 1 quart

   4 quarts = 1 gallon

   You can calculate that a gallon has 16 cups, or eight pints. To help you remember, think of borrowing a cup of sugar. Sugar is sweet, and you have a Sweet 16 birthday party: 16 sweet cups of sugar in a gallon. It may be silly, but the best memory aids usually are.

2. **Length**

   12 inches = 1 foot

   3 feet (36 inches) = 1 yard

   5,280 feet (1,760 yards) = 1 mile

Everyone knows that there are 12 inches in a foot. How many square inches are there in a square foot? If you say 12, you've fallen for the trap. $12 \times 12 = 144$ square inches are in a square foot.

Here's how you may fall for that trap in an otherwise easy problem.

The answer choices are

A if the quantity in Column A is greater.

B if the quantity in Column B is greater.

C if the two quantities are equal.

D if the relationship cannot be determined from the information given.

Column A	_Column B_
Number of square inches in 3 square feet	36

Your first reaction is to think that the columns are equal because there are 12 inches to a foot and $12 \times 3 = 36$. However, a square foot is $12 \times 12 = 144$ inches. Because 144×3 is definitely greater than 36 (don't waste any time doing the math), the answer is A. *Correct Answer:* A.

Bonus: How many cubic inches are there in a cubic foot? Not 12, and not even 144. A cubic foot is $12 \times 12 \times 12 = 1,728$ cubic inches.

3. **Time**

60 seconds = 1 minute

60 minutes = 1 hour

24 hours = 1 day

7 days = 1 week

52 weeks = 1 year

365 days = 1 year

366 days = 1 leap year

Leap year is an interesting concept in terms of math problems. It comes around every four years. The extra day, February 29, makes 366 days in the year. Why do you need to know this? Suppose that you see this problem:

Mr. Pellaton's neon sign flashes four hours a day, every day all year, for four years. If it costs him three cents a day for electricity, how much will he owe for electricity at the end of the fourth year?

You may be tempted to say that this problem is super easy — multiply 365×4 to find the number of days and then multiply that number by .03. Wrong-o! You forgot that extra day for leap year, and your answer is off by three cents. You *know* that the test makers will have that wrong answer lurking among the answer choices just to trap you. Whenever there is a four-year period, look out for the leap year with an extra day.

What's the Point: Decimals

Here's where a calculator would be very helpful. Until the test makers join the twentieth century and let you use a calculator, however, you'll have to rely on brain power, not battery power. (By the way, did you know that students taking the SAT are now allowed to use a calculator? Things are changing.)

Adding and subtracting decimals

Line up the decimal points vertically and add or subtract the numbers.

$$
\begin{array}{r}
3.09 \\
4.72 \\
31.9 \\
\underline{121.046} \\
160.756
\end{array}
$$

 If you're rushed for time and don't want to do the whole problem, go to extremes. The extremes are the far-left and far-right columns. Often, calculating them alone gives you enough information to choose the right answer to a multiple-choice problem. In this case, you can look at the far right, which is the thousands column, and know that it has to end in a 6. Suppose that the answer choices are

(A) 160.999

(B) 160.852

(C) 160.756

(D) 159.831

(E) 159.444

You know immediately that C has to be the correct choice.

Maybe more than one of the answer choices uses the correct digit for the far-right column. Okay, you're flexible; head for the far-left column, which here is the hundreds place. You know in this problem it has to be a 1. The answer choices are

(A) 160.756

(B) 201.706

(C) 209.045

(D) 210.006

(E) 301.786

Only choice A has the correct far-left number.

Multiplying decimals

The biggest trap is keeping the number of decimal points correct. The number of decimal places in the product (the number you get when you multiply the terms together) must be the same as the sum of the number of decimal places in all the terms.

$5.06 \times 3.9 =$

$$
\begin{array}{r}
5.06 \\
\underline{\times\,3.9} \\
19.734
\end{array}
$$

There are two decimal places in the first term and one in the second, for a total of three. Therefore, the final answer must have three decimal places.

The shortcut you learned for addition and subtraction works here as well. Go to extremes. Look at the far-right and far-left terms. You know that $6 \times 9 = 54$, such that the last digit in the answer has to be a 4. You can eliminate wrong answers by using that information. You know that $5 \times 3 = 15$, but you may have to carry over some other numbers to make the far-left value greater than 15 (as it turns out here). At least you know that the far-left digits must be 15 *or more*. An answer choice starting with 14, 13, or anything less than 15 can be eliminated.

Dividing decimals

Turn the decimals into integers by moving the decimal point to the right the appropriate number of places for both terms, the one you are dividing and the one you are dividing by (called the *divisor,* should you happen to care).

$$4.44 \div .06 = {}^{444}\!/_6 = 74$$

I won't spend much time on decimals because you almost certainly won't spend much time on them yourself. Just remember two things:

- Keep a wary eye on the decimal point; its placement is often a trap for the careless.

- Go to extremes: Determine the far-left or far-right digit and use that information to eliminate incorrect answer choices.

Broken Hearts, Broken Numbers: Fractions

Fractions strike fear into the hearts of most mere mortals. Fortunately, the number of fraction problems on the GRE is small and getting smaller all the time.

Adding or subtracting

1. **You can add or subtract fractions only when they have the same denominator.**

$$\frac{1}{3} + \frac{4}{3} = \frac{5}{3}$$

$$\frac{3}{8} - \frac{2}{8} = \frac{1}{8}$$

2. **When fractions have the same denominator, add or subtract the numerators only.**

3. **When fractions don't have the same denominator, you have to find a common denominator.**

You can, of course, multiply all the denominators, but that often doesn't give you the *lowest* common denominator. You end up with some humongous, overwhelming number that you'd rather not work with. Instead, use this little trick:

4. **To find the lowest common denominator, identify the highest denominator and count by it.**

Find the lowest common denominator of 15 and 6. Sure, you can multiply $15 \times 6 = 90$, but that's not the *lowest* common denominator. Instead, count by 15's because it's the larger of the two. 15? No, 6 doesn't go into that. 30? Yes, both 15 and 6 go into 30. That's the *lowest* common denominator.

Try another one: Find the lowest common denominator for 2, 4, and 5. Count by 5s: 5? No, 2 and 4 don't go into it. 10? No, 2 and 4 don't go into it. 15? No, 2 and 4 don't go into it. 20? Yes, all the numbers divide evenly into 20. That number is much smaller than the one you get when you multiply $2 \times 4 \times 5 = 40$.

5. **In many problems, you don't even have to find the lowest common denominator. You can find any common denominator by multiplying the denominators.**

$$\frac{4}{15} + \frac{1}{6} =$$

The common denominator is $15 \times 6 = 90$. Cross-multiply: $4 \times 6 = 24$. The first fraction becomes $^{24}/_{90}$. Cross-multiply: $1 \times 15 = 15$. The second fraction becomes $^{15}/_{90}$. Now add the numerators: $24 + 15 = 39$. Put the sum over the common denominator: $^{39}/_{90}$. Can you reduce? Yes, by 3: $^{13}/_{30}$.

Do the same thing when working with variables instead of numbers.

$$\frac{a}{b} - \frac{c}{d} =$$

Find the common denominator by multiplying the two denominators: $b \times d = bd$. Cross-multiply: $a \times d = ad$. Cross-multiply: $c \times b = cb$. Put the difference of the results of the cross-multiplication over the common denominator: $\frac{(ad - cb)}{bd}$.

Multiplying fractions

This is the easy one. Just do it. Multiply horizontally, multiplying the numerators and then multiplying the denominators.

$$\frac{3}{4} \times \frac{2}{5} = \frac{(3 \times 2)}{(4 \times 5)} = \frac{6}{20} = \frac{3}{10}$$

Always check whether you can cancel before you begin working to avoid having to deal with big, awkward numbers and to avoid having to reduce at the end. In the preceding example, you can cancel the 4 and the 2, leaving you with

$$\frac{3}{{}_2\cancel{4}} \times \frac{\cancel{2}^{\,1}}{5} = \frac{(3 \times 1)}{(2 \times 5)} = \frac{3}{10}$$

You get to the right solution either way; canceling in advance just makes the numbers smaller and easier to work with.

Dividing fractions

To divide by a fraction, invert it (turn it upside down) and multiply.

$$\frac{1}{3} \div \frac{2}{5} = \frac{1}{3} \times \frac{5}{2} = \frac{5}{6}$$

Mixed numbers

A *mixed number* is a whole number with a fraction tagging along behind it, like $2\frac{1}{3}$, $4\frac{2}{5}$, or $9\frac{1}{2}$. Multiply the whole number by the denominator and add that to the numerator. Put the sum over the denominator.

$$2\frac{1}{3} = (2 \times 3) + 1 = 7 \rightarrow \frac{7}{3}$$
$$4\frac{2}{5} = (4 \times 5) + 2 = 22 \rightarrow \frac{22}{5}$$
$$9\frac{1}{2} = (9 \times 2) + 1 = 19 \rightarrow \frac{19}{2}$$

The Stats Don't Lie: Statistics

Don't panic; statistics are tested on the GRE only in the most rudimentary way. If you can master three basic concepts, you can do any statistics on this exam. Those concepts are median, mode, and range.

Median

Simply put, the *median* is the middle number when all the terms are arranged in order. Think of the median strip, which is the middle of the road. Median = middle. Be sure you arrange the numbers in order (increasing or decreasing, it makes no difference) before you find the median.

Find the median of -3, 18, -4, $\frac{1}{2}$, 11.

(A) -3

(B) 18

(C) -4

(D) $\frac{1}{2}$

(E) 11

Put the numbers in order: -4, -3, $\frac{1}{2}$, 11, 18. The one in the middle, $\frac{1}{2}$, is the median. It's as simple as that. *Correct Answer:* D.

Mode

The *mode* is the most frequent number. I suggest you put the numbers in order again. Then look for the one that shows up the most often. It's the mode.

Find the mode of 11, 18, 29, 17, 18, -4, 0, 19, 0, 11, 18.

(A) 11

(B) 17

(C) 18

(D) 19

(E) 29

There are three 18s but no more than two of any other number. *Correct Answer:* C.

Range

The *range* is the distance from the greatest to the smallest. In other words, you take the biggest term and subtract the smallest term and that's the range.

Find the range of the numbers 11, 18, 29, 17, 18, –4, 0, 19, 0, 11, 18.

(A) 33

(B) 29

(C) 19

(D) 0

(E) –4

Ah, did this one getcha? True, 33 is not one of the numbers in the set. But to find the range, subtract the smallest from the largest number: 29 – –4 = 29 + 4 = 33. *Correct Answer:* A.

The only trap you are likely to see in the statistics questions is in the answer choices. The questions themselves are quite straightforward, but the answer choices may assume that some people don't know one term from another. For example, one answer choice to a median question may be the mean (the average). One answer choice to a range question may be the mode. Circle the word in the question that tells you what you are looking for to keep from falling for this trap.

A Picture Is Worth a Thousand Words: Graphs

Each math section of the GRE has one graph followed by five questions (called Data Interpretation) asking you for information gleaned from the graph. Four basic types of graphs show up frequently:

- ✔ **Circle or pie graph:** The circle represents 100 percent. The key to this graph is noting of what total the percentages are part. Below the graph you may be told that in 1994, 5,000 students graduated with Ph.D.s If a 25-percent segment on the circle graph is labelled "Ph.D.s in history," you know to say that the number of history Ph.D.s is 25 percent of 5,000, or 1,250.

- ✔ **Two axes line graph:** A typical line graph has a bottom and a side axis. You plot a point or read a point from the two axes. This is probably the simplest type of graph you will encounter.

- ✔ **Three axes line graph:** This type of graph is rare. It has a left side axis, a bottom axis, and a right side axis. The left axis, for example, may represent the number of crates of a product while the right side axis represents the percentage that those crates are of the whole shipment. You read the points on the graph the same way as you read them on a two axes graph, simply paying special attention that you answer what the question is asking you. If the question asks you for the number of crates, read the left side. If the question asks you for the percentage of crates, read the right side.

- ✔ **Bar graph:** A bar graph has vertical or horizontal bars. The bars may represent actual numbers or percentages. If the bar goes all the way from one side of the graph to the other, it represnts 100 percent.

Some questions use two graphs in one problem. The following is such an example.

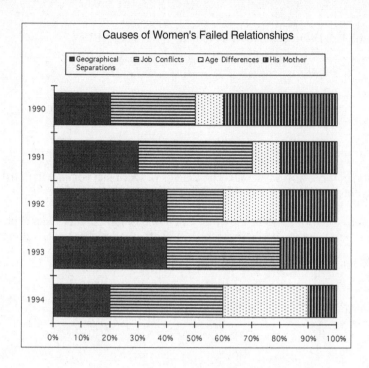

Causes of Women's Failed Relationships

■ Geographical Separations   ⊟ Job Conflicts   ☐ Age Differences   ▥ His Mother

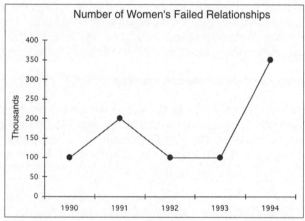

Number of Women's Failed Relationships

Two graphs here must be read in conjunction. The top graph is a bar graph going from 0 to 100 percent. Read the graph by *subtracting* to find the appropriate percentage. For example, in 1990, job conflict begins at 20 and goes to 50, a difference of 30 percent. You'd be falling for a trap were you to say that job conflicts were 50 percent. In 1993, His Mother (as a cause of failed relationships) goes from 80 to 100, or 20 percent.

The second graph gives you the actual number of failed relationships in thousands. Be sure to look at the labels of the axes. For example, in 1990, there were not 100 failed relationships but 100,000. Use the graphs together to find out the number of relationships caused to fail by a particular event or situation. For example, in 1991, there were 200,000 failed relationships. Also in 1991, age differences (from 70 to 80, or 10 percent) made up 10 percent. Multiply 10 percent or $.10 \times 200,000 = 20,000$ relationships.

Ready to try some practice questions? Usually, there are three to five questions below a graph. Answer the following two questions based on the two practice graphs.

How many relationships did women have from 1990 to 1994 inclusive?

(A) 850

(B) 8,500

(C) 85,000

(D) 850,000

(E) It cannot be determined from the information given.

Did I getcha? The title of the graph says it all: The Causes of Women's *Failed* Relationships. You have no way to determine how many relationships worked. *Correct answer:* E.

The number of women's relationships in 1994 that failed due to job conflicts was what percent greater than the number of women's relationships in 1992 that failed due to age differences?

(A) 700

(B) 600

(C) 500

(D) 120

(E) 7

In 1994, job conflicts accounted for 40 percent of women's failed relationships (from 20 to 60). Because there were 350,000 failed relationships in 1994, multiply .40 × 350,000 = 140,000. In 1992, age differences accounted for 20 percent of women's failed relationships (60 to 80). In 1992, there were 100,000 failed relationships. Multiply .20 × 100,000 = 20,000. *Correct answer:* B.

If you chose answer D, you simply subtracted the two amounts: 140,000 − 20,000 = 120,000.

If you chose choice E, 7, or choice A, 700, you fell for the trap. Take the job conflicts number, 140,000, and put it over the age differences number — 20,000. 140,000 ÷ 20,000 = 7. The 7 translates to 700 percent. If you're confused why 7 is 700 percent, not 7 percent, or why 7 times is 600 percent greater than, go back to the percentages section of the math review.

Part IV
Your Number's Up:
Math Questions

The 5th Wave

By Rich Tennant

"THE IMAGE IS GETTING CLEARER NOW...I CAN ALMOST SEE IT...YES! THERE IT IS — THE ANSWER IS $3ab^2 \times 7d^3 - \sqrt{19L} + U\frac{9}{m^4} \div \pm 100.(15)7\frac{9}{5} \Phi Q69$."

In this part . . .

There are two types of people in the world: those who never met an equation they didn't like . . . and those who wish they had never met an equation at all. The following math chapters and practice questions can be a lot of fun for both types.

In these chapters, you learn all sorts of good tricks. Sure, I also sneak in some Real Math (stuff like formulas and rules), but I really focus on the tricks and traps you're likely to see on the GRE, including tips for sidestepping them. But please note: The GRE math has no relation to the Real World. Just review it, ace the math sections, and be done with it.

The two math sections feature two types of problems: Quantitative Comparisons and Problem-Solving questions. Math is a good news/bad news section. The bad news is that you can't use a calculator. The good news is that all questions are in multiple-choice format . . . and there's no penalty for guessing.

Chapter 13

The Incomparable Quantitative Comparisons

In This Chapter
▶ Finding the elusive QC answer choices
▶ Performing a balancing act
▶ Not all columns are created equal
▶ Recognizing and running from built-in traps
▶ Working smarter, not harder

A *riddle for you:* What do quicksand and quantitative comparisons have in common?

Answer: They both can suck you in and pull you down before you realize what's happening.

Quantitative comparisons (QCs) consist of 15 questions with half a zillion traps. The QCs rarely require power math; they require paranoia (to recognize the traps) and finesse (to avoid the traps). Hmmm, "Paranoia & Finesse." Sounds like a firm of attorneys, doesn't it?

Where Did All the Answers Go? The QC Format

A QC question lists a quantity in Column A and another quantity in Column B. The quantities can be numbers, variables, equations, words, figures, compromising photos of you at the last fraternity party — anything. Your job is to compare the quantity in Column A to the quantity in Column B. (Hence the title, "Quantitative Comparisons." I bet some rocket scientist got big bucks for thinking this one up!)

No answer choices are given below the quantities in QC questions. You are to compare the quantities and

> ✔ Choose A if the quantity in Column A is greater than the quantity in Column B.
>
> ✔ Choose B if the quantity in Column B is greater than the quantity in Column A.
>
> ✔ Choose C if the quantity in Column A is equal to the quantity in Column B.
>
> ✔ Choose D if not enough information is provided for you to determine the relationship between the quantities.

Got all that? Just choose A if A is bigger, B if B is bigger, C if they're the same (with C standing for *Same*, if you spell as badly as I do), and D if you can't tell (as in D for *duuuuuh!*).

None of these questions have an E answer. If you fill in an E on your answer grid, it doesn't count for or against you. It's as if you skipped the question. Obviously, you're just wasting your time — and the potential for any Lucky Guess points — if you fill in an E oval.

As Easy as π: Approaching QC Questions

The hardest part of a QC question is knowing where to begin. You can save considerable time — and frustration — if you develop good habits now that carry over to the exam later. Follow this simple three-step approach:

1. **Solve for the quantity in Column A.** You may solve an equation, talk through a word problem, or do nothing but look at what's given. Here are some examples of what you may see in Column A.

   ### Column A

x^2

40% of 340

The number of miles hiked by Ken, who hikes at 3 mph for $6\frac{1}{2}$ hours

2. **Solve for the quantity in Column B.** Again, this can mean solving an equation, talking through a word problem, or just looking at the column. Here are some examples:

   ### Column B

x^3

340% of 40

18

3. **Compare the two columns.**

   Sounds simple enough, right? Wait until you see some of the traps that they can build into the QCs.

Gotchas and Other Groaners: Tips, Traps, and Tricks

QCs have so many tricks and traps that I give you a separate section for each one, with a few examples to illustrate how easily you can fall for the traps.

As unbalanced as the rest of us

If the columns look equal, it's a trap. If two columns appear at first glance to be equal, a trap is almost always involved. Suppose that you see this question:

Column A	Column B
π	3.14

Your gut reaction may be to choose C because they are equal. At school, you've had 3.14 drilled into your head as π. (If you've been out of school for quite a while, you may be very pleased with yourself for remembering that. Put the self-congratulations on hold; you've just fallen for a trap.) But π is only *approximately* 3.14; it is actually larger. The correct answer to this problem is A. For convenience, π is rounded to two decimal places: 3.14. Actually, however, π continues as a nonrepeating, nonterminating decimal: 3.141592. . . . *Correct Answer:* A.

Column A	**Column B**
.0062 × 3600	6200 × .3600

Again, you probably checked that the number of digits and decimal places is the same and chose C. But the answer is B. When you multiply them out, Column A equals 22.32 and Column B equals 2,232. *Big* difference. The moral of the story: If your first reaction is that the problem is a no-brainer — that the answer is obviously, clearly, undoubtedly C — slap yourself upside the head and work through the problem. *Correct Answer:* B.

Problems go from easier to harder. The first five or six questions are probably just as easy as they look. Don't drive yourself crazy trying to find traps *early* in the section; more than enough rear their ugly heads later.

No scale, no sale

If a figure is not drawn to scale, the answer is often choice D. A problem may show a figure. Underneath the picture may appear the words: "Note: Figure not drawn to scale." This message should be a warning buzzer, alerting you to the presence of a built-in trap. If a figure is not drawn to scale, you can't rely on it. Because you can't just eyeball it to figure things out, you need solid information such as the lengths of lines or the measures of angles. If that information is not provided, you often can't determine the relationship between the columns and must choose D.

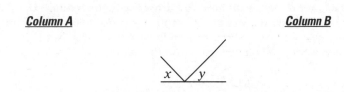

Column A   **Column B**

Note: Figure not drawn to scale.

x	y

Sure, *x* and *y* each appear to be 45 degrees. Go ahead and choose C. You'll blow the GRE, never get into grad school, and end up walking some rich woman's poodles for a living, lamenting, "If only I had noticed that the figure was not drawn to scale!"

Because the figure is not drawn to scale, you can't use it to estimate. You can't look at the figure and deduce that *x* and *y* are equal. Yes, *x* and *y* add up to 90 degrees. That's because angles along a straight line add up to 180 degrees, and you already have a right angle: 180 − 90 = 90. But you *don't* know how much of the 90 is *x* and how much is *y*. Are they 45 and 45? 60 and 30? 89 and 1? The figure is not to scale, so any of those values may be correct. Because you don't have enough information to compare the quantities, choice D is the right answer. *Correct Answer:* D.

Column A   Column B

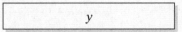

<u>Note:</u> Figure not drawn to scale.

| 2x | y |

If you fell for this one, you can kiss your 800 good-bye. This is a classic D. Yes, yes, the figure appears to be an isosceles right triangle. You know that the two *x*'s are equal and that the angles in a triangle add up to 180 degrees. But no one said that angle *y* is 90 degrees. What's that you say? It *looks* like 90 degrees? Tooooo bad. You can't look at the figure if it's not drawn to scale. As far as you know, angle *y* may be 89 degrees or 91 degrees or all sorts of other possibilities. Maybe *x* = 40, so 2*x* = 80 and *y* = 100. Maybe *x* = 60, so 2*x* = 120 and *y* = 60. What? That can't be, because it's obvious that this is not an equilateral triangle with all angles equal? Nothing is obvious; you can't use the figure if it's not drawn to scale. Because anything is possible, choose D. *Correct Answer:* D.

"Not drawn to scale" problems have fallen out of favor with the GRE lately. In my opinion, these problems were just too easy for students to get right, so the GRE naturally took them off the test. Don't be surprised if you don't see a "not drawn to scale" problem — but be prepared just in case you do. (You will definitely see some on the practice exams. I want you to be prepared for every possibility.)

Win, lose, or draw

If the answer *depends on* how you draw the figure, choose D. Approximately a third of GRE math is geometry. Many of the QC geometry problems are word problems that give no figures or diagrams. These questions often demand that you draw the figure yourself. In that case, the answer may depend on how you draw the figure.

<u>Column A</u>   <u>Column B</u>

| Area of a decagon | Area of a pentagon |

The trap answer is A. True, a decagon has ten sides and a pentagon has five sides, and true, 10 > 5, even in new math. The correct answer, however, depends on how you draw the figures: and how long each side is. For example, I can draw the shapes three different ways:

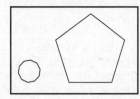 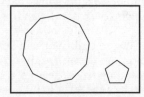 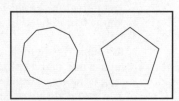

If everything *deeeeee*-pends on the *deeeeee*-rawing, choose D. *Correct Answer:* D.

Column A	*Column B*

A skating rink is 5 miles from a yogurt shop
and 6 miles from a restaurant.

Distance from the yogurt shop to the restaurant	1 mile

Did you fall for the trap answer, C? Two tips come into play here:

✔ **If the columns look equal, it's a trap.**

✔ **If the answer depends on how you draw the figure, choose D.**

Here are a couple ways of drawing the figure:

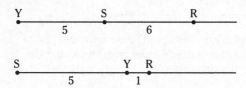

Picture perfect

If a picture is drawn, the answer is rarely D. This is the flip side of the preceding tip. The GRE is rather wishy-washy about figures. The directions say something like this: "Questions have figures that are drawn as accurately as possible, but you should use mathematics, not estimation or measurement based on the figure, to answer the questions." Huh? What does all that mean? It means that the figures really are pretty much drawn to scale, but that the GRE doesn't want you just looking at a figure to get the answer; the GRE wants you to calculate and do things the hard, "official" way. My advice is this: Don't worry about scale. As far as you're concerned, the figures are to scale unless a note specifically says otherwise. Your measurements would have to be incredibly precise for the lack of exact scale to mess you up. The answer, therefore, is rarely D when a figure is given.

Keep in mind that these are just tips, not rules. That means that they work most of the time, but not always. (I have seen, for example, some questions with figures that were unsolvable, requiring a D answer.) Never shut off your own brain in favor of a tip. The purpose of a tip is just to make you think twice before falling for a trap.

Column A	*Column B*

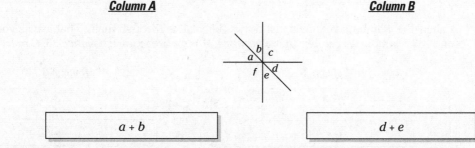

$a + b$	$d + e$

Angle *a* is a vertical angle to angle *d*, meaning that they are opposite and of equal measure. Angle *b* is a vertical angle to angle *e*, meaning that they are opposite and of equal measure. Because each part of Column A is equal to its counterpart in Column B, both columns are equal. *Correct Answer:* C.

At first glance, you may be tempted to choose D for this problem because no numbers are given. It's true that you cannot solve for the exact measure of *a* + *b* or the exact measure of *d* + *e*, but the question doesn't expect you to do so. This section is not about problem solving; it's quantitative comparisons — all you need to do is compare the quantities. You can compare them here (and see that they are equal), so D is wrong.

Column A   **_Column B_**

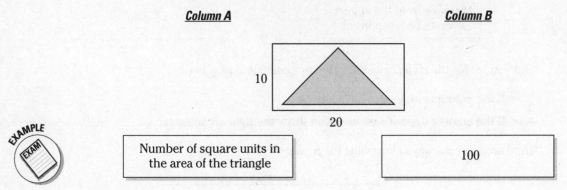

Number of square units in the area of the triangle

100

Fight the temptation to choose D automatically just because you don't have numbers for the lengths of the sides of the triangle. You know that the figure is drawn to scale; you can probably compare the quantities.

The formula for the area of a triangle is ½ *base* × *height*. What is the base? You don't know, but you *do* know that it is less than the base of the rectangle because the sides of the triangle don't extend all the way to the sides of the rectangle. Just call it *less than 20*. How much is the height? You don't know, but you *do* know that it is less than 10 because the top and bottom of the triangle don't touch the top and bottom of the rectangle. Call it *less than 10*. Multiply *less than 10* × *less than 20* = *less than 200*. Half of *less than 200* is *less than 100*. Because *less than 100* is smaller than 100, choose B. *Correct Answer:* B.

Been there, done that

Cancel quantities that are identical in both columns. Think of it as clearing the decks or simplifying the picture. A QC problem is like a scale — a balance. If something is the same on one side as on the other, it doesn't affect the balance — you can ignore it. Be careful that you cancel only *identical* things; –5 does not cancel 5, for example.

Column A   **_Column B_**

$x^2 - 21$ $x^2 - 35$

Cancel the x^2 in both columns; just draw a big ol' line through them. That leaves you with –21 and –35. Caution! Remember that a *negative* 21 is greater than a *negative* 35. *Correct Answer:* A.

Column A   **_Column B_**

$$a > b > c > 2$$

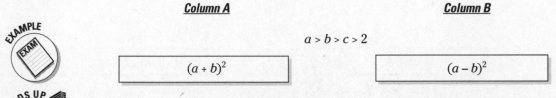

$(a + b)^2$ $(a - b)^2$

You can't cancel out the *a* and *b* on both sides and say that the columns are equal. $(a + b)^2$ is *not* the same as $(a - b)^2$. You should memorize these two expressions (they are discussed in detail in Chapters 10–12):

$$(a + b)^2 = a^2 + 2ab + b^2 \qquad\qquad (a - b)^2 = a^2 - 2ab + b^2$$

Now you can cancel identical terms: slash off the a^2 and the b^2 from both columns. You are left with $+2ab$ in Column A and $-2ab$ in Column B. Because both a and b are greater than 2, you don't need to worry about negatives or fractions. *Correct Answer:* A.

In the preceding problem, you don't need to do any pencil-pushing if you reason the answer out. Because a is greater than b and both a and b are positive numbers (greater than 2), you know that the sum $(a + b)$ must be greater than the sum $(a - b)$. Squaring a larger (positive) number gives you more than squaring a smaller number. You can deduce that Column A is bigger without doing any paperwork.

Six of one, a half dozen of the other

Compare each part of Column A to its counterpart in Column B. Again, think of QCs as a scale. If both parts of Column A are greater, or "heavier," than both parts of Column B, A is greater.

Column A	Column B
$\dfrac{17}{21} + \dfrac{47}{80}$	$\dfrac{19}{81} + \dfrac{23}{97}$

Don't even *think* about reaching for your pencil to work this problem through. Compare each part of Column A to its counterpart in Column B. Which is greater: $^{17}/_{21}$ or $^{19}/_{81}$? Reason that 17 is more than half of 21, whereas 19 is much less than half of 81. The same is true for the second pair of numbers. You know that 47 is more than half of 80; 23 is less than half of 97. Because both parts of Column A are greater than both parts of Column B, A is the answer. No muss, no fuss. *Correct Answer:* A.

Of course, some spoilsport always wants to know what happens if one part of Column A is greater than its counterpart in Column B, but the other part of Column A is less than its counterpart in Column B. Doesn't happen. Why? It ruins the trick that the test makers want you to recognize and use — you'd miss the entire point of the question. The question would reach back to a basic arithmetic, pull-out-your-pencil problem. If lightning strikes and that problem does arise, well, you have no choice but to lift a finger. *Which* finger you lift is up to you.

Keep plugging away

When plugging in numbers, use 1, 2, 0, –1, –2, $^1/_2$ — in that order. This is the best tip you're likely to get outside a racetrack. Whenever you have variables, *plug in numbers.* Instead of randomly choosing any old numbers, plug in these Sacred Six: 1, 2, 0, –1, –2, $^1/_2$. You should memorize these numbers and throw them into a problem whenever possible. These numbers cover most of the contingencies: positive, negative, zero, odd, even, fraction, and 1, which has special properties.

Column A	Column B
x^2	x^4

The *trap* answer is B. Everyone says that, *of course,* something to the fourth power is greater than the same number squared. (A variable must have the same value in Column A as in Column B *within any one problem.* That is, if x is 5 in Column A, it is also 5 in Column B. Always. No exceptions. A rose is a rose is a rose.)

Lite math: Reduced calories, no fat

You should be getting the picture by now that you don't need to do much pencil-pushing to answer QC problems. You can do many problems in a heartbeat just by knowing what the trap is and what to look for. The time you save on these questions is time you can use later in the "real math," or Problem-Solving questions, for which you actually must come up with a solution.

Ah, but whenever you hear yourself saying *"of course,"* you know that you're headed for a trap. Play the *what if* game: What if $x = 1$? Then the two columns are alike, and answer C prevails. What if $x = 2$? Then Column A = 4 and Column B = 16, and the answer is B. Therefore, the answer can be A or it can be B, depending on what you plug in. If an answer *depends* on what you plug in, choose D. *Correct Answer:* D.

Notice that you didn't have to go through all the Sacred Six numbers. As soon as you find that you get two different answers, you can stop. If plugging in 1 and 2 gives you the same answer, you should go on to 0, –1, –2, and $^1/_2$, plugging in as many as necessary. You'll be pleasantly surprised, however, to find out how often 1 and 2 alone get the job done.

Column A	**Column B**
$x \neq 0$	
$^1/x$	$x/_1$

The *trap* answer is B. Most people think that Column A comes out to be a fraction of less than 1. It may . . . or it may not. And who's to say that x is more than 1 in the first place? Play the *what if* game again.

What if $x = 1$? Then the columns are equal, and choice C is correct. What if $x = 2$? Then Column B is greater. It depends on what you plug in, so choose D. *Correct Answer:* D.

On the real exam, you would stop here, but for now, plug in a few more numbers to see what else can happen. You can't plug in 0 because the problem tells you that x is not equal to 0 (division by 0 is undefined). What if $x = -1$? Then Column A is –1 and Column B is –1; they're equal. What if $x = -2$? Then Column A = $-^1/_2$, Column B = –2; now A is bigger. You've seen all the possibilities at this point: A can be bigger, B can be bigger, or the two columns can be the same. I haven't even gotten into fractions yet. And if it's all the same to you, I won't.

Looking like a hundred bucks

Plug in 100 for dollars and percentages. This is an exception to plugging in the Sacred Six (1, 2, 0, –1, –2, $^1/_2$). If a question deals with dollars or percentages, plug in 100 to make it a nice round number. I'm all for an easy life here.

Column A	**Column B**
A book bag costs x dollars.	
Cost of the book bag on sale at 60% off	$.6x$

When pigs fly . . .

Question: Can you ever plug in all the Sacred Six and still fall for the trap?

Answer: Yeah, you can (although it's unlikely). Here's an example:

Column A	Column B

$$x \neq 0$$

$1/x$	3

Now you play the *what if* game. What if $x = 1$? Then Column B is larger. What if $x = 2$? Then Column B is larger. Because x is not equal to 0 (division by 0 is undefined), you skip to the next number in the Sacred Six. What if $x = -1$? Column B is still larger. What if $x = -2$? Yes, yes, Column B is still larger. Finally, what if $x = 1/2$? Then Column A = 2 (to divide by a fraction, invert and multiply) and Column B is still larger. Now, 99 percent of the Thinking World would choose B at this point and feel very confident. And 99 percent of the Thinking World would go straight down the tubes. The answer, in fact, is D. What if $x = 1/3$? Then Column A = 3, and the two columns are equal — choice C. If the answer could be B and could also be C, the answer depends and therefore is choice D.

A problem in which the Sacred Six don't do the job for you is incredibly rare, but it could happen. Sorry about that. This is a *tip*, not a rule. It's not perfect. Close, though. . . .

If you make the book bag cost $100, you can easily determine that 60 percent of 100 is 60; subtract $100 - 60$ and you get 40. In Column B, $.6(100) = 60$. The answer is B. This type of problem is easy to miss because of carelessness. Many people choose C automatically. Of course, you know by now that *if the columns look equal, it's probably a trap*. You should slow down, plug in 100, and work out the problem. *Correct Answer:* B.

Column A	Column B
One year's interest on x dollars at 6% annual interest	$12

Gotcha! I threw this one in to remind you once again that these are *tips,* not rules, and that you should never sacrifice common sense in favor of tips. Sure, if you plug in 100 for x dollars, you know that the interest is $6 and B is the answer. But what if $x = \$1,000,000$? Then Column A is significantly larger. Here, the correct answer *de*pends on which value you plug in for x. Although 100 often works, it is not infallible. Think! *Correct Answer:* D.

Get outta that rut

Plug in consecutive terms first and then nonconsecutive terms. If you need to plug in numbers for two or three variables, first plug in the numbers all in a row: 1, 2, and 3. Then try it again, plugging in numbers that are not in a row: 1, 5, and 7. Sometimes the spacing between the numbers makes a difference.

Column A	Column B

$$a < b < c$$

$\dfrac{a + c}{2}$	b

The normal response is to plug in consecutive numbers: 1, 2, and 3. If you do that, Column A is $1 + 3$, or 4, divided by $2 = 2$. In Column B, b is 2. The columns are equal. *Uh-oh!* You know by now that *if the columns look equal, it's often a trap* and you should double-check your work.

Plug in some nonconsecutive numbers: 1, 5, and 7. Now Column A is 1 + 7 = 8, divided by 2 = 4. In Column B, *b* is 5. Now the answer is B. If the answer *de*pends on which values you plug in for the variables, choose D. *Correct Answer:* D.

Column A	Column B

$$x > y > z$$

$y + z$	x

The *trap* answer is C. The right answer is D because the answer *de*pends on which numbers you plug in. If you plug in 3, 2, and 1, $y + z = 2 + 1 = 3$. Because $x = 3$, the columns are equal. But plug in nonconsecutive numbers: 100, 2, and 1. Now $y + z = 2 + 1 = 3$. But $x = 100$; Column B is larger. The answer can be C or B — it *de*pends on what you plug in. Choose D. *Correct Answer:* D.

Familiarity Breeds Content(ment): A Review

Before going on to the sample questions in the following chapter, review the approach and the tricks described here.

Approach

1. **Solve for the quantity in Column A.**

2. **Solve for the quantity in Column B.**

3. **Compare the two quantities.**

4. **Choose A if the quantity in Column A is greater than the quantity in Column B.**

   Choose B if the quantity in Column B is greater than the quantity in Column A.

   Choose C if the quantity in Column A is equal to the quantity in Column B.

   Choose D if you don't have enough information to determine the relationship between the quantities.

Quantitative comparisons have no answer choice E. Do *not* fill in an answer E under any circumstances!

Tricks

- If the columns look equal, the question is usually a trap.

- If a figure is not drawn to scale, the answer is often choice D.

- If the answer *de*pends on how you draw the figure, choose D.

- If a picture is drawn to scale, the answer rarely is D.

- Cancel quantities that are identical in both columns.

- Compare each part of Column A to its counterpart in Column B.

- When plugging in numbers, use 1, 2, 0, –1, –2, and ½ in that order.

- Plug in 100 for dollars and percentages.

- Plug in consecutive terms first and then nonconsecutive terms.

Chapter 14
Putting It All Together: QC Practice Questions

• •

*I*f you're waiting until someone makes a movie of this stuff, forget it. You're outta luck. The information on quantitative comparisons in the preceding chapter is all she wrote (so to speak). If you didn't read it carefully, please go back and do so now — before you humiliate yourself on this practice exam.

All done? Good. Now, check your ego at the door or it may get trashed on this exam. I've written a dozen problems that incorporate the meanest, the cruelest, the stupidest traps you're likely to see on the real GRE. How many are *you* going to fall for?

The answer choices are

A if the quantity in Column A is greater.

B if the quantity in Column B is greater.

C if the two quantities are equal.

D if the relationship cannot be determined from the information given.

Column A	*Column B*
1. $10\,[(4 \times 3)^2 + 5^0]$	1440

This question tests two concepts: order of operations and the zero exponent. Always do what is inside of the parentheses first: $4 \times 3 = 12$. $12^2 = 144$. Then do what's inside the brackets. $5^0 = 1$. Any number to the zero power equals one. Add: $144 + 1 = 145$. Then multiply by what's outside the brackets: $10 \times 145 = 1450$. *Correct Answer: A.*

If you chose C, you thought that 5^0 was zero, giving you $144 + 0 = 144$; $144 \times 10 = 1440$. Look out for the zero exponent; it is often in tricky questions. Also, double-check all your C answers. I've found more traps in which people choose C than all the other traps combined.

Column A	*Column B*
A cubic box has a total surface area of 600 square units.	
2. Number of cubic units in the volume of the box	1000

The total surface area of a cube is the sum of the areas of all surfaces. A cube has six surfaces: $600 \div 6 = 100$. Each surface of the cube, which is a square, has an area of 100. That means each edge is 10, because the area of a square is *side* $\times$ *side*. The volume of a cube is *edge*^{3}. $10 \times 10 \times 10 = 1000$. *Correct Answer:* C.

Many of the geometry problems ask you to go forwards and backwards. You're given a volume and asked to find a total surface area, or vice versa. You may be given a circumference and asked to find a sector, or vice versa. Be comfortable enough with the geometry formulas to work problems inside out, upside down, and any which way. If you don't know how to find a volume and a total surface area, return to the thrilling pages of Chapter 10.

	Column A	*Column B*
3.	$\sqrt{66 + 85}$	12

First add the numbers under the square root sign. $66 + 85 = 151$. Then take the square root of that. Stop! Don't have a panic attack right here. No, you are not allowed to use a calculator. That's the bad news. The good news is that you don't have to. You don't have to get an exact answer for a QC problem; you just have to compare the quantities in the columns. Look for a perfect square close to 151. How about 144, which is 12^2, or 169, which is 13^2. Because 151 is between 144 and 169, the square of it must be between 12 and 13. You couldn't care less exactly how much it is. (Do not bother finding the exact square root!) As long as it's more than 12, Column A is larger. *Correct Answer:* A.

	Column A	*Column B*
4.	$.10 \times 10 \times 100$	1

You needn't have withdrawal pains from your calculator. This problem is much easier than it looks. Keep in mind that questions in the first half of the QCs are usually relatively simple. Multiply $.10 \times 10$ to get 1. You know that $1 \times 100 = 100$, which is certainly greater than 1. That's all you have to do. If you chose C, you got careless and were swayed by the hypnotic power of the columns. Don't let the C's *mesmerize* (hypnotize) you; double-check them any time you encounter them. *Correct Answer:* A.

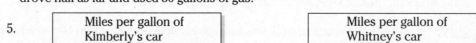

	Column A	*Column B*

On a road trip, Kimberly drove 600 miles and used 45 gallons of gas. Her friend Whitney drove half as far and used 30 gallons of gas.

	Miles per gallon of Kimberly's car	Miles per gallon of Whitney's car
5.		

This is a basic arithmetic problem. To find the mileage, divide the number of miles driven by the gallons used. $600 \div 45$ compared to $300 \div 30$. *Correct Answer:* A.

Before you begin making the pencil scratches, look at both columns. You'll be surprised how often you don't have to work through the actual arithmetic. You know that $300 \div 30$ is 10; you can do that in your head. Is $600 \div 45$ more than 10, equal to 10, or less than 10? It's more than 10, because $600 \div 60$ would be 10. Stop right there. You don't have to work the problem through to the bitter end; just compare the quantities. I want you to be able not only to get all the QC questions correct but to get them correct quickly. Usually, if you have enough time you can get most of the hard multiple-choice problems correct; the difficulty is that you *don't* have enough time. Every second you save here is a second you can use on the "real" math questions, the Problem-Solving questions.

	Column A	**Column B**

6. $\boxed{18y + 18x}$ $\boxed{18y - 18x}$

You didn't fall for the cheezy and *egregious* (heinous, truly terrible) trap built into this very simple question, did you? If so, please consider yourself totally humiliated. One tip you learned in the lecture was to cross off quantities that are identical in both columns. Cancel the 18y. You are now left with 18x compared to –18x. Common sense tells you that 18x is greater. Common sense should take a flying leap. There's nothing common about the QC questions. Play the *what-if* game: What if x = 1? Then A is greater. What if x = 2? Then A is still greater. Ah, but what if x = 0? Then the columns are equal. If the answer *de*pends on what you plug in, choose D. *Correct Answer:* D.

The more variables you have, the greater the likelihood that the answer is D, because those variables could, well, vary. Whenever you plug in, use the Sacred Six you learned in Chapter 13. (If you skipped Chapter 13 and went right to the practice problems, you missed some good stuff. Here's your second chance.) Plug in 1, 2, 0, –1, –2, and ½, in that order. You won't usually have to plug them *all* in. As soon as you get two different possibilities, you know the answer *de*pends on what you plug in, and you choose D.

Column A **Column B**

$$ab = -40$$

7. $\boxed{(a + b)^2}$ $\boxed{(a - b)^2}$

Did you memorize the expanded form of these two expressions $(a + b)^2 = a^2 + 2ab + b^2$? (If you don't know how I got that, go back to the discussion of FOIL methods in Chapter 11.) $(a - b)^2 = a^2 - 2ab + b^2$. Now use the trick also taught in Chapter 11: Cancel quantities that are identical in both columns. Slash off a^2 and b^2. You're left with +2ab, which would be –80, compared to –2ab, which would be +80 (because a negative times a negative is a positive). *Correct Answer:* B.

If you chose A, you got careless with your negative. Keeping the signs straight is one of the most important things you can do in any algebra problem.

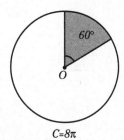

Circle O

$C=8\pi$

Column A **Column B**

8. $\boxed{\text{Area of the shaded region}}$ $\boxed{3\pi}$

A shaded portion of a circle is called a sector. Its area is a fraction of the area of the circle. To find the area of a sector, first find the area of the circle. The formula for the area of a circle is $\pi \times radius^2$. You have to work backwards from the circumference to find the radius. The circumference of a circle is $2\pi \times radius$. Here, the radius is 4, so the area of the circle is 16π.

Next, you know that the degrees in a circle total 360. The shaded portion has a 60-degree angle, making it $\frac{1}{6}$ ($\frac{60}{360}$) of the circle. Multiply the fraction by the area: $\frac{1}{6} \times 16\pi = \frac{16}{6}\pi$ or $\frac{8}{3}\pi$, which is less than 3π. *Correct Answer:* B.

The geometry review section has a good discussion of everything to do with circles, including sectors. Circles, in my not-so-humble opinion, are among the easiest of the geometry problems to get correct. Count on these as "gimmes."

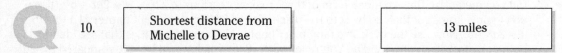

	Column A	**Column B**
9.	$^{47}/_{299} + {}^{18}/_{101}$	$^{17}/_{31} + {}^{7}/_{13}$

Did you see the shortcut? Surely you know by now that you are not expected to do common denominators and go through all the garbage math. If it's a QC problem, there's usually a trick. Use my tip: *Compare each element of Column A to its counterpart in Column B.* That is, compare $^{47}/_{299}$ to $^{17}/_{31}$. Because 47 out of 299 is less than half, and 17 out of 31 is more than half, Column B is larger. Next, compare the remaining two quantities. Because 18 out of 101 is less than half and 7 out of 13 is more than half, Column B is larger here as well. Both parts of Column B are greater than both parts of Column A; B is greater. *Correct Answer:* B.

And for you people who insist on creating drama: No, the test makers will not, repeat, will *not* give you a problem of this sort in which one quantity is larger in Column A but the other quantity is larger in Column B. Doing so would defeat the point that this question is asking. Believe it or not, the test makers don't get a fiendish glee out of watching you do a lot of pencil-pushing. They're trying to see whether you're smart enough to *avoid* doing the work.

Column A   **Column B**

Michelle and Mike begin walking and go 5 miles due north. Their friend Devrae begins at the same point and goes 12 miles due west.

10.	Shortest distance from Michelle to Devrae	13 miles

Did I trick you? True, usually when a geometry problem has no picture drawn, the answer is D. However, if you draw this picture, you see that you get a right triangle of sides 5 and 12.

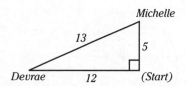

Michelle

13   5

Devrae   12   *(Start)*

You can use the Pythagorean theorem of $a^2 + b^2 = c^2$ and find that $5^2 + 12^2 = (25 + 144) = 169$; $169 = c^2$; $c = 13$. Or you could be grateful you weren't too *parsimonious* (cheap) to plunk the dough down for this book and remember that you learned in the math review one of the Pythagorean Triples, which is 5:12:13. That is, in a right triangle (which is true if one person goes due north and the other person goes due west) if one side is 5, and the other side is 12, the hypotenuse must be 13. You don't have to do the work at all. *Correct Answer:* C.

Did you have trouble figuring out the square root of 169? You should have memorized certain square roots and perfect squares, as given in the math review. If you didn't do so, you could, of course, always work backwards from the Column B quantity: $13 \times 13 =$ (son of a gun!) 169. Once again I say unto you: Don't panic, especially over square roots. In my experience, I've never seen a GRE question that depended on your being able to find an exact square root. I have seen a *plethora* (an abundance), indeed a *superfluity* (an excessive number) of problems that can be answered by knowing the basic Pythagorean Triples, which just happen to be given and explained in the math review.

Column A	Column B
11. The greatest prime factor of 1210	The greatest prime factor of 12,100

A prime factor is a prime number, a number which can be divided only by itself and 1. The prime numbers are 2, 3, 5, 7, 11, and so on. (Notice that 0 and 1 are not prime numbers.) To factor down a number ending in 0, divide by 10. For Column A, that gives you 121×10. You should have memorized your perfect squares and know that $121 = 11 \times 11$. For Column B, dividing by 10 gives you 1210×10. Divide by 10 again to get $121 \times 10 \times 10$. Because 10 factors down into 2 and 5, the greatest prime factor of both columns is 11. *Correct Answer:* C.

Column A	Column B
$9x^2 - 4x = 69$; $3x^2 - 10x = -3$.	
12. $x^2 + x$	15

This is a straightforward algebra problem. Traps are rarely found in algebra problems; they usually are pretty basic. Here, write the two expressions vertically and either add or subtract to make the numerical coefficients (the numbers before the x^2 and the x) the same.

$9x^2 - 4x = 69$

$3x^2 - 10x = -3$

If you add, you get $12x^2 - 14x = 66$, not the same numerical coefficient. Because the numerical coefficients are not the same, no variable "drops out" or can be canceled. On to plan B. If adding the equations doesn't work, subtract the second equation, which means changing the signs on all the numbers.

$9x^2 - 4x = 69$

$-3x^2 + 10x = 3$

You get $6x^2 + 6x = 72$. Divide both sides through by 6 to get $x^2 + x = 12$. *Correct Answer:* B.

Chapter 15

Real Math at Last: Problem Solving

In This Chapter

▶ Developing a plan of attack for Problem-Solving questions

▶ Separating the boring from the bewildering

▶ Sidestepping snares and avoiding built-in traps

*P*roblem Solving is a rather ritzy name for "regular" math problems. A Problem-Solving question, amazingly enough, actually expects you to solve a problem. This is different from the Quantitative Comparison questions (covered in Chapter 13), in which you often don't need to solve the problem through to the bitter end — you just compare the quantities. (Who thinks of these catchy names anyway? How much do they get paid, and where can I apply for the job?)

Strategic Planning: The Attack Strategy

Are you an Algebra Ace? Mathematics Master? Geometry Guru? Me neither. Isn't it lucky that you don't have to be any of those things to do well on the Problem-Solving questions? To improve your chances of acing the material, try to understand and apply the few strategies discussed here.

I realize that some of you reading this book haven't taken math classes in a long, long time. Maybe you are a senior in college and, because you tested out of your math while you were still in high school, never took any math at all in college. Maybe you're returning to school after spending several years off working or having a family or traveling or pursuing the idle and decadent lifestyle of the independently wealthy. Whatever the cause, you may be so rusty in math that your pencil creaks when you pick it up. I realize that you are not going to get every single math question correct; you should realize that you don't have to. The following suggestions help you to maximize your points with a minimum of time and bother.

1. **Read the problem through carefully and *circle what the question is asking for.***

   This crucial point is missed very often, especially by people who are math-phobic. Things are even worse when the very first section on the GRE is math and you haven't had a chance to settle into the rhythm of the test. It's easy to "predict" or "anticipate" what the question is asking for and not take note of what it really wants. Your goal is to give 'em what they want. If the question asks for a circumference, circle the word *circumference* and don't solve for an area. If the question wants you to find the number of hours already worked rather than the total number of hours a job would take, be sure that you supply that figure.

   Of course, of course, *of course,* the answer choices feature trap answers; this goes without saying on the GRE. If you find the area of a figure, it will be a trap answer to a question that wants the perimeter. Just because the answer you got is staring you in the face does not mean that it is the correct answer. It might be . . . or it might be a trap. Circle what the question is asking for — what you are to solve. Before you fill in a bubble on the answer grid, go back and look at this circle: Are you answering the right question?

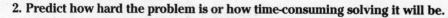

2. **Predict how hard the problem is or how time-consuming solving it will be.**

The difficulty level of questions on the GRE goes from easier to harder. In most cases, you'll be able to answer the first third of the questions without much brain drain. The last third is very hard. The middle third is where most students have to make a conscious decision: Do you solve this problem or blow it off with a quick guess?

Keeping in mind that *there's no penalty for wrong answers,* you don't want to leave any choices blank. The most important thing to remember, however, is that you can penalize yourself if you take too long over a problem. If you can't solve the problem and you're just making a wild guess, guess quickly and go on.

3. **Preview the answer choices; look to see how precise your answer has to be and how careful you have to be on the decimal points.**

If the answer choices are 4, 5, 6, 7, and 8, you probably have to solve the problem to the bitter end, calculating rather than estimating. This type of problem may take a long time. However, if the answer choices are .05, .5, 5, 50, and 500, you know that the digit is definitely going to be a 5 and that you have to keep your decimal point straight. You may be able to use common sense on that problem and estimate the answer without working it out.

4. **Solve the problem forwards and backwards.**

Work out the problem and get an answer; then plug that answer back into the problem to make sure that it makes sense. If you found the average of 4, 6, 7, 9, and 10 to be 36, you can look at the answer and reason that you made a mistake somewhere because the average can't be bigger than the biggest number. (Did you see the mistake? If you got 36, you found the sum of the terms but forgot to divide by the number of terms. "Interim" answers of this sort are common trap answer choices on the GRE.)

Five Commonsense Suggestions

The Problem-Solving questions are much more straightforward than the Quantitative Comparison (QC) problems discussed in Chapter 13. There aren't as many tricks or traps, but you can learn a few good, fairly commonsense techniques that can speed up your work or help you avoid careless mistakes.

Easy problems often have easy answers

This tip is ridiculously simplistic, but it's true. If you're solving question number 5 out of 15, it's exceedingly unlikely that the correct answer will be

$$\sqrt{\frac{5ab^3}{3b-a}}$$

That's just too bizarre and hard of an answer for that early on in the questions. It may (or may not) be correct for a super-hard problem near the end. The test makers know that you all have major insecurities and that you look at an answer and think the harder, the better. Don't immediately choose the easiest answer for an easy question and the hardest answer for a hard question, though; things don't usually work out that neatly. But if you have the answers narrowed down to two, go for the hard one at the end and the easy one at the beginning.

Eliminate illogical (dumb) answer choices

You know how some teachers always reassure students by saying, "Oh, there's no such thing as a dumb question or answer; just try!" Wrong. There *are* such things as dumb answers. If you're asked for the temperature of a liquid and one of the answer choices is –200° Fahrenheit, it's unlikely that a liquid would be that cold; it would freeze and no longer be a liquid! If you're asked for the age of a person and one answer is 217, I'd like to know what kind of vitamins he's been taking! When you preview the answers, dump the ones that seem to make no sense.

Don't choose a "close enough" answer

Suppose that you do a ton of calculations and get the answer 36. One of the answer choices is 38. Don't shrug and say, "Ahh, close enough; I must have made a mistake somewhere." You sure did, and you're about to make a second mistake by being lazy and choosing an answer that's close. *Remember:* Close counts only in horseshoes (which you may want to bring to the exam for luck, come to think of it) and hand grenades (which may be what you feel has hit you when you see some of these math questions!).

Don't let me scare you *too* much about the math. The GRE does not, repeat does *not*, test trigonometry or calculus. It tests basic arithmetic, algebra, and geometry. Even if you haven't had those subjects in years, you can cover enough in a quick math review to do well. As a private tutor, I recently worked with a student in her 60s who wanted to go back to graduate school after her husband passed away. She had never taken geometry in her life because the subject wasn't required when she applied to college 40 years ago. She memorized formulas, went through some sample problems, kept an eye open for tricks, and did just as well as anyone else.

Don't be afraid to skip around

An intelligent Skipper doesn't go down with the ship, if you'll forgive the pun. You'll know by the time you get through with this book which types of questions you ace and which ones drive you crazy. Feel free to skip around in the section, making sure that you get to the questions you're good at and ignoring for the time being those questions that would drive Mother Teresa to drink.

You are not allowed to skip around on the CAT version until you have completed the minimum number of questions required. In fact, on that version, spend extra time double-checking your work to make sure that you ge the first few questions correct.

You want to be absolutely sure that you fill in something for every question (because there is no penalty for wrong answers on the GRE). Therefore, rather than simply skipping a question and leaving it blank on your answer grid, I suggest you fill in something, anything, and put a big arrow in the margin of the test booklet, pointing to the question you guessed at. That way, if you totally run out of time, you won't have any unanswered questions. If you have a few minutes left at the end of the section, go back to the questions with the arrows pointing to them and give them a try.

Questions progress from easier to harder in every section of the GRE. Don't be surprised if you can't answer any of the questions on the last page; that's normal. If you know that the questions are beyond you, forget about them (just make a quick guess) and go back to double-check your work on earlier questions.

Give your pencil a workout

Although you get no scratch paper on the test, there is a lot of blank space on the test booklet — more than enough for you to draw and doodle as necessary. As you'll see when you go through the sample questions and practice exam, writing down formulas and plugging numbers into them or drawing pictures and putting numbers on the pictures is an excellent means of avoiding careless errors and clarifying and organizing thoughts. Don't think you're wasting time by using your pencil; you may actually be saving time by avoiding confusion.

I'm Sure I Know You from Somewhere: A Quick Review

Before going on to the sample questions, let's review the approach and the tricks.

Approach

Although a Problem-Solving question is a basic multiple-choice math question similar to what you've done on exams all your life, using these commonsense suggestions can help you to answer the questions more quickly and with fewer errors.

1. **Read the problem through carefully and *circle what the question is asking for.***

2. **Predict how hard the problem is or how time-consuming solving it will be.**

3. **Preview the answer choices.**

4. **Solve the problem forwards and backwards (plugging in the multiple-choice answers).**

Tricks

The test makers know all the traps students can fall for and delight in building those traps into the questions. Just because the answer you got is one of the answer choices in front of you does not mean that your answer is correct. Keep the following tricks in mind as you go through the Problem-Solving questions:

- Easy problems often have easy answers.
- Eliminate illogical (dumb) answer choices.
- Don't choose a "close enough" answer.
- Don't be afraid to skip around.
- Plug in numbers, write down formulas, and draw pictures. Give your pencil a workout.

Chapter 16

A Chance to Show Off: Problem-Solving Practice Questions

So you think that you understand everything from the lecture? Prove it! I'm calling your bluff. Let's see you ace these practice questions.

1. At a park, the ratio of softball players to volleyball players is 3:4. If the total number of softball and volleyball players is 63, how many more volleyball players than softball players are in the park?

   (A) 3

   (B) 4

   (C) 6

   (D) 9

   (E) 12

The total of a ratio is a multiple of the sum of the numbers in that ratio. In simple English, that means you add the numbers in the ratio: 3 + 4 = 7. Think of seven as the number of athletes in one clique or one batch. In 63, there are 9 cliques or batches, because $^{63}/_7$ = 9. If there are 9 batches of 3 softball players, that's 27. If there are 9 batches of 4 volleyball players, that's 36. 36 − 27 = 9. *Correct Answer:* D.

Ratios should be among the easiest of questions to answer correctly. The math review has a very easy explanation of how to get through these problems without even lifting your pencil.

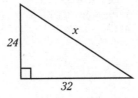

2. What is the length of side x in the figure above?

   (A) 48

   (B) 40

   (C) 35

   (D) 32

   (E) 30

Because the longest side of any right triangle is always the hypotenuse (the side opposite the right or 90-degree angle), you know that answers less than or equal to 32 are wrong. Eliminate choices D and E.

You could of course do this problem the long and boring way, using the Pythagorean theorem to find that $a^2 + b^2 = c^2$. That means you have to square 24, square 32, and then find the square root of whatever humongous number results. (Don't ask me what it is; I'm not about to do all that hard work.) At this stage, you should be reminding yourself that there should be an easier way. And there is.

Right triangles have their sides in specific proportions or ratios, called the Triples. If you haven't learned these yet, go back to Chapter 10 and do so right now. You'll save yourself a lot of work (and points) if you memorize some special triples. The one that works here is the most common on the test: 3:4:5. Each side is a multiple of those terms. The first side is 3×8, or 24. The next side is 4×8, or 32. That means the last side must be 5×8, or 40. Brain overload avoided. *Correct Answer:* B.

3. Given a regular hexagon of side 5, what is the sum of the interior angles?

   (A) 900

   (B) 720

   (C) 540

   (D) 360

   (E) 180

The term *regular* just means that all sides and all angles are equal. For example, an equilateral triangle and a square are regular figures. The interior angles of a figure are found with the formula $(n - 2)$ 180 degrees, where n stands for the number of sides of the figure. Because a hexagon has six sides (think of the x in *six* and the x in *hex* to help you to remember this), your formula is $(6 - 2)$ $180 = (4 \times 180) = 720$. *Correct Answer:* B.

If you chose C, you fell for the trap. You let the 5, which is the *length* of the side, be the number of sides. The two numbers are totally different: six sides, each measuring 5 units. Only the number of sides is important here.

Chapter 10 provides a very good analysis of how to find the interior (and exterior) angles of any figure. Because geometry problems are the easiest to get right once you've learned formulas, I suggest that you spend the majority of your study time working on geometry if you have only a limited time to work on this material.

4. $\boxed{\begin{array}{l} \text{(x)} = x^2 \text{ if } x \text{ is prime.} \\ \text{(x)} = (x + 1)^2 \text{ if } x \text{ is composite.} \end{array}}$

   Solve for ③ + ④.

   (A) 41

   (B) 34

   (C) 25

   (D) 23

   (E) 7

This is a symbolism problem. Talk your way through it, substituting the number in the circle for the x in the directions. First, you have ③. Because 3 is a prime number (a prime number has no positive integer factors other than one and itself), you use the first line of the directions. Square 3 to get 9. Next you have a ④. Because 4 is composite (it has factors other than just one and itself), you use the second line of directions. Add 1 to the 4 first and then square the sum. $1 + 4 = 5$; $5^2 = 25$. Now add the two answers: $9 + 25 = 34$. *Correct Answer:* B.

Did you fall for one of the trap answers? If you added 1 to both terms and squared them, you got choice A. If you didn't add 1 to either term but squared them alone, you got choice C. I want you to avoid a false sense of security. The mere fact that the answer you got is among the answer choices doesn't mean it's the correct answer (although if it's not there, it's definitely the wrong answer).

5. Given that $a \neq 0$, solve for $\dfrac{a^2\, a\, a^3}{a^4}$.

    (A) $a^{3/2}$

    (B) a^1

    (C) a^2

    (D) a^3

    (E) a^9

This is a relatively simple problem, once you know how to work with bases and exponents. When you multiply like bases, you add the exponents. Keeping in mind that a by itself is a^1, you get $a^{(2+1+3)} = a^6$. When dividing like bases, subtract the exponents like this: $a^{(6-4)} = a^2$. The answer is not $a^{3/2}$; even the GRE wouldn't put an answer that nasty on the exam. Well, let me **renege** (take back) that statement. It would put an answer that nasty on the test; the answer just wouldn't be correct. *Correct Answer:* C.

If you chose B, you forgot that a is the same as a^1. You thought it was a^0 and added $a^{(2+0+3)} = a^5$. But any number to the zero power is 1, not that number itself.

Yes, you guessed it: There's an explanation in the math review of working with bases and exponents. It's to your advantage to go back and study it now.

6. $a - 3b + c = 15$; $6a - 2b + 6c = 23$. $b =$

    (A) $^{11}/_{15}$

    (B) 1

    (C) $^{15}/_{11}$

    (D) $^{-60}/_{11}$

    (E) $^{-67}/_{16}$

To find b, you have to make the a and c variables "drop out." That means you need to subtract one equation from the other until you are left only with b. Multiply the first equation by 6 so that you have $6a - 18b + 6c = 90$. Then subtract the second equation from that. It looks like this:

$$6a - 18b + 6c = 90$$
$$\underline{6a - 2b + 6c = 23}$$

When you subtract, you change the signs on the second term. That means you have $6a - 6a$; the a's drop out. You have $-18b + 2b = -16b$. You have $6c - 6c$; the c's drop out. All you have now is $-16b = 67$. Divide both sides through by the -16: $b = {}^{-67}/_{16}$. *Correct Answer:* E.

Hard questions frequently have hard answers. A bizarro answer like $^{-67}/_{16}$ would almost never be correct for the first few problems in the section, but it has a good chance of being correct for the last problems. Don't automatically choose the hardest, most unusual answer just because you're working on a hard problem. But don't be surprised if that weirdo answer is in fact correct.

Part V
Getting into Analysis:
Analytical Ability

In this part . . .

The Analytical Ability section torments you with two types of questions: analytical reasoning (sometimes called logic games) and logical reasoning. In these chapters, you get to play mind games, using logic to make diagrams, identify assumptions, analyze evidence — fun stuff.

Before you go through these sections, check that the schools you're applying to use the Analytical Ability score; many don't. Sweating through stuff that may not even count would be the biggest mind game of all!

Chapter 17

A Section Only Mr. Spock Could Love: Analytical Ability

● ●

In This Chapter

▶ Distinguishing Analytical Reasoning (logic games) from Logical Reasoning (critical thinking) questions

▶ Recognizing and diagramming the four main types of logic games

▶ Finding shortcuts for long and confusing logic passages

▶ Heeding a warning about a possible third Analytical Ability question style

● ●

*N*o, Analytical Ability is not what a potential proctologist must display. Analytical Ability is the reasoning and logic portion of the GRE. Your Analytical Ability score is the third score you'll see on your score report: verbal, math, analytical. Like the verbal and math scores, it ranges from 200 to 800.

Many schools do *not* look at the Analytical Ability scores. Let me repeat that statement, as this information may be critical to your study program: *Many schools do not care about your Analytical Ability scores.* Before you go through this section, before you read any further, read the university bulletins or call the admissions offices of the graduate schools to which you're applying and find out whether the Analytical Ability scores are important to your admission chances. If they are not, congratulations! You don't have to suffer through the rest of this chapter. However, one warning: Don't simply talk to the receptionist in the admissions office and take his or her word for it that the Analytical Ability scores do not count. Get that policy in writing.

For those of you who are still tuned in, welcome to the most bizarre section of the GRE. Analytical Ability is not something tested in everyday life. French doesn't require you to make diagrams or charts of the relationships between things; World History 101 rarely has small passages of which you must find the underlying assumption. In other words, you have not taken a lot of exams with this style of question on it.

Fun and Games: The Format

The GRE has two sections of Analytical Ability. Each section features 25 questions to be done in 30 minutes. A section usually has four logic games (called Analytical Reasoning) with a total of 18–20 questions testing those games. The remaining 5–7 questions are Logical Reasoning questions (sometimes called Critical Reasoning or Critical Thinking).

Logic Games: Analytical Reasoning

I'll start with the games; the fun comes next. A logic game has two basic parts. First is the set of three to seven statements or conditions, sometimes called the facts. These statements describe the relationship between or among people, items, or events. You may, for example, be given statements about colleagues and asked which professors can work together on a committee. You may be told facts about events that can happen on certain days of the week. Perhaps a game will tell you about possible combinations of items. Here are examples of statements you may see in different games:

Amelia cannot sit at the same table as Britta.

Flu shots are given on Mondays, Tuesdays, and Wednesdays except when measles shots are given on the same day.

Justine is taller than Cristina and weighs less than Marco.

Following the statements is a set of three or more questions that tests your understanding of how the statements work together. Each question in a group is independent of the others. That is, you do not have to answer question number 1 correctly to answer question number 2. You may even find that you can answer the last (supposedly hardest) question in a batch without having answered the first few questions. Following are a few sample questions:

How many different groups of at least three people can Amelia be part of?

On which day of the week are no shots given at all?

Which of the following represents the order of the students from tallest to shortest?

Take your time going through a logic game. It's better to get all the questions right on two or three of the games and not even get to the fourth than to get through all the games but not understand any of them and miss nearly all the questions. Frankly, very few people get through all the logic games. If this section is difficult for you, preview the games. Eliminate the one that *cows* (intimidates) you the most. Pretend that game is not even in the section. If you finish the rest of the section and still have time, you can always go back to what you've skipped; if not, you're following your game plan (pun fully intended) and haven't lost a thing.

Here's a basic approach that works for any of the several types of logic games.

You Can't Tell the Players without a Program

Make a "program" of the players by writing down the pool of people or events. For example, if the question talks about five professors, Mahaffey, Negy, O'Leary, Plotnitz, and Quivera, you jot down M, N, O, P, and Q to the side.

My telling you to write down this pool of people may seem simplistic, but your not doing so can cost you points during the heat of the battle. It's very easy to have five people, four of whom are asked about frequently. The fifth poor forgotten soul often is ignored . . . until a trap question near the end. Write the pool down and refer to it often.

Picture This: The Diagram

Usually, you can make a diagram to show the relationship between the people or events. Here are a few of the most common diagrams:

- ✔ **Calendar:** A calendar game is very straightforward; draw a calendar and fill in the events that happen on particular days.

- ✔ **Ordering or sequencing:** You may have an ordering or sequencing relationship game in which some people are taller or heavier than others. You would write a line of people, with A above B if A is taller than B, C at the bottom if she is the shortest, and so on.

- ✔ **Grouping or membership:** This game asks you which items or people could belong to which group. For example, membership in a club might require four out of five characteristics. Often this type of question doesn't require a graph per se but a lot of "if . . . then" statements such as "If A is in the group, then B is not." You can also think of these as mathematical statements: $A \neq B$. I've put a few games of this type in the short quiz that follows in the next chapter; the serious diagramming I'm saving for the Practice Exams 1 and 2 found at the end of the book.

- ✔ **Personal characteristics:** In this game, you are given information about people and asked what those people can or cannot do based on their characteristics. For example, you may be told that Trent has a fear of heights and Lucilla has a fear of horses. If the question asks, "Which of the following could go on a horseback ride along a mountain crest?" you know to eliminate Trent and Lucilla from the group.

The preceding examples are by no means the only types of games you could get; they are simply the most common. Most games you see will be a variation on one of these. As you go through the practice exam, you'll see several different types of games. When you've finished both practice exams, take a few minutes to go back through the analytical games. Label each one by type and decide which types you're great at and which ones you could happily live without.

Artifices, Ruses, and Wiles: A Trap by Any Other Name Still Stinks

Logic games are full of traps; be on the lookout for them. The following suggestions may help you to recognize and overpower the worst of them.

Read the entire game first. Do not start making a diagram as soon as you get to the first statement. You can make several different styles of diagrams; don't decide which type is for you until you've read all the statements.

You cannot and should not make a diagram for every single type of game. Sometimes you will simply write statements such as $A \neq B$ or *If B, then no C*. Occasionally, a game will have more than one diagram. Be flexible and realize that you may have to create two or even three diagrams, any of which could be true under a particular set of conditions.

Focus on an *always/never* statement. Some statements are 100 percent absolute. They give info like "Darnay never goes to the clinic on Tuesdays" or "Puff is the smallest cat." You love those types of statements, as there are no ifs, ands, or buts about them. Look for them first and circle them. You want to keep them in the front of your mind as those statements often let you eliminate answer choices immediately. For example, if a question asks you which is the order of cats from largest to smallest, eliminate any answer that doesn't have Puff at the very end. Usually, you'll be able to narrow your answers down to two or three immediately.

Be alert to multiple contingencies. A game might ask you which clubs a person can join. If you find by going through the statements that Rod could belong to either the swim team or the chess team, be sure to note both possibilities. Maybe the question asks which space Charlene can take at the conference table, and you find she can sit in either seat four or seat five. Make diagrams illustrating both possibilities.

As soon as you see that there is a multiple possibility for one person or item, look for a question on that topic. For example, if Charlene can sit at either seat four or seat five, you will have a question like, "Seat five will be occupied by which of the following?" One answer will be Charlene; the second answer will be "Charlene or nobody."

Don't carry over info given by a preceding question. So there you are. You've created a beautiful diagram, all parts in place, everything perfect. Then you get to question 18 and it adds something new, like, "Boomer decides he doesn't want to sit next to Twyla but must sit next to a blonde. Which of the following could be the seating order?" That piece of new info means you have to go back and redo your entire diagram. Usually doing so chews up a lot of time. I suggest you make a random guess and then mark the question with an arrow so that you know to return to it later. If you decide to do this question in order, be sure not to transfer info to the next question. That is, when you're ready to answer question 19, go back to your original diagram that has Boomer sitting next to Twyla. The test makers know that students have a tendency to carry over info and design answers to trap those who make that mistake.

Don't confuse forward and backward. You may have one game which requires you to make "if . . . then" statements: "If it rains, then I'll go to the library." Don't turn that statement around and say, "If I go to the library, it will be raining." Not necessarily. I may be forced to go to the library on a gorgeous, sunny day because my term paper is due and I can't *procrastinate* (delay) any longer.

It Makes Sense to Me: Logical Reasoning

Logical Reasoning questions consist of short paragraphs, just a sentence or two. You read the passage and then answer questions like these:

Which of the following is the author's underlying assumption?

Which of the following statements would most *weaken* the author's conclusion?

The author's conclusion would be most *strengthened* by which of the following?

Which of the following arguments is most likely to explain the seeming contradiction between the author's statement and his actions?

The author quotes the doctor to make the point that . . .

Which of the following is the best conclusion to the paragraph above?

The statement above follows most logically from which of these statements?

When Nothing is Reason-able: Tricks and Traps

Here are a few suggestions to help you to maximize your points in this section.

Do Logical Reasoning questions first. Most people think that the Logical Reasoning questions, because their format is so similar to that of questions seen every day in school, are easier than the Analytical Reasoning questions. If logic games intimidate you, warm up by doing the Logical Reasoning questions first.

The Logical Reasoning questions are sprinkled among the Aanalytical Reasoning questions. You may see something that says, "Questions 3–7 are based on the following statements." Then questions 8 and 9 will be Logical Reasoning questions. It's easy to overlook this type of question, especially those found near the end of the section.

Underline exactly what the question is asking. The most important step in the Logical Reasoning questions is identifying what the question wants. Are you to identify an assumption? find a strengthening argument? predict what would weaken the argument?

Answer your strongest question types first. I've written these practice exams to give you a smattering of all sorts of Logical Reasoning questions. When you've finished with the tests, go back and identify which types of questions you always get right, and which ones you usually miss. Maybe you're better at questions that require very little reading but a lot of analysis, like parallel reasoning. Maybe you're better at questions that test less formal logic and more reading, like "conclusion to the paragraph" questions. Because most people don't finish this entire section, be sure that you at least answer your best questions.

The New Kid on the Block: Analysis of Explanations

For years now, the GRE has featured just two types of Analytical Ability questions: Analytical Reasoning (logic games) and Logical Reasoning. Lately, a third type has been sneaking into the unscored, experimental section. Questions in the unscored section have a nasty habit of one day turning up in the scored sections. This new style of question is called Analysis of Explanations. While this type of question *probably* won't count on your test, I want you to be prepared so you don't freak out when you see it. ("What's this? No one told me about this!") And of course, there's always the chance that this new question style *will* count by the time you get around to taking the GRE.

A 50-50 chance: The answer choices

The Analysis of Explanations questions are yes/no questions similar to the true/false exams that you took in elementary school. Here's the format.

First, you are given a situation and a result.

<u>Situation</u>: Professor Boniol of Central State University began teaching "Internet Marketing" in fall, 1992. At that time, the course was extremely popular and attracted students from all over campus. As the Internet continued to expand, Professor Boniol felt compelled to add material to his curriculum, making the course workload extremely heavy. Word got around campus that "Internal Marketing" was difficult, and the number of students taking the course steadily declined, falling to such a low level that the university was hard-pressed to justify offering the course in the future. In an attempt to preserve "Internet Marketing," the chancellor insisted that Professor Boniol change his grading policy so that anyone who completed the work in class, regardless of the work's quality, would get at least a C.

Result: One semester later, the number of people taking "Internet Marketing" with Professor Boniol was so low that he was forced to stop teaching it and began concentrating on his research.

Following the statement and result are several questions. The first set presents statements and asks whether the information in each statement is relevant to explaining how the result occurred from the situation. A statement is relevant if it strengthens *or weakens* the result. Keep the words *or weakens* in mind. As long as a statement has some influence on the result or explains it in some way, it is relevant.

Questions 1-4

If true, is the statement relevant to a possible explanation of the result? To be relevant, the statement must either support or weaken that explanation.

1. No other professor has been required to pass all his students.

2. Professor Boniol has never given below a C in his class.

3. Professor Boniol's students are all graduate students who have to get A's or B's to continue in graduate school.

4. Professors at Central State University are in no way obligated to adhere to the chancellor's request

The answer choices are either A or B. Choose A if your answer is Yes, the statement is relevant or B if the answer is No, the statement is not relevant. The answer grid will have bubbles for answers C, D, and E. Be very careful not to fill those in, especially if you're guessing. Because you are not penalized for wrong answers on the GRE, you should always go ahead and guess; even a wild, random guess can help. However, here wild guesses of C, D, and E mean nothing.

Answers and brief explanations to Questions 1-4:

1. The task is to explain why Professor Boniol had to drop his teaching of the course despite his being ordered to ease his grading policy. Other professors are irrelevant. *Correct Answer:* B.

2. One possible explanation is that students received grades lower than a C after the chancellor's intervention, keeping the course's reputation for difficulty intact. (Professor Boniol could have ignored the chancellor or added so much course work that students found it very difficult to complete all the work.) This statement weakens (remember: A relevant statement can strengthen or weaken) this explanation. *Correct Answer:* A.

3. This statement is certainly relevant to an explanation as it points out that a guaranteed C won't help the students taking the course. *Correct Answer:* A.

4. If Professor Boniol is permitted to ignore the chancellor, he may go on with a tough grading policy and cause many students to receive unsatisfactory grades. This statement is relevant to an explanation involving the continued difficulty of the course. *Correct Answer:* A.

Rumors are circulating that ETS may come up with a C answer soon for this style of question. For now, however, the choices are only A and B. I mention this simply because I know that some of you go through this book and then get involved in other things and don't take the exam for a year or two. By then, a C answer may be part of this section.

Another set of questions asks whether the statement provides the basis of an explanation of how the result came about from the situation. These statements are more directly tied to the situation and result than are relevance questions. In explanation questions, you do not have to be concerned with weakeners.

Because explanation questions are more straightforward than relevance questions, do explanation questions first even though they are presented second. Pick up the easy points first. Also, working with the explanation questions will give you a better feel of the relationship between the situation and result and make the relevance questions easier. It's possible that some of the relevance questions will play off of some of the explanation statements. Therefore, do the explanation questions first.

Questions 5-8

If true, could the following statement provide the basis of an adequate explanation of how the result came about from the situation? To be considered an adequate explanation, a statement need not be complete in all particulars.

5. All the smartest students had already taken Professor Boniol's classes; only the barely passing students were left.

6. The university hired a new professor who taught the same subject as Professor Boniol.

7. Many of Professor Boniol's students failed because they found it impossible to complete all required work.

8. The number of companies marketing on the Internet began to decline two months after the chancellor issued his edict.

Answers and brief explanations to Questions 5-8:

5. The barely passing students should still pass as long as they do the work. How is this going to explain why the enrollment numbers dropped to the point that Professor Boniol's course had to be canceled? *Correct Answer:* B.

6. This statement certainly explains why Professor Boniol was forced to stop teaching "Internet Marketing." Students flocked to other professors. *Correct Answer:* A.

7. This statement explains that the course remained difficult after the chancellor's intervention, a plausible reason for the continued decline in enrollments. *Correct Answer:* A.

8. Don't read too much into this statement. Perhaps Professor Boniol will eventually cut down on the amount of material covered in his course, but his doing so is not certain. Even in the unlikely event that he cut down the workload right away and that word of this spread, it would be even more puzzling why Professor Boniol's enrollment figures dropped. This statement makes the situation more confusing; it does not explain. *Correct Answer:* B.

Suggestions and Strategems

Spend your time reading and rereading until you thoroughly understand the situation. Don't let your pumping adrenaline send you right to the questions. Unless you've truly understood the situation, you won't be answering any questions correctly. Repeat the situation to yourself in your own words.

Decide what needs to be explained about the result. What was the result? Was it understandable or very strange? Don't go overboard on the result. If the result were, for example, that a new tax failed in Indiana, don't assume that all similar taxes failed in states throughout the country.

Predict explanations or relevant factors. Use your common sense. What would make this situation happen? What types of factors would you expect to see leading up to the result?

Treat each question separately. Don't carry over info from one statement to another. After you finish with a question, it's history.

All Good Things Must End: Review

The Analytical Ability portion of the GRE has two types of questions: Analytical Reasoning (also called logic games) and Logical Reasoning (also called Critical Reasoning or Critical Thinking). A third type, Analysis of Explanations, *may* be in the unscored section (meaning it won't count).

Analytical Reasoning

When you encounter an Analytical Reasoning question, remember the following:

Approach

- ✔ Three to seven questions are based on a set of statements.
- ✔ Make a pool of the people or events in the game.
- ✔ Read the *entire* game first and then make a diagram showing the relationship between the set of statements.

Tricks

- ✔ Focus on an *always/never* statement.
- ✔ Be alert to different contingencies.
- ✔ Don't confuse forward and backward.

Logical Reasoning

These tips can help you to survive (triumph over!) the Logical Reasoning questions.

- ✔ Carefully — and suspiciously — read short (two-to-five sentence) but often confusing paragraphs.
- ✔ Identify what the question is asking for: an assumption, a strengthening/weakening statement, and so on.
- ✔ Do the Logical Reasoning questions first, as most people consider them easier than the Analytical Reasoning questions (logic games).

Analysis of Explanations

This new style of question is currently found in the unscored/experimental section of the exam; it may be counted soon. Here's an overview of the new kid on the block:

- ✔ Answer choices are either A (yes) or B (no). A choice C may soon be integrated into this exam.
- ✔ Questions are based on a situation and a result. You are asked to identify whether something is relevant to the result or whether the statement is adequate to explain the result.
- ✔ Something is relevant to the result whether it strengthens or weakens that result.

Chapter 18

Just How Logical Are You? Analytical Ability Practice Questions

• •

*N*ow you have your chance to see whether your parents were right when they yelled at you all those years, "Sometimes you make no sense at all!" Use your logic and reasoning skills to answer the following questions.

The good news here (besides the fact that a lot of schools don't even count this analytical section) is that Analytical Ability questions have fewer traps than the rest of the GRE. For a change, you can actually use your common sense and answer these questions directly without having to be paranoid and insecure.

Questions 1–3 are based on the following information.

An independent television station shows movies every day of the week between 8 and 10 p.m. One week, the station must decide on which days it will show movies of the following genres: one western, one romance, two dramas, and three comedies. The selections must conform to the following conditions:

> The western must be shown later in the week than the romance.
>
> A comedy is shown on Wednesday.
>
> The romance may not be shown the night before or night after a drama is shown.
>
> Comedies may not be shown three nights in a row.

ANALYSIS. This game involves arranging a sequence for a given week. A good way to keep track of the information is to draw a calendar for the week.

Su	M	Tu	W	Th	F	Sa
—	—	—	—	—	—	—

You don't really need to label the blanks, given your familiarity with calendars, but doing so may help you to place the movies faster.

Next, go to the rule(s) that can easily be incorporated into the diagram. You don't have to follow the rules in order; start with the one that is the simplest to diagram.

The second rule may be represented as follows:

Su	M	Tu	W	Th	F	Sa
__	__	__	C	__	__	__

Summarize the rule about westerns and romances (westerns must be shown later in the week than romances) by writing something on the order of "R, then W. Not W, then R." This information allows you to deduce, for example, that westerns (W) may not be shown on Sunday and romances (R) on Saturday or else the rule would be violated. Show this on your diagram as follows:

Su	M	Tu	W	Th	F	Sa
__	__	__	C	__	__	__

R, then W. Not W, then R.

Summarize the other two rules by jotting a quick note, such as "no Ð, then R and no R, then Ð" and "no Є, then Є, then Є." Now you've put all the info from words into diagrams or quick notes, and you are ready to tackle the questions.

1. Which of the following is an acceptable lineup for the week's movies?

   (A) drama, western, drama, comedy, romance, comedy, comedy

   (B) comedy, comedy, romance, western, drama, drama, comedy

   (C) comedy, comedy, drama, comedy, romance, drama, western

   (D) drama, drama, comedy, comedy, comedy, romance, western

   (E) drama, comedy, drama, comedy, comedy, romance, western

On the GRE, often the first question after a game simply asks you for the order of an arrangement. Usually, the best way to answer this question is by the process of elimination. The test maker has done all the work for you. You know that one of the sequences must be correct while all the others have at least one thing wrong with them. The best way to approach such a question is to take one rule at a time and eliminate the choice(s) that violate it.

Because W must be after R, choice A is out. No Ð, then R and no R, then Ð? Get rid of choice C. No Є, then Є, then Є? Eliminate choice D. Finally, knock out choice B because a C is not shown on Wednesday. Only the correct answer, choice E, is left. *Correct Answer:* E.

2. If the romance is shown on Friday, which of the following is *not* necessarily true?

   (A) The romance is shown after all the comedies have been shown.

   (B) A comedy is shown on Sunday.

   (C) The western is shown on Saturday.

   (D) Comedies are shown on consecutive nights.

   (E) Both dramas are shown in the first half of the week.

Take the information in the question and add it to your diagram: *Correct Answer:* B.

Su	M	Tu	W	Th	F	Sa
__	__	__	C	__	R	__

R, then W. Not W, then R.

With the R on Friday, the W must shown on Saturday:

Su	M	Tu	W	Th	F	Sa
__	__	__	C	__	R	W

The only movies left are D and D and C and C. Given that D may not go next to R, C must be on Thursday:

Su	M	Tu	W	Th	F	Sa
__	__	__	C	C	R	W

You can't use C, then C, then C, so put a D in Tuesday:

Su	M	Tu	W	Th	F	Sa
__	__	D	C	C	R	W

This is as far as you can go. C can go in Sunday, and D is shown on Monday **or vice versa.**

When you have two options, be sure to keep track of both of them. You frequently encounter questions in which you can have two possibilities; don't arbitrarily choose one. In this case, B may be true, but it is not *necessarily* true. If you are unsure, check the remaining choices. A quick check reveals that the other choices are *definitely* true.

3. If the western is shown the night immediately before the first comedy of the week, how many different sequences of movie genres are possible?

   (A) two

   (B) three

   (C) four

   (D) five

   (E) six

You know that W cannot be shown on Sunday. Because it has to be shown the night before the first comedy, this leaves two possibilities for the western: Monday or Tuesday. See what happens with W on Monday:

Su	M	Tu	W	Th	F	Sa
__	W	C	C	__	__	__

(C is on Tuesday because the W is shown the immediately preceding night.)

Because of "R, then W," R must be shown on Sunday:

Su	M	Tu	W	Th	F	Sa
R	W	C	C	__	__	__

Because of "no C, then C, then C," a D must be shown on Thursday:

Su	M	Tu	W	Th	F	Sa
R	W	C	C	D	__	__

You have two possibilities: D on Friday, and C on Saturday **or vice versa.** This does not make the answer choice A, however. You still have to see what happens with W on Tuesday:

Su	M	Tu	W	Th	F	Sa
—	—	W	C	—	—	—

With this setup, R could go on Sunday:

Su	M	Tu	W	Th	F	Sa
R	—	W	C	—	—	—

Because W must be shown the night before the first C, you can place D only on Monday:

Su	M	Tu	W	Th	F	Sa
R	D	W	C	—	—	—

Now what? "No C, then C, then C," means that the two remaining Cs may be shown on Thursday and Saturday **or** Friday and Saturday. The remaining D simply fills in the night not taken by the Cs. All this produces two more possible sequences, so you're up to four. However (sorry about this!), you are not finished even now. What if R is shown on Monday?

Su	M	Tu	W	Th	F	Sa
—	R	W	C	—	—	—

Put a D in Sunday because W must be shown before the first C.

Su	M	Tu	W	Th	F	Sa
D	R	W	C	—	—	—

Once again, you have two options: Show a C on Thursday and a C on Saturday or show the Cs on Friday and Saturday. These two options bring the total to six, making choice E the answer. *Correct Answer:* E.

 4. *Ricardo:* My wife and I tried to get marital counseling. The counselors who could see us were too expensive, and the counselors whose fees were reasonable were too busy to fit us into their schedules. My wife and I have decided that counseling cannot help us.

Which of the following statements, if true, would most weaken, Ricardo's conclusion?

(A) Marital counseling succeeds only with motivated people who are willing to do the exercises and role-playing suggested by the counselors.

(B) People who go to expensive counselors have better results than those who go to more moderately priced counselors.

(C) Ricardo and his wife will eventually find an affordable counselor who has time for them.

(D) Husbands are often more critical of marital counseling than are wives, who are willing to continue even when frustrated.

(E) Counselors are only human and cannot be as unbiased as they would like to be as they have feelings of their own.

First, identify the conclusion. It is that counseling can't help Ricardo and his wife. Ricardo uses his current inability to find a counselor to leap to this conclusion. He assumes that his wife and he will never see a counselor. The best way to weaken an argument is to contradict the assumption. Choice C does just this. This choice points out that Ricardo can't use the current unavailability of counselors to make a conclusion about future effectiveness.

Eliminate choices D and E right away because they do nothing to indicate that counseling might succeed, which is necessary to contradict Ricardo's conclusion. If you're in a rush and don't have time to figure out the answer, you can guess among choices A, B, and C. *Correct Answer:* C.

5. *Mr. Janowski:* Adolescents should be steered away from a career in dentistry. There are so many breakthroughs in cavity prevention today that the need for a dentist will soon be minimal.

Mrs. Hogan: That's true. The last time I went to a dentist it wasn't for a cavity at all but to get an implant when I knocked my tooth out playing street hockey with my son.

Which of the following may be said of Mrs. Hogan's comment?

(A) It contradicts the point made by Mr. Janowski.

(B) It gives an example that supports the assumption made by Mr. Janowski.

(C) It assumes facts not in evidence.

(D) It redefines terms.

(E) It uses an invalid definition to buttress a weak assumption.

Mrs. Hogan appears to agree with what Mr. Janowski says, but her words in fact contradict his conclusion. He is saying that dentists are not necessary because children no longer get cavities. She shows that a dentist has functions other than to fill a cavity, thus disproving his statement that dentists are no longer necessary.

If you chose B, you fell for the trap. You probably read the "That's true" uttered by Mrs. Hogan and got no further. Reading the whole statement would tell you that while she thought she was agreeing with Mr. Janowski, she was proving his premise wrong.

Choice C means nothing. What facts? What evidence? If you chose this answer, you went for the "best-sounding" choice, the one that sounded the most pretentious and analytical. Choices D and E are wrong because there are no definitions given in the passage, let alone redefined or defined incorrectly. *Correct Answer:* A.

6. Fraud is the intentional misrepresentation upon which a person is intended to rely and upon which he does rely to his detriment. If a person is accidentally misled and suffers an injury (for example, if he is given erroneous financial advice), he may not sue for fraud. If a person relies on something that he was never supposed to find out, the person making the false statement that was not meant to be overheard is not liable for fraud because there was no intentional misrepresentation. Similarly, if the person were intended to rely on the information, and did, but actually benefited from the information, there is no fraud because there was no detrimental effect of the reliance.

Which of the following is best supported by the information above?

(A) If even one element of those required for fraud is absent, there is no fraud.

(B) If an investor loses money after being advised to invest in a restaurant by its new owner, the restaurant owner is not guilty of fraud.

(C) An assembly-line worker warns a machinist that the machinist is about to be fired. If the machinist quits and finds a new job that pays less than half of what he made before, the machinist can rightfully sue the assembly-line worker for fraud.

(D) If there is harm from relying on the information, but the harm eventually turns to gain, there is no fraud.

(E) A physician tells a patient to take some medication and exercise regularly to improve her physical condition. If the patient takes the medication but the condition worsens, the patient has a legitimate case of fraud against the physician.

The passage gives the elements that make up fraud and then provides examples of how not having those elements negates the fraud. Choice B does not necessarily follow from the stimulus because the restaurant owner may have intentionally misled the investor by providing bogus reports of the restaurant's financial health, status, and so on. Choice C is out because the assembly-line worker's information was probably accurate. In addition, the machinist is likely better-off with his new job than he would have been had he stayed and been fired (although unemployment benefits may have been substantial). Choice D is a little tougher to eliminate. The passage does say that there is no fraud if there is no harm. However, it does not say that there is no fraud if the harm eventually turns to gain. Be very careful not to take the information and make more of it than is there. Choice E is no good because the physician may have given very sound advice. The most obvious potential problem is that the patient did not follow the physician's advice regarding exercise. *Correct Answer:* A.

Part VI
It All Comes Down to This: Full-Length Practice GREs

In this part . . .

*J*ust when you think your brain can't be stuffed with one more factoid, relief is at hand. You finally get to download some of the information you've been inputting for the past 18 chapters. Trust me; you'll feel better when you let it all out.

This unit has two full-length exams that are as close to the actual GRE as I can get without having briefcase-bearing barristers battering on my door. I take these tests seriously, and you should, too — do them under actual test conditions, sitting in a quiet room and timing yourself. Open books are definitely out (sorry!). I have spies everywhere; I'll know if you cheat on these tests. There will be a knocking at your door one foggy night. . . . After you've done your duty on these two practice exams, you'll have a good time going through the answer explanations, which are nowhere near as dry and stuffy as the exam itself.

Chapter 19

How to Ruin a Perfectly Good Day, Part I: Practice Exam 1

● ●

*Y*ou are now ready to take a sample GRE. The following exam consists of six 30-minute sections. (The actual GRE has seven sections, but one of them is experimental and doesn't count. Here I won't put you through any more anguish and agony than absolutely necessary. You're welcome.) Two sections are verbal, two are math, and two are analytical. You are familiar with the question formats by now.

Please take this test under normal exam conditions. This is serious stuff here!

1. **Sit where you won't be interrupted (even though you'd probably welcome any distractions).**

2. **Use the answer grid provided.**

3. **Set your alarm clock for the 30-minute intervals.**

4. **Do not go on to the next section until the time allotted for the section you are taking is up.**

5. **If you finish early, check your work for that section only.**

6. **Do not take a break during any one section.**

7. **Give yourself one ten-minute break between sections 2 and 3 and a second ten-minute break between sections 4 and 5.**

When you complete the entire test, check your answers with the answer key at the end of this chapter. You will find a section at the end of Chapter 21 explaining your score.

Go through the answer explanations to ALL the questions, not just the ones you missed. There is a plethora of worthwhile information there, material that provides a good review of everything you've learned in the lectures. I've even tossed in a few good jokes to keep you somewhat sane.

Answer Sheet

Begin with Number 1 for each new section. If any sections have fewer than 50 questions, leave the extra spaces blank.

Section 1	Section 2	Section 3	Section 4
1. Ⓐ Ⓑ Ⓒ Ⓓ Ⓔ	1. Ⓐ Ⓑ Ⓒ Ⓓ Ⓔ	1. Ⓐ Ⓑ Ⓒ Ⓓ Ⓔ	1. Ⓐ Ⓑ Ⓒ Ⓓ Ⓔ
2. Ⓐ Ⓑ Ⓒ Ⓓ Ⓔ	2. Ⓐ Ⓑ Ⓒ Ⓓ Ⓔ	2. Ⓐ Ⓑ Ⓒ Ⓓ Ⓔ	2. Ⓐ Ⓑ Ⓒ Ⓓ Ⓔ
3. Ⓐ Ⓑ Ⓒ Ⓓ Ⓔ	3. Ⓐ Ⓑ Ⓒ Ⓓ Ⓔ	3. Ⓐ Ⓑ Ⓒ Ⓓ Ⓔ	3. Ⓐ Ⓑ Ⓒ Ⓓ Ⓔ
4. Ⓐ Ⓑ Ⓒ Ⓓ Ⓔ	4. Ⓐ Ⓑ Ⓒ Ⓓ Ⓔ	4. Ⓐ Ⓑ Ⓒ Ⓓ Ⓔ	4. Ⓐ Ⓑ Ⓒ Ⓓ Ⓔ
5. Ⓐ Ⓑ Ⓒ Ⓓ Ⓔ	5. Ⓐ Ⓑ Ⓒ Ⓓ Ⓔ	5. Ⓐ Ⓑ Ⓒ Ⓓ Ⓔ	5. Ⓐ Ⓑ Ⓒ Ⓓ Ⓔ
6. Ⓐ Ⓑ Ⓒ Ⓓ Ⓔ	6. Ⓐ Ⓑ Ⓒ Ⓓ Ⓔ	6. Ⓐ Ⓑ Ⓒ Ⓓ Ⓔ	6. Ⓐ Ⓑ Ⓒ Ⓓ Ⓔ
7. Ⓐ Ⓑ Ⓒ Ⓓ Ⓔ	7. Ⓐ Ⓑ Ⓒ Ⓓ Ⓔ	7. Ⓐ Ⓑ Ⓒ Ⓓ Ⓔ	7. Ⓐ Ⓑ Ⓒ Ⓓ Ⓔ
8. Ⓐ Ⓑ Ⓒ Ⓓ Ⓔ	8. Ⓐ Ⓑ Ⓒ Ⓓ Ⓔ	8. Ⓐ Ⓑ Ⓒ Ⓓ Ⓔ	8. Ⓐ Ⓑ Ⓒ Ⓓ Ⓔ
9. Ⓐ Ⓑ Ⓒ Ⓓ Ⓔ	9. Ⓐ Ⓑ Ⓒ Ⓓ Ⓔ	9. Ⓐ Ⓑ Ⓒ Ⓓ Ⓔ	9. Ⓐ Ⓑ Ⓒ Ⓓ Ⓔ
10. Ⓐ Ⓑ Ⓒ Ⓓ Ⓔ	10. Ⓐ Ⓑ Ⓒ Ⓓ Ⓔ	10. Ⓐ Ⓑ Ⓒ Ⓓ Ⓔ	10. Ⓐ Ⓑ Ⓒ Ⓓ Ⓔ
11. Ⓐ Ⓑ Ⓒ Ⓓ Ⓔ	11. Ⓐ Ⓑ Ⓒ Ⓓ Ⓔ	11. Ⓐ Ⓑ Ⓒ Ⓓ Ⓔ	11. Ⓐ Ⓑ Ⓒ Ⓓ Ⓔ
12. Ⓐ Ⓑ Ⓒ Ⓓ Ⓔ	12. Ⓐ Ⓑ Ⓒ Ⓓ Ⓔ	12. Ⓐ Ⓑ Ⓒ Ⓓ Ⓔ	12. Ⓐ Ⓑ Ⓒ Ⓓ Ⓔ
13. Ⓐ Ⓑ Ⓒ Ⓓ Ⓔ	13. Ⓐ Ⓑ Ⓒ Ⓓ Ⓔ	13. Ⓐ Ⓑ Ⓒ Ⓓ Ⓔ	13. Ⓐ Ⓑ Ⓒ Ⓓ Ⓔ
14. Ⓐ Ⓑ Ⓒ Ⓓ Ⓔ	14. Ⓐ Ⓑ Ⓒ Ⓓ Ⓔ	14. Ⓐ Ⓑ Ⓒ Ⓓ Ⓔ	14. Ⓐ Ⓑ Ⓒ Ⓓ Ⓔ
15. Ⓐ Ⓑ Ⓒ Ⓓ Ⓔ	15. Ⓐ Ⓑ Ⓒ Ⓓ Ⓔ	15. Ⓐ Ⓑ Ⓒ Ⓓ Ⓔ	15. Ⓐ Ⓑ Ⓒ Ⓓ Ⓔ
16. Ⓐ Ⓑ Ⓒ Ⓓ Ⓔ	16. Ⓐ Ⓑ Ⓒ Ⓓ Ⓔ	16. Ⓐ Ⓑ Ⓒ Ⓓ Ⓔ	16. Ⓐ Ⓑ Ⓒ Ⓓ Ⓔ
17. Ⓐ Ⓑ Ⓒ Ⓓ Ⓔ	17. Ⓐ Ⓑ Ⓒ Ⓓ Ⓔ	17. Ⓐ Ⓑ Ⓒ Ⓓ Ⓔ	17. Ⓐ Ⓑ Ⓒ Ⓓ Ⓔ
18. Ⓐ Ⓑ Ⓒ Ⓓ Ⓔ	18. Ⓐ Ⓑ Ⓒ Ⓓ Ⓔ	18. Ⓐ Ⓑ Ⓒ Ⓓ Ⓔ	18. Ⓐ Ⓑ Ⓒ Ⓓ Ⓔ
19. Ⓐ Ⓑ Ⓒ Ⓓ Ⓔ	19. Ⓐ Ⓑ Ⓒ Ⓓ Ⓔ	19. Ⓐ Ⓑ Ⓒ Ⓓ Ⓔ	19. Ⓐ Ⓑ Ⓒ Ⓓ Ⓔ
20. Ⓐ Ⓑ Ⓒ Ⓓ Ⓔ	20. Ⓐ Ⓑ Ⓒ Ⓓ Ⓔ	20. Ⓐ Ⓑ Ⓒ Ⓓ Ⓔ	20. Ⓐ Ⓑ Ⓒ Ⓓ Ⓔ
21. Ⓐ Ⓑ Ⓒ Ⓓ Ⓔ	21. Ⓐ Ⓑ Ⓒ Ⓓ Ⓔ	21. Ⓐ Ⓑ Ⓒ Ⓓ Ⓔ	21. Ⓐ Ⓑ Ⓒ Ⓓ Ⓔ
22. Ⓐ Ⓑ Ⓒ Ⓓ Ⓔ	22. Ⓐ Ⓑ Ⓒ Ⓓ Ⓔ	22. Ⓐ Ⓑ Ⓒ Ⓓ Ⓔ	22. Ⓐ Ⓑ Ⓒ Ⓓ Ⓔ
23. Ⓐ Ⓑ Ⓒ Ⓓ Ⓔ	23. Ⓐ Ⓑ Ⓒ Ⓓ Ⓔ	23. Ⓐ Ⓑ Ⓒ Ⓓ Ⓔ	23. Ⓐ Ⓑ Ⓒ Ⓓ Ⓔ
24. Ⓐ Ⓑ Ⓒ Ⓓ Ⓔ	24. Ⓐ Ⓑ Ⓒ Ⓓ Ⓔ	24. Ⓐ Ⓑ Ⓒ Ⓓ Ⓔ	24. Ⓐ Ⓑ Ⓒ Ⓓ Ⓔ
25. Ⓐ Ⓑ Ⓒ Ⓓ Ⓔ	25. Ⓐ Ⓑ Ⓒ Ⓓ Ⓔ	25. Ⓐ Ⓑ Ⓒ Ⓓ Ⓔ	25. Ⓐ Ⓑ Ⓒ Ⓓ Ⓔ
26. Ⓐ Ⓑ Ⓒ Ⓓ Ⓔ	26. Ⓐ Ⓑ Ⓒ Ⓓ Ⓔ	26. Ⓐ Ⓑ Ⓒ Ⓓ Ⓔ	26. Ⓐ Ⓑ Ⓒ Ⓓ Ⓔ
27. Ⓐ Ⓑ Ⓒ Ⓓ Ⓔ	27. Ⓐ Ⓑ Ⓒ Ⓓ Ⓔ	27. Ⓐ Ⓑ Ⓒ Ⓓ Ⓔ	27. Ⓐ Ⓑ Ⓒ Ⓓ Ⓔ
28. Ⓐ Ⓑ Ⓒ Ⓓ Ⓔ	28. Ⓐ Ⓑ Ⓒ Ⓓ Ⓔ	28. Ⓐ Ⓑ Ⓒ Ⓓ Ⓔ	28. Ⓐ Ⓑ Ⓒ Ⓓ Ⓔ
29. Ⓐ Ⓑ Ⓒ Ⓓ Ⓔ	29. Ⓐ Ⓑ Ⓒ Ⓓ Ⓔ	29. Ⓐ Ⓑ Ⓒ Ⓓ Ⓔ	29. Ⓐ Ⓑ Ⓒ Ⓓ Ⓔ
30. Ⓐ Ⓑ Ⓒ Ⓓ Ⓔ	30. Ⓐ Ⓑ Ⓒ Ⓓ Ⓔ	30. Ⓐ Ⓑ Ⓒ Ⓓ Ⓔ	30. Ⓐ Ⓑ Ⓒ Ⓓ Ⓔ
31. Ⓐ Ⓑ Ⓒ Ⓓ Ⓔ	31. Ⓐ Ⓑ Ⓒ Ⓓ Ⓔ	31. Ⓐ Ⓑ Ⓒ Ⓓ Ⓔ	31. Ⓐ Ⓑ Ⓒ Ⓓ Ⓔ
32. Ⓐ Ⓑ Ⓒ Ⓓ Ⓔ	32. Ⓐ Ⓑ Ⓒ Ⓓ Ⓔ	32. Ⓐ Ⓑ Ⓒ Ⓓ Ⓔ	32. Ⓐ Ⓑ Ⓒ Ⓓ Ⓔ
33. Ⓐ Ⓑ Ⓒ Ⓓ Ⓔ	33. Ⓐ Ⓑ Ⓒ Ⓓ Ⓔ	33. Ⓐ Ⓑ Ⓒ Ⓓ Ⓔ	33. Ⓐ Ⓑ Ⓒ Ⓓ Ⓔ
34. Ⓐ Ⓑ Ⓒ Ⓓ Ⓔ	34. Ⓐ Ⓑ Ⓒ Ⓓ Ⓔ	34. Ⓐ Ⓑ Ⓒ Ⓓ Ⓔ	34. Ⓐ Ⓑ Ⓒ Ⓓ Ⓔ
35. Ⓐ Ⓑ Ⓒ Ⓓ Ⓔ	35. Ⓐ Ⓑ Ⓒ Ⓓ Ⓔ	35. Ⓐ Ⓑ Ⓒ Ⓓ Ⓔ	35. Ⓐ Ⓑ Ⓒ Ⓓ Ⓔ
36. Ⓐ Ⓑ Ⓒ Ⓓ Ⓔ	36. Ⓐ Ⓑ Ⓒ Ⓓ Ⓔ	36. Ⓐ Ⓑ Ⓒ Ⓓ Ⓔ	36. Ⓐ Ⓑ Ⓒ Ⓓ Ⓔ
37. Ⓐ Ⓑ Ⓒ Ⓓ Ⓔ	37. Ⓐ Ⓑ Ⓒ Ⓓ Ⓔ	37. Ⓐ Ⓑ Ⓒ Ⓓ Ⓔ	37. Ⓐ Ⓑ Ⓒ Ⓓ Ⓔ
38. Ⓐ Ⓑ Ⓒ Ⓓ Ⓔ	38. Ⓐ Ⓑ Ⓒ Ⓓ Ⓔ	38. Ⓐ Ⓑ Ⓒ Ⓓ Ⓔ	38. Ⓐ Ⓑ Ⓒ Ⓓ Ⓔ
39. Ⓐ Ⓑ Ⓒ Ⓓ Ⓔ	39. Ⓐ Ⓑ Ⓒ Ⓓ Ⓔ	39. Ⓐ Ⓑ Ⓒ Ⓓ Ⓔ	39. Ⓐ Ⓑ Ⓒ Ⓓ Ⓔ
40. Ⓐ Ⓑ Ⓒ Ⓓ Ⓔ	40. Ⓐ Ⓑ Ⓒ Ⓓ Ⓔ	40. Ⓐ Ⓑ Ⓒ Ⓓ Ⓔ	40. Ⓐ Ⓑ Ⓒ Ⓓ Ⓔ
41. Ⓐ Ⓑ Ⓒ Ⓓ Ⓔ	41. Ⓐ Ⓑ Ⓒ Ⓓ Ⓔ	41. Ⓐ Ⓑ Ⓒ Ⓓ Ⓔ	41. Ⓐ Ⓑ Ⓒ Ⓓ Ⓔ
42. Ⓐ Ⓑ Ⓒ Ⓓ Ⓔ	42. Ⓐ Ⓑ Ⓒ Ⓓ Ⓔ	42. Ⓐ Ⓑ Ⓒ Ⓓ Ⓔ	42. Ⓐ Ⓑ Ⓒ Ⓓ Ⓔ
43. Ⓐ Ⓑ Ⓒ Ⓓ Ⓔ	43. Ⓐ Ⓑ Ⓒ Ⓓ Ⓔ	43. Ⓐ Ⓑ Ⓒ Ⓓ Ⓔ	43. Ⓐ Ⓑ Ⓒ Ⓓ Ⓔ
44. Ⓐ Ⓑ Ⓒ Ⓓ Ⓔ	44. Ⓐ Ⓑ Ⓒ Ⓓ Ⓔ	44. Ⓐ Ⓑ Ⓒ Ⓓ Ⓔ	44. Ⓐ Ⓑ Ⓒ Ⓓ Ⓔ
45. Ⓐ Ⓑ Ⓒ Ⓓ Ⓔ	45. Ⓐ Ⓑ Ⓒ Ⓓ Ⓔ	45. Ⓐ Ⓑ Ⓒ Ⓓ Ⓔ	45. Ⓐ Ⓑ Ⓒ Ⓓ Ⓔ
46. Ⓐ Ⓑ Ⓒ Ⓓ Ⓔ	46. Ⓐ Ⓑ Ⓒ Ⓓ Ⓔ	46. Ⓐ Ⓑ Ⓒ Ⓓ Ⓔ	46. Ⓐ Ⓑ Ⓒ Ⓓ Ⓔ
47. Ⓐ Ⓑ Ⓒ Ⓓ Ⓔ	47. Ⓐ Ⓑ Ⓒ Ⓓ Ⓔ	47. Ⓐ Ⓑ Ⓒ Ⓓ Ⓔ	47. Ⓐ Ⓑ Ⓒ Ⓓ Ⓔ
48. Ⓐ Ⓑ Ⓒ Ⓓ Ⓔ	48. Ⓐ Ⓑ Ⓒ Ⓓ Ⓔ	48. Ⓐ Ⓑ Ⓒ Ⓓ Ⓔ	48. Ⓐ Ⓑ Ⓒ Ⓓ Ⓔ
49. Ⓐ Ⓑ Ⓒ Ⓓ Ⓔ	49. Ⓐ Ⓑ Ⓒ Ⓓ Ⓔ	49. Ⓐ Ⓑ Ⓒ Ⓓ Ⓔ	49. Ⓐ Ⓑ Ⓒ Ⓓ Ⓔ
50. Ⓐ Ⓑ Ⓒ Ⓓ Ⓔ	50. Ⓐ Ⓑ Ⓒ Ⓓ Ⓔ	50. Ⓐ Ⓑ Ⓒ Ⓓ Ⓔ	50. Ⓐ Ⓑ Ⓒ Ⓓ Ⓔ

Section 5

1. Ⓐ Ⓑ Ⓒ Ⓓ Ⓔ
2. Ⓐ Ⓑ Ⓒ Ⓓ Ⓔ
3. Ⓐ Ⓑ Ⓒ Ⓓ Ⓔ
4. Ⓐ Ⓑ Ⓒ Ⓓ Ⓔ
5. Ⓐ Ⓑ Ⓒ Ⓓ Ⓔ
6. Ⓐ Ⓑ Ⓒ Ⓓ Ⓔ
7. Ⓐ Ⓑ Ⓒ Ⓓ Ⓔ
8. Ⓐ Ⓑ Ⓒ Ⓓ Ⓔ
9. Ⓐ Ⓑ Ⓒ Ⓓ Ⓔ
10. Ⓐ Ⓑ Ⓒ Ⓓ Ⓔ
11. Ⓐ Ⓑ Ⓒ Ⓓ Ⓔ
12. Ⓐ Ⓑ Ⓒ Ⓓ Ⓔ
13. Ⓐ Ⓑ Ⓒ Ⓓ Ⓔ
14. Ⓐ Ⓑ Ⓒ Ⓓ Ⓔ
15. Ⓐ Ⓑ Ⓒ Ⓓ Ⓔ
16. Ⓐ Ⓑ Ⓒ Ⓓ Ⓔ
17. Ⓐ Ⓑ Ⓒ Ⓓ Ⓔ
18. Ⓐ Ⓑ Ⓒ Ⓓ Ⓔ
19. Ⓐ Ⓑ Ⓒ Ⓓ Ⓔ
20. Ⓐ Ⓑ Ⓒ Ⓓ Ⓔ
21. Ⓐ Ⓑ Ⓒ Ⓓ Ⓔ
22. Ⓐ Ⓑ Ⓒ Ⓓ Ⓔ
23. Ⓐ Ⓑ Ⓒ Ⓓ Ⓔ
24. Ⓐ Ⓑ Ⓒ Ⓓ Ⓔ
25. Ⓐ Ⓑ Ⓒ Ⓓ Ⓔ
26. Ⓐ Ⓑ Ⓒ Ⓓ Ⓔ
27. Ⓐ Ⓑ Ⓒ Ⓓ Ⓔ
28. Ⓐ Ⓑ Ⓒ Ⓓ Ⓔ
29. Ⓐ Ⓑ Ⓒ Ⓓ Ⓔ
30. Ⓐ Ⓑ Ⓒ Ⓓ Ⓔ
31. Ⓐ Ⓑ Ⓒ Ⓓ Ⓔ
32. Ⓐ Ⓑ Ⓒ Ⓓ Ⓔ
33. Ⓐ Ⓑ Ⓒ Ⓓ Ⓔ
34. Ⓐ Ⓑ Ⓒ Ⓓ Ⓔ
35. Ⓐ Ⓑ Ⓒ Ⓓ Ⓔ
36. Ⓐ Ⓑ Ⓒ Ⓓ Ⓔ
37. Ⓐ Ⓑ Ⓒ Ⓓ Ⓔ
38. Ⓐ Ⓑ Ⓒ Ⓓ Ⓔ
39. Ⓐ Ⓑ Ⓒ Ⓓ Ⓔ
40. Ⓐ Ⓑ Ⓒ Ⓓ Ⓔ
41. Ⓐ Ⓑ Ⓒ Ⓓ Ⓔ
42. Ⓐ Ⓑ Ⓒ Ⓓ Ⓔ
43. Ⓐ Ⓑ Ⓒ Ⓓ Ⓔ
44. Ⓐ Ⓑ Ⓒ Ⓓ Ⓔ
45. Ⓐ Ⓑ Ⓒ Ⓓ Ⓔ
46. Ⓐ Ⓑ Ⓒ Ⓓ Ⓔ
47. Ⓐ Ⓑ Ⓒ Ⓓ Ⓔ
48. Ⓐ Ⓑ Ⓒ Ⓓ Ⓔ
49. Ⓐ Ⓑ Ⓒ Ⓓ Ⓔ
50. Ⓐ Ⓑ Ⓒ Ⓓ Ⓔ

Section 6

1. Ⓐ Ⓑ Ⓒ Ⓓ Ⓔ
2. Ⓐ Ⓑ Ⓒ Ⓓ Ⓔ
3. Ⓐ Ⓑ Ⓒ Ⓓ Ⓔ
4. Ⓐ Ⓑ Ⓒ Ⓓ Ⓔ
5. Ⓐ Ⓑ Ⓒ Ⓓ Ⓔ
6. Ⓐ Ⓑ Ⓒ Ⓓ Ⓔ
7. Ⓐ Ⓑ Ⓒ Ⓓ Ⓔ
8. Ⓐ Ⓑ Ⓒ Ⓓ Ⓔ
9. Ⓐ Ⓑ Ⓒ Ⓓ Ⓔ
10. Ⓐ Ⓑ Ⓒ Ⓓ Ⓔ
11. Ⓐ Ⓑ Ⓒ Ⓓ Ⓔ
12. Ⓐ Ⓑ Ⓒ Ⓓ Ⓔ
13. Ⓐ Ⓑ Ⓒ Ⓓ Ⓔ
14. Ⓐ Ⓑ Ⓒ Ⓓ Ⓔ
15. Ⓐ Ⓑ Ⓒ Ⓓ Ⓔ
16. Ⓐ Ⓑ Ⓒ Ⓓ Ⓔ
17. Ⓐ Ⓑ Ⓒ Ⓓ Ⓔ
18. Ⓐ Ⓑ Ⓒ Ⓓ Ⓔ
19. Ⓐ Ⓑ Ⓒ Ⓓ Ⓔ
20. Ⓐ Ⓑ Ⓒ Ⓓ Ⓔ
21. Ⓐ Ⓑ Ⓒ Ⓓ Ⓔ
22. Ⓐ Ⓑ Ⓒ Ⓓ Ⓔ
23. Ⓐ Ⓑ Ⓒ Ⓓ Ⓔ
24. Ⓐ Ⓑ Ⓒ Ⓓ Ⓔ
25. Ⓐ Ⓑ Ⓒ Ⓓ Ⓔ
26. Ⓐ Ⓑ Ⓒ Ⓓ Ⓔ
27. Ⓐ Ⓑ Ⓒ Ⓓ Ⓔ
28. Ⓐ Ⓑ Ⓒ Ⓓ Ⓔ
29. Ⓐ Ⓑ Ⓒ Ⓓ Ⓔ
30. Ⓐ Ⓑ Ⓒ Ⓓ Ⓔ
31. Ⓐ Ⓑ Ⓒ Ⓓ Ⓔ
32. Ⓐ Ⓑ Ⓒ Ⓓ Ⓔ
33. Ⓐ Ⓑ Ⓒ Ⓓ Ⓔ
34. Ⓐ Ⓑ Ⓒ Ⓓ Ⓔ
35. Ⓐ Ⓑ Ⓒ Ⓓ Ⓔ
36. Ⓐ Ⓑ Ⓒ Ⓓ Ⓔ
37. Ⓐ Ⓑ Ⓒ Ⓓ Ⓔ
38. Ⓐ Ⓑ Ⓒ Ⓓ Ⓔ
39. Ⓐ Ⓑ Ⓒ Ⓓ Ⓔ
40. Ⓐ Ⓑ Ⓒ Ⓓ Ⓔ
41. Ⓐ Ⓑ Ⓒ Ⓓ Ⓔ
42. Ⓐ Ⓑ Ⓒ Ⓓ Ⓔ
43. Ⓐ Ⓑ Ⓒ Ⓓ Ⓔ
44. Ⓐ Ⓑ Ⓒ Ⓓ Ⓔ
45. Ⓐ Ⓑ Ⓒ Ⓓ Ⓔ
46. Ⓐ Ⓑ Ⓒ Ⓓ Ⓔ
47. Ⓐ Ⓑ Ⓒ Ⓓ Ⓔ
48. Ⓐ Ⓑ Ⓒ Ⓓ Ⓔ
49. Ⓐ Ⓑ Ⓒ Ⓓ Ⓔ
50. Ⓐ Ⓑ Ⓒ Ⓓ Ⓔ

Section 1

Time: 30 minutes

38 questions

Choose the best answer to each question. Blacken the corresponding oval on the answer grid.

Directions: Each of the following sentences has one or two blanks indicating that words or phrases are omitted. Choose the answer that best completes the sentence.

1. Unable to complete the project yet ---- to admit defeat, Liz worked at the task until she was lucky enough to find a solution that nearly ---- the difficulty.

    (A) proposing . . destroyed

    (B) unwilling . . resolved

    (C) reluctant . . worsened

    (D) eager . . doubled

    (E) determined . . reduced

2. The fire would have spread quickly but for the ---- of the fire chief who pushed his way into the house to douse the fire at its source, ---- great danger to himself.

    (A) bravery . . eliminating

    (B) quick-thinking . . although

    (C) trepidation . . incurring

    (D) fearlessness . . showing

    (E) courage . . despite

3. Mr. Morgan, like others in his family, was of the opinion that the death penalty and corporal punishment in general were ----; consequently, he rarely spanked his own children, preferring instead to speak to them in what he hoped was a ---- manner even when he was furious with their misdeeds and they were even more incensed with him.

    (A) inappropriate . . infuriated

    (B) illegal . . trenchant

    (C) useful . . rational

    (D) ineffective . . conciliatory

    (E) humane . . supercilious

4. After observing the top salesperson garner many awards, several trainees began to ---- her style.

    (A) activate

    (B) emulate

    (C) comprise

    (D) disregard

    (E) outline

5. To criticize a new employee for working slowly may actually be ----, as the employee becomes so flustered that he slows down even further in an attempt to concentrate on his task.

    (A) counterproductive

    (B) praiseworthy

    (C) worthwhile

    (D) essential

    (E) reasonable

6. ---- in his ----, the police officer refused even to consider the bribe and arrested the party who had waved the money in front of his face, who thus learned to his sorrow that — despite the sitcoms to the contrary — police officers are not subject to corruption.

    (A) Vociferous . . acceptance

    (B) Uncompromising . . rectitude

    (C) Redundant . . virtue

    (D) Zealous . . wickedness

    (E) Unwarranted . . virility

7. The feeling that one is being watched is not always mere paranoia; indeed, the ---- and random viewing of citizens by some governmental bureaus is quite probably more ---- than is commonly known.

    (A) intermittent . . widespread

    (B) haphazard . . ironhanded

    (C) arbitrary . . fly-by-night

    (D) flagrant . . surreptitious

    (E) unauthorized . . banal

Go on to next page ⇨

> *Directions:* Each of the following questions features a pair of words or phrases in capital letters, followed by five pairs of words or phrases in lowercase letters. Choose the lowercase pair that most closely expresses the same relationship as that of the uppercase pair.

8. PRACTICE : IMPROVE ::
   - (A) gather : decrease
   - (B) praise : ridicule
   - (C) research : discuss
   - (D) abbreviate : shorten
   - (E) coddle : harm

9. GOSLING : GOOSE ::
   - (A) horse : colt
   - (B) fledgling : bird
   - (C) veal : calf
   - (D) arachnid : spider
   - (E) pod : whale

10. DIRGE : MOURNING ::
    - (A) hymn : praise
    - (B) lament : joy
    - (C) screed : pain
    - (D) sonnet : rhythm
    - (E) diatribe : tranquillity

11. PARSIMONIOUS : SQUANDER ::
    - (A) sophisticated : smile
    - (B) arrogant : boast
    - (C) thrifty : buy
    - (D) fastidious : clean
    - (E) gluttonous : fast

12. TONSORIAL : HAIR ::
    - (A) professorial : job
    - (B) medical : disease
    - (C) stentorian : throat
    - (D) sartorial : apparel
    - (E) canine : teeth

13. SWAGGER : ARROGANCE ::
    - (A) swindle : veracity
    - (B) renege : consistency
    - (C) orchestrate : harmony
    - (D) wheedle : certitude
    - (E) stagger : imbalance

14. RIVET : GIRDERS ::
    - (A) stitch : hem
    - (B) buttress : foundations
    - (C) gargoyle : cathedrals
    - (D) nail : boards
    - (E) frame : photograph

15. OVINE : SHEEP ::
    - (A) dogmatic : dog
    - (B) piscine : fish
    - (C) epicene : earthquake
    - (D) bovine : elephant
    - (E) pulmonary : heart

16. ANGRY : INCENSED ::
    - (A) noticeable : flamboyant
    - (B) obdurate : stubborn
    - (C) ancient : outmoded
    - (D) melodious : euphonious
    - (E) calm : pacific

Go on to next page

Directions : Each passage is followed by questions pertaining to that passage. Read the passage and answer the questions based on information stated or implied in that passage.

Chile's human history apparently began about 10,000 years ago when migrating Indians followed the line of the Andes and settled in fertile valleys and along the coast. The Incas briefly extended (05) their empire into the north, but the area's remoteness prevented any significant effect. In 1541, the Spanish, under Pedro de Valdivia, encountered about one million Indians from various cultures who supported themselves primarily through (10) slash-and-burn agriculture and hunting. Although the Spaniards did not find the gold and silver they had sought there, they recognized the agricultural potential of Chile's central valley, and Chile became part of the Viceroyalty of Peru.

(15) Chilean colonial society was heavily influenced by the *latifundio* system of large landholdings, kinship politics, the Roman Catholic Church, and an aggressive frontier attitude stemming from Indian wars. The drive for independence from (20) Spain was precipitated by usurpation of the Spanish throne by Napoleon's brother Joseph. A national junta in the name of Ferdinand — heir to the deposed king — was formed on September 18, 1810. Spanish attempts to reimpose arbitrary rule (25) during the Reconquista led to a prolonged struggle under Bernardo O'Higgins, Chile's most renowned patriot. Chilean independence was formally proclaimed on February 12, 1818.

The political revolution brought little social (30) change, however, and 19th century Chilean society preserved the essence of the stratified colonial social structure. The system of presidential absolutism eventually predominated, but the wealthy land owners continued to control Chile.

(35) Although Chile established a representative democracy in the early 20th century, it soon became unstable and degenerated into a system protecting the interests of the ruling oligarchy. By the 1920s, the newly emergent middle and working (40) classes were powerful enough to elect a reformist president, but his program was frustrated by a conservative congress. Continuing political and economic instability resulted in the quasidictatorial rule of General Carlos Ibanez (45) (1924–1932).

After constitutional rule was restored in 1932, a strong middle-class party, the Radicals, formed. The Radical Party became the key force in coalition governments for the next 20 years. The 1920s (50) saw the emergence of Marxist groups with strong popular support. During the period of Radical Party dominance (1932–1952), the state increased its role in the economy. However, presidents generally were more conservative than the parties supporting them, and conservative political (55) elements continued to exert considerable power through their influence over the economy and control of rural voters.

17. The primary purpose of this passage is to

   (A) argue that Chile advanced when it became independent of Spanish rule.

   (B) contrast Indian culture with that of the European settlers.

   (C) discuss some key factors in the development of Chilean social structures.

   (D) advocate that Chile adopt a government less dominated by the wealthy class.

   (E) explain how coalition governments resolve some inherent tensions.

18. The author would most probably *disagree* with which of the following statements?

   I. The Incas were the predominant pre-Spanish influence in Northern Chile.

   II. The land mass that includes Chile was most probably formed approximately 10,000 years ago.

   III. The Spaniards used Chile as a source of gold to finance its wars.

   (A) I only

   (B) II only

   (C) III only

   (D) I and II only

   (E) I, II, and III

19. According to the passage, the catalyst for the fight for independence from Spain was

   (A) excessive taxation by the Spanish.

   (B) the *latifundio* system.

   (C) Joseph's usurpation of the Spanish throne.

   (D) Napoleon's abdication of the Spanish throne.

   (E) the Spanish civil war.

Go on to next page

20. From lines 32–34, you may infer that the Chilean government in the 19th century

    (A) included a president who was a figure-head without significant power.

    (B) was ruled by a dictator who had absolute power.

    (C) was secretly ruled by Spain.

    (D) was reigned over by a king.

    (E) was an anarchy, without any formal governmental structure.

21. Which of the following best describes the relationship between congress and the workers in the 1920s?

    (A) They were in opposition.

    (B) They worked together toward the same goals.

    (C) They took turns governing the country.

    (D) They united only once to overthrow the government.

    (E) Congress was composed of workers; they were one and the same.

22. Which of the following was *not* mentioned as being true of the Radical Party?

    (A) It began after constitutional rule was restored.

    (B) It exerted influence for two decades.

    (C) It was composed of members of the working class.

    (D) It was less conservative than the president it supported.

    (E) It had strong support among rural voters.

23. The tone of the passage is

    (A) opinionated.

    (B) heretical.

    (C) objective.

    (D) hidebound.

    (E) dolorous.

Studies have shown that certain components of the immune system behave abnormally in people with chronic fatigue syndrome. Chemicals called interleukin-2 and gamma interferon, which the body produces during its battle against cancer (05) and infectious agents, may not be made in normal amounts. There is evidence that a low-grade battle is being waged by the immune system of CFS patients, given the slight increase in the number of white cells that usually accumulate in the blood (10) when people are fighting off an infection. Natural killer cells, though, that also help the body in this battle are found in slightly reduced numbers. It's important to note that clinical depression has the identical small reduction in natural killer-cell (15) activity. In addition, some depressed patients produce higher amounts of antibodies to certain viruses. There may be more of a connection between depression, the immune system, and chronic fatigue syndrome than is realized even (20) now, which introduces the somewhat controversial aspect of the syndrome, its neuropsychological features.

24. Which of the following does the author mention to support his theory that the immune system may be affected by chronic fatigue syndrome?

    (A) Clinical depression may be more physical than psychological.

    (B) Interleukin-2 and gamma interferon are not produced in normal amounts.

    (C) Antibody levels are higher in depressed people than in nondepressed people.

    (D) White-cell levels in people with neuro-psychological problems tend to decrease.

    (E) Natural killer cells reduce the number of white blood cells.

25. The author mentions the connection between clinical depression and abnormal cellular response in order to

    (A) show that clinical depression is a serious medical condition.

    (B) prove that chronic fatigue syndrome is not unique in its physiological characteristics.

    (C) provide additional evidence of a connection between mental and immunological conditions.

    (D) explain the difference between natural killer and other cells.

    (E) claim that natural killer cells are not crucial in immunological defense.

Go on to next page

26. When the body battles cancer,

   (A) it produces chemicals like gamma interferon.

   (B) it turns against its own immune system.

   (C) it stimulates the condition known as clinical depression.

   (D) it reduces the number of antibodies available to battle viruses.

   (E) it develops abnormal lesions around the area of the cancer.

27. The next paragraph of this passage most likely

   (A) refutes the theory of the connection between cancer and viruses.

   (B) criticizes the underlying assumptions of the passage.

   (C) compares the effects of interleukin-2 to the effects of natural killer cells.

   (D) supports the author's premise that a normal (nondepressed) immune system can successfully kill off cancer cells.

   (E) discusses the neuropsychological aspects of chronic fatigue syndrome.

Directions: Choose the answer choice most nearly opposite in meaning to the question word.

28. TREPIDATION

   (A) caution

   (B) confidence

   (C) beauty

   (D) derision

   (E) insensitivity

29. PRAGMATIC

   (A) cumulative

   (B) unappreciated

   (C) insalubrious

   (D) impractical

   (E) typical

30. PRECARIOUS

   (A) prejudiced

   (B) haughty

   (C) reluctant

   (D) elderly

   (E) safe

31. ANARCHY

   (A) joy

   (B) distress

   (C) veracity

   (D) order

   (E) stress

32. TEDIOUS

   (A) harmonious

   (B) craven

   (C) picayune

   (D) interesting

   (E) dull

33. LUCID

   (A) turbid

   (B) vivacious

   (C) minuscule

   (D) domineering

   (E) spicy

34. OMINOUS

   (A) favorable

   (B) malleable

   (C) unpredictable

   (D) unlucky

   (E) hasty

35. NADIR

   (A) segment

   (B) indigenous

   (C) zenith

   (D) sagacious

   (E) connection

Go on to next page

36. DIFFIDENT
    (A) similar
    (B) unwrinkled
    (C) immaculate
    (D) arrogant
    (E) docile

37. INDIGENOUS
    (A) foreign
    (B) amiable
    (C) satisfactory
    (D) lustrous
    (E) pallid

38. ERUDITE
    (A) timid
    (B) rash
    (C) loquacious
    (D) uneducated
    (E) gargantuan

STOP You may check your work on this section only.
Do not go on to the next section until you are told to do so.

Section 2

Time: 30 minutes

38 questions

Directions: Each of the following sentences has one or two blanks indicating that words or phrases are omitted. Choose the answer that best completes the sentence.

1. Desperate to pass the exam, Bernard ----
   outlined every chapter of the book, noting
   even the most obscure points.

   (A) self-righteously

   (B) rapidly

   (C) playfully

   (D) paranoically

   (E) painstakingly

2. The ---- look on the singer's face underscored
   her ---- at having to perform in front of a
   dinner theater audience that was obviously
   more concerned with the quality of the
   sauce than the singer.

   (A) remorseful . . pleasure

   (B) ecstatic . . shock

   (C) dismayed . . unhappiness

   (D) pleasant . . joy

   (E) vital . . lethargy

3. Reluctant to ---- the man as the complete
   fraud she suspected him to be, Jill chose to
   attack the weaker points of his theory, ----
   them one by one.

   (A) denounce . . debunking

   (B) ridicule . . proving

   (C) castigate . . applauding

   (D) expose . . strengthening

   (E) recommend . . disseminating

4. The news report was anything but ----, but
   those of us who have learned to discount
   such gloomy ---- are optimistic.

   (A) sanguinary . . traps

   (B) pessimistic . . confusion

   (C) pleasant . . prognostications

   (D) heinous . . benefits

   (E) trivial . . magnitude

5. Martin blamed his ---- on his wife's distracting him in the middle of a very difficult
   move; nonetheless, we all can see that he is
   not as ---- at juggling as he claims to be.

   (A) bungling . . adept

   (B) fiasco . . unskilled

   (C) reaction . . maladroit

   (D) fury . . inept

   (E) devastation . . pretentious

6. Annoyed at the politician's ---- comments,
   the reporter pressed harder for a more ----
   response.

   (A) redundant . . repetitive

   (B) tactless . . immediate

   (C) phlegmatic . . lackadaisical

   (D) disputatious . . expiatory

   (E) ambiguous . . direct

7. The ---- her peers the speaker received
   when she presented her report was but a
   small sample of the disdain that she had to
   face daily at the university that was attempting to make her quit despite her tenured
   position.

   (A) abasement by

   (B) plaudits of

   (C) encomium of

   (D) laudation of

   (E) demise of

Go on to next page

> *Directions:* Each of the following questions features a pair of words or phrases in capital letters, followed by five pairs of words or phrases in lowercase letters. Choose the lowercase pair that most closely expresses the same relationship as that of the uppercase pair.

8. KENNEL : DOG ::

   (A) stable : horse

   (B) sty : sheep

   (C) corral : pigs

   (D) coop : fox

   (E) nest : cat

9. THERMOMETER : MEASURE ::

   (A) blanket : decorate

   (B) gauge : predict

   (C) thermos : heat

   (D) anchor : hold

   (E) pencil : sharpen

10. SERENE : PLACID ::

    (A) complicated : easy

    (B) lush : bare

    (C) ungainly : awkward

    (D) ferocious : large

    (E) grainy : clear

11. GORILLA : PRIMATE ::

    (A) doctor : aristocrat

    (B) accountant : bureaucrat

    (C) vertebrate : bird

    (D) water : compound

    (E) flower : mineral

12. VINDICTIVE : REVENGE ::

    (A) wrong : vindication

    (B) irresolute : servility

    (C) jocose : sobriety

    (D) edgy : strength

    (E) blameless : exoneration

13. THIN : EMACIATED ::

    (A) immune : impervious

    (B) imperious : regal

    (C) happy : ecstatic

    (D) sarcastic : sardonic

    (E) insulting : demeaning

14. LIONS : PRIDE ::

    (A) birds : flock

    (B) coyotes : kit

    (C) kangaroos : joey

    (D) swans : cygnet

    (E) wolves : pelt

15. TUXEDO : SUIT ::

    (A) galleon : ship

    (B) computer : circuit

    (C) abode : home

    (D) limousine : car

    (E) hovel : house

16. GARRULOUS : PROLIX ::

    (A) cantankerous : polite

    (B) intrepid : brave

    (C) pedantic : energetic

    (D) asocial : amiable

    (E) gruesome : diligent

Go on to next page ⟹

Directions: Each passage is followed by questions pertaining to that passage. Read the passage and answer the questions based on information stated or implied in that passage.

The Canyon Pintado Historic District in northwest Colorado has been occupied by prehistoric people for as long as 11,000 years, including the Fremont culture who left behind
(05) rock art sites. Fremont rock art has recurring motifs that link it both in time and culture. Strange human-like figures with broad shoulders, no legs, and horned headdresses are similar to the Barrier Canyon style of southwestern Utah. Figures with
(10) shields or shield-like bodies are like Fremont figures from the San Rafael region of Southern Utah.

Some figures have large, trapezoidal shaped bodies, stick-like legs, trapezoidal heads, and in many cases, are adorned with necklaces. Another
(15) motif of the Fremont culture is the mountain sheep, with graceful curvilinear horns. Designs such as concentric circles, snake-like lines, hands, corn plants, and rows of dots are also often found in Fremont art. A unique figure in Douglas Creek is
(20) Kokopelli, the humpbacked flute player of Anasazi mythology. His presence indicates some kind of tie with the more advanced culture of the Four Corners area.

17. The primary purpose of the passage is to

   (A) criticize those who consider Fremont art unsophisticated.

   (B) defend the theory that different cultures progressed at similar rates in their artistic development.

   (C) correct the misapprehension that rock art motifs were merely abstract, without symbolic significance.

   (D) urge readers to take steps to preserve the rock art as historical landmarks.

   (E) discuss the history and style of Fremont culture rock art.

18. It can be inferred from the passage that the author believes which of the following about Fremont rock art?

   (A) Similar figures and themes may suggest connections between the peoples of various times and locations.

   (B) Its primary purpose was to boast of military successes.

   (C) It is secondary in importance to the agricultural breakthroughs accomplished during the same period.

   (D) It was created during one highly artistic period of the natives.

   (E) The animal motif suggest a religion based on worship of animal deities.

19. The passage supplies information for answering which of the following questions?

   (A) What significance is there to the lack of legs on the human-like figures?

   (B) What was the purpose of the rock art?

   (C) Were curved lines absent in Fremont rock art?

   (D) How much of the art work was sacred and how much secular?

   (E) What other cultures besides those in the Four Corners influenced Fremont rock art?

20. The author mentions the connection to the culture of the Four Corners area in order to

   (A) challenge the claim that the Fremont culture was the most advanced of its time.

   (B) refute the assertion that Fremont rock art merely copied art from other cultures.

   (C) suggest that the mimicking of art from other cultures may indicate contact between the cultures.

   (D) prove the relationship between art and the level of civilization.

   (E) ridicule the suggestion that there is a connection between artistic images and warfare success.

A key study has shown that the organic matter content of a soil can be altered to a depth
Line of 10 cm or more by intense campfire heat. As much as 90 percent of the original organic matter
(05) may be oxidized in the top 1.3 cm of a soil. In the surface 10 cm, the loss of organic matter may reach 50 percent if the soil is dry and the temperature exceeds 250° C. The loss of organic matter reduces soil fertility and water-holding capacity
(10) and renders the soil more susceptible to compaction and erosion.

Sandy soils attain higher temperatures and retain heat longer than clayey soils under similar fuel, moisture, and weather conditions. From this
(15) standpoint, it is desirable to locate campgrounds in an area with loam or clay-loam soil. Sandy soils are less susceptible to compaction damage,

Go on to next page

however, and are more desirable for campgrounds from this standpoint.

(20)   A water-repellent layer can be created in a soil
by the heat from the campfire. This condition was
noted only in sandy soils where the temperature
remained below 350° C during the campfire burn.
Campfires often produce temperatures above this
(25) level. By comparison, forest fires are a shorter-
duration event, and soil temperatures produced
are more likely to create water repellency-
inducing conditions. The greater areal extent of
forest fires makes them a more serious threat than
(30) campfires in terms of causing soil water repellency.

If the soil remained moist for the duration of
the campfire, the increased heat capacity of the
soil and heat of water vaporization kept the soil
temperature below 100° C. At this temperature,
(35) little loss of organic matter occurred, and no
water repellency was created. For areas where the
soil remains very moist, campfires probably have
little effect on the soil properties.

Study has shown that softwood fuels burn
(40) faster and produce less heat flow into the soil than
do hardwood fuels under the same conditions.
Elm and mesquite were the hottest burning and
longest lasting fuels tested. In areas where some
choice of fuels is available, the use of softwood
(45) fuels should be encouraged in an effort to minimize the effect of campfires on soil properties.

The effects of campfires on the soil in a
campground can be lessened by restricting the
fire site to the same area, even if permanent
(50) concrete fireplaces are not installed. In this
manner, any harmful effects are restricted to a
minimum area. If campfires are allowed to be
located at random by the user, the harmful effects
tend to be spread over a larger part of the camp-
(55) ground. The placement of a stone fire ring in the
chosen location is one way to accomplish the
objective.

These data support the decision to install
permanent fireplaces in many areas and to restrict
(60) the use of campfires elsewhere in the park. This
eliminates the harmful effects of campfires on the
soil and allows the campground to be located on
sandy soil with low compactibility and good
drainage.

21. The main idea of this passage is that

   (A) excessive campfires will eventually make
       it impossible to grow crops.

   (B) soil temperature affects soil fertility.

   (C) only certain woods allow for high-quality
       campfires.

   (D) soils must be able to absorb water in
       order to sustain organic matter.

   (E) steps can be taken to minimize soil
       damage from campfires.

22. It can be inferred from the passage that
    campfire users generally

   (A) evaluate the amount of soil damage that
       can result before they build a campfire.

   (B) are concerned with the possibility that
       their campfire can cause a forest fire.

   (C) have no regard for the biological
       consequences that result from their
       campfires.

   (D) consider many areas of a campground to
       be suitable for a campfire.

   (E) favor sandy soil over clay-loam soil as a
       campfire site.

23. Long-lasting campfires are more likely than
    short-lived ones to

   (A) create water repellency-inducing
       conditions.

   (B) maintain soil fertility.

   (C) occur with softwood fuels.

   (D) restrict damage to the top 1.3 cm of soil.

   (E) produce higher soil temperatures.

24. The author suggests that elm and mesquite

   I. conduct relatively high heat flow into the
      soil.

   II. should never be used in campfires.

   III. can substantially damage the soil if used
        in campfires.

   (A) I only

   (B) III only

   (C) I and III only

   (D) II and III only

   (E) I, II, and III

25. The purpose of lines 47–64 is to

   (A) demand stringent enforcement of fire
       safety laws.

   (B) support the banning of campfires
       outside fire rings in public parks.

   (C) summarize the effects of campfires on
       soil properties.

   (D) describe means of reducing the harmful
       effects of campfires.

   (E) encourage exploitation of alternative
       energy sources.

Go on to next page

26. The author's attitude toward the use of campfires is best described as one of

    (A) disgust.

    (B) indifference.

    (C) concern.

    (D) admonishment.

    (E) admiration.

27. It can be inferred from the passage that the author would be most likely to agree with which of the following?

    (A) Campfires should be banned as destructive to campfire soil.

    (B) Organic matter decreases soil erosion.

    (C) Clay-loam soil is preferable to sandy soil for campsites.

    (D) The longer the duration of the fire, the higher the resistant soil temperatures.

    (E) Campfires will not burn in areas with moist soil.

Directions: Choose the answer choice most nearly opposite in meaning to the question word.

28. IRRITATE

    (A) badger

    (B) soothe

    (C) pressure

    (D) scratch

    (E) dry

29. AMELIORATE

    (A) invigorate

    (B) placate

    (C) hoard

    (D) gloat

    (E) exacerbate

30. INEPT

    (A) profane

    (B) skilled

    (C) prolific

    (D) thrifty

    (E) indigenous

31. ABSTAIN

    (A) sneer

    (B) participate

    (C) approximate

    (D) meander

    (E) infuriate

32. DORMANT

    (A) patient

    (B) active

    (C) negative

    (D) obstinate

    (E) experienced

33. TERSE

    (A) devoted

    (B) grievous

    (C) poetical

    (D) soporific

    (E) rambling

34. DIFFUSE

    (A) focus

    (B) prognosticate

    (C) exile

    (D) emulate

    (E) confide

35. CREDULOUS

    (A) disbelieving

    (B) inept

    (C) sinister

    (D) boorish

    (E) extravagant

36. FARFETCHED

    (A) fickle

    (B) promiscuous

    (C) probable

    (D) ramshackle

    (E) unseemly

Go on to next page

37. HAPLESS
    (A) saturnine
    (B) fortunate
    (C) cacophonous
    (D) mordant
    (E) ambiguous

38. BURGEON
    (A) garble
    (B) purchase
    (C) aggravate
    (D) wither
    (E) dominate

STOP You may check your work on this section only.
Do not go on to the next section until you are told to do so.

Section 3

Time: 30 minutes

25 questions

Directions: Each question or set of questions is based upon a specific passage or upon a set of conditions. To answer the questions, you may find it useful to draw a diagram or chart. Select the best answer to each question.

Questions 1–3 are based on the following information:

I. Two persons must be of different genders to model together.

II. Two models working together must have different-colored hair.

III. Female clients of agency R have brown hair. Male clients of agency R have red hair.

IV. Male clients of agency B have blond hair. Female clients of agency B have red hair.

V. Male clients of agency Y have blond hair. Female clients of agency Y have red hair.

1. Which of the following combinations of models is *not* possible?

   (A) R agency female, R agency male

   (B) B agency male, Y agency female

   (C) Y agency male, R agency female

   (D) R agency male, Y agency male

   (E) B agency male, R agency female

2. With whom could a male client of agency R model?

   (A) female client of agency B

   (B) female client of agency R

   (C) female client of agency Y

   (D) male client of agency B

   (E) male client of agency Y

3. With whom could a male client of agency B pose?

   I. female client of agency R

   II. female client of agency B

   III. female client of agency Y

   (A) I only

   (B) II only

   (C) III only

   (D) I and III only

   (E) I, II, and III

4. The last time I went to the dentist, he pulled out my tooth. I am not going back to the dentist because I don't want to lose any more teeth.

   The reasoning in the statement above is most closely paralleled in which of the following?

   (A) My last report card had two F's on it. I am not going to take home any more report cards, so I won't be getting any more F's.

   (B) I can't stand loud music. The last time I went dancing, the music was too loud. I am never going dancing again.

   (C) I have only $300 and must use that to pay the rent. Because going out to dinner costs money, I won't go out to dinner.

   (D) Yesterday I went to the doctor, who gave me a shot and charged $50. Because I am broke, I can't go to the doctor any more.

   (E) When I took the lid off the jam jar, I got a cut on my finger. I am not going to open any more jam jars because I don't want to get any more cuts.

5. Children today are learning less than children did ten years ago. Teachers spend too much time on administrative matters, such as report cards, PTA meetings, and field trips, and too little time on teaching the basics.

   Which of the following, if true, would most strengthen the author's argument?

   (A) Teachers spend over 100 school hours on field trips each year.

   (B) The amount children learn is directly related to the amount of time teachers teach the basics.

   (C) Teachers are spending less time in the classroom today than they did ten years ago.

   (D) One out of every twelve students is flunking at least one class in high school.

   (E) Parents are less involved in PTA and similar groups today than they were ten years ago.

Go on to next page

Questions 6–10 are based on the following information:

Larissa wants to plant flowers. She has seven flowers and eight spaces in which she may plant them. She has pink petunias, purple zinnias, white daisies, pink carnations, red roses, purple pansies, and purple lilies.

   I. No flowers of the same color can be planted next to each other.

   II. Pansies must be either in the first space or in the seventh space.

   III. Roses must be right before the zinnias and right after the pansies.

   IV. The lilies must be planted in the last space.

   V. A pink flower must be in spaces four and six.

   VI. A white flower must have exactly one space between it and a purple flower.

6. Which of the following spaces will have no flower planted in it?

   (A) third

   (B) fourth

   (C) fifth

   (D) sixth

   (E) seventh

7. How many flowers will be between the zinnias and the lilies?

   (A) one

   (B) two

   (C) three

   (D) four

   (E) five

8. How many spaces are between the daisies and the closest purple flower?

   (A) one

   (B) two

   (C) three

   (D) four

   (E) five

9. In which space will the carnations be planted?

   (A) two or three

   (B) four or six

   (C) six or seven

   (D) three or five

   (E) one or seven

10. Which of the following statements is not necessarily true?

   (A) There are two spaces between the pansies and a pink flower.

   (B) There are three spaces between an empty space and the zinnias.

   (C) The roses are in space two.

   (D) One space is between the carnations and the roses.

   (E) The zinnias are before the carnations.

11. Few children don't love ice cream. Athalie is a child.

Which of the following would best complete the above statement?

   (A) Therefore, Athalie is a typical child.

   (B) Therefore, Athalie probably loves ice cream.

   (C) Therefore, Athalie eats too much ice cream.

   (D) Therefore, Athalie doesn't like ice cream.

   (E) Therefore, Athalie is an atypical child because she is allergic to ice cream.

12. A study of National Football League Statistics over the last ten years reveals that the losing team threw more interceptions than did the winning team in 82 percent of games played. This statistic clearly indicates that interceptions contribute greatly to team losses.

The conclusion in the preceding argument depends on which of the following assumptions?

   (A) Fumbles do not hurt a team's chances of winning games.

   (B) A team's chances of winning games are greatly reduced if it throws any interceptions during a game.

   (C) A team that throws more interceptions than its opponent throws and still wins the game must have superior players.

   (D) Interceptions do not result from a team's falling behind in a game.

   (E) Interceptions are harmful primarily because they make it easy for the other team to score points.

Go on to next page

Questions 13–17 are based on the following information:

I. A doctor will give shots only on the day that a patient checks into the hospital for an overnight stay.

II. The check-in day for any particular disease is the same day every week.

III. Emphysema patients can check in on Wednesday and every second day thereafter except Tuesday.

IV. Cancer patients can check in only on those days when both emphysema and pneumonia patients check in.

V. Eczema patients can check in only on Tuesday and Thursday.

VI. Pneumonia patients can check in any day when eczema patients are not checking in, except Sunday.

VII. Colitis patients can check in only on the two consecutive days on which no cancer patients check in.

VIII. The hospital will check in patients on Tuesday through Sunday only.

13. On which day(s) can colitis patients be admitted?

(A) Saturday and Sunday

(B) Sunday and Thursday

(C) Thursday only

(D) Tuesday and Wednesday

(E) Wednesday and Friday

14. On which days could the greatest number of patients with different diseases be admitted?

(A) Monday and Friday

(B) Wednesday and Thursday

(C) Wednesday and Friday

(D) Sunday and Friday

(E) Monday and Thursday

15. On which day will pneumonia patients but not cancer patients be admitted?

(A) Sunday

(B) Monday

(C) Wednesday

(D) Friday

(E) Saturday

16. On which days could both cancer and emphysema patients be admitted?

(A) Monday and Tuesday

(B) Tuesday and Wednesday

(C) Wednesday and Thursday

(D) Wednesday and Friday

(E) Thursday and Friday

17. If the schedule were amended and phlebitis patients would also be admitted on every day that neither emphysema patients nor eczema patients were admitted, what days would phlebitis patients be admitted?

(A) Tuesday

(B) Wednesday

(C) Thursday

(D) Friday

(E) Saturday

18. Voice training is not necessary for one to become an opera star. A survey of those who went through voice training for more than two years found that only 2 percent of them were singing with opera companies.

Which of the following, if true, would most effectively undermine the argument?

(A) Nobody has ever become an opera star without voice training.

(B) The survey also revealed that 70 percent of survey respondents were singing in musical comedies.

(C) Many of those surveyed were minors and thereby ineligible to be employed by an opera company.

(D) Most opera stars are freelance performers who do not belong to an opera company.

(E) Stephanie Weiss, rising opera star and lead soprano in the Metropolitan Opera House's new production of Die Fledermaus, went through ten years of voice training.

Go on to next page

19. Eating foods prepared with butter or fried in butter is detrimental to your health. Research has proven that the oils in butter clog arteries and cause heart problems. Therefore, it follows that if you want to lead a long and healthy life, you should eliminate butter from your diet.

    Which of the following, if true, would most weaken the above conclusion?

    (A) No one knows the effects of a completely butter-free diet on the body.

    (B) Butter provides nutrients that are essential for good health and cannot be obtained from other sources.

    (C) Eating a variety of foods in moderation is the key to a long and healthy life.

    (D) Butter substitutes such as margarine also clog arteries and cause heart problems.

    (E) Most people do not believe that butter is detrimental to their health and fail to take precautions to eliminate it from their lives.

20. The opinion polls taken before the 1948 presidential election predicted that the Republican candidate, Thomas Dewey, would defeat the Democratic candidate, Harry Truman, in a landslide. In the actual election, however, Truman was the victor.

    All the following, if true, help to explain the discrepancy between the polls and the actual election EXCEPT

    (A) the last opinion poll was taken more than two weeks before the election.

    (B) the polls were conducted by telephone, and far more Republicans than Democrats owned telephones in 1948.

    (C) Dewey supporters were so confident of victory that they did not bother to vote on Election Day.

    (D) Truman was one of the most effective presidents in history.

    (E) the number of voters polled was far smaller than what mathematicians now consider acceptable to predict a presidential election.

Questions 21–25 are based on the following information:

A lawn mower repairman is fixing three mowers: one orange, one yellow, and one green. After he has reassembled the mowers, he is unhappy to find that he has parts left over: four nuts, two large bolts, one small bolt, and three washers. He must put the parts back according to the following rules:

I. If he puts a large bolt on a mower, he must put a washer and a nut on that bolt.

II. If he puts a small bolt on a mower, he must put a nut on that bolt.

III. He may not put a washer on the green mower.

IV. The small bolt goes on the yellow mower.

V. At least one part must go on each mower.

21. Which of the following is an acceptable distribution of parts?

    (A) Orange: one nut, large bolt; Yellow: two nuts, large bolt, small bolt, three washers; Green: nut

    (B) Orange: two nuts, two large bolts, two washers; Yellow: two nuts, one bolt, one washer; Green: no parts

    (C) Orange: two nuts, one large bolt, two washers; Yellow: one nut, one small bolt; Green: one nut, one large bolt, one washer

    (D) Orange: one nut, one large bolt, one washer; Yellow: two nuts, one large bolt, one small bolt, two washers; Green: one nut

    (E) Orange: two nuts, one large bolt, one small bolt, two washers; Yellow: one nut, one large bolt, one washer; Green: one nut

22. Which of the following statements must be false?

    (A) A nut is on the yellow mower.

    (B) There are more washers than large bolts on the yellow mower.

    (C) There are more parts on the yellow mower than on any other mower.

    (D) A washer is on the orange mower.

    (E) There are two parts on the green mower.

Go on to next page

23. If only one nut goes on the orange mower, what is the maximum number of parts that can be on the orange mower?

    (A) three

    (B) four

    (C) five

    (D) seven

    (E) eight

24. If both large bolts go on the yellow mower, which of the following must be true?

    (A) The orange mower has more parts than the green mower.

    (B) The yellow mower has an odd number of parts.

    (C) All three washers are on the yellow mower.

    (D) The green mower has two nuts.

    (E) The orange mower has only a washer.

25. If the repairman is allowed to put a washer on the green mower and each mower must have fewer than five parts, where do the large bolts go?

    (A) on the orange and green mowers

    (B) on the orange and yellow mowers

    (C) both on the orange mower

    (D) on the yellow and green mowers

    (E) both on the green mower

STOP You may check your work on this section only.
Do not go on to the next section until you are told to do so.

Section 4

Time: 30 minutes

30 questions

Notes:

All numbers used in this exam are real numbers.

All figures lie in a plane.

Angle measures are positive; points and angles are in the position shown.

Directions: Questions 1 – 15 feature two columns with a quantity in each. Compare the quantities.

Choose A if the quantity in Column A is greater than the quantity in Column B.

Choose B if the quantity in Column B is greater than the quantity in Column A.

Choose C if the quantities in Column A and Column B are equal.

Choose D if you cannot determine which quantity is greater from the information given.

You will not be given credit for choosing answer E.

A letter (*a, b, c,* or *x, y, z*) or symbol means the same thing throughout one problem but may not be the same in different problems.

Information that is centered between two columns applies to both columns in that problem.

Examples:

Column A	**Column B**	**Sample Ovals**

1.

2^3	4	● Ⓑ Ⓒ Ⓓ Ⓔ

2.

$x°$	45°	Ⓐ Ⓑ Ⓒ ● Ⓔ

3. $$3x + y = 3x$$

0	y	Ⓐ Ⓑ ● Ⓓ Ⓔ

The answer choices are

    A if the quantity in Column A is greater.

    B if the quantity in Column B is greater.

    C if the two quantities are equal.

    D if the relationship cannot be determined from the information given.

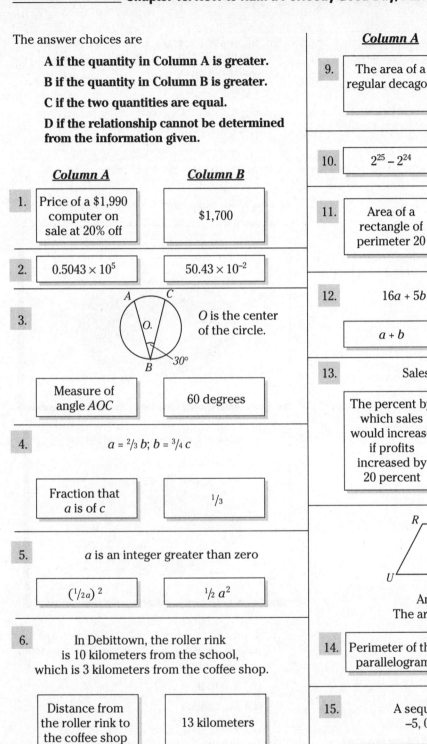

	Column A	_Column B_
1.	Price of a $1,990 computer on sale at 20% off	$1,700
2.	0.5043×10^5	50.43×10^{-2}
3.	*O* is the center of the circle. Measure of angle *AOC*	60 degrees
4.	$a = \frac{2}{3}b; b = \frac{3}{4}c$ Fraction that *a* is of *c*	$\frac{1}{3}$
5.	*a* is an integer greater than zero $\left(\frac{1}{2a}\right)^2$	$\frac{1}{2}a^2$
6.	In Debittown, the roller rink is 10 kilometers from the school, which is 3 kilometers from the coffee shop. Distance from the roller rink to the coffee shop	13 kilometers
7.	300% of 30	60% of 15
8.	$\boxed{x} = (3x)^2 - \frac{1}{3}x$ $\boxed{-3}$	$\boxed{3}$

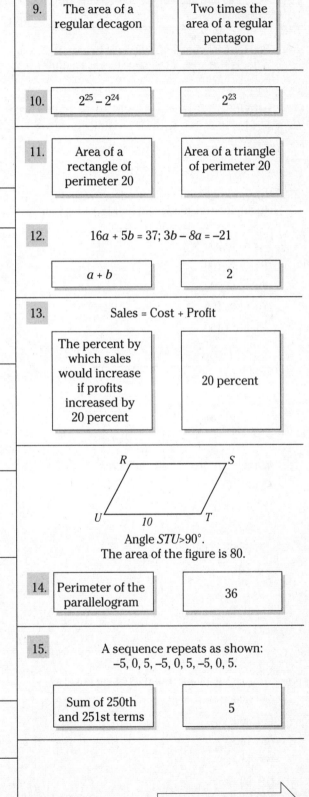

	Column A	_Column B_
9.	The area of a regular decagon	Two times the area of a regular pentagon
10.	$2^{25} - 2^{24}$	2^{23}
11.	Area of a rectangle of perimeter 20	Area of a triangle of perimeter 20
12.	$16a + 5b = 37; 3b - 8a = -21$ $a + b$	2
13.	Sales = Cost + Profit The percent by which sales would increase if profits increased by 20 percent	20 percent
14.	Angle *STU* > 90°. The area of the figure is 80. Perimeter of the parallelogram	36
15.	A sequence repeats as shown: −5, 0, 5, −5, 0, 5, −5, 0, 5. Sum of 250th and 251st terms	5

Go on to next page

> *Directions:* Each of the following questions (16–30) has five answer choices. Select the best choice.

16. The longest chord of a circle is two units. What is the area of the circle in square units?

    (A) 4π

    (B) 2π

    (C) 1π

    (D) $\frac{1}{2}\pi$

    (E) $\frac{1}{4}\pi$

17. Roger earns $100 dollars a day, every day (including weekends and holidays) for four years. How much does he earn?

    (A) $140,000

    (B) $142,100

    (C) $146,000

    (D) $146,100

    (E) $149,100

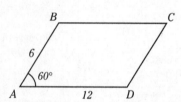

18. What is the area of parallelogram *ABCD*?

    (A) $3\sqrt{3}$

    (B) $15\sqrt{3}$

    (C) 36

    (D) $36\sqrt{3}$

    (E) 72

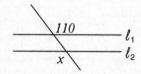

19. What is the number of degrees in angle *x*?

    (A) 360

    (B) 260

    (C) 180

    (D) 110

    (E) 80

20. In four years, Mary Alice will be twice as old as she was last year. Mary Alice is how many years old now?

    (A) 12

    (B) 9

    (C) 8

    (D) 7

    (E) 6

Use the following graphs to answer questions 21–25.

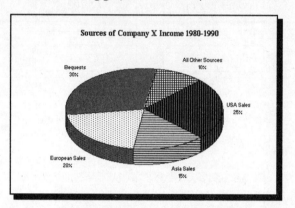

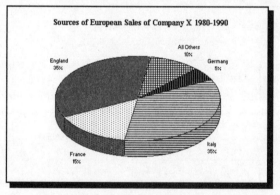

21. If total income from 1980 to 1990 was $10 million, how much of that income came from sales to Germany?

    (A) $10 million

    (B) $1 million

    (C) $100,000

    (D) $10,000

    (E) $1,000

22. Sales to Italy account for what percent of Company X's income?

    (A) 87.5

    (B) 35

    (C) 25

    (D) 15

    (E) 7

Go on to next page

23. If Company X received $50,000 in bequests from 1980 through 1990, how much money did it receive from sales to France?

    (A) $16,666

    (B) $3,333

    (C) $5,000

    (D) $333

    (E) $250

24. The 1980 sales to England were what percent of the sales to Italy?

    (A) 100

    (B) 50

    (C) 35

    (D) 25

    (E) It cannot be determined.

25. If sales to Italy accounted for $1 million more than sales to France, how much income came from U.S. sales?

    (A) $200,000

    (B) $6,250,000

    (C) $5 million

    (D) $25 million

    (E) It cannot be determined.

26. This year a $42 coat will be marked up 200%. What will be its new price?

    (A) $242

    (B) $142

    (C) $126

    (D) $84

    (E) $42

27. Lael took seven exams. Her average score was 82. Her first six scores were 75, 91, 85, 89, 74, and 79. What was her seventh score?

    (A) 90

    (B) 87

    (C) 82

    (D) 81

    (E) 80

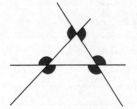

28. What is the sum of the degrees in the shaded angles?

    (A) 1080

    (B) 720

    (C) 360

    (D) 180

    (E) It cannot be determined from the information given

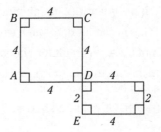

29. A 4-by-4 meter plot of land shares a corner with a 4-by-2 meter plot of land as shown. Approximately how much shorter will a walk that goes in a straight line from A to E be than a walk from A to B to C to D to E?

    (A) 1 meter

    (B) 4 meters

    (C) 8 meters

    (D) 10 meters

    (E) 14 meters

30. Two cans each have a height of 10. Can A has a circumference of 10π. Can B has a circumference of 20π. Which of the following represents the ratio of the volume of Can A to the volume of Can B?

    (A) 1:10

    (B) 1:8

    (C) 1:4

    (D) 1:2

    (E) 1:1

 STOP You may check your work on this section only. Do not go on to the next section until you are told to do so.

Section 5

Time: 30 minutes

30 questions

Notes:

All numbers used in this exam are real numbers.

All figures lie in a plane.

Angle measures are positive; points and angles are in the position shown.

Directions: Questions 1 – 15 feature two columns with a quantity in each. Compare the quantities.

Choose A if the quantity in Column A is greater than the quantity in Column B.

Choose B if the quantity in Column B is greater than the quantity in Column A.

Choose C if the quantities in Column A and Column B are equal.

Choose D if you cannot determine which quantity is greater from the information given.

You will not be given credit for choosing answer E.

A letter (a, b, c, or x, y, z) or symbol means the same thing throughout one problem but may not be the same in different problems.

Information that is centered between two columns applies to both columns in that problem.

Examples:

Column A	**Column B**		**Sample Ovals**
1.			
2^3	4		● Ⓑ Ⓒ Ⓓ Ⓔ

Column A	**Column B**		**Sample Ovals**
2. $x°$	$45°$		Ⓐ Ⓑ Ⓒ ● Ⓔ

3. $$3x + y = 3x$$

Column A	**Column B**		**Sample Ovals**
0	y		Ⓐ Ⓑ ● Ⓓ Ⓔ

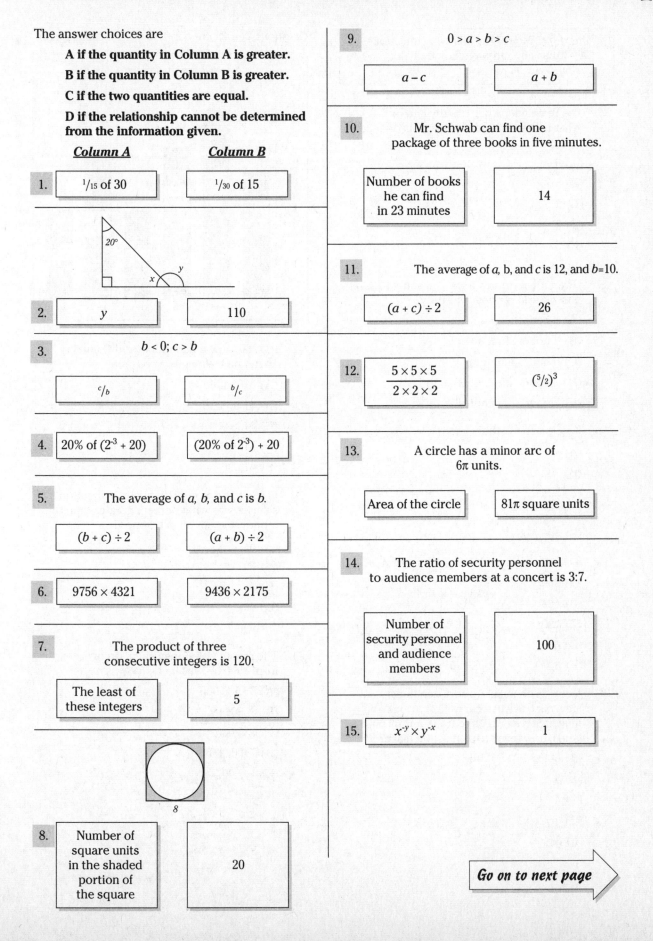

The answer choices are

    A if the quantity in Column A is greater.

    B if the quantity in Column B is greater.

    C if the two quantities are equal.

    D if the relationship cannot be determined from the information given.

    <u>**Column A**</u>   <u>**Column B**</u>

1. $1/15$ of 30 $1/30$ of 15

2. y 110

3. $b < 0; c > b$

     c/b b/c

4.   20% of $(2^{-3} + 20)$ (20% of 2^{-3}) + 20

5.   The average of a, b, and c is b.

     $(b + c) \div 2$ $(a + b) \div 2$

6. 9756×4321 9436×2175

7.   The product of three consecutive integers is 120.

     The least of these integers   5

8.   Number of square units in the shaded portion of the square   20

9. $0 > a > b > c$

     $a - c$ $a + b$

10.   Mr. Schwab can find one package of three books in five minutes.

     Number of books he can find in 23 minutes   14

11.   The average of a, b, and c is 12, and $b=10$.

     $(a + c) \div 2$ 26

12. $\dfrac{5 \times 5 \times 5}{2 \times 2 \times 2}$ $(5/2)^3$

13.   A circle has a minor arc of 6π units.

     Area of the circle 81π square units

14.   The ratio of security personnel to audience members at a concert is 3:7.

     Number of security personnel and audience members   100

15. $x^{-y} \times y^{-x}$ 1

Go on to next page ➡

Directions: Each of the following questions (16–30) has five answer choices. Select the best choice.

16. The remainder when *n* is divided by 5 is 4. What is the remainder when 3*n* is divided by 5?

    (A) 0

    (B) 1

    (C) 2

    (D) 3

    (E) 5

17. Gwendolyn studies from 9:30 a.m. to 12:27 p.m. How long does she study?

    (A) 3 hours 57 minutes

    (B) 3 hours 27 minutes

    (C) 3 hours 3 minutes

    (D) 2 hours 57 minutes

    (E) 2 hours 27 minutes

18. If $\triangle\!x\!\triangle = x^2 + 2$, then $\triangle\!4\!\triangle =$

    (A) 16

    (B) 18

    (C) 324

    (D) 326

    (E) 106,278

19. If *O* is the center of the circle, angle *AOC* =

    (A) 360°

    (B) 180°

    (C) 120°

    (D) 60°

    (E) 30°

20. A carton contains three dozen items. Steven's truck can carry 432 cartons at a time. If Steven wants to transport 60,000 items, how many trips must he make?

    (A) 6

    (B) 5

    (C) 4

    (D) 3⁴/₅

    (E) 3

Questions 21 – 25 are based on the following graph.

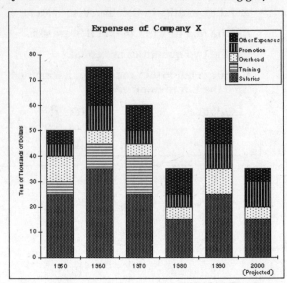

21. In 1960, how much money did Company X spend on training?

    (A) $10 million

    (B) $1 million

    (C) $100,000

    (D) $10,000

    (E) $1,000

22. In 1970, the money Company X spent on salaries was what percent greater than the money it spent on promotion?

    (A) 5

    (B) 20

    (C) 25

    (D) 400

    (E) 500

23. The amount of money spent on overhead from 1950 to 1990 inclusive was

    (A) $3,500,000

    (B) $350,000

    (C) $35,000

    (D) $400,000

    (E) $4,000,000

Go on to next page

24. If the money spent on salaries in 1980 were increased to equal that of 1970 but all other 1980 expenses remained constant, then 1980's salaries would be what percent of that year's total expenses?

    (A) 71

    (B) 56

    (C) $33^{1}/_{3}$

    (D) 25

    (E) It cannot be determined.

25. The amount of money spent on television advertising in 1970 is what percent of that estimated to be spent in the year 2000?

    (A) 200

    (B) 100

    (C) 50

    (D) 10

    (E) It cannot be determined.

26. $x * y * z = \dfrac{^{1}/_{2}x + y^{3}}{y - z}$

    Solve for 6 * 2 * 9.

    (A) 108

    (B) 21

    (C) 17

    (D) $-^{11}/_{7}$

    (E) $-^{1}/_{6}$

The diameter of the circle = 10

27. The area of the shaded portion of the square is

    (A) $100 - 25\pi$

    (B) $100 - 10\pi$

    (C) $40 - 25\pi$

    (D) $40 - 10\pi$

    (E) It cannot be determined from the information given.

28. It takes three painters ten hours to paint four rooms. How many hours would it take nine painters to paint twelve rooms?

    (A) $1^{1}/_{3}$

    (B) $3^{1}/_{3}$

    (C) 6

    (D) 10

    (E) 30

29. Bob traveled 40 percent of the distance of his trip alone, went another 20 miles with Anthony, and then finished the last half of the trip alone. How many miles long was the trip?

    (A) 240

    (B) 200

    (C) 160

    (D) 100

    (E) 50

30. How many sides are in a polygon with interior angles that average 140 degrees each?

    (A) 9

    (B) 8

    (C) 7

    (D) 4

    (E) It cannot be determined from the information given.

STOP You may check your work on this section only. Do not go on to the next section until you are told to do so.

Section 6

Time: 30 minutes

25 questions

Directions: Each question or set of questions is based upon a specific passage or upon a set of conditions. To answer the questions, you may find it useful to draw a diagram or chart. Select the best answer to each question.

Questions 1–5 are based on the following information:

I. Seven batters are ready to play at the league's softball game. Four veterans (John, Karl, Larry, and Moe) played last year. The other three are rookies (Frank, Gary, and Harold).

II. For a rookie to bat, he must be preceded by and followed by a veteran.

III. Gary bats second while his good friend Larry is the last veteran at bat.

IV. The last batter is a veteran.

V. Karl must bat before Moe but after John.

1. Which of the following could be the correct order of batters from first to last?

   (A) John, Gary, Karl, Frank, Moe, Harold, Larry

   (B) John, Gary, Frank, Moe, Karl, Harold, Larry

   (C) Karl, Frank, Larry, Gary, Moe, Harold, John

   (D) Karl, Harold, Moe, Frank, Larry, John, Gary

   (E) Moe, Harold, Larry, John, Gary, Karl, Frank

2. Which of the statements was unnecessary for solving the batting order?

   (A) I

   (B) II

   (C) III

   (D) IV

   (E) V

3. If Karl and Frank have a fight and Frank refuses to bat next to Karl, which of the following would be the correct batting order?

   (A) Larry, Harold, Moe, Frank, Gary, Karl, John

   (B) Larry, Harold, Frank, Moe, Karl, Gary, John

   (C) Larry, Frank, Moe, Harold, Karl, Gary, John

   (D) John, Gary, Karl, Harold, Moe, Frank, Larry

   (E) John, Gary, Moe, Karl, Harold, Frank, Larry

4. If an additional player, Deb, were added at the end of the batting order, which of the following statements would be true?

   (A) She would have to be a novice.

   (B) She would have to bat five places after Karl.

   (C) There would be three batters between Frank and her.

   (D) She would be the best batter.

   (E) She would bat right after Harold.

5. Which of the following is not necessarily a true statement?

   (A) Harold bats after Gary.

   (B) Frank bats before Moe.

   (C) Larry bats after all the rookies.

   (D) Gary is the first rookie at bat.

   (E) Moe bats between Karl and Larry.

Go on to next page ⟹

6. Physicians correctly warn that for a rash to improve, one must stop scratching it no matter how badly it itches. Unfortunately, the lotions and salves physicians prescribe do almost no good. Recent research has shown that keeping ice packs on the rash helps because the skin becomes so numb that the itching ceases.

   If all the above statements are true, which of the following is most likely true?

   (A) Physicians are incapable of estimating the severity of a skin rash on another person.

   (B) No prescription medication is effective in treating skin rash.

   (C) Some readily obtainable treatments work better than physician-prescribed medications.

   (D) Patients have a greater awareness of what feels good to them than their physicians do.

   (E) One suffering from a rash should try over-the-counter lotions and salves before consulting a physician.

7. Larry told Mimi that he had to save enough money to buy a motorcycle because everyone was riding motorcycles, and if he didn't have one, he would not be accepted by the gang.

   Based on the above passage, which of the following assumptions may be drawn?

   (A) Gang membership is very prestigious.

   (B) Motorcycle ownership ensures acceptance by the gang.

   (C) The gang requires its members to own motorcycles.

   (D) Motorcycles are expensive.

   (E) Mimi does not want Larry to have a motorcycle.

8. All of the finalists in the Miss Universe contest last year were blondes. Therefore, in order to get more dates this year, I am going to dye my hair blond.

   The author of the above passage fails to recognize which of the following?

   (A) This year all the contestants may be redheads, and blondes will be out of fashion.

   (B) What appeals to Miss Universe judges may not be what attracts her potential dates.

   (C) The Miss Universe contestants were not chosen solely because they were blondes.

   (D) There are too many blondes already; redheads are less common and thus get more attention.

   (E) Men do not like to date Miss Universe finalists.

Questions 9 - 11 are based on the following information:

International Day Camp has two vehicles at its disposal to transport campers to a tour of a dairy. One vehicle is a minivan that can seat seven, including the driver. The other is a sedan that seats five, including the driver. The available counselors are Alban, Brown, and Chen, who must select from the camper roster of Kang, Leon, Madrid, Nguyen, Oliphant, Pascal, Quint, Robinson, Smith, Toorani, Umdekar, and Valdez. The selections of counselors and campers must conform to the following conditions:

   I. Counselors must drive the vehicles.

   II. The number of campers on the field trip must not be more than three times the number of counselors.

   III. If Alban is selected, Valdez is also selected.

   IV. Robinson and Smith may not both be selected.

   V. If Nguyen is selected, Chen will not be selected.

   VI. Valdez will not be selected unless Smith is selected.

9. Which of the following groups may go to the dairy?

   (A) Alban, Brown, Chen, Kang, Leon, Madrid, Smith, and Valdez

   (B) Alban, Brown, Leon, Madrid, Quint, Robinson, Toorani, and Umdekar

   (C) Alban, Chen, Madrid, Pascal, Quint, Robinson, Smith, and Valdez

   (D) Brown, Chen, Kang, Madrid, Nguyen, Robinson, Toorani, and Umdekar

   (E) Brown, Chen, Kang, Madrid, Oliphant, Toorani, Umdekar, and Valdez

Go on to next page

10. The inclusion of which of the following guarantees that at least one of the vehicles will have empty seats?

    (A) Alban

    (B) Leon

    (C) Nguyen

    (D) Smith

    (E) Quint

11. If Robinson is selected, all the following will be rejected for the trip EXCEPT

    (A) Alban

    (B) Nguyen

    (C) Pascal

    (D) Smith

    (E) Valdez

Questions 12 – 17 are based on the following information:

I. A survey is made of six dogs, Rover, King, Spot, Lassie, Fido, and Prince. They are ranked in terms of their intelligence and the number of movie contracts they have received.

II. Spot is less intelligent than all the other dogs with the exception of Lassie (who gets the fewest movie contracts of all the dogs).

III. King gets more movie contracts than any other dog even though he is not the most intelligent.

IV. Prince is the fourth most intelligent dog but gets the third highest number of movie contracts because he is so friendly.

V. Rover is the most intelligent dog but gets fewer movie contracts than any other dog except Fido and Lassie.

12. Which of the following is the order of dogs ranging from the one with the fewest movie contracts to the one with the most?

    (A) King, Prince, Rover, Spot, Fido, Lassie

    (B) King, Spot, Prince, Rover, Fido, Lassie

    (C) Lassie, Rover, Spot, King, Fido, Prince

    (D) Lassie, Fido, Rover, Prince, Spot, King

    (E) Lassie, Prince, Rover, Fido, King, Spot

13. Which of the following could be the order of dogs ranging from the most intelligent to the least intelligent?

    (A) Prince, Fido, King, Rover, Spot, Lassie

    (B) Prince, Rover, Fido, King, Spot, Lassie

    (C) Rover, Fido, King, Prince, Spot, Lassie

    (D) Rover, Spot, Prince, Fido, King, Lassie

    (E) Lassie, Spot, Prince, Fido, King, Rover

14. Assuming that Fido is exactly twice as intelligent as Spot, which of the following must be true?

    I. He gets twice as many movie contracts as Spot gets.

    II. He is four times as intelligent as Prince.

    III. He is less friendly than Spot but friendlier than Rover.

    (A) None

    (B) I only

    (C) I and II only

    (D) I and III only

    (E) I, II, and III

15. Which of the following dogs is less intelligent than Prince but gets more contracts?

    (A) Fido

    (B) Rover

    (C) Spot

    (D) Lassie

    (E) King

16. Which of the dogs has the least disparity between its position in order of intelligence and its position in order of movie contracts awarded?

    (A) Rover

    (B) Fido

    (C) Lassie

    (D) Prince

    (E) King

Go on to next page

17. If a seventh dog, Rex, were added to the group and he had half the movie contracts of Prince, which of the following must be true?

    (A) He has more intelligence than Spot.

    (B) He has less intelligence than Prince.

    (C) He gets fewer movie contracts than Spot.

    (D) He gets more movie contracts than King.

    (E) He is friendlier than Prince.

Questions 18–22 are based on the following information:

Alphabet Communications is linked by computer terminals A, B, C, D, E, and F. Messages are sent from one terminal to another by way of systems X and Y.

I. System X allows only the following messages to be sent:

    A to B
    B to C
    C to B
    C to E
    D to C
    E to A
    A to E

II. System Y allows the following messages to be sent:

    A to D
    D to A
    D to F
    E to B
    F to A

III. Messages from one terminal to another may be relayed through one or more other terminals. Messages may switch from X to Y.

18. Which of the following messages requires use of both systems?

    (A) A to E

    (B) A to F

    (C) C to B

    (D) C to F

    (E) D to B

19. One leg of a message along system X takes one second, while a similar connection along system Y takes three seconds. Which of the following takes the least time?

    (A) B to E

    (B) C to D

    (C) A to F

    (D) B to F

    (E) F to B

20. Which of the following routes does not require a relay through terminal A?

    (A) E to B along system X

    (B) F to C

    (C) F to B

    (D) D to E when both systems are used

    (E) B to E

21. If terminal E breaks so that it cannot send or receive messages, which message is impossible?

    (A) D to B along system X

    (B) D to A along system X

    (C) C to B

    (D) F to B

    (E) A to B when system Y is used part of the way

22. System Y is discontinued, but the following connections are added to system X: C to F; F to C; E to D. Which of the following requires the fewest relays?

    (A) D to A

    (B) F to A

    (C) C to A

    (D) A to F

    (E) E to F

Go on to next page

23. The cost for sending a fax outside of your local calling area consists of long-distance charges for the time the phone lines are connected to send the fax. The first fax machines required six minutes to send a two-page document. The resultant cost of sending such a document outside of your calling area was twice that of sending the document by regular mail. Even the slowest fax machine currently in use is four times as fast as the first fax machines. Long-distance phone charges for the first minute and each subsequent minute have not changed since fax machines were first used.

Which of the following is the conclusion to which the author of the above paragraph is leading?

(A) Sending a fax of a two-page document is better than mailing it outside of your calling area.

(B) Sending a fax of a two-page document is cheaper than mailing it outside of your calling area.

(C) Sending any document by fax is now cheaper than sending it by regular mail.

(D) Sending a fax of a two-page document is cheaper than sending the document by mail only when its destination is outside the local calling area.

(E) There are no advantages in sending documents by regular mail rather than sending them by fax.

24. Persons who consume large amounts of Vitamin C often have fewer colds and more cheerful dispositions than the average person. Therefore, I am going to start taking extra Vitamin C right away because I don't want to be depressed.

The author makes which of the following assumptions?

(A) Colds cause depression.

(B) Vitamin C is necessary in extra supplements because the average diet doesn't supply enough.

(C) Cheerfulness is not the result of a physical condition that also leads to increased uptake of Vitamin C.

(D) Vitamin C quickens healing from injuries.

(E) It is impossible to overdose on Vitamin C.

25 The professors at Stanford, Harvard, and Yale all agree that computers are useful instructional tools. Therefore, many colleges have made budget requests for funds to purchase many computers this year.

The reasoning in the above passage is most nearly paralleled by which of the following?

(A) Everyone who flunked math this semester used Mr. Mammana as a tutor. I am going to get a tutor other than Mr. Mammana as quickly as possible.

(B) All of us who are winning race car drivers have had at least one serious accident; all racers are virtually certain to have accidents sometime in their driving careers.

(C) The presidents of the large corporations endorse company dental plans; most businesses now are trying to get dental insurance coverage for their employees.

(D) The teachers and the principal disagree over the value of study hall; the principal has refused to let the school discontinue it.

(E) Political analysts all agree that the Federal Reserve Board should cut interest rates. Many political leaders now feel the same way.

STOP You may check your work on this section only.

Answer Key for Practice Exam 1

Section 1	Section 2	Section 3	Section 4	Section 5	Section 6
1. B	1. E	1. D	1. B	1. A	1. A
2. E	2. C	2. B	2. A	2. C	2. D
3. D	3. A	3. E	3. C	3. B	3. D
4. B	4. C	4. E	4. A	4. B	4. B
5. A	5. A	5. B	5. B	5. D	5. B
6. B	6. E	6. E	6. D	6. A	6. C
7. A	7. A	7. C	7. A	7. B	7. C
8. D	8. A	8. A	8. A	8. B	8. B
9. B	9. D	9. B	9. D	9. A	9. A
10. A	10 C	10. D	10. A	10. B	10. C
11. E	11. D	11. B	11. D	11. B	11. C
12. D	12. E	12. D	12. C	12. C	12. D
13. E	13. C	13. A	13. D	13. D	13. C
14. D	14. A	14. C	14. A	14. D	14. A
15. B	15. D	15. E	15. B	15. D	15. C
16. A	16. B	16. D	16. C	16. C	16. C
17. C	17. E	17. E	17. D	17. D	17. C
18. E	18. A	18. A	18. D	18. D	18. D
19. C	19. C	19. B	19. D	19. C	19. A
20. A	20. C	20. D	20. E	20. C	20. E
21. A	21. E	21. D	21. C	21. C	21. B
22. C	22. D	22. E	22. E	22. D	22. C
23. C	23. E	23. B	23. C	23. B	23. B
24. B	24. C	24. E	24. E	24. B	24. C
25. C	25. D	25. A	25. B	25. E	25. C
26. A	26. C		26. C	26. D	
27. E	27. B		27. D	27. A	
28. B	28. B		28. B	28. D	
29. D	29. E		29. D	29. B	
30. E	30. B		30. B	30. A	
31. D	31. B				
32. D	32. B				
33. A	33. E				
34. A	34. A				
35. C	35. A				
36. D	36. C				
37. A	37. B				
38. D	38. D				

Chapter 20

Practice Exam 1: Answers and Explanations

Section 1

1. **B.** The only excuse for missing a question like this one is laziness or carelessness. So many of the Sentence Completion questions test very hard vocabulary that when you get to one like this with very easy vocabulary you should take your time and go through each answer choice carefully to ensure that you find the correct one.

   To **resolve** a difficulty is to solve the problem. If Liz kept working, she was unwilling to abandon the project. Only choices B and C work for the first blank; the second blank in C is just the opposite of what the sentence intends to say.

2. **E.** This easy question is put here to trap careless readers who zoom through the question and don't plug in every answer choice. You can predict that the fire chief was brave and that there was danger to himself. Thinking that the first word is bravery, it's easy to choose A and not worry about the second blank.

   Always plug your answer back into the original question to make sure that the new sentence makes sense. The few seconds you save by not doing so won't make up for all the points you'll lose.

   In choice C, **trepidation** is a word you know from your roots: **trep** means fear. Trepidation is just fearfulness, as in, "I approached the GRE with trepidation."

3. **D.** If Mr. Morgan rarely spanked his own children, he probably didn't believe spanking was of any use. Predict that the first word is something like useless. Choices A, B, and D work. Eliminate choices C and E (**humane** means kind and gentle, the way the Humane Society treats the animals it takes care of). If he *hoped* he were speaking in some way to his children, that way must be good. Eliminate second words that are negative, like **infuriated** (very angry) and **supercilious** (arrogant, conceited, stuck-up). Only choice D is left.

   Trenchant means sharp, cutting, effective, energetic. A trenchant comment cuts through the baloney and gets to the heart of the matter. **Conciliatory** means tending to reconcile or soothe the anger of. You may have heard this word in another form in divorce courts: irreconcilable differences.

4. **B.** The trainees watched someone succeed. They probably reasoned that she did things right and would therefore want to copy her style. Which word comes closest to "copy"? Choice D is exactly the opposite of what you are looking for. Choices A, C, and E are remotely similar to *copy,* but they sound awkward when plugged into the sentence (don't forget to take the vital final step of rereading the sentence with your selection inserted). By the process of elimination, **emulate** (which just happens to mean *copy,* as a matter of fact!) is the correct answer. Notice that you could get this question right even without knowing the exact definition of the word.

5. **A.** The gist of the sentence is that criticizing the employee for working slowly makes him work even more slowly. The action, therefore, hurts rather than helps the situation and is **counterproductive**, meaning having a different result or consequence than what was intended. For example, staying up late studying the Friday night before the GRE may actually be counterproductive; you will be so tired that you may do worse on the exam than you would have had you studied less and slept more.

Try to predict whether the word to fit in the blank should be a "good" or positive word, or a "bad" or negative word. You know that if the employee gets flustered and slows down, something bad has happened. Looking for a negative word allows you to eliminate choices B, C, D, and E.

6. **B.** Did you eliminate choice B immediately, thinking that to compromise is to meet in the middle, to give a little and get a little? That's one definition of compromise, but to *compromise* can also mean to undermine or sabotage, as in compromising your virtue by doing things you know are wrong. *Rectitude* means correctness, integrity, the state of being right. You may know this word in another form, *rectify*. To *rectify* is to make something right or correct. The officer refused to sabotage his integrity by taking a bribe.

You could immediately eliminate choice A because the officer in fact did not accept the bribe. *Vociferous* means loud, literally "full of voice." In choice E, *virility* means manliness. It is impossible to "sabotage manliness," short of extreme surgery in a Scandinavian country. And *unwarranted* means uncalled for, not justified. An unwarranted insult in a hot game of hockey can get you decked. In choice C, the second word fits well, but *redundant* means repeated. How could he be "repeated in his virtue?" If you chose this, you probably didn't go back and reread the entire sentence with the new words inserted. Never skip that last step, even if you're rushed for time.

7. **A.** Vocabulary is the key to this sentence. You probably could predict relatively easily what types of words go in the blanks; the trouble is finding the words with those definitions. Start with the second blank. Say: The practice is probably more *common* than realized. *Widespread* means common, spread about everywhere.

Ironhanded means severe, strong. Have you heard the expression "rules with an iron fist"? That type of ruler is ironhanded.

Throughout this book, I have used clichés and expressions common to English, like "rules with an iron fist." If you don't understand those expressions or aren't comfortable with them, get someone to explain them to you. Many vocabulary words on this exam are parts of sayings or proverbs, or *aphorisms* (sayings) or *adages* (sayings). I suggest that you pull out an index card and write the cliché or saying on the card, along with an explanation of how it is used and what words are related to it (such as ironhanded). *Fly-by-night* is another cliché. It means temporary, not permanent. This came from the idea that a less-than-honest company would pack up in the middle of the night and leave town, taking its customers' money with it. It would, in effect, fly away in the middle of the night: fly-by-night.

Surreptitious means secretive, concealed. *Banal* means dull or stale from overuse. A cliché is banal.

Here's the vocabulary for the first blanks. *Intermittent* means off and on, not constant. Don't confuse this word with *interminable,* which means endless, or seemingly endless. A lecture can be interminable; a good lecturer will use jokes intermittently to try to keep the listeners' attention. *Haphazard* means nonsystematic, unplanned. *Arbitrary* means dependent on individual discretion and not fixed by law. You make an arbitrary choice when you buy a grab bag.

8. **D.** *Practice* and *improve* have a purpose or function relationship: You *practice* in order to *improve;* you *abbreviate* in order to *shorten*. (Did you notice the root *brev*, which means short? A harder word with this root is *brevity*, which means briefness. You may have heard the cliché, the overused saying, that brevity is the soul of wit. That means that if you keep it short, they'll think you're smart.) *Coddle,* choice E, means to pamper or treat carefully. Coddled eggs are cooked without having their yolks broken. *Coddle* would be a great name for a dog or cat you spoil rotten.

9. **B.** A *gosling* is a baby goose. A *fledgling* is a baby bird. (The word *fledgling* has come into the language to mean anyone new, a novice, but its original and exact meaning is a baby bird.) Choice A is backwards; a *horse* is not a baby colt, but vice versa. Choice C is rather *macabre* (gruesome). Veal is the meat of a calf, which is a baby cow. In D, a spider is a member of the arachnid class. In E, a *pod* is a group of whales. (My best friend always mentions when we eat chocolate together that we are turning into a pod!)

10. **A.** Make your sentence, "A dirge is a song of mourning." (If you don't know what a dirge was, you can simply say that a *dirge* is mourning. Assume that unknown words are synonyms.) A *hymn* is a song of praise. A *lament*, in B, is a statement of grieving. You lament that you didn't know the word *dirge* if you missed this question. A *screed* is a long, dull speech or piece of writing. When your friend makes you read her term paper, you can mutter under your breath that you don't have time to slog through such a screed. A *sonnet* is a type of poem. A *diatribe* is not the name of some aborigines recently discovered near the equator but rather a *tirade*, a bitter and abusive speech. (When your friend gets a D on her screed, she indulges in a diatribe about the idiot professor who doesn't know genius when he sees it.)

11. **E.** Someone who is *parsimonious* (extremely frugal, cheap) will not *squander* (waste). Someone who is *gluttonous* (overindulging) will not *fast* (refrain from eating).

If you missed this question, did you think of *fast* as an adverb, as in, " I wish this day would go fast and be over with" instead of as a verb? Because words can function as more than one part of speech, it's important to identify how the word is used by looking at its counterparts. The second words in all the answer choices are verbs, meaning *fast* must be a verb as well.

Someone sophisticated may or may not smile. When your sentence is " may or may not," you often can eliminate the answer. An *arrogant* (stuck up, conceited) person is likely to boast. Choice C is the trap. Yes, *parsimonious* (cheap) and *thrifty* (frugal, careful with money) have somewhat similar meanings (they are not exact synonyms), but it would not be right to say that a thrifty person will not buy. He may buy; he will just be careful and buy wisely. A *fastidious* (picky, fussy) person is likely to keep things clean.

Suppose that you don't know the word *parsimonious* and make the sentence, " A parsimonious person will squander." As soon as you see that both choices B and D feature the "will" relationship (an arrogant person will boast; a fastidious person will clean), you should realize that because two answers can't be correct, they are both wrong, and you must have the relationship wrong. Make a 180-degree turn and say, " A parsimonious person will not squander."

12. **D.** *Tonsorial* means pertaining to hair. No one really expects you to know this word. Instead, assume that unknown words are synonyms and make your sentence, "Tonsorial is hair." Then you can probably narrow the answers down to the two words you don't know (stentorian and sartorial) and make a quick guess. (If I'm underestimating your genius and your vocabulary, I abjectly apologize.) *Sartorial* means pertaining to clothing or apparel. If you want to get your money's worth out of this book, tell your mother that she is looking sartorially resplendent when she asks how her new outfit looks on her. And to be sure that she gets the message, bellow it in a *stentorian*, or loud, voice. In Homer's poetry, Stentor was a character who "has the voice of 50 men." In other words, he was a loudmouth. (I once had a less-than-erudite boyfriend who pouted when I talked about Homer's poetry, telling me that it wasn't polite to discuss former sweethearts and their love poems in front of him!)

Professorial does not mean pertaining to a job. That word would be *professional*, pertaining to a profession or job. *Professorial* means like a professor. In B, *medical* means pertaining to medicine, not pertaining to a disease. Choice C may have made you pause for a moment. Yes, we have canine teeth, but *canine* actually means pertaining to a dog, not pertaining to teeth. Our canine teeth are called that because they are pointed, like dogs' teeth.

13. **E.** To *swagger* is to walk with arrogance, or to strut your stuff. Remember all those bad war movies you watched on Saturday afternoons back in the good old days when all your time wasn't spent studying for this exam? The evil commandant often had a short stick tucked under his arm. That was called a swagger stick, because it was a symbol of his authority and *arrogance* (conceit). To *stagger* is to teeter, to walk with difficulty, or to have trouble maintaining your balance. (You swagger off the football field when you score the winning touchdown. You stagger out of the locker room after drinking too much champagne to celebrate your winning touchdown.)

To *swindle* is to cheat; *veracity* is truthfulness (*ver* means truth; *-ity* makes the word a noun). You don't cheat someone with truthfulness — you cheat someone with dishonesty.

If a word in English is difficult, try pronouncing it with the accent of your native language. You may find that the word pronounced in your native accent will sound like a word in your own language that is similar in meaning. For example, *verdad* in Spanish means truth. Knowing that would help you make a connection with *veracity.*

To *renege* is to go back on your word, or to not be consistent at all. (If you tell your friends that you'll split your lottery winnings with them and then a miracle happens and you actually do win ten gazillion dollars, would you *renege* on your promise? That all depends on your *veracity* in making the statement in the first place.)

To *orchestrate* is to arrange to achieve a maximum effect. For example, a good hostess orchestrates a dinner party, arranging the seating and the entertainment to give the maximum pleasure to the guests. If you fell for this answer, hang your head in shame. The connection between orchestra and harmony is just a little too hokey, don't you think? One of my goals is to get you thinking the GRE way (don't worry, the condition is not permanent) so that you can recognize cheap tricks like this one.

And finally, to *wheedle* is to beg or flatter. It has nothing to do with *certitude*, which is just what it looks like (certainty, confidence, or assurance). Someone sure of himself or herself probably wouldn't have to beg or wheedle.

14. **D.** A *rivet* is a bolt that connects two *girders*, which are steel beams. A *nail* connects boards. If you didn't know these question words, you could say, "A rivet is girders." Unfortunately, that wouldn't help you this time because any of the answer choices sort of fits into that sentence. Therefore, this is the first question in this batch of analogies for which I would say to you, "If you don't know the words, Guess and Go: Make a quick guess and go on."

In choice B, a *buttress* is a support beam (like the buttress of a wall). When I am feeling particularly *corpulent* (fat), I lament the fact that I need a buttress to support my butt. In choice C, a *gargoyle* is a grotesque carving, usually in the shape of a head. You've probably seen pictures of the gargoyles on the walls of cathedrals.

15. **B.** Don't let this question pull the wool over your eyes: *Ovine* means like a sheep. *Piscine* means fish-like or pertaining to fish (no one likes a "piscine" kisser). If you didn't know the words, you could simply say, "Ovine is sheep." Doing so allows you to eliminate at least a few of the answers. You know that *dogmatic* doesn't mean like a dog; that word is canine. *Dogmatic,* in fact, means stubborn and opinionated, or not veering from accepted dogma or rules.

Choice C is a California joke. Epicene is not the same as *epicenter*, which is the center of an earthquake. *Epicene* means of indeterminate sex, or characteristic of both sexes. Long hair is an epicene look. *Bovine* means pertaining to a cow or an ox, but not to an elephant. And finally, *pulmonary* means pertaining to the lungs, not to the heart.

16. **A.** The relationship is from lesser degree to greater degree. First, you're angry, and then you become *incensed*, which means furious, or burning mad (think of burning incense). Choice A also moves from a lesser to a greater degree. Something may be *noticeable*, like a new haircut; however, when you dye your hair neon green, the hairdo turns from noticeable to *flamboyant*, very noticeable or showy.

The pair of words in choice B are synonyms: *obdurate* means stubborn. You can remember this by pairing obdurate with a more familiar *ob* word, *obstinate* (also meaning stubborn). *Outmoded* means out of fashion. Something ancient may or may not be out of fashion; as the song says, "Everything old is new again." In choice D, *melodious* and *euphonious* are synonyms. You can figure out euphonious with roots: *eu* means good; *phon* means sound; *-ous* means full of. Something *euphonious* is full of good sound, or melodious. Choice E also lets you use your roots: *pac* means calm.

17. **C.** The primary purpose question demands that you walk a fine line: Find an answer that is broad enough to cover the entire passage but not so broad that it brings up issues that are beyond the scope of the passage.

Pay special attention to the first word (typically a verb) in the answers to a primary purpose question. The first word should match the passion or style shown by the author in the passage. The tone of this passage is neutral, which knocks out choices A and D. The author is simply laying out some information for us. She does not take a stand. In addition, these choices contain ideas that the author mentions as parts of an overall development. They are too detailed to be the answer to a primary purpose question. Choice B also contains a verb that doesn't quite match the passage. In the beginning of the passage, the author discusses Indian agriculture and empire and then mentions that the Spanish picked up on these Indian developments. While there were undoubtedly many differences between the Indians and the Spanish, the author does not describe any in this passage. The verb in choice C, *discuss,* clearly matches the author's tone.

Three verbs are often correct answers to primary purpose questions: *discuss*, *describe*, and *explain*. The purpose of many passages is to *discuss* an idea, *describe* an event, or *explain* a philosophy. This choice includes social structures, which are mentioned in every paragraph in the passage. Development matches the historical aspects of the passage. Choice E contains a verb that is tempting but doesn't fit as well as *discuss*. The author is not lecturing to you. More importantly, the substance of choice E is too broad for this passage: The author does not discuss coalition governments in general. Even worse, the author does not provide you with any resolutions.

18. **E.** This question is tricky. The author would disagree with every statement. Although the Incas were in the north, the area's remoteness prevented any significant effect (lines 5 and 6). Although Chile's human history began 10,000 years ago, the land mass must have been there before that because the Indians migrated to it (lines 2 – 4). As for III, the passage states that the Spaniards did not find the gold and silver they sought in Chile (lines 10 – 12).

19. **C.** Lines 19 – 21 tell you that "the drive for independence from Spain was precipitated by the usurpation of the Spanish throne by Napoleon's brother Joseph."

A question that begins "According to the passage" is usually extremely simple and straightforward. This is the type of question you always want to do.

20. **A.** Lines 32 – 34 say that although presidential absolutism prevailed, "the wealthy landowners continued to control Chile." From this, you may infer that, although there was a president, he was merely a figurehead without any real power.

21. **A.** In lines 38 – 42, you are told that the conservative congress frustrated the program of a reformist president who had been elected by the workers. From this, you may infer that the congress and the workers were in opposition.

22. **C.** Line 47 tells you that the Radical party was composed of members in the middle class, not of the working class. (How do you know that the middle class and the working class were two separate classes? Lines 39 and 40 in the preceding paragraph mention them separately. You often find a correct answer a few lines above or below the "obvious" answer.) This question requires very careful, *meticulous*, detailed, *painstaking* reading.

23. **C.** No way did you miss this one. What's my favorite word? Objective! This answer is often (but not always) correct for a tone or attitude question. Here, the passage is narrative, neutral. It simply states the facts. *Opinionated* means unreasonably stubborn, holding to your own opinion. It's just the opposite of *objective*, which means open-minded, not prejudging a situation. *Heretical* means opposed to customary doctrine, especially of a church. (You may be more familiar with another form of the word: *heretic*. A *heretic,* or disbeliever, is often martyred, like Joan of Arc, whose principles were, uh, at stake.) *Hidebound* means stubborn, inflexible. *Dolorous* means sad, mournful . . . what you are if you chose this answer.

24. **B.** The first two sentences of the passage tell you that " . . . certain components of the immune system behave abnormally in people with chronic fatigue syndrome" and ". . . interleukin-2 and gamma interferon . . . may not be made in normal amounts." This is a simple detail or fact question.

Choice C is a trap answer. The author does in fact say that antibody levels are higher in depressed people; however, he does not make that statement to support the theory that the immune system may be affected by chronic fatigue syndrome. Just because a statement is true does not mean that it is the correct answer; be sure to address what the question is asking.

Remember, questions usually go in order through the passage, especially through science passages (which require you to find specific facts rather than make inferences). Because this is the first question, go back to the first sentence or two.

25. **C.** The author begins by stating that there is a correlation between chronic fatigue syndrome and changes in the immune system. He uses this evidence to speculate about the presence of neuropsychological (physical and mental aspects of the brain) features. The existence of such features would seem more plausible with additional examples of a connection between a psychological state and immune response. The clinical depression data provide such an example. Choice C states this and thus is the answer. Choice A is probably a true statement, given that clinical depression affects the immune system, but it misrepresents the author's purpose in mentioning clinical depression.

Do not choose an answer simply because it makes a true statement. Be sure that the statement answers specifically what the question is asking. Here, keep in mind that the author's conclusion has to do with connections. The best way to eliminate choice B is to note the word *prove*, which is very strong.

Eliminate choices with powerful, dramatic verbs, such as *prove* (and *demand*, and *urge*). Passages rarely *prove* anything, and the author of this very short passage has certainly not provided any proof. In addition, this statement leaves out consideration of how the author concludes the passage. If choice D were what the author was trying to do, he didn't do a very good job. You have little info regarding how these cells differ. Choice E is not the author's purpose and is probably not true.

26. **A.** This is a very simple detail or fact question. Lines 3 – 5 tell you that the body produces chemicals such as interleukin-2 and gamma interferon during its battle against cancer.

As you have probably noticed by now, the questions on science passages are often easier than questions on other types of passages. Even if the science passages themselves are boring or difficult to understand, the questions relating to them are usually quite straightforward; frequently, you just have to skim for a specific fact or detail. If you know you are not going to finish all the questions or all the section, try those in the science passage first.

27. **E.** The last sentence of the passage introduces the idea of neuropsychological features of chronic fatigue syndrome. It's reasonable to assume the next paragraph will go on to discuss that topic.

Discuss is one of the Big Three words you should love by now: *discuss, describe, explain.* Those are nice vague verbs that are often found in correct answers.

Did you immediately eliminate answers A and B? Negative answer choices are rarely correct. You should always look at them because you never know when a passage has a particularly *nefarious* (wicked, evil) exception to this generalization, but you can usually feel quite *sanguine* (cheerfully optimistic) about dumping the negative answers.

28. **B.** *Trepidation* is fear (*trep* means fear). The opposite is confidence (*fid* means faith). You may know a more common form of the word, *intrepid*, meaning not afraid (*in-* means not). I may never be intrepid enough to try Bungee jumping; my trepidation will keep me firmly on the ground. In D, *derision* means ridicule (*de-* means to put down). My decision not to Bungee jump was treated with derision by my more intrepid friends.

29. **D.** *Pragmatic* means practical. A pragmatic college student asks for money for his birthday rather than for more new clothes. The opposite is impractical (*im-* means not). *Kudos* (praises) to you if you were able to use your roots to define choice C. *Insalubrious* means not healthful (*in-* means not; *sal* means health; *-ous* means full). Whiskey is an insalubrious drink.

30. **E.** *Precarious* means difficult or dangerous. Walking a tightwire is a precarious activity. The opposite is safe. In choice B, *haughty* means arrogant, conceited, stuck-up. Someone skilled enough to excel at a precarious activity like walking a tightwire may be haughty, thinking he's above (so to speak!) everyone else.

31. **D.** *Anarchy* is without government or laws (*an-* means without or not; *arch* is government or rule). When a substitute teacher is taking over for the regular professor, the class may disintegrate into anarchy. The opposite is order. *Veracity* means truthfulness (*ver* means truth; *-ity* makes a word a noun).

If you speak Spanish, you know that *verdad* means truth, which can help you to remember veracity.

Go back and put *adamant* on your flashcard with all the other "stubborn" words you have learned: *refractory, obstinate, obdurate, froward,* and *recalcitrant.* See how useful learning is? The first time you're searching for a word to call your Significant Other when he or she won't see things your way you can rattle off, "You obstinate, obdurate, recalcitrant, refractory, adamant dolt, you!" and feel you've gotten your money's worth out of this book.

32. **D.** *Tedious* means boring or tiresome. The opposite is interesting. Choice C, *picayune,* means minor, or unimportant. In your graduate school essay, see whether you can get away with belittling the GRE as a picayune aspect of your overall application. No one will buy it, but at least you'll impress others with your vocabulary. If you're too *craven* (afraid) to be so witty, you're sentencing the readers to yet another tedious essay.

33. **A.** You probably got this question right by the process of elimination. *Lucid* means clear (*luc* means light or clear). A lucid explanation elucidates, or makes clear, the material. *Turbid* means thick, cloudy, dense. When you stir up waters that are muddy, they become turbid. If you put ice cubes into a glass of Oozo (Greek wine), the liquid becomes turbid. *Vivacious* means lively, full of life (*vi* means life; *-ous* means full of). *Minuscule* means very small.

Do not confuse *turbid* with *turgid*. *Turgid* means swollen or distended. A corpse floating in turbid waters after a few days would become turgid. (Where else but in *The GRE For Dummies,* 2nd Edition can you read answer explanations that manage to work in both Greek wine and floating corpses?)

34. **A.** *Ominous* means foreboding or portentous. The opposite is *favorable*. Choice B, *malleable,* means pliable, or capable of being shaped. The personality of a young child is malleable.

35. **C.** A *nadir* is the lowest point. You may jokingly say that the nadir of your life is having to study for the GRE when all your friends are out partying. The *zenith* is the highest point. The zenith of your life may come when you receive your excellent GRE scores and find that all your studying paid off (especially because you can now gloat over your friends)!

Choice B, *indigenous*, means native to. Cacti are indigenous to the Southwest. Choice D, *sagacious*, means wise. If you have more degrees than a thermostat, you're sagacious.

36. **D.** *Diffident* means reserved, or not assertive. A diffident person digs his toe in the carpet when he says, "Uh . . . Er . . . Um, I don't suppose you'd rather go out with me than study for the GRE tonight, would you?" (If he only knew!) Choice E, *docile,* means easily taught or handled. A diffident person is probably also docile.

37. **A.** *Indigenous* means native to. Monsters are indigenous to the spaces under children's beds. Something not native to an area is foreign to it.

    Amiable means friendly (hint: think of *ami*, which is *friend* in French, or *amigo*, which is *friend* in Spanish). *Lustrous* means shiny (*lus* means light or clear). *Pallid* means pale.

38. **D.** *Erudite* means well-educated, scholarly. The opposite is uneducated. *Timid* means shy. *Rash* in this context means overly hasty. *Loquacious* means talkative (*loq* means talk; *-ous* means full of or very). *Gargantuan* means huge. Loquacious, erudite people have gargantuan vocabularies and are not timid about using them.

Section 2

1. **E.** If Bernard noted even obscure points, he paid attention to detail. *Painstaking* is a word you've seen before; it means "taking pains" over something, paying attention to what you're doing. Bernard carefully outlined the chapter in order to get a good score. Choice D, *paranoically*, means unwarrantedly, suspiciously paranoid. (Sure I'm paranoid, but am I paranoid *enough?*) This word is too hard for the first question.

   Self-righteous means virtuously indignant, sure that you're correct and upset over being challenged. I personally become self-righteous when someone looks at my last name and tells me, "You've misspelled it; there are no vowels!" Excuse me, but I do know how to spell my own name, thank you very much.

2. **C.** Predict that the singer was unhappy at having to perform in front of an audience that didn't care about her performance. She therefore would have a sad look on her face. Both blanks require negative words. By eliminating any answers with positive words, you can cross off choices A, B, D, and E. *Vital* means lively, energetic. *Lethargy* is laziness or indifference. *Remorseful* means sad, apologetic.

3. **A.** You can predict the types of words you need to fill in the blanks. Jill was reluctant to show the man to be a fraud, so she attacked or put down or criticized the weaker points of his theory. To *denounce* is to criticize, to speak harshly of. To *debunk* is to disprove. (*de* = down from, away from, to put down). The first words in choices B, C, and D fit well; the second do not. To *castigate* is to criticize or punish. (For you men who are crossing your legs, relax. *Castigate* does not mean castrate, although both are certainly punishing!) In choice E, to *disseminate* is to spread, to disburse.

4. **C.** Predict that the news report is negative because those who *discount* it (attach no importance to it, ignore it) are optimistic, or positive. The "anything but" means "not," such that the first blank must be positive. (This is definitely confusing. You have to read a sentence this *convoluted*, or twisting and turning, a few times until you are clear what is expected. Take your time.) If the first word has to be positive or good, you can eliminate B and maybe E (*trivial* means minor, unimportant). Choice A doesn't seem to fit; what would a gloomy "trap" have to do with a news report? *Sanguinary* means blood-thirsty; a coach tries to get his football players in a sanguinary state of mind before they take the field. A *prognostication* is a prediction, something foretold. (*pro* means before; *gnos* means knowledge.)

   Choice D, *heinous,* means wicked, criminal. The musical *Kiss Me, Kate* (based loosely on Shakespeare's *The Taming of the Shrew*) has this great couplet in one of its songs:

   > "If she says your behavior is heinous
   > Kick her right in her Coriolanus!"

5. **A.** If you read the sentence carefully, you can probably get the gist: Martin messed up, blamed his wife, but we know better. Predict that the first blank needs a word meaning "to mess up." To *bungle* is to perform badly, to make a mess of. Choice B, however, also works in the first blank because a *fiasco* is a big mistake, a bad situation. And you may even argue that the first word in C works. Eliminate choices D and E. On to the second blank.

Predict that the second blank has to be filled with a word meaning skillful. That eliminates B, C, D, and E (*pretentious* means false, insincere). To be *adept* is to be skillful, competent. To be *maladroit* and *inept* is to be unskilled.

Did you get confused on the second blank? You know that Martin is unskilled, maladroit, inept. But the sense of the sentence is that Martin is *not as good* as he thinks he is, not *not as bad*.

6. **E.** Because the reporter is annoyed, you can predict that the first blank will be filled with a negative word. Unfortunately, that won't eliminate any answers here (unless you know *phlegmatic*, which most people don't. If you don't know what a word means, you can't eliminate it but have to leave it in as a "maybe"). You can tell we're getting closer to the end; the tricks don't help as much. Predict that the second word will be something good, because the reporter is pressing to get it, wants to hear it. That also doesn't help us to eliminate any answers except choice C. *Lackadaisical* means mellow, not energetic. You can predict that the blanks will be filled with words that are pretty much the opposite (eliminating choice A because *redundant* means repeated, repetitive). At this point, it's all a matter of vocabulary. If you don't know what the words mean, do yourself a favor — guess and go.

    Ambiguous means unclear, capable of being understood in two or more possible senses. An ambiguous response doesn't give much clear-cut information; a good reporter would press for a more direct, understandable response.

    Redundant means repetitive (or did I already say that?). *Tactless* means imprudent, without any manners or diplomacy, and isn't the opposite of *immediate*. *Phlegmatic* and *lackadaisical* both mean calm, composed, laid-back and mellow. *Disputatious* is just what it looks like, full of dispute, argumentative. *Expiatory* means tending to expiate or cleanse of guilt. (Gold merchants can never expiate themselves of their association by gilt.)

7. **A.** If the university is trying to make the speaker quit, she receives disdain (contempt, scorn) daily, and the response to her report was a small sample of that contempt. Predict that the blank requires a negative word. If (and this is a big if, I know!) you know the definitions of the words, you can eliminate choices B, C, and D. *Plaudits*, *encomium*, and *laudation* all mean praise (think of ap*plaud* for *plaud*its and *laud*). *Demise* means death. The speaker may have planned a million deaths for her ungrateful audience, but it's unlikely her listeners died during the presentation. That leaves only *abasement*. To *abase* is to humble or humiliate.

The last question in a segment often has very difficult vocabulary. If you don't know the words and can't narrow the answers down, make a quick guess and go on. Remember that the GRE has no penalty for wrong answers. It's to your advantage to guess, but guess *quickly*. The only way you can hurt your score on a question like this is to spend a lot of time agonizing over the words.

8. **A.** A *kennel* is where a dog is kept; a *stable* is where a horse is kept. Choice B, a *sty,* is the home to a pig, not to a sheep. Choice C, a *corral,* is the place to keep horses, not pigs (yee ha, wrangle them little piggies!). Choice D, a *coop,* is the place for hens and chickens, and you *fervently* (strongly) hope no fox enters there. A *nest* is a place for birds, not cats. If the cats are in the nest, the birds are in big trouble.

9. **D.** The purpose of a *thermometer* is to measure. The purpose of an *anchor* is to hold. If you chose choice C, you fell for the trap. Don't think of the meanings of the words; think of the relationships between them. Just because thermometers have to do with heat doesn't mean an answer with the word *heat* in it is correct. As a matter of fact, this type of answer is usually the trap answer.

    Don't out-think yourself on the other answers. While a blanket may be used for decoration, that's not its primary purpose.

10. **C.** Choices A, B, and E contain antonyms. Because all three answers can't be correct, they must all be wrong. Now you know that *serene* and *placid* can't be opposites. Make the sentence, "Serene *is* placid." Choice D is slightly tricky, but something ferocious doesn't *have* to be large. A cornered rat can be ferocious. By the process of elimination, you can choose C even if you don't know that **ungainly** means awkward, clumsy. Both **serene** and **placid** mean calm, peaceful (the root *plac* means calm).

11. **D.** This connection is a classic on the GRE: One word is a type of the other. A gorilla is a type of primate (the order of mammals that includes monkeys, apes, and humans).

    Choice C is the trap. It involves animals, which is a reason to examine it carefully, but the relationship is backwards. A bird is a type of vertebrate but not vice versa. Choices A and B may or may not be true. A doctor may be an aristocrat (a member of the privileged class), but he or she doesn't have to be. Accountants aren't necessarily bureaucrats, or people overly concerned with official details. Choice D fits perfectly. Water is a type of compound (H_2O, to be exact).

12. **E.** If you are vindictive, you are seeking revenge. **Vindictive** means vengeful, looking to get even. (You are vindictive towards the moron who left a dent in your car in the parking lot and left a note with the phone number of Dial-a-Prayer!)

    If you are **blameless**, you are seeking exoneration. To **exonerate** is to exculpate, to free from a charge. (When you accuse your neighbor of slamming into your car, she can exonerate herself by proving that she was in another state at the time of the dent.)

    Choice A is the trap answer. Don't choose it just because vindication looks like vindictive. **Vindication** means being proven correct. When you disprove your friend's alibi by showing that her twin was in another state and that she herself in fact was here and did dent your car, you are vindicated. Someone in the right is looking for vindication, not someone in the wrong.

    Irresolute means indeterminate, or wishy-washy. That type of person looks for strength, not for **servility** (the state of being like a servant, or submissive). **Jocose** means jolly, or fun-loving. A jocose person may or may not be looking for sobriety; it depends on how he became jocose in the first place! Someone **edgy** is nervous, fidgety, or on edge. He is not necessarily looking for strength but rather for peace and tranquillity.

    When you look at the words, look for their salient or distinctive features. Don't choose an answer that's "good enough" but rather hold out for one that fits perfectly. (A blameless person is definitely looking for exoneration whereas a jocose person may or may not be looking for sobriety.)

13. **C.** The relationship is lesser to greater, or weaker to stronger. First, you are thin, and then you are overly thin, or **emaciated**. First, you are happy, and then you are overly happy, or **ecstatic**.

    The pair of words in choice A are synonyms. To be **impervious** to something is to be immune to it. A teacher is often impervious to the **blandishments** (flattery) of her students who want to raise their grades. **Imperious** means regal. You may know this word in a more common form, *imperial*. (Think of Imperial margarine, with the crown on the box.) They both mean kingly, somewhat haughty and acting like royalty. **Sarcastic** means sardonic. In choice E, **demeaning** means insulting. The prefix *de-* means down from or away from, and it often precedes a word that means to put down, in the sense of insulting. A demeaning insult puts you down, criticizes you, and insults you.

14. **A.** A group of lions is a *pride*. A group of birds is a *flock*. Some of these other words are hard, especially if English is not your first language. A *kit* is a baby coyote; a *joey* is a baby kangaroo; a *cygnet* is a baby swan. A *pelt* is the fur of a wolf.

TIP

If you think the GRE is a beastly exam, you're right. There are often questions in the analogies requiring you to know the terms for the young of animals, groups of animals, or where animals live; therefore, I'd advise you to learn the terms. Use flash cards. Label one *young animals,* and write on it such terms as kit, joey, and cygnet. Label a second card *habitats* and write things like den, corral, and sty. Label a third card *groups of animals* and write down pride, pod, and flock. A few minutes of memorization can pay off here, as there are no roots, prefixes, or suffixes to help you define these types of words.

15. **D.** A *tuxedo* is a fancy suit worn on formal occasions. A *limousine* is a fancy car, used on formal occasions. The salient, or distinguishing feature, of the relationship between each pair of words is the idea of formality.

In choice A, *galleon* is an old-fashioned type of ship. (Columbus may have been the first "green" explorer in terms of energy conservation. After all, he got thousands of miles to the galleon!)

An *abode* is a home and a *hovel* is a ramshackle, dilapidated house, not a fancy one.

16. **B.** The last word in the set often features difficult words. If you recall that *in-* usually means not and *trep* means fear, you can analyze that *intrepid* means not having fear, or brave. Roots also help you to define *prolix*. *Pro-* means big or much; *lix* means speech or talk. Someone *prolix* has "big or much talk," is talkative. *Garrulous* also means talkative.

Eliminate choice E: What do gruesome and *diligent* (hard working) have to do with each other? Choice C may be a slight trap. *Ped* can be a root meaning foot; a pedestrian is a person who goes on foot (which makes him more energetic than a couch potato like me, who jumps in the car to go to the mailbox). However, *pedantic* means scholarly and has no connection to the foot. Someone *asocial* is not sociable (*a-* means not or without), not very friendly. *Amiable* (*ami* means friend, like *mon ami* in French, or *amigo* in Spanish) means friendly. In choice A, *cantankerous* means grumpy or grouchy.

17. **E.** The correct answer to a primary purpose question is rarely negative; passages almost never set out to criticize something. Eliminate choice A. A passage also rarely tries to convince the readers to take action; eliminate choice D with "urge." Choices B and C imply that the author is arguing against something, which is not the case here. Instead, he is merely giving the facts, discussing the rock art.

TIP

Three key words are often correct answers to a primary purpose question: *discuss, describe, explain.* These terms are neutral (even innocuous!) enough that they are frequently used.

18. **A.** Don't you just love the wishy-washy, noncommittal language in choice A? Dramatic answers are rarely right; the more wimpy (wimpier?) the language, the greater the odds that answer is correct. An expression like "may suggest" is difficult to argue with. The author does, in fact, say that recurring motifs link the art (and by inference, the peoples who created the art) in time and culture. He even states that the presence of Kokopelli indicates a tie with another culture. Choice B is outside the scope of the passage. Although shields are mentioned, there is no discussion of military successes. Agriculture is only indirectly mentioned ("corn plants"), eliminating choice C. Choice D is too strong ("highly artistic"); besides, nothing was said about how long the art evolved. It may have been done all at once, but it may, for all you know, have been done in bits and pieces over a long period of time. Choice E is also extraneous. Nothing was mentioned about religion.

19. **C.** Choice A sounds like something that would be interesting to know (Hmmm . . . just why *didn't* the figures have a leg to stand on?), but the passage doesn't supply the answer. Choice B is the trap. Logically, you'd think that a passage about rock art would discuss the purpose of the art, but this very short passage doesn't provide that information. You may be tempted to throw out choice C after you read that sheep were depicted with curvilinear lines and that circles were a frequent motif. However, this information serves to answer the question in choice C with a definitive "no." The question simply asks which question can be answered. It makes no difference whether the answer is "yes" or "no." Choice D is completely irrelevant; nothing was said about religion. Choice E may have tempted you. The author did mention a possible connection between the Fremont artists and people of the Four Corners area, but you should not take the information further. Nothing was said about people from other cultures beyond those of the Four Corners area.

20. **C.** First, use the verbs to help to eliminate wrong answers. Passages are rarely negative and don't ridicule anything (choice E). This very factual passage does not *refute* (deny, disprove) anything, eliminating choice B. A strong word like "prove" (choice D) is rarely correct (and how much can be proven in one paragraph, anyway?). Just by examining the verbs, you have narrowed your answers down to a 50-50 guess. (Although the GRE has no penalty for wrong answers, meaning you should always guess, a 50-50 shot is a real gift.) Choice A would be tempting except that nowhere does the author make the claim that the Fremont culture was the most advanced, so how can that claim be challenged? Choice C fits with the same motif as that discussed in the previous two questions: Recurring motifs between cultures may indicate connections between those cultures.

21. **E.** This passage contains a lot of dry detail about how certain campfire factors damage soil and its ability to support life. Throughout the passage, the author uses these details to recommend a certain action. The author is concerned that campfires damage soil and wants to minimize this damage. Choice E fits this perfectly. Choice A is too extreme. Choices B and D are true statements, but these are just two of several factors mentioned by the author.

Just because a statement is true does not mean it is the correct answer; in a main idea question, all five choices may in fact be true. Choice C is also a detail but is wrong primarily because the author is concerned that certain woods will lead to soil damage, not with how well the woods will work with the campfire per se.

22. **D.** The last two paragraphs of the passage urge measures to restrict campfire location. Without such measures, the author claims that campfires will be built just about every-where and that soil damage will be widespread. It can be inferred from this that campfire users, when left to their own devices, will build a campfire just about anywhere. This leads to choice D as the answer. Because the opposite of choice A appears to be true, eliminate this choice. Choice B is plausible, but there is no mention of a connection between campfire users and forest fires. Forest fires were discussed briefly in paragraph three in relation to water repellency. Choice C goes overboard. There is no information to indicate whether campfire users favor a certain type of soil, eliminating choice E. The scientific findings discussed in paragraph two point to an advantage of one type or the other, but you can't tell whether the campfire users actually consider this evidence.

23. **E.** Common sense suggests that E is the right answer. Paragraph three helps to confirm this. This paragraph mentions that short-lived forest fires are more likely than campfires to create water repellency-inducing conditions (knocking out choice A). This information implies that campfires last longer. Combine this reasoning with the explicit mention that campfires typically exceed 350 degrees and you've got your answer. Choice C is directly contradicted by paragraph four. Choices B and D don't make sense. The passage often mentions that heat flow into the soil damages it. A long-lasting campfire will produce more heat flow than a short-lived one.

While you certainly do not need to have any background knowledge to answer Reading Comprehension questions (all information necessary is given or implied in the passage), don't hesitate to use your common sense, especially with science passages. Common sense is a good place to start, but do be sure to check your "logical" answer with the facts given in the passage.

24. **C.** All the information needed to answer this question comes from the fifth paragraph. The author does not directly state option I but comes close by saying that elm and mesquite were the hottest burning fuels. In addition, the author says that elm and mesquite are long-lasting, suggesting that they are not softwoods, which burn quickly. Because they are not softwoods, elm and mesquite will not be associated with little heat flow into the soil. Option II goes too far. The author recommends that softwood use be encouraged when a choice of wood is available. The author would probably permit elm and mesquite use if they were the only woods available. Option III follows from option I and is consistent with the entire paragraph. Elm and mesquite conduct heat into the soil, which damages it, and as hardwoods, are not the woods of choice. With I and III in and II eliminated, the answer has to be C.

25. **D.** This was almost the same question as number 21 and very similar to number 24; did you notice? The questions following reading passages are often very similar, like variations on a theme. Think of them as spokes emanating from the hub, or the central idea. After you've identified the central idea, the other answers will all cover the same territory. Here, the central idea is that campfires have negative effects on soil. The last few paragraphs get very specific on how to reduce that negative impact, via proper fuel selection and using campfire rings.

Choice B looks good at first glance, but it is too dramatic, too strong, too intense. Lines 56 – 58 talk about using fire rings but don't say anything about banning fires outside of them. Be sure not to "take the next step," to read too much into a statement. Most passages don't get that demanding.

Choice C is also tricky. If you didn't actually go back and skim over lines 47 – 64 again, you probably chose this answer. Summarizing the effects of campfires on soil properties was the theme of the *first* half of the passage, not of the second. The second half shifted ideas from what campfires do to soil to how to prevent them from doing it.

Choice E has a few problems. The author does suggest using softwoods, but is that really "an alternate energy source?" Even if it is, the suggestion isn't the theme of lines 47 – 64, just one paragraph's worth. This answer is too specific for the question.

Just because your answer was mentioned in the passage does not mean it's the best answer to this specific question.

26. **C.** To answer a tone/attitude question, begin by deciding whether the material is positive, negative, or neutral. Here, the author clearly has some reservations about campfire use, so eliminate the positive and neutral choices, E and B, respectively. Choice A goes overboard and can be eliminated. The GRE will rarely, if ever, give you a passage that contains such an extreme emotion. How about choice C? The author is concerned about what campfires can do to soil but is not ranting and raving about it. This choice fits nicely and is the answer. Choice D misses the mark because the author's tone does not match that of one who is lecturing to somebody after she has done something wrong, which is what "admonishment" suggests.

27. **B.** The last sentence of the first paragraph states that the loss of organic matter reduces water-holding capacity and renders the soil more susceptible to erosion.

Note that this question basically required your truly understanding the whole passage. If you didn't read this passage carefully but just skimmed for specific answers to specific questions, this questions would have been a good question just to guess at.

28. **B.** To *irritate* is to annoy. The opposite is to soothe. Choice A, *badger,* is to harass, bother, annoy. Occasionally, the answer choices feature a word that is a synonym to the question word. It's easy to choose this one, because uppermost in your mind is the definition. "Badger, hmmm. That means to annoy, to irritate. Oh, there it is!" Keep in mind that the name of the game is *antonyms.*

29. **E.** To *ameliorate* is to make more tolerable or improve. Studying in the same room as your *pulchritudinous* (beautiful) sweetheart will ameliorate the situation. Choice E, *exacerbate,* means to make more violent or severe, to aggravate. If you don't feel like studying, being in the same room as your pulchritudinous sweetheart will exacerbate your lack of interest . . . in the exam, that is. Choice B, *placate,* is to calm down (*plac* means calm; *-ate* means to make). To *hoard* is to save secretly. I hoard the last ice cream bar in the freezer by hiding it behind the broccoli.

30. **B.** *Inept* means bungling or foolish. An inept person makes a mess of anything he attempts. The prefix *in-* means not; someone inept is not adept, not skillful. Choice C, *prolific,* means abundant or producing much. An inept person is prolific at creating chaos. Choice E, *indigenous,* means native to. Long-legged blondes are indigenous to California beaches.

31. **B.** To *abstain* is to refrain, to hold back (*ab-* means away from). You may abstain from voting in the student elections if you don't like any of the candidates. The opposite is to participate. In choice D, to *meander* is to wander aimlessly, to ramble. To *infuriate* is to annoy greatly, to make furious. A good public speaker will abstain from meandering too much because rambling can infuriate the audience.

32. **B.** Something *dormant* is inactive. The opposite, logically enough, is active.

    In Spanish, *dormir* means to sleep. Think of something dormant as sleeping and thus not being active. *Obstinate* means stubborn (*ob-* means block or against; someone obstinate or stubborn may block or be against the plans of others).

33. **E.** *Terse* means concise, succinct. A terse comment gets to the point quickly. The opposite is rambling. *Soporific* means causing sleep. Many of the test prep tomes on the market are soporific.

34. **A.** *Diffuse* means to disperse, to spread widely. The opposite is to focus, to converge. To *prognosticate* is to predict (*pro-* means before; *gnos* means knowledge; *-ate* means to make. "To make knowledge before" is to predict.) To *emulate* is to imitate.

35. **A.** *Credulous* means full of trust, gullible (*cred* means trust or belief; *-ous* means full of or very). The opposite is disbelieving. *Inept* means unskilled. *Sinister* means ominous. Sinister music may alert viewers to the presence of an inept doctor in a soap opera. *Boorish* means crude.

36. **C.** *Farfetched* means illogical or improbable. Getting a perfect GRE score without studying at all is farfetched. Choice A, *fickle,* means changeable or inconstant. Choice B, *promiscuous,* means without discrimination, without being selective, or picky. A fickle person is probably promiscuous in his choice of girlfriends. Choice D, *ramshackle,* means poorly constructed, ready to collapse. Choice E, *unseemly,* means inappropriate. It would be unseemly for the president of the United States to live in a ramshackle building.

37. **B.** *Hapless* means unlucky. (*hap* means luck; a mishap is bad luck; *haphazard* means depending on luck or chance; *hapless* is without luck, unlucky.) Choice A, *saturnine,* means gloomy or morose. Choice C, *cacophonous,* means bad-sounding, raucous. (*caco* means bad; *phon* means sound; *-ous* means full of.) My friends who have to listen to my cacophonous singing voice are saturnine (actually, they become sanguinary, which means bloodthirsty, but that's another story). Choice D, *mordant,* means sarcastic, caustic. Choice E, *ambiguous,* means uncertain, able to be interpreted in two or more ways. (*ambi* means both; *-ous* means full of. Ambiguous is "full of both," unclear.) An ambiguous response is often the best answer to a no-win question such as, "Does this outfit make me look fatter than before?"

38. **D.** To *burgeon* is to blossom and grow. The opposite is to wither. To *garble* is to distort or jumble. A student may garble her words and mispronounce this question as "surgeon" or even (my favorite) "sturgeon." Pretty hard to find the opposite of sturgeon, wouldn't you say?

Section 3

Questions 1 – 5

	Female	Male
Agency		
R	brown	red
B	red	blond
Y	red	blond

Make a simple box grid. Because statement I tells you that only a man and woman can work together, label the grids male and female along the top. There are three agencies, R, B, and Y; label those along the side of the grid. Now put the appropriate hair color in the box, as indicated by the statements. The information given in statement II doesn't fit neatly into the grid (don't box me in!) and should be noted briefly to the side: something simple such as, "2 diff. color hair."

After you have the grid filled in, answering the questions takes only a few seconds.

1. **D.** Statement I tells you that people must be of different genders (sexes) to model together. A male cannot model with a male, regardless of hair color or agency affiliation. This question is a big time-waster; you probably went through all the answer choices checking the grid carefully. You can save a few seconds by skimming the answer choices to eliminate *egregiously* (flagrantly bad) wrong answers, ones that jump off the page at you.

2. **B.** A male cannot model with another male (the law according to statement I). Choices D and E are immediately eliminated.

   If you chose A or C, pack your bags, you're going on a guilt trip. You forgot to look to the side of the box for the information from statement II: Models must have different colored hair. A male model from agency R has red hair and thus cannot model with a female with red hair.

3. **E.** All the answer choices feature women; no answers can be quickly eliminated based on the requirement that models be different sexes. A male client of agency B has blond hair. He can pose with a female client of agency R who has brown hair. Circle I; eliminate answers B and C. Remember to eliminate wrong answers as you go to prevent the chance of making a careless mistake by choosing one. A male client of agency B can pose with a female client of agency B, who is a redhead. Circle II; eliminate answer D because it does not include II. You don't even have to bother evaluating III; choice E must be correct.

4. **E.** Put the reasoning in A-B form as follows: When A, then B. No more A because I cannot afford more B. Answer E follows that same reasoning: when A (when I took the lid off the jam jar), then B (I got a cut finger). No more A (I am not going to open any more jam jars) because I cannot afford more B (I can't afford to get any more cuts).

   Choice A takes the argument too far. There is no reason to assume that taking home the report card is the cause of the F's; therefore, not taking it home any more does not ensure a *paucity* (lack of) of F's in the future.

   Choice B can be written as No A (I can't stand loud music). When B, then A (when dancing, then loud music). No B. That is not at all the same sequence as in the question.

   Choice C introduces too many aspects. A (I have $300), and B (must use it to pay the rent). Because C (going out to dinner) uses A (uses the money), no C (no going out to dinner).

   Choice D is the most tempting; you might have chosen this one. Close, but no cigar. (Smoking is *detrimental* [harmful] to your health anyway.) Think of it as A (went to the doctor), and then B (gave a $50 shot). Because no B (no $50), no A.

This type of question often takes a lot of time . . . and is frequently missed anyway. If you can't make a quick "If A, then B" type statement, or if you're not absolutely sure of your statement, just skip this problem. There's no *dearth* (lack of, paucity) of other questions to torment you.

5. **B.** First, identify the argument. The argument is that children today are learning less than children did ten years ago. This conclusion is based on evidence that says that teachers spend less time on basics and more time on administrative matters. For this to be true, the author must assume that more teacher time on basics contributes to learning while more teacher time on administrative matters detracts from learning. To strengthen the argument, support this assumption. Choice B does so by stating that time spent on basics does indeed contribute to student learning.

Choice A is a "so what?" How do you know whether 100 hours a year is a larger number of hours or a smaller number than field trips a decade ago? You have no basis of comparison.

Choice C is very, very tempting. Just because teachers are spending less time in the classroom, however, does not mean children are learning less. Maybe the teachers are showing kids more via computers or cable TV shows. There are all sorts of other ways children can learn besides having a teacher in front of them. They could read *scintillatingly* (sparkling, giving off flashes of light) brilliant books like this one, for example.

Choice D doesn't give you enough information. You need to know how many children were flunking at least one class in high school ten years ago before you can support the statement that children are learning less today than they did ten years ago.

Choice E also discusses just one facet of learning. Just because parents are less involved in their children's education does not necessarily mean children are learning less. If my own father, for instance, had been *less* involved in my calculus homework, I'm quite sure I would have learned it faster and a lot less painfully.

Questions 6 – 12

Because there are so many flowers to keep straight, make a list or "pool" of them. To the side, jot down the flowers: pink petunias, purple zinnias, white daisies, pink carnations, red roses, purple pansies, purple lilies.

Draw eight spaces. Keep in mind that one space will be empty because there are only seven types of flowers. You can drive yourself crazy trying to figure out what goes in that space if you forget this disparity between flowers and available spaces.

Statement I gives information that is written off to the side, not in a chart. Jot down a brief note, such as "same colors not together."

Statement II allows you to write purple pansies above space 1 and again above space 7.

Be careful to put the note in *both* spaces; you don't know yet which one will finally get the flower.

Statement III tells you that the order is pansies-roses-zinnias. From this, you know that the pansies cannot be in space 7 because there is no room for two types of flowers after space 7. Scratch off the purple pansies from space 7; you have ascertained they go in space 1.

Statement IV puts the lilies in the last space. I don't know about you, but this is my favorite type of statement. Brief, to the point, no-nonsense. Let's have more of these.

Statement V puts a pink flower, either petunias or carnations, in spaces 4 and 6. Be sure to write *both* petunias and carnations in the blanks. You cannot arbitrarily decide petunias go in 4 and carnations in 6, or vice versa. Keep your options open.

Statement VI deals with a white flower. The only white flower is the daisies. It must go in space 5, resulting in one space between it and the purple zinnias. The other purple flowers are the pansies and lilies. To be one space away from the pansies, the daisies would have to go in space 3, which is already taken up with the zinnias. To be one space away from the purple lilies, the daisies would have to go in space 6, which is already filled with either the petunias or the carnations. Space 5 it is.

Your chart now looks like this.

purple pansies	red roses	purple zinnias	pink petunias or carnations	white daisies	pink petunias or carnations		purple lilies
1	2	3	4	5	6	7	8

You can now look at the chart and answer any question with *celerity*. (No, not a dieter's worst nightmare; that's celery. *Celerity* means speed.) Note especially that space 7 is empty.

6. **E.** You could predict that this would be a question, right? If you forgot to leave an empty space, you would lose a lot of time going back and trying to figure out which space is blank. By drawing in the lines and numbering them right away, you avoid making this mistake.

7. **C.** If you chose D, you fell for the trap. Sure, there are four SPACES between the zinnias and the lilies, but the question asks how many FLOWERS there are between the zinnias and the lilies. There are three.

8. **A.** The closest purple flower is the zinnias, only one space away. Keep in mind that this type of question is not trying to trick or trap you; once you have your chart made, the answers are all straightforward.

9. **B.** You determined that carnations can go in either space 4 or space 6.

10. **D.** The carnations can be in space 4, making them two spaces away from the roses, *or* the carnations can be in space 6, making them four spaces away from the roses. Note how cunningly the question is phrased: "is not necessarily true." That means the statement could be true, but it doesn't have to be.

    When you have an "open option" on a chart, a space that "could be" one thing or "could be" another, you will almost always see a question on asking about the options. Watch for it.

11. **B.** Because negatives can be so confusing, try to rewrite the statement in a positive form. If *few* children *don't* love ice cream, *many* children *do* love ice cream. If many children do love ice cream, and Athalie is a child, she probably loves ice cream.

    The word *probably* is a great word to buddy up to. It is such a wimp, such a namby-pamby hedging, *equivocating* (deceptive) word that it can fit into nearly any situation. While few things are *always* true or *never* true, many things are *probably* or *sometimes* true. When I see the word *probably*, I "assume it's guilty until proven innocent." I head straight for it.

    Choice A does not follow the argument. If Athalie is a child, there is no reason to assume she is a typical child. Maybe she wants to grow up to take the GRE and is looking forward to the event. How bizarre.

    Choice C goes overboard. Just because Athalie is a child and most children love ice cream doesn't mean Athalie pigs out on the stuff. She might love it but not get too much of it because of her nutrition-conscious (that is, spoilsport) parents.

    Choice D is totally wrong. If few children don't like ice cream, most do; it's not logical to assume that Athalie is one of the few who don't. Be careful: If the question said, "Which may be true . . ." choice D *may* be true. It's not likely, but it is possible. Always note what the question is asking for.

    Choice E again is out in left field. We don't know whether most children are or are not allergic to ice cream; we know only that few don't love ice cream.

12. **D.** For all you gridiron-challenged types, don't panic. You don't even need to know the difference between a touchdown and a rubdown to answer this question. The key is to recognize that the second sentence is the conclusion, which states that interceptions are one of the major causes of football game losses. The first sentence provides the evidence for the conclusion, and it says that there is a relationship between the number of interceptions thrown and game losses. Does this establish with certainty that the interceptions have a lot to do with causing the losses? No, for all you know, the interceptions could come about as a result of a team's losing a game. (Football aficionados know that a team that is losing starts throwing more passes and is thereby likely to throw more interceptions.) For the argument to be valid, its author must assume that interceptions are a cause rather than a result of losing. Choice D points to this very thing.

Choice A is out because the stimulus says nothing about fumbles. The argument does not claim that interceptions are the only thing that can hurt a football team. Choice B is too extreme: The author does not have to assume zero interceptions. Choice C is a possible, but hardly definite, inference, as the author doesn't *have* to assume it. The author discusses how interceptions contribute to losses. He is not concerned with how a team can overcome an interception. Perhaps bad officiating allows a team to win despite throwing more interceptions; who knows? Choice E provides one good reason why interceptions might contribute to losing games, but it is not a necessary assumption. It could be, for example, that interceptions interfere more about a team's ability to score than about whether they make it easy for the opponent to score.

Questions 13 – 20

Create a week's calendar. Statement I gives info that doesn't fit into the calendar. Put it to the side in case you need it later. "No shots unless check-in." Statement II again has info that doesn't fit neatly onto the calendar. Put a note to the side: "same disease, same day." Statement III finally gives you something to write on the calendar. Put **Emp** on Wednesday, Friday, and Sunday. If you put down Tuesday, scratch it off; the statement tells you Tuesday is an exception. Statement IV has to be postponed. You don't know when pneumonia patients check in yet. Put a big mark in the margin to remind you to come back to this statement later. Statement V tells you to put **Ec** under Tuesday and Thursday. Statement VI tells you to put **Pn** under Monday, Wednesday, Friday, and Saturday. Sunday is the exception. You always have to be careful to note the exceptions. You may want to circle them in the statements.

Note: Now you can go back to statement IV. You know that emphysema and pneumonia patients check in on Wednesdays and Fridays; put **Ca** for cancer patients in on those days. *Don't forget to go back to statements you skipped earlier.*

Statement VII means that **Cl** (colitis) patients can check in only on Saturday, Sunday, Monday, and Tuesday because those are the consecutive days with no cancer patient check-ins. BUT look out for the next statement. Statement VIII won't allow patients to check in on Mondays, which means that Monday and Tuesday disqualify for consecutive days for **Cl** (colitis) patients, who have to settle for Saturday and Sunday. This means that you must remove **Pn** from Monday.

Your final calendar looks like this:

Sun	Mon	Tues	Wed	Thurs	Fri	Sat
Emp			Emp		Emp	
		Ec		Ec		
			Ca		Ca	
Cl						Cl
			Pn		Pn	Pn

A calendar game is one of the easiest games to diagram and one of the quickest to finish. If you are running short of time and you know that you won't be able to do all the games, head for the calendar one. Think of it as a gift from the GRE fairy.

13. **A.** A look at the chart gives you this information.

14. **C.** On Wednesday and Friday, patients with three diseases, emphysema, cancer, and pneumonia, can be admitted.

15. **E.** On Saturday, pneumonia patients are admitted but not cancer patients. On both Wednesday and Friday, both pneumonia and cancer patients are admitted.

16. **D.** On Wednesday and Friday, both cancer and emphysema patients can be admitted.

17. **E.** Every day except Saturday (and Monday, in which no one is admitted) has either eczema or emphysema patients.

Everything, but everything, depends on the chart, graph, or diagram you make. If it is off even a little bit, you are probably going to miss every question. Be the Degas of Diagrams, the Chagall of Charts. Spend your time on the pictures, and then you can zoom through the problems.

18. **A.** This argument misses the mark. The conclusion has to do with whether voice training is necessary for operatic stardom, but the evidence runs along the lines of saying that voice training does not guarantee a career in opera. The evidence would be better used to support a conclusion that stated that voice training is not sufficient for one to become an opera star. Even if the evidence stated that only one in a million voice training graduates became an opera star, it still might be the case that the voice training was necessary. A great way to weaken the argument would be to establish that, no matter how difficult it is to become an opera star, it is impossible to become an opera star without voice training. This is pretty much what choice A states.

Choice B would work well if the conclusion stated that voice training is largely unsuccessful in helping one land a role as a singer. It does nothing to establish that voice training is necessary to become an opera star.

Choice C suggests that the 2 percent figure will go up after some voice training graduates age. However, it can't be established that voice training is necessary for operatic stardom. It still could be the case that many opera stars made it on raw talent alone.

Choice D suggests that opera company membership is not the place to look for the existence of opera stars, but it does not say anything about whether voice training is necessary or not. Maybe all those opera stars had voice training, but maybe they did not.

Choice E provides a single example (typically not a great weakener) of voice training paying off. Voice training may have worked for Stephanie, but maybe she would have made it anyway. What about other stars? Did they go through voice training?

19. **B.** The conclusion that you should eliminate butter is predicated on butter's clogging arteries and causing heart problems. This argument assumes that arteries and heart problems are the only factors that matter in regard to the consumption of butter. Perhaps there is a positive factor associated with butter that outweighs the artery and heart problems. Such a factor would argue for the use of butter and thus weaken the conclusion. Choice B does just this. In fact, it argues that one *must* consume butter.

Most of the answer choices seem reasonable, but they don't address the question, which is what weakens the conclusion. Just because most people don't believe butter is detrimental to their health (choice E), for example, does not weaken the conclusion that butter in fact is detrimental. Choice C is probably the second best answer. If eating a variety of foods is the key to a healthy life, butter may be part of that variety; however, choice B discusses butter specifically and thus is a slightly better answer.

Choice A is similar to choice C in that it is too indirect to be a good answer. Choice D would fit in to some extent if the conclusion said that butter is the only thing to eliminate, but this choice is out primarily because one could shoot back with, "Then eliminate butter and all substitutes."

20. **D.** For a small-group survey to reflect the opinions of a larger population, it must be large enough and, more importantly, have various groups present in the proportion that they appear in the larger group. To take an extreme example, a poll taken at the Republican National Convention would not be valid to predict a presidential election because the percentage of people at the convention who will end up voting for the Democratic candidate in November is far smaller than the percentage of Americans who will vote for the Democrat. Sample size is also important, in that randomly picking a group of five people is more likely to produce, say, 80 percent Republicans than will a random selection of 1,500 people. Choices B and E point to these sampling problems and thus serve as possible explanations for the discrepancy between the polls and the actual election. Eliminate them, remembering that you are looking for something that does *not* explain the discrepancy.

Choices A and C are also plausible explanations. It could be that Truman came on strong in the last two weeks (choice A) or that Dewey didn't collect all the votes the polls indicated he should have gotten because the Dewey faithful didn't show up (choice C).

By the process of elimination, you have choice D. Whether this statement is true or false is not important. What is critical is what the poll participants and voters of 1948 thought. The Truman voters may have thought this way on Election Day, but then why did Truman trail in the polls? Additionally, the choice D statement may have become evident only after Truman left office in January, 1953. This choice does not explain the discrepancy.

Questions 21 – 25

Did just reading through this game make you think of a Stephen King garden fantasy gone amuck? Before going through the answer explanations, keep four things in mind:

1. This is a very hard game, found at the end of the section. You may not even get this far.

2. There is no penalty for wrong answers on the GRE. Go ahead and guess.

3. Some schools don't put much emphasis on the Analytical Ability score.

4. You have friends and family who still love you.

In this game, you must distribute the parts amongst the mowers. A good way to represent this is to draw three circles for the three mowers. Use letters for the parts and put these in the circles. Here's the initial setup:

N N N N
B B b (small b = small bolt)
W W W

Remember to start with the most concrete information. The small bolt (b) goes on the yellow mower.

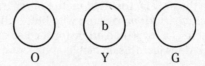

Another simple rule is that W may not appear in the green circle.

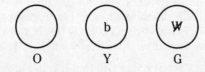

You may combine the second rule (small bolt means put on nut) with your diagram to lead to the following:

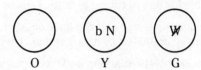

Symbolize the first rule to make it easier to remember: B → W + N works well. This does not mean that W + N → B. B guarantees W + N but is not necessary for W + N. This means that W + N may be present without B. What you can deduce is that no W and/or no N means no B because to have a B without W and/or N would violate the first rule.

Are you still with me? These games get easier with practice, I promise.

Because N and W aren't in the green circle, B can't be either; you can show that there is no B in the green circle.

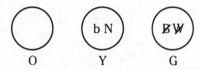

Put an asterisk by the last rule to help you to remember it. What does this rule tell you about the green circle? Because there has to be at least one part on each mower, there must be an N in G. Your final diagram (and you thought the day would never come; o ye of little faith!) and roster are as follows:

NN~~NN~~
Bb~~b~~
W W W

Crossed out parts are those that have been used.

After all that work, answering the questions is the easy part.

21. **D.** An effective way to answer this question is to select a rule and eliminate the choice(s) that violate the rule.

   Take the simple third rule (no W on G). Choice C violates it; dump choice C. Look at the fourth rule (small b on Y) and eliminate choice E. Choice B violates the fifth rule. Choice A violates the first rule (by gad, this is a violent exam!) because the orange mower must have a washer to go with the large bolt. Only choice D is left.

22. **E.** As soon as you find one possibility for a choice, you know that the choice need not be false. Take a look at choice D for number 21, which you know is a possibility that doesn't violate any rules. This shows that choices A, B, C, and D could be true and leaves choice E as the answer. To check, try to make E true:

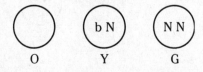

Remember that you may not put a W or a B in G. The problem is that the two large bolts must go in O or in Y, but there is only one nut left. A large bolt must have a nut, but this is now impossible for one of the large bolts. Choice E must be false.

23. **B.** First, use common sense and eliminate choice E. You can see from your master diagram that at least three of the ten parts are not in O, which makes eight parts for O impossible.

    Make a quick copy of the diagram and try to put in as many parts as possible into O:

    It's easy to put a B and a W with the N (see first rule). Can you add anything to B N W? Forget the other B because B → N + W, but this question does not allow for a second N. See whether you can add a W.

    This is fine because the second B may go in Y along with the final N and the final W:

24. **E.** This question provides a lot of information, so work with it. Put the two large bolts (which also means two nuts and two washers) in the yellow circle:

    There is only one part left (a W) and because of the fifth rule, it must go in O.

25. **A.** Once you put a B in a circle, you must add N + W. The yellow already has two parts, so adding a B would produce the following *un*acceptable grouping:

    This eliminates choices B and D, which put a large bolt on the yellow mower.

    Putting both large bolts on a single mower would produce two B N W combinations, or six parts, on a mower. This eliminates choices C and E. Choice A works. Here is one possibility:

Section 4

1. **B.** You know that 20 percent = $^1/_5$. You can divide 1,900 by 5, get 398, and then subtract that from 1,990 to get 1,592. That's the official way. Here's the much easier Dummies way: Estimate that 1,990 is actually 2,000. $^1/_5$ of 2,000 (you can figure in your mind) is 400. Subtract 400 from 2,000 to get 1,600. That's close enough estimation for a problem in the easy questions at the start of the exam.

Keep in mind that the name of the game here is quantitative comparisons, not problem solving. You don't have to solve each problem through to the final solution – just until you can compare the two quantities.

2. **A.** You know that when you multiply by a power of ten, you move the decimal point that many places. If the power of ten is positive, move the decimal to the right. If the power of ten is negative, move the decimal to the left. In Column A, move the decimal five places to the right, which gives you 50,430. In Column B, move the decimal two places to the left, giving you .5043.

3. **C.** An inscribed angle has one half the degree measure of its intercepted arc. In plain English, that means when two angles have the same endpoints (in this case points A and C), the angle with its vertex in the center of the circle is twice as big as the angle with its vertex actually on the circle. This concept was covered in Chapter 10.

Geometry problems are, in my opinion, the easiest of the math questions to get correct, as a rule. They reward you for memorizing formulas. You rarely have to do any deep analysis (as in word problems) or worry about keeping things straight (as in algebra problems). You just have to know and apply the rules. If I were running short on time or brain power (or both), I'd head for the geometry problems first.

4. **A.** Are you a fraction-phobe, like most of us? Then avoid fractions altogether and simply plug in numbers. Work backwards and plug in a number for c that will be divisible by both 4 and 3. Try 12. If c = 12, then b = $^3/_4 \times 12$ = 9. If b = 9, then a = $^2/_3 \times 9$, or 6. Now $^a/_c$ = $^6/_{12}$, or $^1/_2$. Because $^1/_2$ is greater than $^1/_3$, A is the answer. While this will work no matter what number you plug in for c, why not make life easy and plug in a nice round number? If you plug in something like 10, then b = $^3/_4 \times 10$ or $^{30}/_4$ and that's a pain in the fundament (that portion of your body upon which you are sitting even as we speak).

If you want to do the problem "the real way," it's not hard. You just have to know that "of" means $\times$ and multiply the whole shebang. $^2/_3$ of $^3/_4$ of c = $^2/_3 \times ^3/_4 \times c$ = $^6/_{12} \times c$ = $^1/_2 \times c$. It comes out the same.

5. **B.** Plug in numbers. Suppose that a = 1. Then Column A is $^1/_2 \times 1$, which is $^1/_2$, and then $^1/_2{}^2$ which is $^1/_4$. Column B requires you to square the 1 first, which is simply 1, and then multiply by $^1/_2$ to get $^1/_2$. So far, Column B is bigger. Try a different number. Suppose that a = 2. Then Column A is $^1/_2$ of 2, which is 1. You know that 1^2 = 1. Column B is $^1/_2$ of 4 (because 2^2 = 4) and Column B is still greater. No matter what you plug in (and you should always plug in more than once, or you'll never know whether the answer depends on what you plug in), Column B is larger.

Do you remember the Sacred Six you are to plug in for variables? They are 1, 2, 0, –1, –2, and $^1/_2$. Usually, just plugging in 1 and 2 will do the job for you, especially on the easy problems near the beginning of the exam.

6. **D.** Please tell me you didn't fall for this trap. Did you pick up your pencil and start to draw a picture of the roller rink, the school, and the coffee shop? As soon as you have to draw a picture, you should be thinking choice D. The answer *de*pends on how you draw the picture. If you put the roller rink, the school, and the coffee shop all in a straight line in that order, then the coffee shop and the rink are in fact 13 kilometers apart. But (and this is a big but, because whenever you see a C answer, you should be paranoid and double-check it) what if you put the coffee shop three kilometers to the other side of the school, between the rink and the school? Then the distance from the rink to the coffee shop is only 7 kilometers, and now the answer is B. If the answer changes *de*pending on how you draw the figure, choose D.

Problems that require you to find a distance between places or people are often D because the distance depends on the sequence those places or people are in. When you see a "line 'em up" problem, think D.

7. **A.** It's easy to do this problem if you convert the percent to decimals (all right-thinking people despise percentages) and remember that *of* means ×. Column A, therefore, is 3.0 (300 percent is the same as 3, or 3.0) × 30 = 90. Column B is .60 × 15 = 9.

Did you fall for the trap and choose C? Don't be *disheartened* (sad); it happens to the best of us. You were thinking of only the numerals and forgetting your decimal places. You could have avoided all this grief by using your brain instead of your yellow #2. You know quickly that 300 percent of 30 is more than 30. You know just as quickly that 60 percent of 15 is less than 15. Because more than 30 is greater than less than 15, Column A is greater. Whenever possible, try to talk the problem through rather than solving it precisely. No one really cares what the answer is.

8. **A.** Ah, if you chose C, you got careless.

Whenever you see a choice C, double- and triple-check it. More traps lie in the C answers than in most of the rest of the answers. If your first instinct is to choose C, you're probably just making some nasty test maker's day by falling for his trap.

First, you have to say to yourself in English what the symbols means. Say, "I have something in a triangle. First, I multiply that something by 3. Then I square that answer. Then I take a third of that something. Then I subtract the second from the first." In other words, substitute the number in the triangle for the *x* in the equation. For Column A, you have 3×-3, which is -9. Then $-9^2 = 81$. Next, $\frac{1}{3}$ of $-3 = -1$. Finally, $81 - (-1)$ means $81 + 1 = 82$. For Column B, you have $3 \times 3 = 9$. Then $9^2 = 81$. Next, $\frac{1}{3}$ of $3 = 1$. Finally, $81 - 1 = 80$. You had to keep your negatives and positives straight.

Whenever a problem has a negative variable, double-check your signs. You can easily make a careless mistake with them.

9. **D.** If a geometry problem is all words and no pictures, the answer is often choice D. You have no formulas for the area of a decagon in the math review; that should be a hint that you don't have to know how to find the area of a decagon for this exam. Because you have no numbers at all, you can't find the exact area for column A. However, before choosing D automatically, be sure to read Column B. You can often compare quantities even without being able to find precise answers.

You have no way of knowing the area of a regular pentagon.

Just because a pentagon has five sides and a decagon has ten sides does not mean the area of a decagon is twice the area of a pentagon. Everything depends on how big the sides of the figures are. You can draw a decagon in which each side is 1 unit long and a pentagon in which each side is 100 units long; then two times the area of the pentagon would certainly not be equal to the area of the decagon.

The word *regular* is put here as a red herring: It just means that all sides and all angles are equal. For example, an equilateral triangle is a regular triangle. The word doesn't give you any information about the lengths of the sides of the figure.

10. **A.** What do I mean by giving you a problem like this without allowing you access to your calculator? Well, you have two choices (murder and mayhem are not among them). You can make a quick guess on this problem and pretty much blow it off entirely. Or you can be very smart and realize that if a principle is valid with a large number, it is usually valid with a small number. In other words, instead of 2^{25} or 2^{24}, make it 2^5 and 2^4. You can quickly figure 2^5 as $2 \times 2 \times 2 \times 2 \times 2 = 32$. Then 2^4 is 16, and $32 - 16 = 16$. Therefore, $2^5 - 2^4$ is 2^4, just as $2^{25} - 2^{24}$ is 2^{24}, not 2^{23}.

11. **D.** When a geometry problem has no figure drawn, the answer is often choice D because it *de*pends on how the figure is drawn. A rectangle of perimeter 20 can have, for example, sides of 1 and 9 and 1 and 9, making the area 9. Or it can have sides of 6 and 4 and 6 and 4, making the area 24. (The area of a rectangle is *length* times *width*. If you forgot this, return to the geometry portion of the math review.) A triangle of perimeter 20 can have sides of

4, 7, and 9, or a *plethora* (abundance) of other combinations. And because you don't know whether the triangle is a right triangle, you have no idea what the height is. That height could be a leg of the triangle, be inside the triangle, or be outside the triangle. There is not enough information to compare the quantities.

12. **C.** It's amazing how many questions that require you actually to do the work and solve the problem turn out to be choice C. I'm not saying that you should choose C as soon as you start shoving the pencil around, but the more calculations you do, the more often the answer seems to be C. (That's the flip of the tip in the lecture that if the quantities appear to be equal at first glance, without doing any work, there's probably a trap.) Here, set the equations up vertically:

$$16a + 5b = 37$$

$$-8a + 3b = -21$$

You want to either add or subtract to get the same numerical coefficient (the number that goes in front of the variable) for the a and the b. When you add the equations here (and notice how I've moved the a to the front of the second equation, to make the variables add up neatly), you get $8a + 8b = 16$. Divide both sides by 8 to get $a + b = 2$.

You didn't have to go through the whole mess of substitution. That is, you didn't have to say for the first equation that $16a = 37 - 5b$, and then say that $a = {}^{37}/_{16} - {}^{5b}/_{16}$, and then substitute that for the value of a in the second equation. I'd call that *gratuitous* (uncalled for, unearned, unnecessary) violence. When you have two equations, line them up vertically and work so that either one of the variables drops out (for example, you may have $3b - 3b$) or so that the variables have the same numerical coefficients.

13. **D.** If you chose C, didn't you feel guilty thinking this was just a little bit too easy, especially for a question this close to the end? Besides, if the columns look equal, there's usually a trap. A percentage means that you must know a part and a whole. For example, if the sales were \$100 and the profits went up from 25 to 30, then the sales went up from 100 to 105 (assuming the costs remained the same) and the percent increase was 5 percent. But say that the original sales were \$150 and the profits were \$10. Then if the profits go up 20 percent to \$12, the sales go up only two dollars as well, to \$152, and $^2/_{152} = .013$, or roughly $1\,^1/_3$ percent. The answer *depends* on the original values for both the sales and the profit.

I am less concerned, as a teacher, with your getting the question right than I am with your not missing the question. That may sound *circuitous* (arguing in a circle), but it's not really. You have to be sure that you don't miss the question by falling for a trap before your brain has time to process the information and solve the problem. Think of this rather like the physician's creed: First, do no harm.

14. **A.** The area of a parallelogram is *base* × *height.* You know the base is 10. The height is a straight line from the tallest point of the figure to the base.

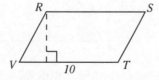

Because the area is 80, the height must be 8 (because $10 \times 8 = 80$). That means that the slanted line which is the side of the parallelogram must be more than 8, because a slanted line is longer than a straight line (the shortest distance between two points is a straight line, to indulge in a *hackneyed,* or overused, expression). You don't know what the length of the side actually is, but you know it's more than 8. Ten plus "more than 8" is "more than 18." Two times "more than 18" is "more than 36." Who cares how much more than 36 it is? Not I. You don't have to find the exact perimeter (the sum of the lengths of all the sides); you only have to compare the quantities.

When a figure is given in a QC problem, the answer is rarely D. Usually — but not always, she says, *equivocating* (hedging) madly — the figure provides enough information to compare the quantities, even if there is not enough to come up with a precise answer.

15. **B.** There are three terms in the sequence. That means that every third term is 5. Divide 250 by 3 to get 83 with a remainder of 1. That means that the 249th number is 5 (because 249 divides evenly by 3), the 250th number is –5, and the 251st number is 0. Add –5 + 0 = –5.

This question was put in to get people to waste their time. Oh sure, you could have counted on your fingers up to the 250th term, but who has that sort of time? Find the closest number that divides by 3 and then work from there.

Did you choose D for this problem? If so, you probably confused "It depends" with "Don't have a clue — duuuh!" Choice D does not mean *you* don't know how to do the problem but rather that no one could do the problem with the *paucity* (lack) of information presented in the problem. Don't take it personally, in other words. Just because you can't do a problem yourself does not indicate it is undoable, or a choice D.

16. **C.** A chord connects any two points on the circumference of a circle. The longest chord in any circle is the diameter. The area of a circle is πr^2. A diameter is $2r$; here, $r = 1$, and $1^2 = 1$.

If your answer was 3 or 4, or 9 or 16, you multiplied by or squared π. The problem was worded to avoid having you do so. Circle what the problem is asking for, to avoid making this type of careless mistake.

If you didn't know what "the longest chord in a circle" was, you might have wanted a "It cannot be determined from the information given" answer. Well, surprise! There is no such answer among the choices. That's a clue that you *can* solve this problem; think about it a little more. Fill in something, anything. **Remember:** There is *no* penalty for a wrong answer.

17. **D.** If you said there are 365 days in a year, times 4 years times $100, you got $146,000, trap answer C. You forgot that one of those four years is a leap year, with 366 days. Add another day, another $100.

Keep leap year in mind when you work with problems that cover a range of years. Leap year comes along once every four years and has an extra day, February 29.

18. **D.** If you chose E, you have no right to show your face among decent people (although the rest of them probably fell for that trap answer, too!). You can't simply multiply two sides of a parallelogram $6 \times 12 = 72$ and think that's the area. What's the formula for the area of parallelogram? $A = bh$ (*area = base × height*). Sure, the base is 12, but what's the height?

Drop an altitude (height). The height is a straight line from the tallest point perpendicular to the base.

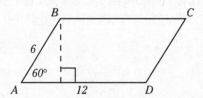

Because a height is perpendicular, the angle it makes is a right or 90-degree angle. The dropped line creates a 30:60:90 triangle (the angles in a triangle must total 180 degrees; you already have 60 + 90 = 150; the remaining angle must be 30 degrees). Now you are rewarded for memorizing all those Pythagorean Triples in Chapter 10. (You *did* memorize them, didn't you? If not, you probably were stumped by this problem right here and couldn't figure out the next step.) The sides of a 30:60:90 triangle are in the ratio *side*: *side* $\sqrt{3}$: 2*side*. You know the "2 *side*" segment is 6. That means *side* = 3. The base of the little 30:60:90 triangle is 3. And the dashed line here is side $\sqrt{3}$, or $3\sqrt{3}$.

You now know the height — $3\sqrt{3}$ — and the base — 12 — of the parallelogram. Multiply to get $36\sqrt{3}$.

If you chose A, you forgot what the question was asking. Choice A is only the height of the parallelogram; you were directed to find the area. Choice B is also a trap for people who somehow add $12 + 3\sqrt{3}$ and get $15\sqrt{3}$. Just imagine how bummed you'd be to do all this work and then fall for a cheesy trap like that.

If you skimmed over the geometry math review, figuring you could live without it, here's your last chance to go back and make amends. A few minutes invested now in memorizing important formulas and ratios (like the Pythagorean Triples) will save you those precious minutes later on the actual test.

19. **D.** Number the angles as shown in the figure.

All odd-numbered angles are equal; all even-numbered angles are equal. Because x is an odd-numbered angle, it is equal to 110, also an odd-numbered angle.

This is a very simple problem if you know how to "number angles of parallel lines around a transversal." (See Chapter 10.) This concept works, regardless of where you start numbering the angles, as long as you number them clockwise and start in the same position for both sets of angles.

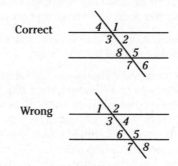

20. **E.** The equation is $x + 4 = 2(x - 1)$ where x is Mary Alice's current age. Distribute the terms: $x + 4 = 2x - 2$. Move the x's to the right, the non-x's to the left, remembering to change the signs. $6 = x$.

If you are not good at making equations or want to double-check your work, "plug n' chug": Plug in the answer choices and try them one by one. Start with choice A. If Mary Alice is 12 years old now, in four years she will be 16. Is that twice as old as she was last year, when she was 11? No; try another answer. This time, let's check our answer, E. If Mary Alice is 6, in four years she will be 10. Is that twice as old as she was last year, when she was 5? Yes, the answer works.

21. **C.** Use both graphs to answer the question. The total income was $10 million. From graph one, you know that European sales accounted for 20 percent or $\frac{1}{5}$ of total sales, for $2 million. From the second graph, you know that Germany accounted for 5 percent of $2 million, or $100,000.

Here's an easy way to find 5 percent of $2 million in your head without doing all sorts of pencil work. Figure that ten percent is $\frac{1}{10}$ or $200,000. Five percent is one half of that, or $100,000.

Be sure to keep your decimal points straight. Note that all the answers have the same numerals, only the number of zeros is different.

Use your common sense to eliminate answers if you're in too big of a hurry to work the whole problem through. The total income of Company X was $10 million; obviously, Germany didn't account for *all* of that, meaning you can eliminate answer A. All of European sales were only $2 million; because Germany's sales were not half of all European sales, you can eliminate answer B. You should be able to eliminate answer E as being way too small. That leaves a 50–50 guess.

22. **E.** All European sales accounted for 20 percent; the sales to Italy must be less than that. Eliminate answers A, B, and C. Sales to Italy were 35 percent of 20 percent, or $.35 \times .20$. Look only at the digits: You're going to get a 7 when you multiply it out. Because only one answer has a 7 digit, choose it.

Always keep an eye on how careful you have to be with your decimal point. In question number 21, all the digits were identical; the decimal was the decisive factor. In this question, the digits are different; you can ignore the decimal.

23. **C.** Bequests account for 30 percent of total income. *Hint:* Ignore the zeros; just let the equation be $50 = .3x$. Divide both sides through by .3 to get x (total income) = 166.67. Then European sales were 20 percent of that, or $166.67 \times .20 = 33.3$. Sales to France were 15 percent of that: $.15 \times 33.3 = 5$.

Estimate wildly. The answer choices are so far apart that you can get away with murder here. Say that Bequests are about a third of the total, making the total 15. Then European sales are 20 percent or a fifth of that, for 3. Then French sales are 15 percent of that, or .45. The only answer even remotely close to that is choice C. If this question really slows you down, just guess.

24. **E.** Read the title on the graphs: They show income and sales from 1980 through 1990. You cannot figure out sales in one particular year. If you chose A, you fell for the trap. And shame on you for being so *credulous* (gullible). You should have been more paranoid than that. If something looks too good to be true, it probably is.

25. **B.** Good problem. If you got this question right, *kudos* and *accolades* and *encomium* (praises) to you. This question takes a lot of backtracking.

Sales to Italy are 20 percent more than sales to France (35 percent – 15 percent), meaning that 20 percent = 1 million, or $\frac{1}{5}$ = 1 million, thus 100 percent = 5 million. But this is 100 percent of the second graph, which is still only 20 percent of the first graph. In other words, the total 5 million in the second graph is 20 percent or $\frac{1}{5}$ of the first graph, such that the total of the first graph is 25 million. (Are you totally confused yet? Just keep reading and no one will get hurt.) USA sales are 25 percent or $\frac{1}{4}$ of that: $.25 \times \$25$ million is — hey, stop right there; don't actually do the work out. Estimate. A fourth of 25 is just over 6; the only possible correct answer is B. Don't do all the work until you've checked out the answer choices; often, you can do just a rough estimate and get the correct answer.

26. **C.** One hundred percent markup is doubling the price; two hundred percent markup is tripling the price, and $42 \times 3 = 126$.

If you said 84, you got confused on the difference between a 200 percent increase (which is three times as much) and doubling (which is two times as much). Go back to the percentages section of Chapter 12.

27. **D.** Find the total number of points by multiplying the average times the number of items: $82 \times 7 = 574$. Find the subtotal by adding: $75 + 91 + 85 + 89 + 74 + 79 = 493$. Subtract the subtotal from the total: $574 - 493 = 81$.

Another way of saying this is with an equation: Average = $^{\text{Sum of all terms}}/_{\text{number of terms}}$. First, $82 = (75 + 91 + 85 + 89 + 84 + 79 + x) / 7$. Cross multiply: $82 \times 7 = 75 + 91 + 85 + 89 + 84 + 79 + x$. Then $574 = 493 + x$. Finally, $x = 81$.

28. **B.** There are two separate sets of exterior angles here; $360 \times 2 = 720$.

You've seen a problem like this before in the geometry review. It makes no difference what kind of polygon you're dealing with; the exterior angles still total 360. If you can't remember this, just picture yourself "running around in circles" outside of the polygon, trying to measure its exterior angles. You already know a circle has 360 degrees.

29. **D.** The distance A to B to C to D to E is 14 meters (just add up the sides: $4 + 4 + 4 + 2$). If you chose E, you didn't answer what the question asked. Also, you didn't keep in mind where you were in the exam: This close to the end, a question will not be so easy to answer. In fact, you can eliminate choice E immediately because you have to subtract

some other distance from that 14 meters. Even if you're making a wild guess (and guessing can't hurt because there's no penalty for wrong answers), it takes only a few seconds to eliminate an obviously incorrect answer.

Draw a picture connecting points *A* and *E*.

The line segment *AE* can be drawn as a hypotenuse of a right triangle. From *E* to *D* is 2 units. From *D* to *A* is 4 units. Use the Pythagorean theorem: $a^2 + b^2 = c^2$. First, $4^2 + 2^2 = c^2$. Then $16 + 4 = c^2$. Next, $20 = c^2$, so $c = \sqrt{20}$. Then $c = \sqrt{5} \times \sqrt{4}$. Finally, $c = 2\sqrt{5}$. Because $\sqrt{5}$ is slightly greater than 2, estimate $2\sqrt{5}$ as approximately 4, and $14 - 4 = 10$.

30. **C.** The volume of any figure is (*area* of *base*) × *height*. The base of a cylinder is a circle. Because the area of a circle is πr^2, the volume of a cylinder is $\pi r^2 h$.

    The circumference of a circle is $2\pi r$. Therefore, the radius of Can A = 5; the radius of Can B = 10. Volume Can A = $5^2\pi \times 10 = 250\pi$. Volume Can B = $10^2\pi \times 10 = 1000\pi$. Finally, $250\pi : 1000\pi = 1:4$.

You may — *or may not* — be given the necessary formulas to solve this type of question. Don't take any chances: Have the geometry formulas memorized. They're all given in the math review.

Section 5

1. **A.** You didn't actually bother working this out, did you? Think about it logically. In column A, you are taking a larger portion (because $\frac{1}{15}$ is greater than $\frac{1}{30}$) of a larger number (because 30 is greater than 15). In column B, you are taking a smaller portion of a smaller number. Without dealing with those gawd-awful fractions (any number that's not all there is not a number I want to mess with), you can compare the quantities.

   You do not have to find the exact solution to each problem, only compare the quantities. You often just waste time if you work the problem all the way through.

2. **C.** There are two ways you can approach this problem. The sum of the angles in any triangle is 180 degrees. Because you know two angles are 90 degrees (the box indicates a right or 90-degree angle) and 20 degrees for a sum of 110 degrees, you know the remaining angle must be 70 degrees (180 – 110 = 70). That angle and the *y* angle are along a straight line, which means they are supplementary and add up to 180 degrees. Subtract 70 from 180 and you get 110.

   There's an even easier way to do this problem. The exterior angle is equal to the sum of the two remote interior angles. In simple speech, that means an angle outside the triangle is the same as the sum of the two angles away from it inside the triangle. In this problem, angle *y* = 90 + 20 = 110.

   Most geometry problems simply require you to know the properties of angles and figures. I can't emphasize enough the importance of memorizing everything you can wrestle your brain cells around in geometry. Learn the rules until you can mutter them in your sleep and they'll return to you in your hour of need.

3. **B.** If you chose A, you fell for the trap. When something looks too good to be true, it's a GRE question. You know that *b* is less than zero, making it negative. When a bigger number is over a smaller number, that number is usually greater than one, such as $\frac{3}{2}$ or $\frac{5}{4}$. But the negative can change matters. Say that *b* is –2 and that *c* is –1. Then column A is $\frac{-1}{-2} = \frac{1}{2}$. Column B is $\frac{-2}{-1} = 2$. So far, B is bigger. You may have been tempted to stop there, but whenever you see variables, you should be suspicious in case the answer is D. Plug in something else.

   Keep *b* as –2 but let *c* = 4. Now $\frac{c}{b} = \frac{4}{-2} = -2$. And $\frac{b}{c} = \frac{-2}{4} = -\frac{1}{2}$. Because $-\frac{1}{2}$ is greater than –2, the answer is still B. With negatives and fractions, everything is inside out, upside down, backwards, and just plain strange. Expect the worst.

4. **B.** This question tests order of operations. Do what's in the parentheses first. A number to the negative power is the same as the reciprocal (or upside down version) of that number to the positive power. In other words, do the number as if it were positive, and then stick a 1 over it. 2^3 is 8; 2^{-3} is $\frac{1}{8}$.

A number to a negative power is not a negative number; it is a positive fraction. That trap has caught too many students over the years.

The parentheses in Column A come out to be 20 $\frac{1}{8}$. Twenty percent, or one fifth of that is just over 4 (because a fifth of 20 is 4, and a fifth of $\frac{1}{8}$ is too much bother to figure out precisely). The quantity in Column B is much larger. You are taking a fifth of $\frac{1}{8}$, which is a minuscule number you needn't bother figuring out, plus 20. That means you have 20 and something in Column B, compared to 4 and something in Column A.

When it comes to fractions, less work is more intelligent. Don't do any calculations unless and until you see that they are absolutely necessary. Often you can ignore the fraction entirely or make a good guesstimate.

5. **D.** If you chose A, you assumed too much. You do not know that the numbers are consecutive integers or even that they are different. They could all be 1, all be 0, or all be 2,001. Or they could in fact be something simple like 1, 2, 3, such that Column A would be greater than Column B. Because the answer depends on the numbers you plug in, choose D.

The more variables you have, the greater the chances that the answer is D. Don't immediately see an alphabet soup and start filling in the D oval, but because variables have so many different values, often the answer depends on which values you plug in.

6. **A.** Please tell me you didn't pick up your pencil and start doing calculations! I'd take it personally if you felt compelled to do that much work. Instead, use the tip you were given in the lecture: Compare each element of Column A to its counterpart in Column B. First, the 9756 in Column A is greater than the 9436 in Column B. Next, the 4321 in Column A is greater than the 2175 in Column B. Because you are multiplying a bigger times a bigger in column A, Column A is larger.

As soon as you start doing a lot of arithmetic operations, stop and ask yourself whether you've missed a shortcut somewhere. *Nefarious* (wicked and evil) though the test makers are, they're really not so mean as to make you do a lot of pencil pushing. I can't recall ever seeing a problem that actually made you multiply out two four-digit numbers.

If you chose C, you fell for the trap. Sure, the digits are the same in both columns, but you can't simply cancel them out. The tip to cancel quantities that are identical in both columns doesn't work here because the quantities aren't identical, only the digits. That would be like saying 25 is the same as 52 because the digits are the same.

7. **B.** Oh sure, you could do this the algebraic way. Let x be the smallest of the three consecutive integers, which are then x, $x + 1$, and $x + 2$ (because *consecutive* means in a row). Your equation is $x \times x + 1 \times x + 2 = 120$. But now what? You are going to have to deal with an x^3 and an x^2 — forget it. Your best bet is trial and error: Plug in numbers. Start, as always, with 1: $1 \times 2 \times 3$? No, that's way too small. Take a leap, say to $3 \times 4 \times 5 = 60$. Not yet. Next: $4 \times 5 \times 6 = 120$. See, that didn't take too long, did it?

Don't let your ego overshadow your common sense. That is, don't insist on doing math The Real Way when The Sneaky Way is so much easier and faster. It may be slightly tedious to plug in numbers and have to do several multiplication problems, but it also may be easier than working with a long equation.

8. **B.** Think of a shaded area as a leftover. It's what's left over after you have subtracted the unshaded area from the figure as a whole. Because Column A tells you that the figure is a square, you find its area by multiplying side times side: $8 \times 8 = 64$. The diameter of the circle is the same as the length of the square, 8. The radius of a circle is half the diameter, or 4. The area of a circle is $\pi \, radius^2$, or 16π. Find the shaded area by subtracting $64 - 16\pi$.

Do not, I repeat, do not bother actually figuring out how much 16π is. You know that π is slightly larger than 3.14, but I wouldn't even make things that complicated. Just say that π is bigger than 3. Multiply $16 \times 3 = 48$. Subtract $64 - 48 = 16$. The actual area will be even smaller than that because you'll be subtracting some number larger than 48 (whatever you get when you multiply 3.14×16, which I am not about to do, and neither should you). Because 16 is smaller than 20, and the "real" answer will be even smaller than 16, Column B is bigger.

If you've forgotten how to do shaded areas, return to Chapter 10, which discusses a simple three-step approach.

9. **A.** You have absolutely no excuse for missing this problem, even if you did get a brain cramp when you first looked at it. Remember my tip from Chapter 13: Cancel quantities that are identical in both columns. Slash off the a in both columns. That leaves you with $-c$ and $+b$. Because c is negative, a negative c is a double negative, which is actually positive. In Column B, b remains negative (because a positive times a negative is negative). Because any positive is greater than any negative, Column A is larger.

Did you look at all the variables and choose D, thinking the answer depended on what you plugged in? That's a very good first reaction, but then be sure to do the actual plugging. Say that the numbers are -1, -2, and -3. (Be careful not to get messed up and put -3, -2, -1. With negatives, everything is backwards: -1 is greater than -2.)

Column A is $-1 - (-3) = -1 + 3 = 2$. Column B is $-1 + (-2) = -3$. Please, please be careful not to overuse and abuse my tips. They are glorious tips and will help you if you treat them with respect. That means when you use a tip, make a commitment to it: Work it through to the end. If you decide that the answer is going to depend on what you plug in, *actually plug in numbers* and work the problem through.

Usually, there are three times when a choice D is valid. You think D when you have a geometry problem with no picture. You think D when a picture specifically says it is not drawn to scale (something that is very rare on the GRE). And you choose D when you have *actually* plugged in different values for variables, *actually* done the work, and *actually* gotten different answers.

10. **B.** You didn't actually work this problem through with fractions, did you? Think logically: You cannot find a fraction of a book. Either you find the whole book, or you don't find the book. (Now, don't argue. It doesn't count if you go into remote flights of fancy like saying, "But what if he finds just the first chapter which has been ripped out of the book . . ." The problem makes it clear that the books come in packages of 3. Don't make life any harder than it already is.)

Instead of making a big equation, why not just count? In 5 minutes, Mr. Schwab finds 3 books. In 10 minutes, he finds 6 books. In 15 minutes, he finds 9 books. In 20 minutes he finds 12 books. In 25 minutes — uh oh. Mr. Schwab doesn't have 25 minutes. That means he'll still be searching for his next books when time runs out. The most he'll find is 12 books.

11. **B.** The formula for an average is the sum divided by the number of terms. In this case, you know that the average is 12. That means that $12 = (a + 10 + c) \div 3$. Cross multiply the 3 and the 12 to get 36 for the total of all three numbers, the sum. If the sum of the three terms is 36 and one term is 10, the sum of the remaining two terms must be 26. That means that $a + c$ *together* equals 26.

If you divide $(a + c)$, which is 26, by 2, you get 13, making Column B larger. If you chose C, you fell for the trap of looking at the numbers and forgetting to do the division. Remember the tip: If the columns look equal, there's a trap. Any C answer should be carefully scrutinized for signs of betrayal and *perfidy* (disloyalty).

12. **C.** If you have some sort of sick fetish for fractions, you can of course multiply this all out: $5 \times 5 \times 5 = 125$. Next, $2 \times 2 \times 2 = 8$. In Column B, $(5/2)^3$ means $5/2 \times 5/2 \times 5/2$. Because you multiply fractions horizontally (multiply all the *numerators,* the top numbers, and then multiply the *denominators,* the bottom numbers), you are performing the same work as you did in Column A.

The point of this problem is to make you waste time. Before you begin doing any actual calculations, read both columns. You may find that you don't need to do the work after all. You don't care what the actual solution to the problem is; you care only which column is greater. If you are going to perform the same operations with the same numbers in both columns, you are going to get the same solutions (barring careless mistakes, that is, which is another good reason not to do all the work).

13. **D.** When a geometry problem gives only words and not figures, it is often a choice D, because the answer depends on what the figure is going to look like, what its dimensions are. The goal of this problem was to dazzle you with terminology and thus blind you to the fact that the critical numbers are missing. A minor arc is the smaller of two arcs formed on a circle. An arc is a portion of the circle's circumference. If you knew the fraction that the arc is of the circle, you could find the circle's circumference and eventually find its area. For example, maybe the minor arc is $\frac{1}{3}$ the circle. Then the whole circumference is 18π and the radius is 9. (The circumference of a circle is 2π radius.) The area then would be $\pi\ radius^2$, or 81π. But what if the arc is only $\frac{1}{10}$ of the circumference of the circle? Then the circumference is 60π, making the radius 30, and the area 900π. Because the answer depends on information you aren't given, choose D.

14. **D.** The number of security personnel and audience members could be 100, with 30 security and 70 audience. Or it could be 200, with 60 security and 140 audience members. Or it could be just 10, with 3 security and 7 audience members. The point is that the number could be any multiple of the sum: $3 + 7 = 10$; any multiple of 10 could be the answer. Because the answer can change depending on the values you plug in, choose D.

Chapter 11 has a great section on how to do ratios in your head, the quick and easy way. A ratio problem is nearly a freebie, something you should never miss.

15. **D.** If you chose C, you fell for the trap. You cannot simply multiply the exponents of two unlike bases. For example, if you were to multiply 5^{-2} (which is $\frac{1}{5^2}$ or $\frac{1}{25}$) $\times 2^{-5}$ (which is $\frac{1}{2^5}$, or $\frac{1}{32}$), the answer would not be 1. The answer depends on the values of x and y: Are they positive? negative? fractions? With this many possibilities, the answer is D.

The more variables you have, the better your chances of getting a D answer. Don't immediately choose D when you see a lot of x and y variables, but you should entertain the possibility that the answer will depend on the numbers you plug in.

Will the end of the QCs have a lot of D answers like this? Not necessarily. However, because questions go from easier to harder and because the hard or tricky questions often have answer D, don't be surprised if you do have what seems a disproportionate number of D's at the end of the exam.

16. **C.** You know the remainder cannot be 5; you cannot have 5 left over when you divide by 5. (Think of $\frac{10}{5}$: It's not "5 remainder 5," but 2.) Eliminate choice E.

A great way to simplify a remainder problem is to *plug in numbers*. Choose a number that fits the criterion of the problem: a number divided by 5 has a remainder of 4. How about 9 (because $\frac{9}{5} = 1$ with 4 left over)? Make $n = 9$. Then $3n = 27$. When 27 is divided by 5, the remainder is 2 ($\frac{27}{5} = 5$ with 2 left over). Still skeptical? Try another number. Say that $n = 14$ (because $\frac{14}{5} = 2$ remainder 4). Then $3n = 14 \times 3 = 42$. Finally, $\frac{42}{5} = 8$ remainder 2.

17. **D.** From 9:30 to 12:30 is 3 hours. Gwendolyn studies for 3 minutes less than that, or 2 hours and 57 minutes. Notice that you don't have to go through all the fuss n' bother of converting to minutes, subtracting, and then converting back to hours. Round the study time to three hours, and then subtract three minutes. Don't do more work than you have to; there's no prize for the most equations, you know.

18. **D.** This problem isn't as hard as it looks. It is a symbolism problem (covered in Chapter 11). First, you say to yourself in words what the triangle means, as explained in the question stem: "I have a number inside of a triangle. That means I square the number first and then add 2 to it." For triangle 4, you square 4 and add 2 to it: $4^2 + 2 = 16 + 2 = 18$.

If you chose A or B, you didn't finish the problem. Always remind yourself that the mere fact that the answer you got is one of the answer choices does not mean you can stop working. The test makers are notorious for supplying incremental answers among the choices (in other words, if solving the problem takes five steps, the answer to the first step may be choice A, the answer to the second step may be choice B, and so on).

Because the first triangle is inside a second triangle, you have to do the whole operation over again. It's as if you're starting anew with a triangle 18. Square 18 and add 2 to it: $18^2 = 324 + 2 = 326$.

If you chose C, you forgot to add the 2 at the end and did all that work for nothing. If you chose E, you acted as if there were a third triangle, squaring 326 and adding 2 to it. Naturally, the answer you get after doing all that wasted work is among the answer choices. Hey, there's no limit to the depths of the test's *depravity* (corruption, wickedness).

19. **C.** An inscribed angle is $\frac{1}{2}$ the measure of the central angle with the same endpoints. Because *A* and *C* are the endpoints of both *ABC* and *AOC*, *ABC* = $\frac{1}{2}$ of *AOC*, which there-fore equals 120.

    Choice E is backwards, since it is half of *ABC* instead of twice *ABC*. You could just look at the angles and know that *AOC* is more than *ABC*, eliminating answers D and E. ***Remember:*** Unless a problem *specifically* says that a figure is not drawn to scale, it *is* drawn to scale and you may use it to help you find an answer.

20. **C.** Multiply 432×36 (three dozen is 36) = 15,552 to find the number of items the truck can carry at one time. Divide that into 60,000 to get *more than* 3 but *less than* 4. The trap answer is E, 3. Even though the truck is partially empty on the fourth trip, it does have to make four complete trips, or some of the cartons will be left behind. Answer D is illogical; how can the truck make $\frac{4}{5}$ of a trip? Don't be tricked into choosing this just because your answer is approximately 3.8 or $3\frac{4}{5}$. If the truck makes that $\frac{4}{5}$ trip, it never gets to its final destina-tion but sits in the middle of the road and causes a heck of a traffic jam.

21. **C.** The first question after the graph is usually quite straightforward, relatively easy. Here, if you remembered to skim the answer choices before doing the work, you saw that the question was basically asking you how many zeros would be in the answer. If you look at 1960, training costs went from about 35 to about 45, for a total of about ten. But it is "ten tens of thousands" of dollars: 10 (ten) 0 (ten) 000 (thousands) or 100,000.

For those of you who hate estimating, relax. The GRE does not try to trap you with estimating, making it difficult to tell whether something is 10 or 11 or 9.5 units. If you can eyeball the graph and get a guesstimate, that's good enough.

22. **D.** Did you fall for trap answers A or E? In 1970, salaries went from 0 to 25, for a total of 25. Promotion went from 45 to 50, a total of 5. While 25 is 5 times as much as 5, it is only 4 times greater, or 400 percent greater. (This percentage jazz comes up a lot on the exam and was covered in detail in the math review. If you're confused by this problem, go back to the percentages section of Chapter 12 and lock yourself in a room with it until only one of you emerges alive.)

23. **B.** Just add up all the overhead amounts: approximately 10 + 5 + 5 + 5 + 10 = 35. But again, this is 35 tens of thousands, or 350,000.

If you chose D or E, you included the 10 that was projected to be spend on overhead in 2000. The question specifically asks for the amount spent from 1950 through 1990. Careless reading could cost you points here.

24. **B.** This question is designed to confuse you with the wording, not the math. Take it one step at a time. Salaries in 1980 are brought up to equal salaries in 1970, meaning they increase from 15 to 25, an increase of 10. All other 1980 expenses remain constant, which means you have to add 10 to the total for 1980, bringing it from 35 to 45. Now, 25 is what percent of 45? Use the $^{is}/_{of}$ formula: $^{25}/_{45}$ = STOP! Don't actually work this one out; estimate. You know that 25 is just over half of 45, so the percentage must be just over 50 percent. The only answer close is B.

25. **E.** Make my day and tell me that I got you to do a lot of useless calculating on this problem. If you found the total promotion in 1970 and then the promotion in 2000 and figured out the percentage, I gotcha. You know only how much was spent on promotion; you can't break that promotion down to television and other types of media blitzes.

26. **D.** Substitute numbers for letters in the original formula; put a 6 where the x is, a 2 for the y, and a 9 for the z. This gives you $1/2 (6) + 2^3$, all divided by $2 - 9$. This equals $3 + 8$ all divided by -7 or $-11/7$. This problem tests the concept of symbolism, which often requires substitution. Note that there is no such thing as a * operation; the * means something different in every problem and applies only to that particular problem.

27. **A.** To find a shaded area, subtract the area of the unshaded portion from the area of the total figure. If the diameter of the circle is 10, the side of the square is 10.

    Because the area of a square is $side^2$, the area of this square is $10 \times 10 = 100$. If the diameter of a circle is 10, the radius is 5. The area of a circle is πr^2, or $5 \times 5 \times \pi = 25\pi$. Subtract: $100 - 25\pi$. Don't actually multiply π out. In most problems, π is left in that form. Look at the answer choices before you do too much work.

    The easy way to do a shaded area problem is to think of it as a "leftover," what remains when the area of the unshaded part has been subtracted from the area of the entire figure. Chapter 10 covered shaded areas.

    If you got choice B, you found the circumference ($2\pi r = 10\pi$) of the circle instead of the area. If you chose C, you used the perimeter of the square ($10 + 10 + 10 + 10 = 40$) rather than the area. If you chose D, you messed up absolutely everything (!), finding the perimeter of the square instead of its area and finding the circumference of the circle instead of its area. Isn't it vicious how the test makers anticipate just about every mistake you can make? They must be psychic . . . or is that psycho?

28. **D.** Choice E is a sucker bet. Just because both the number of painters and the number of hours are multiplied by three does not mean the number of hours is multiplied by three. A problem toward the end of the section is not going to be that simple and straightforward.

    If three times as many painters are working, they can do the job in one-third the time it takes just one painter. If this is confusing, reword the problem in your own terms. Suppose that it takes you three hours to mow a lawn. If your two fraternity buddies chip in and help you, the three of you can work three times as fast and get the job done in just one hour. The same is true here. Three times the number of painters (from 3 to 9) means the job can be done in $1/3$ the time: $10/3 = 3\ 1/3$.

    If you chose $3 1/3$, you didn't finish the problem. Nine painters would do the *same* job, that is, paint 4 rooms, in $3 1/3$ hours. But the number of rooms is three times what it was, so this factor triples the amount of time needed. Triple $3 1/3$ to get 10 hours. Yup, you're back to the original amount of time, which unfortunately was probably the first answer your "common sense" told you to eliminate.

    Think about this logically. It takes $1/3$ the time, but the painters do three times the work. The $1/3$ cancels out with the three to get you right back where you started from.

29. **B.** If the last half of the trip were alone, then the 40 percent and the 20 miles are the first half, or 50 percent. Since 50 percent – 40 percent = 10 percent, 20 miles = 10 percent. It may be easier to think in terms of fractions: 10 percent = $1/10$. One-tenth of *something* is 20; that *something* is 200. (Arithmetically: $1/10 x = 20$. Divide both sides through by $1/10$, which means inverting and multiplying by $10/1$, and $20 \times 10 = 200$.) This was a good problem to talk through; you needed reasoning, not arithmetic.

30. **A.** The formula for the average measure of an interior angle of a polygon is $\frac{(n-2)\ 180}{n}$,

    where n stands for the number of sides. Solve for n. Here, set up the equation:

    $\frac{(n-2)\ 180}{n} = 140.$

Cross multiply: $(n-2)\,180 = 140n$.

$180n - 360 = 140n$

$40n = 360$.

$n = 9$.

If you chose C, you found $(n-2)$. That represents the number of triangles, not the number of sides.

Section 6

Questions 1 – 9

First, jot down the pool of men, broken into two categories.

Rookies= Frank, Gary, Harold

Veterans= John, Karl, Larry, Moe

Next, draw seven dashes or spaces to represent the order in which the men will bat. Use the information given in the statements to fill in the spaces.

Statement I gives you the pool of players, which you have already jotted down.

Statement II tells you that a rookie cannot be first or last, because he must be preceded by and followed by a veteran.

Because statement III says that Gary bats second; put him in space 2. If Larry is the last veteran at bat, he must be the last batter, period, because you have already ascertained (from statement II) that the last batter cannot be a rookie.

Statement IV tells you that the last batter is a veteran. You already knew this.

When a series of statements repeats information, pay attention. You often will see a question along the lines of "Which statement is unnecessary?" or "Which two statements give the same information?"

Statement V tells you that John-Karl-Moe bat in that order . . . but don't assume that they are consecutive batters. There must be rookies between them, because rookies are preceded by and followed by veterans (per statement II). Since a veteran must be before and after Gary, you know that John must be first, followed by Gary and then by Karl.

Your final chart looks like this:

John   Gary   Karl   Frank or Harold   Moe   Frank or Harold   Larry

Note that spaces 4 and 6 could be filled by either Frank or Harold. When a logic game gives you options, when a space may be filled by more than one person, or when a job may be done in more than one way, you will often see a question on that option.

1. **A.** Just look at the chart. You'll notice how carefully the question is phrased: Which of these *could* be the correct order of batters? You don't know which one *must* be the order; you have two options, based on Frank and Harold's positions.

2. **D.** I warned you that this question was coming. (Have I lied to you yet? That you know of, I mean. And did I mention that I'm tall, blond, *svelte*, *pulchritudinous* . . . .) Statement IV gives you information you already deduced from statement II, that a veteran must be the last batter.

If you chose C, you fell for a trap. Statement III tells you that Larry is the last veteran at bat. That is not *superfluous* (extra, unnecessary) information; you didn't know it before. You already knew that the last batter was a veteran, but you didn't know who that veteran was.

3. **D.** From the chart, you know that Frank could be in spaces 4 or 6. If he won't bat next to Karl, he can go only in space 6. Look at the chart to see the only possible order.

4. **B.** If she is the last batter, Deb has to be a veteran because statement II makes clear that the last batter is a veteran. (Remember that a rookie must be *both* preceded by *and* *followed by* a veteran.) The last batter is in space 8, five spaces after Karl.

If you chose either C or E, you fell for a trap. Spaces 4 and 6 could be occupied by *either* Frank or Harold. Choice C may or may not be true. If Frank is in space 4, choice C is correct. If Frank is in space 6, choice C is not correct. The same is true for choice E. Harold could be in space 4, in which case choice E is wrong. Or Harold could be in space 6, in which case choice E is correct. Be very, very careful to note the options on any diagram. When a person could be in more than one place, don't arbitrarily assign him to one space; keep your options open and noted.

5. **B.** The question is wonderfully vague and *ambiguous* (uncertain; capable of being understood in more than one way). It doesn't ask which is false, or which must be wrong, but which "is not necessarily true." This is GRE-speak for looking at the options. You know that Frank could be in space 4, in which case B is true. But Frank could be in space 6, in which case B is false. Therefore, depending on Frank's placement, choice B is "not necessarily true."

6. **C.** In terms of logic, *some* means at least one, making choice C a true statement. The ice works better than the prescription lotions and salves, so there is at least one treatment that is superior. Choice E goes too far, though. You cannot infer anything about over-the-counter medications from the research about ice. Choice B is a tempting wrong answer, but all you know from the stimulus is that prescription lotions and salves aren't very effective. Perhaps some other prescriptions will do wonders. Choice D seems to make a lot of sense. However, it does not deal with the information in the stimulus, which has to do with treatment effectiveness. Choice A is too extreme and most likely false. Physicians may be very good at estimating the severity of a rash but may be incapable of prescribing a lotion or salve to take care of it.

7 **C.** Larry feels that the lack of a motorcycle will make it impossible to be accepted by the gang. He does not state or imply that a motorcycle will be sufficient for gang membership, so choice B is out. His feeling, though, is very consistent with choice C; such a statement will reinforce what Larry is stating and is the answer.

Gang membership seems to be important to Larry, but he never claims that he wants to belong to the gang because of any prestige. You can eliminate choice A because it does not fall into Larry's line of reasoning.

Choice D deals somewhat with the first part of Larry's argument, but it doesn't have any bearing on the main conclusion. In one sense, this statement could even *weaken* Larry's argument in that a motorcycle may be so expensive that it will be fruitless for him to try to save up for one.

Choice E has nothing to do with the connection between motorcycles and gangs. If Larry is interested in gaining Mimi's favor, which is likely, this choice could also *weaken* the argument somewhat.

8. **B.** The author makes a couple of giant leaps here. First, there was a correlation between hair color and being a Miss Universe finalist but nothing to prove that being blond caused the women to be finalists. More critically, who is to say that being a finalist in a Miss Universe has anything to do with this author's ability to get a date? Fortunately for those of us who are not Miss Universe, some men are happy with mere mortals.

Choice A is possibly true and, as such, would mess up the author's reasoning. Nevertheless, it is too indirect to be a good answer. You can't fault the author for not thinking about such a specific possibility — and one that has only a chance of being true.

Choice B expresses the real problem with what the author is thinking. The author is using a beauty pageant result to make a conclusion about her ability to get a date. What if she has an absolutely abominable personality? Will hair color make a difference? What if the men she is attracted to prefer women of her hair color?

Choice C does get to the correlation versus causation question, but it is not strong enough. Even though the finalists may not have been picked <u>solely</u> because they were blond, the blond hair may have had a lot to do with their selection. Choice C would have been good had it said that the contestants were picked solely for reasons other than hair color.

You may eliminate choice D the same way you eliminated choice A. In addition, choice D mentions the vague word *attention*. What about getting dates?

Choice E is close, but the fact may remain that men are attracted to blondes. There could be many reasons why men don't like to date Miss Universe finalists, but hair color may not be one of them.

Questions 9–11

The task with this game is to select from a large pool. A good way to keep track of who is selected is to list all the counselors and campers and circle those selected. You can distinguish between the counselors and campers by using capital letters for the counselors and small letters for the campers. Your pool may look like this:

A B C

k l m n o p q r s t u v

Incorporate statement I into this listing by writing "2 or more" by the counselor row.

You must have *at least* two counselors because two drivers are needed, but don't assume that there will be *only* two counselors. The third counselor could go on the trip as a passenger in one of the vehicles.

A B C (2 or more)

k l m n o p q r s t u v

Next, work with the two rules that involve Valdez. (You don't have to go through the rules in any particular order; approach whichever one you think is the easiest to work with.)

Statement III can be summarized as $A \to v$. This rule also means that *not v → not A*. This is true because once *v* is out, *A* has to be out because the presence of *A* could bring on *v* and produce a contradiction.

Do not make the mistake of thinking *not A → not v*, or *v → A*. The presence of *A* guarantees that *v* is included, but *v* could be there even if *A* is not there.

Statement VI says that *s* is necessary for *v*. This means *not s → not v*. Think of it this way: *s* is a requirement or a prerequisite for *v*. If *s* fails to show, *v* has to be left home because the requirement was not fulfilled. Therefore, *not s → not v* leads to the further deduction of *v → s*. This means if *v* is there, its requirement, *s*, has to be there.

Combine the third and last rules to get the following:

$A → v$ and *not s → not v → not A*

Statement IV may be summarized as *no(rs.)*

The next-to-last (**penultimate**, for those of you with spectacular vocabularies) rule may be summarized as *n → not C*, which allows the deduction of *C → not n*.

Statement II is hard to summarize. Put a mark next to it to ensure that you will remember it and use the information that if only two counselors go, no more than six campers may go on the trip.

Next, make a rough sketch of the number of available seats.

Minivan				*Sedan*		
—	—			—	—	
—	—	—		—	—	—
—	—					

9. **A.** The most efficient way to answer this question is to take one rule at a time and eliminate any violators. Choice B has Alban but no Valdez, so it is out, as per statement III. Choice C is eliminated because it has Robinson and Smith together, which you learned in statement IV is not possible. Toss out choice D because Chen and Nguyen are together, a violation of the penultimate (next to last) rule. Finally, choice E is eliminated because it has Valdez without Smith. According to the last rule, Smith must be there for Valdez to be present. By the process of elimination, choice A is the only combination that works.

10. **C.** Decode this question: Which condition would most limit the number of people included? Because the camper:counselor ratio cannot exceed 3:1, choosing only two counselors would mean that a maximum of only six campers could go on the trip. In other words, only eight people would go on the trip, resulting in four empty seats.

Choice C would force out one of the counselors because *n → C*. With counselor *C* out, only two counselors are going on the trip.

If you are completely stuck on this last question, you can at least eliminate choices B and E. Leon and Quint are not mentioned in any of the rules; therefore, their presence does not restrict anyone else from going on the trip. Although the GRE does not subtract points for wrong answers (meaning that you should always guess), it's worth taking a few seconds to eliminate obviously incorrect answers to help your odds.

11. **C.** Choice C looks promising because Pascal is not mentioned in any of the rules. Someone not mentioned in the rules should be able to go on the trip unless all the spaces are taken. To confirm this, draw the roster and circle *r*.

A B C

k l m n o p q (r) s t u v

Robinson's inclusion means that *s* is out, which in turn eliminates *v* and *A*.

A̶ B C

k l m n o p q (r) s t u s̶l̶v̶

Once counselor *A* is knocked out, counselors *B* and *C* must be included. Because *C* is in, *n* must be eliminated. You still have plenty of room for Pascal.

Questions 12 – 17

First, write down the various dog's names for the pool: Rover, King, Spot, Lassie, Fido, Prince. (A lot of original thought went into those names, eh? The pooches may as well be called *Cliche*, *Banal*, *Trite*, and *Hackneyed*.)

Next, make two sets of dashes. Put six dashes for the ranking of movie contracts, six more dashes for the ranking of intelligence. Then use the information given in the statements to fill in the spaces.

Statement II tells you to put Spot in the second-to-last (*penultimate*, if you want to use a *pedantic*, *pretentious* term, and why not?) space. Lassie goes in the last space. Lassie also goes in the last space of the movie contracts chart.

Statement III tells you to put King in the first space of the movie contracts chart but not in the first space of the intelligence chart.

Statement IV puts Prince in space 4 on the intelligence chart and space 3 on the movie contracts chart.

Statement V puts Rover in the first spot of the intelligence chart and in the third to last space (*antepenultimate*) of the movie contracts chart. You also get the information that Fido must be in the second to last space of the movie contracts list (you already know that Lassie is in the last or ultimate space).

Your final charts should look like the following:

Movie contracts

King	Spot	Prince	Rover	Fido	Lassie
1	2	3	4	5	6

Intelligence

Rover	(Fido or King)	(Fido or King)	Prince	Spot	Lassie
1	2	3	4	5	6

Did you take special notice of the fact that spaces two and three in the intelligence chart could be filled by either Fido or King? When you have a double option like this, you often have a question about it.

12. **D.** I'd almost bet that you fell for the trap, chose B, and are starting to bluster and argue with me right now. Go back and read the question. It asks for the order FROM FEWEST TO MOST. You have to read the chart backwards. Questions on this exam often ask the unexpected. If normal people order items from top to bottom, the test goes from bottom to top. If your first reaction is to read something left to right, check that the question isn't asking you to read it right to left.

13. **C.** Look at the chart, from most intelligent to least intelligent. The question carefully asks which *could be* the order, not which *must be* the order. Spaces 2 and 3 could be filled with Fido and King or King and Fido. Either is okay.

14. **A.** Nothing in the question tells you that there is a direct correlation between movie contracts and intelligence. In fact, you're told in statement III that King is not the smartest dog but has the most movie contracts. Eliminate I. Go down through the answer choices, scratching off anything with I in it . . . *voilà!* The right answer must be choice A. You don't even have to go through the rest of the choices.

For those of you who are skeptics, I'll finish the question out. Because you don't know of a direct or proportional level of intelligence from one ranking to another, you can't assume II is true. Spot may be just two and a half times as intelligent as Prince or ten times as intelligent. You know nothing about the friendliness rankings (III) and can't make any assumptions about them. Friendliness was mentioned only once, in statement IV as a reason Prince gets a lot of movie contracts.

15. **C.** Just look at the charts.

16. **C.** Lassie is the least intelligent dog and has the fewest movie contracts. This is a very easy question to answer . . . assuming that your charts are correct. Always double-check them.

17. **C.** Spot has more movie contracts than Prince. If Rex has fewer movie contracts than Prince, he must also have fewer movie contracts than Spot.

Choice A may or may not be true. Because you don't know of any direct correlation between intelligence and movie contracts, you can't make any assumptions. The same is true for choice B. Choice D is wrong. King has the most movie contracts of all the dogs. You don't know enough about the ranking of friendliness of the dogs to know whether choice E is true or not.

Questions 18 – 23

Does this game make you think your mental confusion is, uh, terminal? In your opinion, is Alphabet Communications right up there with other Communicable Diseases? Okay, calm down, take a deep breath, and approach this maze one step at a time (and keep reminding yourself: "This is the last game in the section; I may not even get to it.").

In most mapping games, the actual locations are not important. The games typically reward your ability to keep track of the connections. Put the terminals in a circle (as in Figure 1):

Indicate the connections with arrows. The simplest way to do this is to point the arrows towards the ending point of a connection (see Figure 2). Double-headed arrows indicate that the connections go both ways (e.g., *B* to *C* and *C* to *B*). Be sure to represent the two different systems (system *X* and system *Y*) with different types of lines. Use a legend, as a map does, to remind you of which system is which.

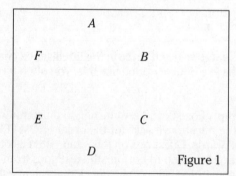

Figure 1

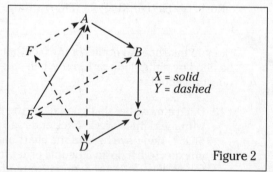

X = solid
Y = dashed

Figure 2

18. **D.** Choice A can readily be eliminated as *A* and *E* are connected by *X*. *A* to *D* to *F* can be done with *Y*, so choice B is out. *C* to *B* goes along *X*, so choice C is out. As for choice D, *C* could go to *B*, which won't get anywhere, or *E*. To move toward *F*, *E* must go to *A* and switch from system *X* to system *Y* to move to *D*. Finally, the message will go from *D* to *F*. Note that choice E is out because a *D* - *C* - *B* relay along *X* will do the job.

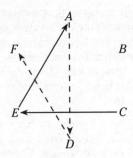

19. **A.** Here are the fastest paths for each choice.

    (A)   *B (X) C (X) E*   2 seconds

    (B)   *C (X) E (X) A (Y) D*   5 seconds

    (C)   *A (Y) D (Y) F*   6 seconds

    (D)   *B (X) C (X) E (X) A (Y) D (Y) F*   9 seconds

    (E)   *F (Y) A (X) B*   4 seconds

20. **E.** If *E* must transmit on system *X*, it must go to *A,* so choice A is out. Choices B and C are similar. *F* must go to *A,* so both choices are out. To use both systems from *D* to *E*, the connection is *D - F - A - E*, so choice D is out.

21. **B.** Draw a diagram for this problem (see Figure 1). Be sure to disconnect terminal *E*. A quick inspection of the connections reveals that choices A, C, and D are all possible, so eliminate those choices. Choice E is possible (see figure 2):

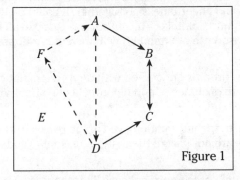

Figure 1

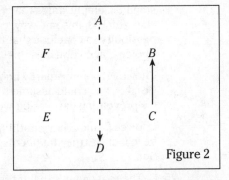

Figure 2

This leaves choice B as the answer. D can go to C which can go to B, but the message stops there.

22. **C.** Draw a system *X* diagram for this problem. Following are the paths:

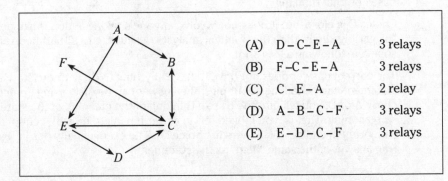

    (A)   D – C– E – A   3 relays

    (B)   F –C – E – A   3 relays

    (C)   C – E – A   2 relay

    (D)   A – B – C – F   3 relays

    (E)   E – D – C – F   3 relays

23. **B.** Some simple math will give you the right answer. One piece of information the stimulus gives you is that a six-minute phone connection costs twice what mailing a letter cost when fax machines were first in use. These days you can send a fax in two minutes as

opposed to six minutes, which means that sending a fax outside of your calling area will cost you no more than a two-minute call. A two-minute connection costs one-third as much as a six-minute connection; therefore, the charge to send a two-page document by fax is one-third what it was when fax machines were first used. This makes sending documents by fax cheaper than sending them by mail, which is one-half the cost of a fax when fax machines were first used (or even more than one-half if postal rates go up). Whew! Choice B makes sense.

Choice A looks good, but it says "better" rather than "cheaper," making it subjective and incorrect. Who's to say what's better? What if an original is necessary? A fax won't do much good then, no matter how cheap it is. The word *better* goes too far. Choice E can be eliminated by similar reasoning.

Choice C mentions "any" document, pushing it too far as well. What about a 50-page document or a 500-page one? Such a document might occupy the lines for a long time and push the fax charges to the stratospheres.

Choice D is wrong for two reasons. First, the stimulus does not discuss charges that are not outside the local calling area. Second, it is probable that the advantage of a fax over regular mail is even greater inside the local calling area in that such phone line connections are cheaper than long-distance connections, but mail costs are the same inside or outside a local calling area.

24. **C.** If you chose B, you fell for the trap. Maybe the average diet doesn't have enough Vitamin C, but you are concerned here only with the speaker's diet. She does not necessarily assume that she has to take supplements because the *average* diet doesn't supply enough, but because *her* diet does not supply enough. She does make the assumption that Vitamin C is a causative agent in the prevention of depression. Because of this assumption, she must assume that the cause/effect is not reverse. The information in the stimulus simply states that Vitamin C and cheerfulness go together. It could be that cheerfulness, in some way, causes Vitamin C uptake. The author has to close off this possibility to conclude that her increased use of Vitamin C will prevent her depression. Choice C accomplishes this.

Choice A is out primarily because the author is concerned with depression, not colds. Besides, she could assume the opposite of choice A, and her conclusion about Vitamin C's preventing depression would still stand.

Choices D and E have nothing to do with the informationgiven in the passage. They may be in fact be true statements, but they are not part of the writer's reasoning and assumption.

25. **C.** The reasoning is that if the "big shots" (presitgious colleges like Standford, Harvard, and Yale) think something, many other people in the same field are going to take action that follows from that thinking. Choice C parallels that reasoning. The "big shots" (presidents of large corporations) think something; most others are now takingaction taht is based on that thinking

Choice C is close, but it does not involve anyone's taking action. Also, political leaders are "bigger big shots" than the political analysts. As such, this situation does not have someone following a "big shot."

The correct answer does not have to have anything to do with the statement. The statement can be talking about pigs; the answer can be discussing French wine. If you chose A or D, you fell into the trap of thinking of the meaning of the statement rather than its reasoning. That is, you looked for an aswer having to do with school or education (tutuoring in choice A, teachers in choice D). The exam usually has at least one wrong/ trap answer in the same "field" as the statement.

Chapter 21

How to Ruin a Perfectly Good Day, Part II: Practice Exam 2

● ●

*A*re you bloody but unbowed and ready to have another go at it? The following exam consists of six 30-minute sections. (You were kind enough to laugh at my jokes; I'm kind enough to leave out the experimental seventh section.) Two sections are verbal, two are math, and two are analytical. You are familiar (practically *intimate*) with the question formats by now.

Please take this test under normal exam conditions. This is serious stuff here!

1. **Sit where you won't be interrupted (even though you'd probably welcome any distractions).**

2. **Use the answer grid provided.**

3. **Set your alarm clock for the 30-minute intervals.**

4. **Do not go on to the next sextion until the time allotted for the section you are taking is up.**

5. **If you finish early, check your work for that section only.**

6. **Do not take a break in the middle of any one section.**

7. **Give yourself one ten-minute break between sections 2 and 3 and a second ten-minute break between sections 4 and 5.**

After you finish, check your answers with the answer key. A sample scoring chart is provided at the end of this chapter. Take a few minutes to go over the answer explanations to all the questions, not just the ones you missed. This is your last chance to pick up one more nugget of knowledge, that final bit of information that could put you over the top.

There are no penalties for wrong answers on the GRE. Guess, guess, guess! Don't leave any answers blank.

Answer Sheet

Begin with Number 1 for each new section. If any sections have fewer than 50 questions, leave the extra spaces blank.

Section 1	Section 2	Section 3	Section 4
1. Ⓐ Ⓑ Ⓒ Ⓓ Ⓔ	1. Ⓐ Ⓑ Ⓒ Ⓓ Ⓔ	1. Ⓐ Ⓑ Ⓒ Ⓓ Ⓔ	1. Ⓐ Ⓑ Ⓒ Ⓓ Ⓔ
2. Ⓐ Ⓑ Ⓒ Ⓓ Ⓔ	2. Ⓐ Ⓑ Ⓒ Ⓓ Ⓔ	2. Ⓐ Ⓑ Ⓒ Ⓓ Ⓔ	2. Ⓐ Ⓑ Ⓒ Ⓓ Ⓔ
3. Ⓐ Ⓑ Ⓒ Ⓓ Ⓔ	3. Ⓐ Ⓑ Ⓒ Ⓓ Ⓔ	3. Ⓐ Ⓑ Ⓒ Ⓓ Ⓔ	3. Ⓐ Ⓑ Ⓒ Ⓓ Ⓔ
4. Ⓐ Ⓑ Ⓒ Ⓓ Ⓔ	4. Ⓐ Ⓑ Ⓒ Ⓓ Ⓔ	4. Ⓐ Ⓑ Ⓒ Ⓓ Ⓔ	4. Ⓐ Ⓑ Ⓒ Ⓓ Ⓔ
5. Ⓐ Ⓑ Ⓒ Ⓓ Ⓔ	5. Ⓐ Ⓑ Ⓒ Ⓓ Ⓔ	5. Ⓐ Ⓑ Ⓒ Ⓓ Ⓔ	5. Ⓐ Ⓑ Ⓒ Ⓓ Ⓔ
6. Ⓐ Ⓑ Ⓒ Ⓓ Ⓔ	6. Ⓐ Ⓑ Ⓒ Ⓓ Ⓔ	6. Ⓐ Ⓑ Ⓒ Ⓓ Ⓔ	6. Ⓐ Ⓑ Ⓒ Ⓓ Ⓔ
7. Ⓐ Ⓑ Ⓒ Ⓓ Ⓔ	7. Ⓐ Ⓑ Ⓒ Ⓓ Ⓔ	7. Ⓐ Ⓑ Ⓒ Ⓓ Ⓔ	7. Ⓐ Ⓑ Ⓒ Ⓓ Ⓔ
8. Ⓐ Ⓑ Ⓒ Ⓓ Ⓔ	8. Ⓐ Ⓑ Ⓒ Ⓓ Ⓔ	8. Ⓐ Ⓑ Ⓒ Ⓓ Ⓔ	8. Ⓐ Ⓑ Ⓒ Ⓓ Ⓔ
9. Ⓐ Ⓑ Ⓒ Ⓓ Ⓔ	9. Ⓐ Ⓑ Ⓒ Ⓓ Ⓔ	9. Ⓐ Ⓑ Ⓒ Ⓓ Ⓔ	9. Ⓐ Ⓑ Ⓒ Ⓓ Ⓔ
10. Ⓐ Ⓑ Ⓒ Ⓓ Ⓔ	10. Ⓐ Ⓑ Ⓒ Ⓓ Ⓔ	10. Ⓐ Ⓑ Ⓒ Ⓓ Ⓔ	10. Ⓐ Ⓑ Ⓒ Ⓓ Ⓔ
11. Ⓐ Ⓑ Ⓒ Ⓓ Ⓔ	11. Ⓐ Ⓑ Ⓒ Ⓓ Ⓔ	11. Ⓐ Ⓑ Ⓒ Ⓓ Ⓔ	11. Ⓐ Ⓑ Ⓒ Ⓓ Ⓔ
12. Ⓐ Ⓑ Ⓒ Ⓓ Ⓔ	12. Ⓐ Ⓑ Ⓒ Ⓓ Ⓔ	12. Ⓐ Ⓑ Ⓒ Ⓓ Ⓔ	12. Ⓐ Ⓑ Ⓒ Ⓓ Ⓔ
13. Ⓐ Ⓑ Ⓒ Ⓓ Ⓔ	13. Ⓐ Ⓑ Ⓒ Ⓓ Ⓔ	13. Ⓐ Ⓑ Ⓒ Ⓓ Ⓔ	13. Ⓐ Ⓑ Ⓒ Ⓓ Ⓔ
14. Ⓐ Ⓑ Ⓒ Ⓓ Ⓔ	14. Ⓐ Ⓑ Ⓒ Ⓓ Ⓔ	14. Ⓐ Ⓑ Ⓒ Ⓓ Ⓔ	14. Ⓐ Ⓑ Ⓒ Ⓓ Ⓔ
15. Ⓐ Ⓑ Ⓒ Ⓓ Ⓔ	15. Ⓐ Ⓑ Ⓒ Ⓓ Ⓔ	15. Ⓐ Ⓑ Ⓒ Ⓓ Ⓔ	15. Ⓐ Ⓑ Ⓒ Ⓓ Ⓔ
16. Ⓐ Ⓑ Ⓒ Ⓓ Ⓔ	16. Ⓐ Ⓑ Ⓒ Ⓓ Ⓔ	16. Ⓐ Ⓑ Ⓒ Ⓓ Ⓔ	16. Ⓐ Ⓑ Ⓒ Ⓓ Ⓔ
17. Ⓐ Ⓑ Ⓒ Ⓓ Ⓔ	17. Ⓐ Ⓑ Ⓒ Ⓓ Ⓔ	17. Ⓐ Ⓑ Ⓒ Ⓓ Ⓔ	17. Ⓐ Ⓑ Ⓒ Ⓓ Ⓔ
18. Ⓐ Ⓑ Ⓒ Ⓓ Ⓔ	18. Ⓐ Ⓑ Ⓒ Ⓓ Ⓔ	18. Ⓐ Ⓑ Ⓒ Ⓓ Ⓔ	18. Ⓐ Ⓑ Ⓒ Ⓓ Ⓔ
19. Ⓐ Ⓑ Ⓒ Ⓓ Ⓔ	19. Ⓐ Ⓑ Ⓒ Ⓓ Ⓔ	19. Ⓐ Ⓑ Ⓒ Ⓓ Ⓔ	19. Ⓐ Ⓑ Ⓒ Ⓓ Ⓔ
20. Ⓐ Ⓑ Ⓒ Ⓓ Ⓔ	20. Ⓐ Ⓑ Ⓒ Ⓓ Ⓔ	20. Ⓐ Ⓑ Ⓒ Ⓓ Ⓔ	20. Ⓐ Ⓑ Ⓒ Ⓓ Ⓔ
21. Ⓐ Ⓑ Ⓒ Ⓓ Ⓔ	21. Ⓐ Ⓑ Ⓒ Ⓓ Ⓔ	21. Ⓐ Ⓑ Ⓒ Ⓓ Ⓔ	21. Ⓐ Ⓑ Ⓒ Ⓓ Ⓔ
22. Ⓐ Ⓑ Ⓒ Ⓓ Ⓔ	22. Ⓐ Ⓑ Ⓒ Ⓓ Ⓔ	22. Ⓐ Ⓑ Ⓒ Ⓓ Ⓔ	22. Ⓐ Ⓑ Ⓒ Ⓓ Ⓔ
23. Ⓐ Ⓑ Ⓒ Ⓓ Ⓔ	23. Ⓐ Ⓑ Ⓒ Ⓓ Ⓔ	23. Ⓐ Ⓑ Ⓒ Ⓓ Ⓔ	23. Ⓐ Ⓑ Ⓒ Ⓓ Ⓔ
24. Ⓐ Ⓑ Ⓒ Ⓓ Ⓔ	24. Ⓐ Ⓑ Ⓒ Ⓓ Ⓔ	24. Ⓐ Ⓑ Ⓒ Ⓓ Ⓔ	24. Ⓐ Ⓑ Ⓒ Ⓓ Ⓔ
25. Ⓐ Ⓑ Ⓒ Ⓓ Ⓔ	25. Ⓐ Ⓑ Ⓒ Ⓓ Ⓔ	25. Ⓐ Ⓑ Ⓒ Ⓓ Ⓔ	25. Ⓐ Ⓑ Ⓒ Ⓓ Ⓔ
26. Ⓐ Ⓑ Ⓒ Ⓓ Ⓔ	26. Ⓐ Ⓑ Ⓒ Ⓓ Ⓔ	26. Ⓐ Ⓑ Ⓒ Ⓓ Ⓔ	26. Ⓐ Ⓑ Ⓒ Ⓓ Ⓔ
27. Ⓐ Ⓑ Ⓒ Ⓓ Ⓔ	27. Ⓐ Ⓑ Ⓒ Ⓓ Ⓔ	27. Ⓐ Ⓑ Ⓒ Ⓓ Ⓔ	27. Ⓐ Ⓑ Ⓒ Ⓓ Ⓔ
28. Ⓐ Ⓑ Ⓒ Ⓓ Ⓔ	28. Ⓐ Ⓑ Ⓒ Ⓓ Ⓔ	28. Ⓐ Ⓑ Ⓒ Ⓓ Ⓔ	28. Ⓐ Ⓑ Ⓒ Ⓓ Ⓔ
29. Ⓐ Ⓑ Ⓒ Ⓓ Ⓔ	29. Ⓐ Ⓑ Ⓒ Ⓓ Ⓔ	29. Ⓐ Ⓑ Ⓒ Ⓓ Ⓔ	29. Ⓐ Ⓑ Ⓒ Ⓓ Ⓔ
30. Ⓐ Ⓑ Ⓒ Ⓓ Ⓔ	30. Ⓐ Ⓑ Ⓒ Ⓓ Ⓔ	30. Ⓐ Ⓑ Ⓒ Ⓓ Ⓔ	30. Ⓐ Ⓑ Ⓒ Ⓓ Ⓔ
31. Ⓐ Ⓑ Ⓒ Ⓓ Ⓔ	31. Ⓐ Ⓑ Ⓒ Ⓓ Ⓔ	31. Ⓐ Ⓑ Ⓒ Ⓓ Ⓔ	31. Ⓐ Ⓑ Ⓒ Ⓓ Ⓔ
32. Ⓐ Ⓑ Ⓒ Ⓓ Ⓔ	32. Ⓐ Ⓑ Ⓒ Ⓓ Ⓔ	32. Ⓐ Ⓑ Ⓒ Ⓓ Ⓔ	32. Ⓐ Ⓑ Ⓒ Ⓓ Ⓔ
33. Ⓐ Ⓑ Ⓒ Ⓓ Ⓔ	33. Ⓐ Ⓑ Ⓒ Ⓓ Ⓔ	33. Ⓐ Ⓑ Ⓒ Ⓓ Ⓔ	33. Ⓐ Ⓑ Ⓒ Ⓓ Ⓔ
34. Ⓐ Ⓑ Ⓒ Ⓓ Ⓔ	34. Ⓐ Ⓑ Ⓒ Ⓓ Ⓔ	34. Ⓐ Ⓑ Ⓒ Ⓓ Ⓔ	34. Ⓐ Ⓑ Ⓒ Ⓓ Ⓔ
35. Ⓐ Ⓑ Ⓒ Ⓓ Ⓔ	35. Ⓐ Ⓑ Ⓒ Ⓓ Ⓔ	35. Ⓐ Ⓑ Ⓒ Ⓓ Ⓔ	35. Ⓐ Ⓑ Ⓒ Ⓓ Ⓔ
36. Ⓐ Ⓑ Ⓒ Ⓓ Ⓔ	36. Ⓐ Ⓑ Ⓒ Ⓓ Ⓔ	36. Ⓐ Ⓑ Ⓒ Ⓓ Ⓔ	36. Ⓐ Ⓑ Ⓒ Ⓓ Ⓔ
37. Ⓐ Ⓑ Ⓒ Ⓓ Ⓔ	37. Ⓐ Ⓑ Ⓒ Ⓓ Ⓔ	37. Ⓐ Ⓑ Ⓒ Ⓓ Ⓔ	37. Ⓐ Ⓑ Ⓒ Ⓓ Ⓔ
38. Ⓐ Ⓑ Ⓒ Ⓓ Ⓔ	38. Ⓐ Ⓑ Ⓒ Ⓓ Ⓔ	38. Ⓐ Ⓑ Ⓒ Ⓓ Ⓔ	38. Ⓐ Ⓑ Ⓒ Ⓓ Ⓔ
39. Ⓐ Ⓑ Ⓒ Ⓓ Ⓔ	39. Ⓐ Ⓑ Ⓒ Ⓓ Ⓔ	39. Ⓐ Ⓑ Ⓒ Ⓓ Ⓔ	39. Ⓐ Ⓑ Ⓒ Ⓓ Ⓔ
40. Ⓐ Ⓑ Ⓒ Ⓓ Ⓔ	40. Ⓐ Ⓑ Ⓒ Ⓓ Ⓔ	40. Ⓐ Ⓑ Ⓒ Ⓓ Ⓔ	40. Ⓐ Ⓑ Ⓒ Ⓓ Ⓔ
41. Ⓐ Ⓑ Ⓒ Ⓓ Ⓔ	41. Ⓐ Ⓑ Ⓒ Ⓓ Ⓔ	41. Ⓐ Ⓑ Ⓒ Ⓓ Ⓔ	41. Ⓐ Ⓑ Ⓒ Ⓓ Ⓔ
42. Ⓐ Ⓑ Ⓒ Ⓓ Ⓔ	42. Ⓐ Ⓑ Ⓒ Ⓓ Ⓔ	42. Ⓐ Ⓑ Ⓒ Ⓓ Ⓔ	42. Ⓐ Ⓑ Ⓒ Ⓓ Ⓔ
43. Ⓐ Ⓑ Ⓒ Ⓓ Ⓔ	43. Ⓐ Ⓑ Ⓒ Ⓓ Ⓔ	43. Ⓐ Ⓑ Ⓒ Ⓓ Ⓔ	43. Ⓐ Ⓑ Ⓒ Ⓓ Ⓔ
44. Ⓐ Ⓑ Ⓒ Ⓓ Ⓔ	44. Ⓐ Ⓑ Ⓒ Ⓓ Ⓔ	44. Ⓐ Ⓑ Ⓒ Ⓓ Ⓔ	44. Ⓐ Ⓑ Ⓒ Ⓓ Ⓔ
45. Ⓐ Ⓑ Ⓒ Ⓓ Ⓔ	45. Ⓐ Ⓑ Ⓒ Ⓓ Ⓔ	45. Ⓐ Ⓑ Ⓒ Ⓓ Ⓔ	45. Ⓐ Ⓑ Ⓒ Ⓓ Ⓔ
46. Ⓐ Ⓑ Ⓒ Ⓓ Ⓔ	46. Ⓐ Ⓑ Ⓒ Ⓓ Ⓔ	46. Ⓐ Ⓑ Ⓒ Ⓓ Ⓔ	46. Ⓐ Ⓑ Ⓒ Ⓓ Ⓔ
47. Ⓐ Ⓑ Ⓒ Ⓓ Ⓔ	47. Ⓐ Ⓑ Ⓒ Ⓓ Ⓔ	47. Ⓐ Ⓑ Ⓒ Ⓓ Ⓔ	47. Ⓐ Ⓑ Ⓒ Ⓓ Ⓔ
48. Ⓐ Ⓑ Ⓒ Ⓓ Ⓔ	48. Ⓐ Ⓑ Ⓒ Ⓓ Ⓔ	48. Ⓐ Ⓑ Ⓒ Ⓓ Ⓔ	48. Ⓐ Ⓑ Ⓒ Ⓓ Ⓔ
49. Ⓐ Ⓑ Ⓒ Ⓓ Ⓔ	49. Ⓐ Ⓑ Ⓒ Ⓓ Ⓔ	49. Ⓐ Ⓑ Ⓒ Ⓓ Ⓔ	49. Ⓐ Ⓑ Ⓒ Ⓓ Ⓔ
50. Ⓐ Ⓑ Ⓒ Ⓓ Ⓔ	50. Ⓐ Ⓑ Ⓒ Ⓓ Ⓔ	50. Ⓐ Ⓑ Ⓒ Ⓓ Ⓔ	50. Ⓐ Ⓑ Ⓒ Ⓓ Ⓔ

Section 5	Section 6
1. Ⓐ Ⓑ Ⓒ Ⓓ Ⓔ	1. Ⓐ Ⓑ Ⓒ Ⓓ Ⓔ
2. Ⓐ Ⓑ Ⓒ Ⓓ Ⓔ	2. Ⓐ Ⓑ Ⓒ Ⓓ Ⓔ
3. Ⓐ Ⓑ Ⓒ Ⓓ Ⓔ	3. Ⓐ Ⓑ Ⓒ Ⓓ Ⓔ
4. Ⓐ Ⓑ Ⓒ Ⓓ Ⓔ	4. Ⓐ Ⓑ Ⓒ Ⓓ Ⓔ
5. Ⓐ Ⓑ Ⓒ Ⓓ Ⓔ	5. Ⓐ Ⓑ Ⓒ Ⓓ Ⓔ
6. Ⓐ Ⓑ Ⓒ Ⓓ Ⓔ	6. Ⓐ Ⓑ Ⓒ Ⓓ Ⓔ
7. Ⓐ Ⓑ Ⓒ Ⓓ Ⓔ	7. Ⓐ Ⓑ Ⓒ Ⓓ Ⓔ
8. Ⓐ Ⓑ Ⓒ Ⓓ Ⓔ	8. Ⓐ Ⓑ Ⓒ Ⓓ Ⓔ
9. Ⓐ Ⓑ Ⓒ Ⓓ Ⓔ	9. Ⓐ Ⓑ Ⓒ Ⓓ Ⓔ
10. Ⓐ Ⓑ Ⓒ Ⓓ Ⓔ	10. Ⓐ Ⓑ Ⓒ Ⓓ Ⓔ
11. Ⓐ Ⓑ Ⓒ Ⓓ Ⓔ	11. Ⓐ Ⓑ Ⓒ Ⓓ Ⓔ
12. Ⓐ Ⓑ Ⓒ Ⓓ Ⓔ	12. Ⓐ Ⓑ Ⓒ Ⓓ Ⓔ
13. Ⓐ Ⓑ Ⓒ Ⓓ Ⓔ	13. Ⓐ Ⓑ Ⓒ Ⓓ Ⓔ
14. Ⓐ Ⓑ Ⓒ Ⓓ Ⓔ	14. Ⓐ Ⓑ Ⓒ Ⓓ Ⓔ
15. Ⓐ Ⓑ Ⓒ Ⓓ Ⓔ	15. Ⓐ Ⓑ Ⓒ Ⓓ Ⓔ
16. Ⓐ Ⓑ Ⓒ Ⓓ Ⓔ	16. Ⓐ Ⓑ Ⓒ Ⓓ Ⓔ
17. Ⓐ Ⓑ Ⓒ Ⓓ Ⓔ	17. Ⓐ Ⓑ Ⓒ Ⓓ Ⓔ
18. Ⓐ Ⓑ Ⓒ Ⓓ Ⓔ	18. Ⓐ Ⓑ Ⓒ Ⓓ Ⓔ
19. Ⓐ Ⓑ Ⓒ Ⓓ Ⓔ	19. Ⓐ Ⓑ Ⓒ Ⓓ Ⓔ
20. Ⓐ Ⓑ Ⓒ Ⓓ Ⓔ	20. Ⓐ Ⓑ Ⓒ Ⓓ Ⓔ
21. Ⓐ Ⓑ Ⓒ Ⓓ Ⓔ	21. Ⓐ Ⓑ Ⓒ Ⓓ Ⓔ
22. Ⓐ Ⓑ Ⓒ Ⓓ Ⓔ	22. Ⓐ Ⓑ Ⓒ Ⓓ Ⓔ
23. Ⓐ Ⓑ Ⓒ Ⓓ Ⓔ	23. Ⓐ Ⓑ Ⓒ Ⓓ Ⓔ
24. Ⓐ Ⓑ Ⓒ Ⓓ Ⓔ	24. Ⓐ Ⓑ Ⓒ Ⓓ Ⓔ
25. Ⓐ Ⓑ Ⓒ Ⓓ Ⓔ	25. Ⓐ Ⓑ Ⓒ Ⓓ Ⓔ
26. Ⓐ Ⓑ Ⓒ Ⓓ Ⓔ	26. Ⓐ Ⓑ Ⓒ Ⓓ Ⓔ
27. Ⓐ Ⓑ Ⓒ Ⓓ Ⓔ	27. Ⓐ Ⓑ Ⓒ Ⓓ Ⓔ
28. Ⓐ Ⓑ Ⓒ Ⓓ Ⓔ	28. Ⓐ Ⓑ Ⓒ Ⓓ Ⓔ
29. Ⓐ Ⓑ Ⓒ Ⓓ Ⓔ	29. Ⓐ Ⓑ Ⓒ Ⓓ Ⓔ
30. Ⓐ Ⓑ Ⓒ Ⓓ Ⓔ	30. Ⓐ Ⓑ Ⓒ Ⓓ Ⓔ
31. Ⓐ Ⓑ Ⓒ Ⓓ Ⓔ	31. Ⓐ Ⓑ Ⓒ Ⓓ Ⓔ
32. Ⓐ Ⓑ Ⓒ Ⓓ Ⓔ	32. Ⓐ Ⓑ Ⓒ Ⓓ Ⓔ
33. Ⓐ Ⓑ Ⓒ Ⓓ Ⓔ	33. Ⓐ Ⓑ Ⓒ Ⓓ Ⓔ
34. Ⓐ Ⓑ Ⓒ Ⓓ Ⓔ	34. Ⓐ Ⓑ Ⓒ Ⓓ Ⓔ
35. Ⓐ Ⓑ Ⓒ Ⓓ Ⓔ	35. Ⓐ Ⓑ Ⓒ Ⓓ Ⓔ
36. Ⓐ Ⓑ Ⓒ Ⓓ Ⓔ	36. Ⓐ Ⓑ Ⓒ Ⓓ Ⓔ
37. Ⓐ Ⓑ Ⓒ Ⓓ Ⓔ	37. Ⓐ Ⓑ Ⓒ Ⓓ Ⓔ
38. Ⓐ Ⓑ Ⓒ Ⓓ Ⓔ	38. Ⓐ Ⓑ Ⓒ Ⓓ Ⓔ
39. Ⓐ Ⓑ Ⓒ Ⓓ Ⓔ	39. Ⓐ Ⓑ Ⓒ Ⓓ Ⓔ
40. Ⓐ Ⓑ Ⓒ Ⓓ Ⓔ	40. Ⓐ Ⓑ Ⓒ Ⓓ Ⓔ
41. Ⓐ Ⓑ Ⓒ Ⓓ Ⓔ	41. Ⓐ Ⓑ Ⓒ Ⓓ Ⓔ
42. Ⓐ Ⓑ Ⓒ Ⓓ Ⓔ	42. Ⓐ Ⓑ Ⓒ Ⓓ Ⓔ
43. Ⓐ Ⓑ Ⓒ Ⓓ Ⓔ	43. Ⓐ Ⓑ Ⓒ Ⓓ Ⓔ
44. Ⓐ Ⓑ Ⓒ Ⓓ Ⓔ	44. Ⓐ Ⓑ Ⓒ Ⓓ Ⓔ
45. Ⓐ Ⓑ Ⓒ Ⓓ Ⓔ	45. Ⓐ Ⓑ Ⓒ Ⓓ Ⓔ
46. Ⓐ Ⓑ Ⓒ Ⓓ Ⓔ	46. Ⓐ Ⓑ Ⓒ Ⓓ Ⓔ
47. Ⓐ Ⓑ Ⓒ Ⓓ Ⓔ	47. Ⓐ Ⓑ Ⓒ Ⓓ Ⓔ
48. Ⓐ Ⓑ Ⓒ Ⓓ Ⓔ	48. Ⓐ Ⓑ Ⓒ Ⓓ Ⓔ
49. Ⓐ Ⓑ Ⓒ Ⓓ Ⓔ	49. Ⓐ Ⓑ Ⓒ Ⓓ Ⓔ
50. Ⓐ Ⓑ Ⓒ Ⓓ Ⓔ	50. Ⓐ Ⓑ Ⓒ Ⓓ Ⓔ

Section 1

Time: 30 minutes

38 questions

Directions: Each of the following sentences has one or two blanks indicating that words or phrases are omitted. Choose the answer that best completes the sentence.

1. Although many of us consider Marshall to be the most ---- of men, he has been known to become extremely ---- when confronted with a situation beyond his control.

   (A) quixotic . . angry

   (B) placid . . agitated

   (C) peaceful . . apologetic

   (D) attractive . . joyous

   (E) irritable . . calm

2. Although he lacked the ---- that he would like to have in the field, Dr. Dickstein felt confident enough of his premise to continue arguing ---- against the physician, whom he considered to be a dangerous quack and a charlatan.

   (A) fidelity . . exhaustively

   (B) grace . . indifferently

   (C) skill . . lackadaisically

   (D) expertise . . vehemently

   (E) ability . . tentatively

3. Some of the less reputable psychologists simply take money for telling their patients what they want to hear, but such ---- rarely stay in business long, soon found by the public and the disciplining agencies to be the ---- that they are.

   (A) charlatans . . frauds

   (B) misers . . skinflints

   (C) fussbudgets . . heroes

   (D) lechers . . winners

   (E) malefactors . . benefactors

4. Despite his ---- the ---- of the program, the government official was forced to sign the paperwork that continued funding of what everyone knew was a failed experiment that was costing the taxpayers millions of dollars annually.

   (A) demanding . . enhancement

   (B) suggesting . . implementation

   (C) rejecting . . termination

   (D) advocating . . demise

   (E) predicting . . continuation

5. While some see in a(n) ---- appearance a challenge to authority and a self-actualizing personality, free of the demands and orthodoxy of Society, I think that a person with so little ---- as to let himself look like that has more deeply rooted psychological problems than he realizes.

   (A) attractive . . self-indulgence

   (B) unkempt . . self-esteem

   (C) slovenly . . dissonance

   (D) comely . . disgust

   (E) foppish . . popularity

6. Ironically, for most people, the importance of material possessions has dwindled even though the state of society as a whole enables them to be more ---- than ever; most people now can afford a plethora of items that their parents and grandparents could only dream about.

   (A) insolvent

   (B) diversified

   (C) miserly

   (D) duplicitous

   (E) affluent

Go on to next page

7. The - - - - look with which the defendant accepted his fate left the jury - - - - whether they in fact had done the correct thing in finding him guilty.

   (A) insolent . . inquisitive about

   (B) complacent . . wondering

   (C) plaintive . . ambivalent about

   (D) quiescent . . irresolute over

   (E) giddy . . befuddled by

Directions: Each of the following questions features a pair of words or phrases in capital letters, followed by five pairs of words or phrases in lowercase letters. Choose the lowercase pair that most closely expresses the same relationship as that of the upper-case pair.

---

8. SHIELD : WARRIOR ::

   (A) assignment : student

   (B) helmet : cyclist

   (C) resume : employee

   (D) bet : gambler

   (E) paddle : canoeist

9. HARDY : STRONG ::

   (A) puny : grandiose

   (B) unruly : disorganized

   (C) stubborn : flexible

   (D) dubious : ineligible

   (E) lucid : clouded

10. STAPLE : ATTACH ::

    (A) button : sew

    (B) carpet : impede

    (C) water : dehydrate

    (D) incision : open

    (E) petition : review

11. DOLT : MORONIC ::

    (A) sycophant : ill

    (B) martinet : severe

    (C) hermit : gregarious

    (D) runner : pedantic

    (E) patron : patriotic

12. COVEY : BIRDS ::

    (A) hive : ants

    (B) sow : pig

    (C) buck : doe

    (D) lobster : invertebrate

    (E) gaggle : geese

13. REFUGEE : ASYLUM ::

    (A) charlatan : charisma

    (B) miser : paranoia

    (C) congregation : leader

    (D) plaintiff : redress

    (E) escapee : safety

14. HEIRLOOM : ANCESTOR ::

    (A) red herring : magician

    (B) bequest : testator

    (C) instrument : musician

    (D) rules : renegade

    (E) throne : usurper

15. ACRIMONIOUS : SWEET ::

    (A) begrudging : eager

    (B) depraved : possessive

    (C) itinerant : experienced

    (D) lascivious : lustful

    (E) protean : changeable

16. DIFFIDENT : RESERVED ::

    (A) disaffected : loyal

    (B) rapacious : altruistic

    (C) discerning : indiscriminate

    (D) ominous : dire

    (E) ravenous : indifferent

Go on to next page

Directions: Each passage is followed by questions pertaining to that passage. Read the passage and answer the questions based on information stated or implied in that passage.

Due to the involuntary, simultaneous contraction of 15 facial muscles, the upper lip is raised, partially uncovering the teeth and effecting a downward curving of the furrows that extend from
(05) the wings of both nostrils to the corners of the mouth. This produces a puffing out of the cheeks on the outer side of the furrows. Creases also occur under the eyes and may become permanent at the side edges of the eye. The eyes undergo
(10) reflex lacrimation and vascular engorgement. At the same time, an abrupt strong expiration of air is followed by spasmodic contractions of the chest and diaphragm resulting in a series of expiration-inspiration microcycles with interval pauses. The
(15) whole body may be thrown backward, shaken, or convulsed due to other spasmodic skeletal muscle contractions. We call this condition laughter.

Of all human expressive behaviors, laughter has proven a most fascinating enigma to philoso-
(20) phers and scientists alike. Its psychology, neurology, and anthropological origins and purpose are only partially defined. But its effects and uses are becoming increasingly apparent to health care professionals.

(25) Laughter is considered to be an innate human response which develops during the first few weeks of life. Evidence of the innate quality of laughter is seen in its occurrence in deaf and blind infants and children who are completely without
(30) visual or auditory clues from their environment. Darwin propounded in his *Principle of Antithesis* that laughter develops as the infant's powerful reward signal of comfort and well-being to the nurturing adult. This signal is totally antithetical
(35) perceptually to the screams or cries of distress associated with discomfort. Laughter seems to play an important role in the promotion of social unity, production of a sense of well-being, communication of well-being, and as a mechanism for
(40) coping with stressful situations. Physiologically, both reflexive (tickle-response) and heart-felt (mental response) laughter effect changes to the human system which may be significant in the treatment and prevention of illness. These include
(45) laughter's association with an increase in pulse rate, probably due to increased levels of circulatory catecholamines (blood catecholamine levels vary directly with the intensity of laughter). There is an increase in respiration. There is a decrease in

blood CO_2 levels. There is a possible increase in (50) secretion of brain and pituitary endorphins — the body's natural anesthetics which relieve pain, inhibit emotional response to pain, and thus reduce suffering. There is a decrease in red blood cell sedimentation rate ("sed rate" is associated (55) with the body's level of infection or inflammation).

While it is possible that the effect laughter and other salutary emotions have is primarily one of a placebo, this in no way minimizes the therapeutic potential for these emotions. Hippocrates (60) propounded that the mind and body are one. It may be possible that there is a physical chemistry associated with the will to live. Further investigation of the effects of positive emotions upon health and well-being may give us the keys to (65) unlocking the power of the life force.

17. The purpose of the first paragraph is to

(A) describe the physical features of laughter.

(B) list the causes of laughter.

(C) urge people to laugh more.

(D) propose a plan for developing muscular control.

(E) analyze the damaging effects of laughter on the central nervous system.

18. In lines 29–34, the author uses the example of blind and deaf infants to make the point that

(A) laughter has salubrious physical effects.

(B) all children love to laugh.

(C) the ability to laugh is inborn, not acquired.

(D) sighted and hearing children laugh at different things and in different ways than do blind and deaf children.

(E) laughter is a socializing event, drawing people together.

Go on to next page ⇨

19. It can be inferred from the passage that an infant unable to laugh would
    (A) be unable to convey to adults when he is distressed.
    (B) never have increased catecholamine levels.
    (C) have certain handicaps in his ability to interact with others.
    (D) be likely to cry more often than an infant who is able to laugh.
    (E) not benefit from any placebo effects.

20. According to the passage, laughter
    (A) is associated with the contraction of many muscles.
    (B) increases blood pressure.
    (C) directly lowers the sed rate.
    (D) increases CO_2 levels in the lungs.
    (E) is essential for pain reduction.

21. The author responds to the possibility that laughter has a placebo effect by
    (A) discounting the benefits of laughter.
    (B) continuing to discuss a link between laughter and health.
    (C) denying that the physiological responses discussed in the previous paragraph are real.
    (D) emphasizing that laughter is a learned response.
    (E) recommending other preventative measures.

22. The best title for this passage might be
    (A) How to Develop a Sense of Humor
    (B) Why We Laugh
    (C) Cultural Differences in Humor
    (D) The Physical and Emotional Side Effects of Laughter
    (E) Laughter: America's Favorite Medicine

23. The author most likely would disagree with all of the following EXCEPT
    I. Laughter's effects are primarily mental or psychological, not physical.
    II. Laughter is a learned response.
    III. Pain is decreased by pituitary endorphins released by laughter.

    (A) I only
    (B) III only
    (C) I and II only
    (D) I and III only
    (E) I, II, and III

Community property is a legal concept that is growing in popularity in the United States. A few years ago only the western states had community property laws and few people east of the Mississippi had ever heard the expression "community property." Now several states have adopted or modified laws regarding community property. (05)

Community property is jointly owned by both wife and husband. Generally, the property that was owned by a spouse before the marriage is known as separate or specific property. It remains the property of the original possessor in case of a separation or divorce. Community property is anything gained by the joint effort of the spouses. (10)

Gifts specifically bestowed upon only one party, or legacies to only one spouse, are separate property. However, courts often determine that a donor had the intention to give the gift to both parties, even though his words or papers may have indicated otherwise. Community property goes to the surviving partner in case of the death of one spouse. Only that half of the property owned by the testator can be willed away. (15) (20)

24. According to the passage, which of the following would NOT be separate property?
    (A) a gift given specifically to one spouse
    (B) property owned by one spouse before marriage
    (C) a family business
    (D) property willed away by a deceased spouse
    (E) a legacy willed to one spouse

Go on to next page

25. The best title for this passage might be

    (A) The History of Community Property

    (B) The Rights of a Surviving Spouse

    (C) A Definition of Real and Personal Property

    (D) An Argument to Abolish Community Property

    (E) Distinguishing Separate and Community Property

26. You may infer that the author would most likely agree with which of the following?

    (A) Community property is the fairest settlement concept for marital property.

    (B) Community property laws currently discriminate against the working spouse in favor of the homemaker spouse.

    (C) Community property laws will probably continue to increase in number throughout the U.S.

    (D) Community property laws will be expanded to include all property acquired during the marriage, regardless of its source.

    (E) All inheritances received by one party during the marriage are in theory, if not in fact, community property.

27. In which of the following instances would a gift to one party become community property?

    I. when the court determines the intent of the donor was to make a gift to the couple

    II. when the property is real (land) rather than personal (possessions)

    III. when the court determines that the intent to give the gift was formed by the donor prior to the party's marriage

    (A) I only

    (B) II only

    (C) I and III only

    (D) II and III only

    (E) I, II, and III

Directions: Choose the answer choice most nearly opposite in meaning to the question word.

28. AMUSING

    (A) humorous

    (B) stalwart

    (C) temporary

    (D) exasperating

    (E) unbelievable

29. FRENETIC

    (A) willful

    (B) tardy

    (C) toxic

    (D) worldly

    (E) placid

30. DOCILE

    (A) rebellious

    (B) tactless

    (C) tawdry

    (D) vulnerable

    (E) inexplicable

31. ANTEDILUVIAN

    (A) intrepid

    (B) contemporary

    (C) capricious

    (D) wet

    (E) solemn

32. ILLICIT

    (A) expedient

    (B) insufficient

    (C) legal

    (D) affable

    (E) coarse

Go on to next page

33. NADIR
    (A) euphemism
    (B) query
    (C) zenith
    (D) rancor
    (E) weakness

34. QUIXOTIC
    (A) pragmatic
    (B) rancid
    (C) warped
    (D) oleaginous
    (E) lackadaisical

35. GARNER
    (A) fret
    (B) efface
    (C) respect
    (D) parch
    (E) disperse

36. PERFIDIOUS
    (A) loyal
    (B) empirical
    (C) esteemed
    (D) dogmatic
    (E) repentant

37. PROGENITORS
    (A) sentries
    (B) oracles
    (C) fops
    (D) progeny
    (E) skinflints

38. NOXIOUS
    (A) froward
    (B) salubrious
    (C) inane
    (D) erudite
    (E) vapid

STOP You may check your work on this section only.
Do not go on to the next section until you are told to do so.

Section 2

Time: 30 minutes

38 questions

Directions: Each of the following sentences has one or two blanks indicating that words or phrases are omitted. Choose the answer that best completes the sentence.

1. Shocked to hear the students jeering at his proposal that they work on the school grounds to help the school save on grounds-keeping fees, the principal ---- said that the commitment was completely ---- and no one would be penalized for not showing up.

   (A) swiftly . . mandatory

   (B) hastily . . voluntary

   (C) loudly . . irregular

   (D) scornfully . . illegal

   (E) predictably . . necessary

2. It is unfortunate that Heather's first day on the job was filled with so many mistakes that her supervisor felt ---- his original recommendation not to hire her.

   (A) justified in

   (B) discontented with

   (C) objective about

   (D) vituperative regarding

   (E) innovative in

3. Although the athlete's explanation is ----, we can understand enough to know that he is furious because his coach benched him for what the athlete considered but a(n) ---- offense.

   (A) garbled . . immoral

   (B) incoherent . . trivial

   (C) pithy . . egregious

   (D) lucid . . minor

   (E) disdainful . . heinous

4. Because she is usually quiet and ----, Mrs. Kinoshita surprised us when she suddenly leaped into the middle of the dance floor and performed a flamenco dance, whirling and stomping.

   (A) exuberant

   (B) reticent

   (C) unpredictable

   (D) energetic

   (E) honorable

5. Although often ----, James Michael realized the importance of proceeding slowly with his task and deliberately forced himself to examine all the options available to him before making the decision on the best way to proceed.

   (A) impetuous

   (B) pensive

   (C) uncouth

   (D) dilatory

   (E) unenthusiastic

6. Anything but ----, the student unabashedly challenged what the (in her opinion) ---- professor was teaching, claiming that he should check his facts more carefully before presenting such an unorthodox point of view.

   (A) jejune . . reactionary

   (B) froward . . callow

   (C) bourgeois . . pulchritudinous

   (D) reticent . . heretical

   (E) withdrawn . . skinflint

7. At the ---- of his career, Ken basks in the kudos and ---- of judges and audiences alike.

   (A) apogee . . plaudits

   (B) lapse . . reproofs

   (C) apex . . fecklessness

   (D) genesis . . effrontery

   (E) nascency . . perjury

Go on to next page

> *Directions:* Each of the following questions features a pair of words or phrases in capital letters, followed by five pairs of words or phrases in lowercase letters. Choose the lowercase pair that most closely expresses the same relationship as that of the uppercase pair.

8. TRUANT : SCHOOL ::

   (A) scholar : library

   (B) worker : office

   (C) deserter : army

   (D) ogre : home

   (E) politician : Congress

9. IRON : BLACKSMITH ::

   (A) fabric : mason

   (B) wood : carpenter

   (C) pork : butcher

   (D) brides : matchmaker

   (E) pranks : jester

10. LAYERS : CAKE ::

    (A) strata : atmosphere

    (B) spokes : rim

    (C) keys : piano

    (D) threads : tapestry

    (E) gases : balloon

11. CREDULOUS : TRUST ::

    (A) ludicrous : money

    (B) ominous : size

    (C) precious : belief

    (D) dubious : doubt

    (E) bibulous : religion

12. INSTIGATE : REBELLION ::

    (A) join : club

    (B) initiate : conclusion

    (C) spawn : offspring

    (D) arraign : guilt

    (E) challenge : victory

13. EUPHONIOUS : SOUND ::

    (A) pusillanimous : pus

    (B) savory : taste

    (C) dissonant : shade

    (D) expired : life

    (E) hapless : luck

14. WEAK : IMPREGNABLE ::

    (A) rambunctious : rowdy

    (B) quixotic : practical

    (C) slovenly : sloppy

    (D) fastidious : careful

    (E) senescent : old

15. EUPHORIC : LACHRYMOSE ::

    (A) affluent : destitute

    (B) dexterous : skillful

    (C) lax : casual

    (D) weary : fatigued

    (E) jovial : intelligent

16. PERFUME : PUTRID ::

    (A) dotard : fond

    (B) leader : beneficent

    (C) flowers : fragrant

    (D) sponge : absorbent

    (E) slime : immaculate

Go on to next page

The UTM grid location, or reference, of a point may easily be found if the point can be located on a map with UTM grid marks along its edges or with a UTM grid superimposed. USGS (United States Geographical Survey) quadrangles published since 1959, and many published before then, have these ticks, which are printed in blue. If no USGS map with UTM ticks exists for a location, then latitude, and longitude coordinates, or certain local grid coordinates, may be converted to UTM references by a mathematical formula. However, computer programs are necessary to perform such a task. It is always preferable to record locations initially in UTM terms rather than to use translated values.

The simplicity of the UTM grid method follows from certain assumptions, which do not seriously compromise the accuracy or precision of measurements made on the common types of USGS topographical maps. The primary assumption is that narrow sections of the earth's nearly spherical surface may be drawn on flat maps with little distortion. Larger sections, however, such as the contiguous United States, cannot be drawn on a single flat map without noticeable distortion.

In the UTM system, the earth is divided into 60 zones, running north and south, each six degrees wide. Mapping on flat sheets within one of these narrow zones is satisfactory for all but the most critical needs. Each zone is numbered, beginning with zone 1 at the 180th meridian near the International Date Line with zone numbers increasing to the east. Most of the United States is included in Zones 10 through 19. On a map, each zone is flattened, and a square grid is superimposed upon it. Any point in the zone may be referred to by citing its zone number, its distance in meters from the equator ("northing") and its distance in meters from a north-south reference ("easting"). These three figures — the zone number, easting, and northing — make up the complete UTM Grid Reference for any point and distinguish it from any point on earth.

Northings for points north of the equator are measured directly in meters, beginning with a value of zero at the equator and increasing to the north. To avoid negative northing values for points south of the equator, the equator is arbitrarily assigned a value of 10 million meters, and points are measured with decreasing, but positive, northing values heading southward. For clarity, a minus sign usually precedes northing

figures for points south of the equator. The explanation may seem complicated, but experience has shown that dealing with negative values (55) for measurements and having to specify the direction of measurements from a reference line are more complex and less reliable. When actually working with maps, especially at the scales commonly used for locating historic sites, the (60) UTM grid system becomes extremely clear and straightforward to use.

17. By "ticks," the author most likely means

(A) beats.

(B) sounds.

(C) insects.

(D) marks.

(E) watches.

18. You may infer from the passage that which of the following is the most likely reason the author prefers not to use translated values?

(A) They are inaccurate.

(B) They are difficult or inconvenient to obtain.

(C) They are appropriate only for large-scale maps.

(D) They measure longitude but not latitude.

(E) They quickly become obsolete.

Go on to next page

19. In line 18, the author uses the word *compromise* to mean

    (A) lessen.

    (B) come to an agreement.

    (C) promise.

    (D) match.

    (E) predict.

20. You may infer which of the following from the passage?

    I. The zone number of Florida is higher than the zone number of California.

    II. The zone numbers of the United States and Mexico are identical.

    III. Zone 15 is farther north of the equator than is Zone 10.

    (A) I only

    (B) II only

    (C) III only

    (D) I and II only

    (E) I, II, and III

21. The purpose of the last sentence of this passage is to

    (A) list possible uses for UTM grids.

    (B) criticize the use of negative numbers in the UTM grid system.

    (C) justify the choice of arbitrary values of points.

    (D) distinguish northing from easting.

    (E) reassure readers as to the feasibility of using the UTM grid system.

22. This passage would be mostly likely to appear in which of the following?

    (A) an encyclopedia entry on the U.S. Geographical Survey

    (B) a backpacking and hiking booklet

    (C) a geography textbook

    (D) a magazine article about using computers to create more accurate maps

    (E) an advertisement for a map-reading course

23. Which of the following additional topics would be most useful if added to this passage?

    (A) how to use the computer system that converts local grid coordinates to UTM references

    (B) specific situations in which mapping on flat sheets does not provide sufficiently accurate data

    (C) the distinctions between the UTM grid system and other map reading systems

    (D) the qualifications of the author to write this passage

    (E) an example of how to find the specific UTM grid location for one city

The lungs, shaped roughly like triangles or pyramids, rest in the chest cavity on the diaphragm (a muscular tissue that separates the abdominal cavity from the chest). They are separated by the large blood vessels, the esophagus, and the heart. (Line 05)

The main function of the lungs is to keep the body supplied with oxygen (lungs are unnecessary in water-dwelling animals as water removes the waste gases and supplies the cells with the needed oxygen). When oxygen enters the lungs, it permeates the walls of the air sacs and is absorbed into the bloodstream. The blood travels through the body, giving oxygen to the tissues and receiving carbon dioxide. (10) (15)

The lungs, consisting primarily of air sacs, average between three and four pounds. Healthy lungs are gray and blotchy in appearance. The idea of the bright pink lung is widespread but erroneous. However, lungs do become grossly discolored by disease and smoking. (20)

More than five hundred million alveoli (air sacs) are in the lungs. The alveoli are hollows formed by the bronchioles, which are the smallest version of the air passages known as the bronchial tubes. The alveoli are clusters (something like soap suds) that are found at the end of the bronchioles. The right lung has three lobes (large cluster of alveoli), while the left lung has two. (25)

Go on to next page

24. According to the passage, a smoker is likely to have lungs that

    (A) have pink color.

    (B) have fewer alveoli than a normal lung.

    (C) are impaired in their ability to allow oxygen to be absorbed into the bloodstream.

    (D) are not gray and blotchy in appearance.

    (E) allow more carbon dioxide to stay in tissues.

25. What separates the right and left lungs?

    (A) the diaphragm

    (B) the number of alveoli

    (C) the number of lobes

    (D) large blood vessels

    (E) bronchial tubes

26. Blood vessels travel to and from the lungs. It can be inferred from the passage that which of the following is (are) true?

    I. The blood vessel traveling away from the lungs has a relatively high concentration of oxygen.

    II. The blood vessel traveling towards the lungs will approach the alveoli.

    III. The blood vessel traveling towards the lungs has a relatively low concentration of carbon dioxide.

    (A) I only

    (B) II only

    (C) III only

    (D) I and II only

    (E) I, II, and III

27. The main purpose of the passage is to

    (A) demonstrate how smoking interferes with normal lung function.

    (B) outline the path oxygen takes after it enters an animal.

    (C) compare how land animals and sea animals differ in regard to oxygen intake.

    (D) describe the basic appearance and function of lungs.

    (E) explain how the lungs function to pass oxygen to the bloodstream.

Directions: Choose the answer choice most nearly opposite in meaning to the question word.

28. DANDY

    (A) philistine

    (B) slob

    (C) curmudgeon

    (D) slattern

    (E) visionary

29. WILY

    (A) sporadic

    (B) straightforward

    (C) fallacious

    (D) somber

    (E) urbane

30. INGENUOUS

    (A) alien

    (B) stupid

    (C) rash

    (D) earthy

    (E) sophisticated

31. EXTROVERTED

    (A) bombastic

    (B) unnecessary

    (C) shy

    (D) stationary

    (E) ubiquitous

32. PRODIGIOUS

    (A) bold

    (B) minuscule

    (C) agile

    (D) menacing

    (E) immature

Go on to next page

33. QUERULOUS
    (A) brash
    (B) pristine
    (C) dormant
    (D) unconscionable
    (E) uncomplaining

34. EXTIRPATE
    (A) abolish
    (B) exacerbate
    (C) introduce
    (D) adulate
    (E) seethe

35. REVERE
    (A) prattle
    (B) buttress
    (C) waft
    (D) disdain
    (E) saunter

36. DESICCATE
    (A) admire
    (B) beatify
    (C) interpolate
    (D) hydrate
    (E) plummet

37. PONTIFICATING
    (A) scintillating
    (B) fawning
    (C) burnishing
    (D) desiccating
    (E) self-effacing

38. SANGUINE
    (A) supple
    (B) stygian
    (C) doting
    (D) morose
    (E) voracious

STOP You may check your work on this section only.
Do not go on to the next section until you are told to do so.

Section 3

> Time: 30 minutes
>
> 25 questions
>
> *Directions:* Each question or set of questions is based upon a specific passage or upon a set of conditions. To answer the questions, you may find it useful to draw a diagram or chart. Select the best answer to each question.

Questions 1–3 are based on the following information:

Five men, Jared, Anthony, Eric, Kato, and Bob, are seated in six chairs in a row in the theater.

 I. Anthony cannot sit next to Kato but must have persons on both sides of him.

 II. Bob sits in either the first seat or the last seat.

 III. Eric sits three spaces to the left of Bob.

 IV. There are two spaces between Jared and the empty seat.

 V. Kato is in seat five.

1. Which seat is empty?

   (A) first

   (B) second

   (C) fourth

   (D) fifth

   (E) sixth

2. If Eric sits three spaces to the right of Bob rather than three spaces to the left of Bob, which of the following must be true?

   (A) Anthony is in seat three.

   (B) Seat five is empty.

   (C) Anthony is next to Eric.

   (D) Anthony is next to Bob.

   (E) Eric is next to the empty seat.

3. From which of the following statements did you deduce in which seat Bob sits?

   (A) I and II

   (B) I and III

   (C) II and III

   (D) I only

   (E) I, II, and III

4. My dentist said that she would use the drill when I visit her today. She used the drill when she filled my bicuspid, put a crown on my molar, and gave me a root canal. I felt a lot of pain on each occasion. I know that I will feel pain today.

   The argument above depends on which of the following assumptions?

   (A) The drill emits a high-frequency sound that can hurt ears.

   (B) The drill will be used for a routine teeth cleaning.

   (C) The patient will get a filling, crown, or root canal today.

   (D) The drill was the only source of pain for the patient during past visits to the dentist.

   (E) Use of the drill always leads to pain for the patient.

5. Cancer is less curable now than it was 100 years ago. In 1895, only 5 percent of all deaths were caused by cancer whereas cancer is responsible for 25 percent of all deaths today.

   Which of the following most weakens the argument?

   (A) Scientists have developed many cures for cancer over the past 100 years.

   (B) Immunizations and other health care measures protect humans from non-cancer diseases that were fatal 100 years ago.

   (C) Heart disease causes a higher percentage of deaths now than it did 10 years ago.

   (D) New technologies produce many cancer-causing agents.

   (E) Modern medicine alleviates the pain that cancer patients endure.

Go on to next page ➡

Questions 6–10 are based on the following information:

Five vacancies have just opened up on the Board of Directors. These vacancies must be filled by three newcomers and two veterans. The newcomers interested in the job are Rusty, Susan, Tawny, Virginia, and Yolanda. The veterans interested in the job are Hank, Ingrid, and Jack.

  I. Hank will not serve with Ingrid.

  II. Neither Tawny nor Virginia will serve with Jack.

  III. Yolanda will not serve with Hank

6. How many possible groups of persons can serve on the board?

(A) one

(B) two

(C) three

(D) four

(E) five

7. If Yolanda were replaced by Zane, who has no restrictions on the people with whom he will serve, how many different groups are possible?

(A) one

(B) two

(C) three

(D) four

(E) five

8. If Hank may serve with Ingrid but all other rules remain in force, which of the following groupings is *not* possible?

  I. Hank, Rusty, Susan, Tawny, Virginia

  II. Ingrid, Jack, Rusty, Susan, Yolanda

  III. Hank, Ingrid, Susan, Tawny, Virginia

  IV. Ingrid, Jack, Rusty, Susan, Virginia

(A) I only

(B) III only

(C) I and IV only

(D) I, III, and IV only

(E) I, II, III, and IV

9. Which of the following cannot serve on the board if Ingrid serves?

(A) Tawny

(B) Rusty

(C) Jack

(D) Yolanda

(E) Susan

10. If the Board agrees to have six members, three veterans and three novices, how many groupings are possible?

(A) 0

(B) 1

(C) 2

(D) 3

(E) 4

11. A passbook savings account is a great investment because it allows one to accumulate a fortune. All people who have become wealthy through their investments have invested in a passbook account.

Which of the following arguments has a flaw in the reasoning most similar to that found in the statement above?

(A) Calculus is a valuable subject because calculus helps you to master GRE math. All calculus students do well on the math portion of the GRE.

(B) Penicillin is a useful drug because it cures many diseases. Penicillin kills the bacteria that causes several diseases.

(C) This rectangle could be a square because rectangles and squares share many properties. All squares are rectangles.

(D) The run-and-shoot offense is ineffective because teams that use it usually lose. Defensive coaches have devised ways to stop the run-and-shoot offense.

(E) Training wheels on a bicycle typically do more harm than good because they make it harder for a child to learn to ride a bike. Training wheels provide too much support and thereby make it impossible for a child to develop a sense of balance.

Go on to next page

12. Professor Garcia uses a 100-point grading scale in her astronomy class. Class attendance accounts for 25 of these points. Students lose five of their attendance points for each day that they are absent. Therefore, a student who is absent three or more days will not be able to earn an A.

    If the above statements are true, which of the following is most probably also true?

    (A) No other factor accounts for more than 25 points.

    (B) Students who miss the final will not earn an A.

    (C) Students who miss five or more classes will not earn a B.

    (D) An A requires more than 85 points.

    (E) Professor Garcia automatically lowers a grade one level when a student is absent three or more times.

Questions 13–17 are based on the following information:

Gregory is planting four pea plants in his garden. The peas on the plants are characterized by color (yellow or green), shape (round or wrinkled), and size (large or small). Each plant has only one type of pea (that is, one plant won't have both a large pea and a small pea, or a round pea and a wrinkled pea, or a yellow pea and a green pea). Each characteristic is found on at least one of the plants. The following information is known about the peas:

> The number of plants with yellow peas does not equal the number of plants with green peas.
>
> Plant number two has large peas.
>
> There are no round yellow peas.
>
> If a plant has round peas, those peas are large.
>
> Plant number four has yellow peas.

13. Which of the following is a possible set of characteristics?

    (A) plant number one: yellow wrinkled; number two: yellow round; number three: green wrinkled; number four: yellow wrinkled

    (B) plant number one: yellow wrinkled; number two: green round; number three: green wrinkled; number four: yellow wrinkled

    (C) plant number one: green wrinkled; number two: yellow wrinkled; number three: green round; number four: green wrinkled

    (D) plant number one: yellow wrinkled; number two: green round; number three: yellow wrinkled; number four: yellow wrinkled

    (E) plant number one: yellow wrinkled; number two: yellow wrinkled; number three: green wrinkled; number four: yellow wrinkled

14. If plants number two and three have round peas, the peas on plant number one must be

    (A) green

    (B) yellow

    (C) round

    (D) wrinkled

    (E) large

15. Which information would allow you to determine all the characteristics of plant number four?

    (A) plant number one is small; plant number three is round

    (B) plant number one is round; plant number three is large

    (C) plant number two is yellow; plant number three is yellow

    (D) plant number two is green; plant number three is wrinkled

    (E) plant number two is green; plant number four is wrinkled

Go on to next page

16. If the peas on plant number one are small and those on plant number three are round, how many possible combinations are there for the four plants?

    (A) three

    (B) four

    (C) five

    (D) six

    (E) seven

17. If plant number two is the only plant with large peas, which plants(s) must have green peas?

    (A) number one

    (B) number two

    (C) number three

    (D) both number one and number three

    (E) both number two and number three

18. Diamonds are a more popular investment among the extremely rich than are yachts. Ten thousand times as many people who can afford both buy a diamond as buy a yacht.

    Which of the following, if true, would most weaken the argument above?

    (A) Owning a private yacht is more prestigious than owning a diamond.

    (B) There are fewer yacht brokers than there are diamond brokers.

    (C) It is harder to resell a yacht than to resell a diamond.

    (D) The ratio of people who can afford diamonds to the people who can afford yachts is a million to one.

    (E) People with diamonds are less likely to be audited by the IRS than are people with yachts.

19. Rock fan: This bootleg tape is definitely a recording of an early Beatles jam session. The choice of chords, the voice timbre, even the bantering is typical of the Beatles.

    The rock fan presupposes which of the following?

    (A) The chords of a song are its most distinctive feature.

    (B) The Beatles bootleg jam sessions are very rare and consequently very valuable.

    (C) Music is the only form of art with characteristics that allow the audience to identify the artist immediately.

    (D) No other musicians used the chords or had the voice timbre and bantering found in the tape.

    (E) The Beatles used chords, voice timbre, and bantering that differed greatly from those of any other group.

20. Last year, there was only one fatality among circus performers who did acts without a net on the trapeze or the high wire. There were more than five hundred deaths from skateboarding accidents. Therefore, it is more dangerous to skateboard than to perform without a net on the trapeze or high wire in a circus.

    The absurdity of the conclusion in the preceding material would be best illustrated by which of the following?

    (A) comparing the death rates as percentages of all skateboarders vs. all circus performers on the trapeze or high wire who work without a net

    (B) graphing the history of the number of deaths from circus acts vs. the number of deaths from skateboarding over a longer period, such as 10 years

    (C) identifying more specifically the causes of the deaths: lack of qualification for the task, equipment failure, outside forces, and so on

    (D) counting severe injuries as well as deaths from the two activities

    (E) comparing the age groups of the average trapeze or high wire artist to the age group of the average skateboarder and finding the number of deaths as a percentage of that age group

Go on to next page

Questions 21–25 are based on the following information:

An academic team coach must select five players to compete in an upcoming match. To maximize her team's chances of winning, she must include two strong math players, a strong humanities player, and a strong social science player. Her roster includes Ann, Beth, and Carlos, who are strong math players; Damien and Elaine, who are strong humanities players; Fahid, Gail, and Haroon, who are strong social science players; and James.

The coach's selections must conform to the following conditions:

> If she selects Carlos, she must select Fahid.
>
> If she selects James, she may not select Fahid.
>
> Elaine is chosen for the team.
>
> The team may not include two or more social science players.

21. Which of the following is an acceptable group of five players?

    (A) Ann, Beth, Elaine, Gail, Haroon
    (B) Ann, Carlos, Damien, Elaine, Haroon
    (C) Ann, Carlos, Damien, Elaine, Fahid
    (D) Ann, Damien, Elaine, Haroon, James
    (E) Ann, Beth, Carlos, Damien, Fahid

22. If the coach selects James, the team must also include

    (A) Damien
    (B) Beth
    (C) Gail
    (D) Carlos
    (E) Haroon

23. If Damien is chosen and Gail is not, how many different teams are possible?

    (A) one
    (B) two
    (C) three
    (D) four
    (E) five

24. Which of the following is _not_ possible?

    (A) Carlos and James are both chosen.
    (B) Damien and Gail are both chosen.
    (C) Carlos is chosen, and Haroon is not chosen.
    (D) Three math players are chosen.
    (E) Ann and Haroon are both chosen.

25. James will be selected if which of the following is/are rejected?

    (A) Ann
    (B) Damien and Gail
    (C) Gail and Haroon
    (D) Damien and Fahid
    (E) Carlos and Fahid

STOP You may check your work on this section only.
Do not go on to the next section until you are told to do so.

Section 4

Time: 30 minutes

30 questions

Notes:

All numbers used in this exam are real numbers.

All figures lie in a plane.

Angle measures are positive; points and angles are in the position shown.

Directions: Questions 1 – 15 feature two columns with a quantity in each. Compare the quantities.

Choose A if the quantity in Column A is greater than the quantity in Column B.

Choose B if the quantity in Column B is greater than the quantity in Column A.

Choose C if the quantities in Column A and Column B are equal.

Choose D if you cannot determine which quantity is greater from the information given.

You will not be given credit for choosing answer E.

A letter (a, b, c, or x, y, z) or symbol means the same thing throughout one problem but may not be the same in different problems.

Information that is centered between two columns applies to both columns in that problem.

Examples:

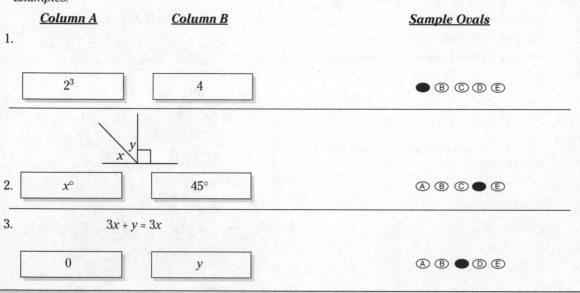

<u>**Column A**</u>	<u>**Column B**</u>	<u>**Sample Ovals**</u>
1.		
2^3	4	● Ⓑ Ⓒ Ⓓ Ⓔ
2. $x°$	45°	Ⓐ Ⓑ Ⓒ ● Ⓔ
3. $3x + y = 3x$		
0	y	Ⓐ Ⓑ ● Ⓓ Ⓔ

	Column A	_Column B_

1.

The number of days in four years	The number of years in forty decades

2. $a \neq 0, 1$

a^2	1

3.

20 percent of 120	120 percent of 20

4.

The area of a pentagon with perimeter 15	The area of a rectangle with perimeter 20

5. $3a + 5b = 12; 3b + 5a = 28$

$3(a + b)$	15

6. $-20 \leq x < 0$

Greatest possible value of x^3	0

7. A right cylinder of volume 200π cubic units has a height of 8.

Circumference of the base	10

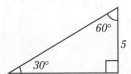

8.

Area of the triangle	$25\sqrt{3}$

	Column A	_Column B_

9.

$\dfrac{1}{\left(1 - {}^1\!/_6\right)^2}$	1

10. $a\,{}^{\#}\,b\,{}^{\#}\,c = 3a + 4b - {}^1\!/_2 c$

$3 * 6 * 12$	27

Area of circle O=36π

11.

Length of arc NP	36π

12.

$10(\sqrt{10})(\sqrt{10})10$	$\sqrt{10^3}$

13.

The average (arithmetic mean) of $10^2, 11^2,$ and 12^2	11

14. Five less than six times one-third of the workers at a plant are laid off. There were originally x workers at the plant.

Number of workers laid off	$2x - 5$

15. $1 < m < 5$

m is a whole number

2^{m-6}	1

Go on to next page

Directions: Each of the following questions (16 – 30) has five answer choices. Select the best choice.

16. A dunce cap in the shape of a cone sits on Buddy's floor. The cap has a diameter of 8 feet and rises 1.5 feet. Which of the following represents the volume of the cap in cubic feet?
(Volume of a cone = $\frac{1}{3}\pi r^2 \times$ height)

   (A) 8π

   (B) 7.5π

   (C) 7π

   (D) 6.33π

   (E) 6π

17. A box of candy contains three types of candy: 20 creams, 15 chews, and 12 nuts. Each time LaVonne reaches into the box, she pulls out a piece of candy, takes a bite out of it, and throws it away. She pulls out a cream, a nut, a chew, a nut, a cream, and a chew. What is the probability that on the next reach, she will pull out a nut?

   (A) $^{15}/_{47}$

   (B) $^{13}/_{41}$

   (C) $^{10}/_{41}$

   (D) $^{13}/_{15}$

   (E) $^{11}/_{15}$

18. Rachel and Shayna are looking at a shelf of 84 books at the library. The difference between the number of books that they look at and put back and the number of books that they look at and check out is 20. How many books did they put back? (They put back more books than they took out.)

   (A) 24

   (B) 32

   (C) 35

   (D) 52

   (E) 64

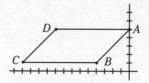

Note: Each tick mark represents one unit.

19. What is the number of square units in the area of parallelogram *ABCD*?

   (A) 40

   (B) 36

   (C) 32

   (D) 26

   (E) 24

20. In Li's store, his profit is 320% of his cost. If his costs increase by 25% but his selling price remains constant, approximately what percent of selling price is the profit?

   (A) 30

   (B) 70

   (C) 100

   (D) 250

   (E) 286.70

Go on to next page

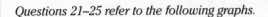

Questions 21–25 refer to the following graphs.

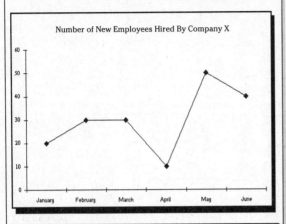

Number of New Employees Hired By Company X

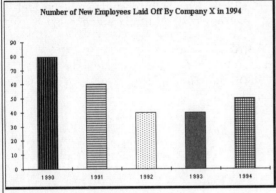

Number of New Employees Laid Off By Company X in 1994

21. The number of new employees hired by Company X from January through June of 1994 was

(A) 180

(B) 160

(C) 140

(D) 120

(E) 100

22. If no additional new employees are hired by Company X in 1994, the number of employees in Company X will be

(A) 180

(B) 160

(C) 140

(D) 120

(E) It cannot be determined.

23. From 1990 through 1994 inclusive, Company X laid off how many employees?

(A) 280

(B) 250

(C) 200

(D) 80

(E) It cannot be determined.

24. If new employees hired in May 1994 were $\frac{1}{5}$ of the total employees, new employees laid off in 1994 would be what percent of the total employees in the company?

(A) 60

(B) 50

(C) $33\frac{1}{3}$

(D) 24

(E) 20

25. In 1995, the increase in the percentage of new employees laid off over that of the previous year was the same as the increase in the percentage of new employees hired between January and February of 1994. How many new employees were laid off in 1995?

(A) 10

(B) 20

(C) 50

(D) 60

(E) 75

26. Devrae travels twice as far as Michelle but only a third as fast. Michelle starts at Point A at noon on Monday and travels to Point B, 300 kilometers away, by 9 p.m. the same day. If Devrae starts three hours later than Michelle, when will Devrae reach Point C, exactly twice as far as point B? (She makes no stops along the way and travels at a steady pace.)

(A) 6 p.m. Tuesday

(B) Noon Wednesday

(C) 6 p.m. Wednesday

(D) 9 p.m. Wednesday

(E) Midnight Wednesday

Go on to next page

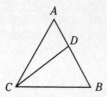

27. In this figure, the number of interior degrees in the triangle ABC is what percent of the number of interior degrees in triangle ADC?

(A) 45

(B) 50

(C) 100

(D) 200

(E) It cannot be determined from the information given.

28. Gigi and Neville, working together at the same rate, can mow the estate's lawn in 12 hours. Working alone, what fraction of the lawn can Gigi mow in three hours?

(A) $^1/_{24}$

(B) $^1/_{12}$

(C) $^1/_8$

(D) $^1/_4$

(E) $^1/_3$

29. If $x \neq 4$, solve for

$$\frac{\sqrt{x}+2}{\sqrt{x}-2}$$

(A) -1

(B) $\dfrac{x+4}{x-4}$

(C) $-\sqrt{x}-1$

(D) $\sqrt{x}+4$

(E) $\dfrac{x+4\sqrt{x}+4}{x-4}$

30. If ten plums cost a cents and six apples cost b cents, what is the cost of two plums and two apples in terms of a and b?

(A) $\dfrac{3a+5b}{15}$

(B) $3a+5b$

(C) $15ab$

(D) $5a+\dfrac{3b}{15}$

(E) $\dfrac{1}{15ab}$

STOP You may check your work on this section only. Do not go on to the next section until you are told to do so.

Section 5

Time: 30 minutes

30 questions

Notes:

All numbers used in this exam are real numbers.

All figures lie in a plane.

Angle measures are positive; points and angles are in the position shown.

Directions: Questions 1–15 feature two columns with a quantity in each. Compare the quantities.

Choose A if the quantity in Column A is greater than the quantity in Column B.

Choose B if the quantity in Column B is greater than the quantity in Column A.

Choose C if the quantities in Column A and Column B are equal.

Choose D if you cannot determine which quantity is greater from the information given.

You will not be given credit for choosing answer E.

A letter (a, b, c, or x, y, z) or symbol means the same thing throughout one problem but may not be the same in different problems.

Information that is centered between two columns applies to both columns in that problem.

Examples:

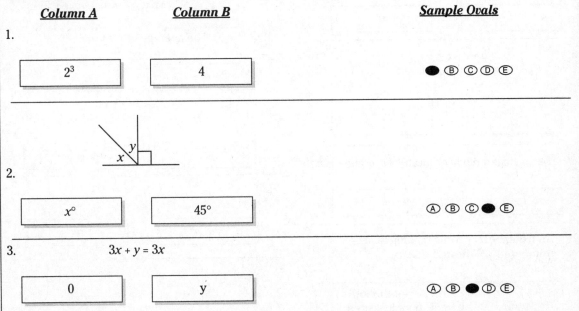

	Column A	**Column B**	**Sample Ovals**
1.	2^3	4	● Ⓑ Ⓒ Ⓓ Ⓔ
2.	$x°$	45°	Ⓐ Ⓑ Ⓒ ● Ⓔ
3.	$3x + y = 3x$		
	0	y	Ⓐ Ⓑ ● Ⓓ Ⓔ

Column A	Column B

1. $a \times b = c$

| c | b |

2.

| $^1/_{32}$ of 16 | $^1/_{16}$ of 32 |

3. $x > 1$

| Fifty percent more than $^1/_2$ of x | x |

4.

| $2a$ | c |

5. $a > b > c > d > 0$
a, b, c, d are integers

| $\dfrac{b + c}{d}$ | $\dfrac{d + c}{b}$ |

6. The average (arithmetic mean) of a, b, and c is b.

| $c - a$ | b |

7. An usher seats people holding tickets numbered 226 through 252.

| 26 | Number of people seated by the usher |

8.

| 40 | Perimeter of trapezoid $ABCD$ |

Column A	Column B

9. A rectangular patio measures 6' × 8'. Each square tile is 3" × 3".

| Number of tiles needed to cover the patio | 600 |

10.

| $x^6 \times x^5 \times x \times x^{-3}$ | x^9 |

11. x is a prime number > 5; y is a composite number < 9.

| x | y |

Note: Figure not drawn to scale

12. The average of $x + y = 90$.

| a | 90 |

13.

| a^2 | $(a + 5)(a - 5)$ |

14.

| $a^{10} \times a^5 \times {}^1/_{a^3}$ | a^{12} |

15.

| Distance BC | $2\sqrt{5}$ |

Go on to next page

Go on to next page

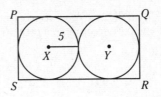

Directions: Each of the following questions (16–30) has five answer choices. Select the best choice.

16. A teacher walks down the aisle, checking homework. He checks the math for the first student, the English for the second, the science for the third, and the history for the fourth. If he continues this pattern, what homework will he check for the 38th student?

    (A) math

    (B) English

    (C) science

    (D) history

    (E) It cannot be determined from the information given.

17. A plane flies from Los Angeles to New York at 600 miles per hour and returns along the same route at 400 miles per hour. What is the average (arithmetic mean) flying speed for the entire route?

    (A) 460 mph

    (B) 480 mph

    (C) 500 mph

    (D) 540 mph

    (E) It cannot be determined from the information given.

18. Women's shoes of the following sizes were sold on Saturday: 8, 7$\frac{1}{2}$, 6$\frac{1}{2}$, 5$\frac{1}{2}$, 6, 6$\frac{1}{2}$, 8, 7, 6, 8$\frac{1}{2}$, 8. What is the difference between the mode and the median?

    (A) 0

    (B) $\frac{1}{2}$

    (C) 1

    (D) 1$\frac{1}{2}$

    (E) 2

19. Area of circle X = area of circle Y

    What is the area of rectangle $PQRS$?

    (A) 200

    (B) 180

    (C) 150

    (D) 100

    (E) 25

20. Marking flags are placed along a building site. If the orange flag is twice as far from the red flag as the red flag is from the green flag, which of the following represents this ratio:

    $$\frac{\text{distance from red to orange flag}}{\text{distance from orange to green flag}}$$

    (A) 4:1

    (B) 3:1

    (C) 2:1

    (D) 3:2

    (E) It cannot be determined from the information given.

Company X

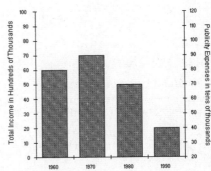

21. The total income of Company X from 1960 through 1990 was

    (A) $20,000,000

    (B) $2,000,000

    (C) $200,000

    (D) $20,000

    (E) $200

22. In 1970, publicity expenses were approximately what percentage of total income?

(A) 10

(B) 13

(C) 20

(D) 23

(E) 40

23. If publicity expenses doubled in 1980, approximately what percentage of total income was spent on publicity?

(A) 10

(B) 20

(C) 25

(D) 45

(E) 50

24. The amount of money spent by Company X on television advertising in 1980 was

(A) $ 5,000,000

(B) $700,000

(C) $500,000

(D) $70,000

(E) It cannot be determined.

25. Company X's publicity expenses in 1970 were what percent greater than those in 1990?

(A) 500

(B) 250

(C) 225

(D) 125

(E) It cannot be determined.

26. $\boxed{\begin{array}{l} ⓧ = x + x^2 \text{ for all prime numbers} \\ ⓧ = x^2 - x \text{ for all composite numbers} \end{array}}$

④ + ⑤ =

(A) 50

(B) 42

(C) 40

(D) 32

(E) 15

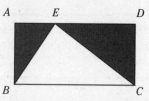

27. Given that the area of triangle *EBC* = 36, what is the area of the shaded portion of the figure?

(A) 72

(B) 54

(C) 40

(D) 36

(E) 18

28. What is the perimeter of a regular polygon of side 3 whose interior angles measure 135 degrees each?

(A) 27

(B) 24

(C) 21

(D) 8

(E) It cannot be determined.

29. A hubcap with an area of 16π has a radius of exactly one-half that of the wheel it is on. If the wheel were to roll down a 400-foot hill, approximately how many revolutions would it make?

(A) 16

(B) 10

(C) 8

(D) 6

(E) 4

30. $\dfrac{6\, a^{10}\, b^5\, c^7}{3\, a^5\, b^9\, c^7} =$

(A) $2\, a^2\, b^4\, c$

(B) $\dfrac{2\, a^2\, b^4}{c}$

(C) $\dfrac{2\, a^5\, b^4}{c}$

(D) $2\, a^5\, b^4$

(E) $\dfrac{2\, a^5}{b^4}$

STOP You may check your work on this section only.
Do not go on to the next section until you are told to do so.

Section 6

Time: 30 minutes

25 questions

Directions: Each question or set of questions is based upon a specific passage or upon a set of conditions. To answer the questions, you may find it useful to draw a diagram or chart. Select the best answer to each question.

Questions 1–3 are based on the following information:

I. Edgar is richer than Roxanne but poorer than Julie.

II. Glenn is less rich than Lauren.

III. Roxanne is richer than Glenn but less rich than Julie.

1. Which of the following must be true?

(A) Roxanne is richer than Edgar.

(B) Glenn has no money.

(C) Edgar is richer than Lauren.

(D) Julie is richer than Glenn.

(E) Lauren has more money than anyone else.

2. If the additional information "Lauren is richer than Julie" is added, what is the order of persons from poorest to richest?

(A) Glenn, Roxanne, Edgar, Julie, Lauren

(B) Lauren, Julie, Edgar, Roxanne, Glenn

(C) Glenn, Roxanne, Julie, Lauren, Edgar

(D) Lauren, Julie, Roxanne, Glenn, Edgar

(E) Glenn, Julie, Roxanne, Edgar, Lauren

3. Which of the following pieces of information is superfluous?

(A) Edgar is richer than Roxanne.

(B) Glenn is less rich than Lauren.

(C) Roxanne is richer than Glenn.

(D) Roxanne is less rich than Julie.

(E) Julie is richer than Edgar.

4. UCLA basketball fan: I am so glad that college basketball changed its rules and put in a shot clock. When there was no shot clock, a team with inferior ability could keep the ball away from the other team by passing the ball around the entire game. The winning team should be the one that is better at shooting baskets, not at playing keep-away.

North Carolina basketball fan: I disagree. The object of basketball is to win. If playing keep-away is the way for a team to win, it should do so.

The North Carolina fan's response indicates that he has misunderstood the UCLA fan's remark to mean

(A) games without a shot clock are boring.

(B) true basketball does not involve a game of keep-away.

(C) it is unwise to utilize a keep-away strategy, even when permitted to do so.

(D) a game with a shot clock is better than a game without one.

(E) Teams with superior ability have a very difficult time winning when a keep-away strategy is used.

Go on to next page

5. Angelica has great grades and high SAT scores and is her high school's student body president. She has been accepted to Harvard. Angelica will certainly attend Harvard next year.

   The author's conclusion that Angelica will attend Harvard would be most strengthened if it were true that

   (A) Angelica was accepted under the early decision program, which binds accepted applicants to the school and prohibits them from attending any other college.

   (B) grades are the most important factor for admission to Harvard.

   (C) students who are accepted to Harvard attend Harvard.

   (D) Harvard is the most prestigious college in the world.

   (E) Harvard has tougher admission standards than does any other college in the United States.

Questions 6–10 are based on the following information:

   I.   To get a ticket to see Hootie and the Blowfish, Valerie must have a ride from her friend, get cash from the bank, and have a day off from work.

   II. Valerie will get a ride from her friend only when she can get her husband to take the friend's children to the park.

   III. Valerie's husband is available to go to the park on any day except Sunday, Thursday, and Friday.

   IV. Valerie can get off work to go to the concert only when the bank is open in the afternoon. The bank's hours are 9 a.m. to noon on Monday, Tuesday, Friday, and Saturday; 9 a.m. to 5 p.m. Wednesday and Thursday; and closed Sunday. Valerie works Monday through Saturday.

6. On what day can Valerie get the tickets?
   (A) Monday
   (B) Tuesday
   (C) Wednesday
   (D) Thursday
   (E) Friday

7. If the bank changed its hours such that it is open every afternoon except weekends, how many additional days may Valerie buy tickets?
   (A) five
   (B) four
   (C) three
   (D) two
   (E) one

8. If Valerie's friend were willing to lend her the cash such that Valerie did not have to go to the bank, on what days could she get tickets?
   (A) Monday, Tuesday, and Sunday
   (B) Wednesday and Saturday
   (C) Tuesday, Wednesday, and Saturday
   (D) Wednesday and Thursday
   (E) Wednesday

9. If Valerie can get a ride on the bus which runs every day, and if the bank is open every weekday afternoon except Tuesday and the ticket office is closed on the weekends, on which days can she purchase tickets?
   (A) Wednesday only
   (B) Wednesday and Thursday
   (C) Wednesday and Sunday
   (D) Wednesday, Friday, and Sunday
   (E) Monday, Wednesday, Thursday, and Friday

10. If an additional piece of information, "Valerie's husband can go to the bank to get the cash instead of taking the kids to the park," is added, on which days can Valerie buy tickets?
   (A) Monday, Tuesday, Wednesday, Thursday, and Friday
   (B) Wednesday only
   (C) Wednesday, Thursday, Friday, and Saturday
   (D) Monday only
   (E) Monday and Friday

Go on to next page

11. Parents frequently criticize schools for not doing their job. Most notably, they blame schools for low student achievement scores. Surprisingly, the most frequent and vociferous complaints come from those who live in districts where the achievement scores are high.

All of the following, considered individually, help to explain the apparent paradox *except*

(A) parents from districts of high achievers are very involved with the schools and are therefore more likely to make critical comments.

(B) Parents of children who use an interdistrict transfer to attend a school in a high-achieving district do not hesitate to complain when they feel their children are being ignored in favor of those students who live in the district.

(C) high scores cause parents' expectations to rise, leading parents to demand that students achieve even more.

(D) high-scoring districts contain high-profile students whose parents are very likely to complain when they observe that their children's scores do not match those of children who live nearby.

(E) most complaints about schools come from political activists, most of whom live in high-achieving districts.

12. Newspaper advertisement: Enroll in Apogee Test Prep! Apogee GRE students average 570 in the verbal, 640 on the quantitative, and 660 on the analytical. Raise your scores to the Apogee!

Which of the following would be most useful in evaluating the ad's claim?

(A) the number of years Apogee Test Prep has been working with GRE students

(B) the national averages for GRE scores

(C) the number of hours of instruction offered by Apogee Test Prep

(D) the GRE scores for Apogee students before they took the course

(E) whether Apogee's students' scores were high enough to get the students admitted to the graduate schools of their choice

Questions 13–17 are based on the following information:

A university chemistry department must circulate a journal among Professors Ewing, Filbig, Geffen, Hurst, Ito, Jenn, Kinoshita, and Ludwig. Professor Ewing, the department chair, receives the journal first. Each professor who receives the journal reads it for one day and passes it to another professor the very next day. The journal is circulated in the following manner:

Ewing to Filbig or Geffen

Filbig to Kinoshita

Geffen to Hurst

Hurst to Ito or Jenn

Ito to Filbig or Jenn

Jenn to Kinoshita or Ludwig

Kinoshita to Ewing

Ludwig to Kinoshita

A professor may receive the journal more than once. Each time she/he receives it, she/he reads it for a day and passes it on the next day.

13. What is the minimum number of days required for everyone to see the journal?

(A) eight

(B) nine

(C) ten

(D) eleven

(E) twelve

14. Suppose that the journal must be circulated to Ewing, Filbig, Hurst, and Kinoshita, but the other professors need not see it. Who besides Ewing, Filbig, Hurst, and Kinoshita must end up seeing the journal?

(A) nobody

(B) Geffen only

(C) Geffen and Ito

(D) Geffen and Jenn

(E) Geffen, Ito, and Jenn

Go on to next page

15. The professors are tired of having at least one person see the journal twice. If the routes remain the same, which of the following researchers should become the first one to look at the journals?

    (A) Filbig

    (B) Geffen

    (C) Hurst

    (D) Kinoshita

    (E) Ludwig

16. The journal never stops circulating. If Geffen receives it on January 1, what's the earliest she may receive it again?

    (A) January 4

    (B) January 5

    (C) January 6

    (D) January 7

    (E) January 8

17. If nobody receives the journal twice as it circulates from Ewing to Kinoshita, how many ways are there for the journal to get from Ewing to Kinoshita?

    (A) three

    (B) four

    (C) five

    (D) six

    (E) seven

18. Cars are safer than planes. Fifty percent of plane accidents result in death, while only one percent of car accidents result in death.

    Which of the following, if true, would most seriously weaken the argument above?

    (A) Planes are inspected more often than cars.

    (B) The number of car accidents is several hundred thousand times higher than the number of plane accidents.

    (C) Pilots never fly under the influence of alcohol, while car drivers often do.

    (D) Plane accidents usually involve just one plane while car accidents often involve other vehicles or a pedestrian, increasing the number of potential fatalities.

    (E) The percentage of car accidents that result in death is far higher on roads that allow cars to travel at high speeds.

19. You will not take Economics 101C unless you complete Economics 101B. You will take Economics 101B only if you complete Economics 101A. If you complete Economics 101A, you must take Economics 102A.

    Which of the following is inconsistent with the information above?

    (A) You are taking Economics 101C, so you completed Economics 101A.

    (B) You completed Economics 101A but will not take Economics 101B.

    (C) You completed Economics 101A but are not eligible for Economics 101B.

    (D) You completed Economics 101A and 101B, and you will take Economics 101C.

    (E) You will not take Economics 102A, but you did take Economics 101B.

Questions 20–25 are based on the following information:

In the Derby of Legends, horses Rive Ridge, Secretariat, and Tim Tam finish first, second, and third, but not necessarily in that order. The horses are ridden by jockeys Arcaro, Baeza, and Cordero, in no particular order, and are trained by Jolley, Lukas, and Whittingham, in no particular order.

The following information is known:

> The horse ridden by Arcaro finishes ahead of the horse ridden by Cordero.
>
> Lukas trains the horse ridden by Baeza.
>
> The horses trained by Lukas and Jolley do not finish in consecutive order.
>
> Secretariat finishes first.

20. Which of the following would make it necessary that Cordero ride the horse that finished second?

    (A) Rive Ridge finished second.

    (B) The horse ridden by Baeza finished first.

    (C) The Whittingham-trained horse finished second.

    (D) Tim Tam was ridden by Cordero.

    (E) The Lukas-trained horse finished third.

Go on to next page

21. Which of the following is possible?

    (A) Tim Tam finished second.

    (B) Arcaro's horse finished third.

    (C) The horse trained by Jolley finished second.

    (D) Lukas trained the horse ridden by Cordero.

    (E) Rive Ridge finished first.

22. Which of the following must be true?

    (A) If Rive Ridge is ridden by Cordero, Rive Ridge finishes second.

    (B) If Secretariat is ridden by Arcaro, the Jolley-trained horse finishes third.

    (C) If Tim Tam is ridden by Cordero, Rive Ridge finishes third.

    (D) If Tim Tam is ridden by Baeza, Rive Ridge finishes second.

    (E) If Tim Tam is trained by Whittingham, Tim Tam finishes third.

23. If Rive Ridge is second and ridden by Arcaro, which of the following is true of Jolley?

    (A) His horse finishes first.

    (B) His horse finishes second.

    (C) His horse finishes third.

    (D) He trains the horse ridden by Baeza.

    (E) He trains the horse that finishes ahead of the horse trained by Whittingham.

24. If Jolley trains Secretariat, who trains the horse ridden by Arcaro?

    (A) Whittingham

    (B) Jolley

    (C) Lukas

    (D) Rive Ridge's trainer

    (E) Tim Tam's trainer

25. If the horse trained by Whittingham finishes ahead of the horse trained by Jolley, which of the following must be false?

    (A) Cordero rides Tim Tam.

    (B) Lukas trains Cordero's horse.

    (C) Riva Ridge is the next horse to finish after Secretariat.

    (D) Arcaro rides Tim Tam.

    (E) Baeza rides Secretariat.

STOP You may check your work on this section only.

Answer Key for Practice Exam 2

Section 1		Section 2		Section 3		Section 4		Section 5		Section 6	
1.	B	1.	B	1.	C	1.	A	1.	D	1.	D
2.	D	2.	A	2.	D	2.	D	2.	B	2.	A
3.	A	3.	B	3.	C	3.	C	3.	B	3.	D
4.	D	4.	B	4.	E	4.	D	4.	C	4.	C
5.	B	5.	A	5.	B	5.	C	5.	A	5.	C
6.	E	6.	D	6.	A	6.	B	6.	D	6.	C
7.	C	7.	A	7.	B	7.	A	7.	B	7.	D
8.	B	8.	C	8.	C	8.	B	8.	B	8.	E
9.	B	9.	B	9.	A	9.	A	9.	A	9.	E
10.	D	10.	A	10.	A	10.	C	10.	C	10.	B
11.	B	11.	D	11.	A	11.	B	11.	D	11.	B
12.	E	12.	C	12.	D	12.	A	12.	D	12.	D
13.	D	13.	B	13.	D	13.	A	13.	A	13.	B
14.	B	14.	B	14.	A	14.	C	14.	C	14.	B
15.	A	15.	A	15.	B	15.	B	15.	C	15.	A
16.	D	16.	E	16.	D	16.	A	16.	B	16.	C
17.	A	17.	D	17.	B	17.	C	17.	B	17.	D
18.	C	18.	B	18.	D	18.	D	18.	C	18.	B
19.	C	19.	A	19.	D	19.	B	19.	A	19.	E
20.	A	20.	A	20.	A	20.	B	20.	E	20.	E
21.	B	21.	E	21.	C	21.	A	21.	A	21.	A
22.	D	22.	C	22.	B	22.	E	22.	B	22.	D
23.	B	23.	E	23.	D	23.	E	23.	C	23.	C
24.	C	24.	D	24.	A	24.	E	24.	E	24.	B
25.	E	25.	D	25.	D	25.	E	25.	D	25.	B
26.	C	26.	D			26.	D	26.	B		
27.	A	27.	D			27.	C	27.	D		
28.	D	28.	B			28.	C	28.	B		
29.	E	29.	B			29.	E	29.	C		
30.	A	30.	E			30.	A	30.	E		
31.	B	31.	C								
32.	C	32.	B								
33.	C	33.	E								
34.	A	34.	C								
35.	E	35.	D								
36.	A	36.	D								
37.	D	37.	E								
38.	B	38.	D								

Scoring Worksheet GRE

Here's a quick review of what you learned earlier.

On the GRE, you get one point for every question you answer correctly, and zero points for every omitted answer (anything you leave blank). There is no penalty for incorrect answers.

Analytical

Add the number of questions you answered correctly in sections three and six. Round the sum to the nearest whole number. Check your score on the Analytical score chart.

Analytical raw score: _____

GRE Analytical Score Chart

You calculated a raw score on the worksheet. Look for that score in the following table and then move to the right to find your 200–800 score.

Raw	GRE		Raw	GRE		Raw	GRE
50	800		34	610		19	390
49	800		33	600		18	380
48	800		32	580		17	360
47	790		31	570		16	350
46	760		29	550		14	330
44	750		28	530		13	310
43	730		27	520		12	290
42	710		26	500		11	280
41	700		25	480		10	260
40	690		24	470		9	250
39	680		23	450		8	240
38	670		22	440		7	230
37	660		21	430		6	210
36	640		20	410		0–5	200
35	620						

Math

Add the number of questions you answered correctly in sections four and five. Round the sum to the nearest whole number. Check your score on the Math score chart.

Math raw score: _____

GRE Math Score Chart

You calculated a raw score on the worksheet. Look for that score in the following table and then move to the right to find your 200–800 score.

Raw	GRE	Raw	GRE	Raw	Gre	Raw	GRE
60	800	46	670	32	510	18	340
59	800	45	660	31	500	17	330
58	800	44	650	30	490	16	310
57	790	43	640	29	480	15	300
56	780	42	630	28	470	14	290
55	770	41	620	27	460	13	270
54	760	40	600	26	440	12	250
53	750	39	590	25	430	11	240
52	730	38	580	24	420	10	230
51	720	37	570	23	400	9	220
50	710	36	560	22	400	8	200
49	700	35	550	21	390	7	200
48	690	34	540	20	370	6	200
47	680	33	530	19	360	0–5	200

Verbal

Add the number of questions you answered correctly in sections one and two. Round the sum to the nearest whole number. Check your score on the Verbal score chart.

Verbal raw score: _____

GRE Verbal Score Chart

You calculated a raw score on the worksheet. Look for that score in the following table and then move to the right to find your 200 - 800 score.

Raw	GRE	Raw	GRE	Raw	Gre	Raw	GRE
72-76	800	55	590	38	420	21	270
71	790	54	580	37	410	20	260
70	770	53	570	36	400	19	250
69	760	52	560	35	390	18	240
68	750	51	550	34	380	17	240
67	730	50	540	33	370	16	230
66	720	49	530	32	360	15	220
65	710	48	520	31	360	14	210
64	700	47	510	30	350	13	200
63	690	46	500	29	340	12	200
62	670	45	490	28	330	11	200
61	660	44	470	27	320	10	200
60	650	43	460	26	310	9	200
59	640	42	450	25	300	8	200
58	620	41	440	24	300	7	200
57	610	40	430	23	290	6	200
56	600	39	430	22	280	0–5	200

Chapter 22

Practice Exam 2: Answers and Explanations

· ·

Section 1

1. **B.** Look at the second blank first. (The second blank is often the key to a Sentence Completion question. When I'm taking a test, I make it a matter of habit to begin there.) Marshall probably doesn't like being confronted with a situation beyond his control; few of us would. Therefore, the second word will be something negative, such as angry or upset. Eliminate choices C, D, and E. The *although* at the beginning of the sentence tells you that Marshall is considered by us to be the opposite of what the second blank calls him. Therefore, if he is upset or angry in the second blank, he is content or happy in the first blank. *Placid* means calm, peaceful. You know the root *plac*, meaning calm. *Placate*, to make calm, is another frequently tested version of this word.

   In choice A, *quixotic* means unrealistically idealistic. It's quixotic to think that most people know words like *quixotic*. It's also irrelevant. Don't expect words this hard to be the correct answer to the very first question. Questions go from easier to harder. A word like *quixotic* would rarely be right in the first half of the questions but may very well be the correct answer to a more difficult second-half question.

2. **D.** Focus on the second blank. If Dr. Dickstein felt that the man against whom he was arguing was dangerous, he would argue pretty strongly against him. Eliminate choice B (*indifferently* means not caring one way or the other), choice C (*lackadaisically* means in a mellow, laid-back, nonenergetic way), and choice E (*tentatively* means hesitantly or uncertainly). The second word in A is possible; *exhaustively* means thoroughly. (It does not mean the same thing as exhausted, although an exhaustive search of the house for your missing car keys may leave you exhausted.) The first word, however, doesn't fit. *Fidelity* means faithfulness, as in fidelity between a loving couple (or Fido the faithful companion). (*fid* = faith.) That leaves choice D. *Vehemently* means strongly-felt and powerfully.

   Do you know the words *charlatan* and *quack* in the question? A *charlatan* or a *quack* is a fraud or nonexpert. A GRE tutor who tells you that you'll get a 1600 if you stand naked in the light of the full moon and bury a toad in your backyard is a charlatan.

3. **A.** Don't panic if you don't know all the vocabulary. You can use the process of elimination to narrow the answers down quickly. First, predict that both of the blanks must be filled by negative words. We're talking about bad people here. Eliminate any answer with positive words: choices C, D, and E. As quickly as that, you're down to two choices. If you're in a hurry, guess and go.

   You probably know that the word *miser* (choice B) means a cheapskate, a penny-pincher. That wouldn't fit into the idea of the sentence, making A the best answer. Let's review the rest of the vocabulary. A *skinflint* is a miser, a cheapskate. A *charlatan* is a fake, a fraud, one who holds himself up as an expert, especially in medicine. Did you notice that these words were in question 2, too? I used them twice to fix them permanently in your brain. Many people who are terminally ill and desperate for help will turn to charlatans who hold out any hope. A *fussbudget* is just what it looks like, a person who fusses excessively and nit picks over everything. A teacher who is a fussbudget flunks you if your margins aren't straight. A *lecher* is person given to extreme sexual indulgence. A *malefactor* is an evil-doer; a *benefactor* is one who does good deeds.

4. **D.** The second blank is the key to this question. If the official were *forced* to sign paperwork, you infer that he didn't want to do so and therefore was against the continuation of the program. He would want the program stopped. The second word must be something like stopped, narrowing the choices down to C and D. The *demise* is the death or conclusion of something. As soon as you have the answers narrowed down to two, if you're in a rush, this is a good time to guess and go.

To ***advocate*** is to defend or support a cause. The official would support the end or death of the program.

Circle any key words or connectors/changers you encounter. These are words that can change the whole sentence, such as *despite, but, even though, although, nevertheless,* and *nonetheless.* Had the word *despite* not been here, you could have read the sentence to mean that the official wanted the program to continue and therefore signed the paperwork. Choices A, B, and E would work in that case.

5. **B.** Predict that the second blank will be positive. If the person has deeply seated problems, he must not be feeling good about himself, and thus has *little* of something good. (If you missed the *little* by careless reading, you probably missed this whole question.) Eliminate A, C, and D. In choice D, ***comely*** means pretty or attractive, exactly the opposite of what the question means. ***Self-esteem*** is self-respect. ***Unkempt*** means disorderly. ***Dissonance*** is a clashing of sounds or a lack of harmony. To be ***self-indulgent*** is to pamper yourself.

As for the other words, ***slovenly*** means sloppy; ***foppish*** means foolish or conceited, especially about personal appearance.

Don't forget to predict positive or negative. In some sentences, usually the easy ones towards the beginning, you may be lucky enough to predict the exact word that fits into the blank. But in the more difficult sentences towards the end, you should still be able to say to yourself, "The word that goes in this blank must be something good," or "I need a bad word here." Usually, doing so narrows the choices down quickly.

6. **E.** If the person can afford items that his parents could only dream about, he must have more money than they had. Predict that the blank has a word meaning having money. You can eliminate choice B. ***Diversified*** means varied, not all the same. Eliminate choice C. ***Miserly*** means cheap, stingy. If you know your roots, you can eliminate choice D. ***Duplicitous*** means deceptive, double-dealing (*dup-* means double; *-ous* means full of, very). Now you have a 50-50 chance of getting this question right. Because *in-* usually means not, you can deduce that insolvent is a negative word. You want a positive word, like wealthy. ***Insolvent***, in fact, means bankrupt, unable to pay bills, just the opposite of what you're looking for. ***Affluent*** means wealthy, rich.

7. **C.** The second half of the sentence leads you to believe that the jury was having second thoughts. Unfortunately, in this case, that doesn't narrow down the answers because all the second words have to do with being confused or uncertain. ***Inquisitive*** means curious. ***Ambivalent*** means unclear or of two minds. (The root *ambi* means both. An ambivalent person could go both ways, take either side of an issue.) ***Irresolute*** means undetermined, wishy-washy. ***Befuddled*** means confused.

If the defendant's actions in accepting his fate gave the jury those second thoughts, he must be acting as if he is innocent. That means he is not ***complacent*** (unconcerned) or ***insolent*** (disrespectful). He would not be ***quiescent,*** which means the same as complacent. And ***haughty*** means arrogant or conceited. If the defendant were arrogant, chances are the jury would be glad to have convicted him, not worried whether they had done the right thing. That leaves only ***plaintive,*** which means sorrowful, melancholy. Think of the plaintive look on your dog's face when he realizes you are going to eat all your dinner and not give him any morsels.

8. **B.** A shield protects a warrior; a helmet protects a cyclist. Be sure to look for the salient feature of the word, the reason that particular word and no other was chosen. Pretend that you are trying to define the word to a friend: A shield is what a warrior uses to prevent injury to himself.

9. **B.** *Hardy* means strong. You'd get this question right even if you didn't know the words and assumed that they are synonyms and made the *is* sentence: "Hardy is strong." (When you were young, did you ever read the adventure series of books about the Hardy boys? That name expressed the type of young men the main characters were.) *Unruly* means unable to be ruled, uncontrollable. A group of elementary school kids is unruly when a substitute teacher tries to take over the class. Roots could help you to define choices D and E. *Dubious* means doubtful: *dub-* means doubt; *-ous* means full of. *Lucid* means clear: *luc-* means light or clear. Unless someone has a lucid explanation of why he wants to borrow your car, it's dubious you'll let him take it.

10. **D.** The purpose of a staple is to attach something; the purpose of an *incision* (a cut) is to open something. A surgeon makes an incision to get into your chest, for example.

    If you chose A, you fell for a trap. Although a button is sewn on, the purpose of a button is not to sew. Don't fall for a trap answer by looking at the meanings of the words. Just because buttons and staples both attach items doesn't have any relevance here. You are to look at the relationships between the words, not at their meanings.

    The purpose of a carpet is not to *impede*, which is to hold back, to hinder. If you want to go roller skating, then roller skating across a carpet would impede your progress; but impeding progress is not a carpet's primary function. The purpose of water is to hydrate, or moisten something, not to *dehydrate*, or dry something out. The purpose of a *petition* is to suggest or demand that something happen, not to review what happened. If you get up a petition about the GRE, your purpose is to suggest that the exam be abolished from polite society, not to review the status of the exam.

11. **B.** Don't know the word *dolt?* That's normal; you don't need to feel like a dolt because of your lack of knowledge. A *dolt* is a dumb person. If you don't know the words, you can assume that they are synonyms and correctly say a dolt is *moronic* (like a moron).

    While the answer choices have a hard vocabulary, it's too early to throw up your hands and make a wild guess. Choice A, a *sycophant*, is a yes-man, an over-flatterer, a kiss-up. Even without knowing that, you could realize that *sycophant*, just because it sounds like *sick,* doesn't necessarily mean the same thing. Answers like that almost have neon signs proclaiming "TRAP! TRAP!"

    A hermit likes to be alone. The root *greg-* means group or herd; *-ous* means full of. A *gregarious* person is "full of the group" or in the center of a group and sociable (just the opposite of a hermit).

    Choice D is another stupid pet trick. True, *ped-* does mean foot. And true, a runner uses his or her feet. But *pedantic* actually means overly precise, like a teacher. A teacher or professor is pedantic; a runner is not necessarily so.

    And a *patron*, one who supports a cause or a person (as in *a patron of the arts*), doesn't have to be patriotic.

    You can deduce the answer by the process of elimination. A *martinet* is a rigid disciplinarian, usually a military officer. You may think of your coach who refuses to let you out of two-a-day practices even in Indian summer as a martinet.

12. **E.** A *covey* is a group of birds; a *gaggle* is a group of geese.

    You should have (if you've been going through these exams in order and following my suggestions) a group of cards with the categories "group of animals," "young of animals," and "living places of animals." Add *gaggle* and *covey* to the "group of animals" card. And now make a new card: "male and female of the species." Write on it: A *sow* is a female pig. A *buck* is a male deer; a *doe* is a female deer.

13. **D.** A *refugee* seeks asylum. A *plaintiff* (one who files a lawsuit, the person doing the suing of the defendant) seeks *redress* (the setting right of what is wrong).

In choice A, a *charlatan* is a fake, a fraud. While he may have *charisma* (leadership quality) that fools people into following him, he doesn't *seek* charisma. (Notice how important it is to get your sentence exactly right? The verb you choose for your sentence, in this case *seek*, makes all the difference.) In choice B, a *miser* (a cheapskate, a penny-pincher, like Silas Marner) may suffer from *paranoia* (a feeling that someone is out to get you), but that doesn't mean he is seeking paranoia. He is seeking ever more money. Choice C is tempting. A *congregation* is a group of people, but they are not necessarily seeking a leader. The relationship is close, but not as good as choice D.

If you fell for the trap in E, you got dazzled and *bamboozled* (fooled) by the meanings of the words and didn't use the sentence. Sure, an escapee may be close to a refugee, and safety is like asylum, but you would not say that an escapee seeks safety. He or she is usually escaping *from* an overly secure place, like a prison. *Remember:* Words that have meanings similar to the question words are often the trap answers.

14. **B.** Now this is a hard question because so many of the answer choices are similar. The best sentence is that an *heirloom* is something left to you by an ancestor. A *bequest* (a gift to an heir) is left to you by a *testator* (one who makes the Last Will and Testament). While a magician may incorporate a *red herring* (something that tries to mislead or trick) into his act, he doesn't leave you one. While a musician uses an instrument, he doesn't leave you one. A *renegade* is a person who breaks the rules, a rebel. He leaves you with nothing. A *usurper* is one who takes without authority or right. He takes the throne; he doesn't leave it to you.

15. **A.** The prefix *acr-* means harsh or bitter. Gin can have an acrid taste; a divorce can be acrimonious. (That's one of the society columnists' favorite clichés: The acrimonious divorce between Mr. X and his third wife. Don't knock clichés. They can help you to define a word from its context.) Therefore, something acrimonious would *not* be sweet. Something *begrudging* is given grudgingly, not eagerly. Do you remember the prefix *be-?* It's as useless as your appendix. You can just ignore it — the prefix, not your appendix. Think of begrudging as simply grudging. (To help you remember this prefix, think of a belated birthday card: It's simply late. Ignore the *be-*.)

Choice B has a sloppy trap in it. If you are *deprived*, you are without something, like deprived of the common sense to look for traps like this. But the word here is not *deprived*, it is *depraved* (people often confuse or misread the two words). If you are *depraved*, you are degenerate, without good moral sense. The people who write traps like this one are degenerate. In choice C, *itinerant* means traveling or wandering. You may be more familiar with the word in another form: *itinerary*, which is your travel schedule. Therefore, being itinerant has no connection to being experienced. In choice D, *lascivious* means full of lust, lustful. A lascivious glance at the itinerant salesperson will get you a reputation for depravity. In choice E, *protean* means constantly changing. Madonna is a protean star, always changing her hairstyle and appearance to keep the audience interested.

16. **D.** This is a good question to guess at randomly if you don't know the vocabulary. There are no roots, prefixes, or suffixes to help you to define the words, many of which are very hard. Assume that the words in the question are synonyms: *diffident* is reserved. Someone diffident is laid back, not at all aggressive or assertive. Something *ominous* is *dire*, dangerous. You find yourself in dire straits if you ignore the Coast Guard's warnings and take the boat out in a storm.

Choice A is a lovely word. *Disaffected* does not mean not affected; it means not loyal, disloyal. During political campaigns, each side tries to get the disaffected voters from the other parties. In choice B, *rapacious* means excessively greedy, grasping. It is the opposite of *altruistic*, which means unselfish. Choice C also has opposites. To be *discerning* is to discriminate, to recognize something as separate or distinct. For example, a discerning shopper can tell the difference between polyester and silk. An *indiscriminate* shopper buys everything she can fit into her cart, not making any distinction between quality and shoddy goods. In choice E, *ravenous* means voracious, eager for food. By the time you finish studying for this exam, your brain will be starved for more nutrition and you will be ravenous.

17. **A.** The first paragraph describes the physical changes that occur when you laugh. The word *describe* is one of the three words that often are used as correct answers to main-purpose questions. (These words are *describe, discuss,* and *explain.*) Many times, the main purpose or primary concern of a passage is to describe, discuss, or explain something.

18. **C.** The purpose of any example is to support the main idea, either of the passage as a whole or of the paragraph in which the example appears. Here, the main idea of the paragraph is stated in the topic sentence: "Laughter is considered to be an innate human response which develops during the first few weeks of life." In other words, the ability to laugh is pretty much there when a baby is born; it is not slowly developed as the child grows up. The word *innate* is tricky if you use roots. For example, *nat* = birth, as in going to the hospital for prenatal (before-birth) care. But although most of the time *in-* = not, in this case, *in-* = inside. Something innate is "in at birth," or inborn. (Remember that *in-* has three meanings: not, inside, and beginning.)

Some of the other answers may be true, especially A, but that's not what the question is asking for. The question wants to know the purpose of one specific example. Be very careful not to choose any old answer that is true, but one that answers the question; otherwise, the process is like writing "The area of a triangle is $1/2$ *base* × *height*" when a professor asks you to name the capital of Bosnia. Yeah, it may be true, but what does that have to do with anything?

19. **C.** The third paragraph discusses many social and physiological effects of laughter. Choices B and C both bring up topics discussed in the paragraph, but choice B is too extreme.

Remember: The GRE shies away from dramatic or extreme answers. Moderate or even wishy-washy answers seem to be preferred.

While laughter leads to increased catecholamine levels, nothing in the passage indicates that laughter is the *only* way to increase these levels. Choice C is a safe answer. Lines 31-40 point out several social benefits derived from laughter. These benefits may come about in the absence of laughter, but given laughter's important role in these functions, it's fair to say that someone unable to laugh would be at a disadvantage. Choice A is completely illogical: It would make more sense if the question asked about an infant who is unable to cry, not unable to laugh. Choice D cannot be inferred from the passage. Crying occurs when the infant is distressed. While an infant who is unable to laugh may have more frequent stressful episodes than a normal infant, this is not certain. The best conclusion is that an infant who is unable to laugh won't be able to signal comfort as often as a normal infant does. Choice E is similar to choice B. An infant who is unable to laugh may benefit from placebo effects, just not necessarily those produced by laughter.

20. **A.** Pay careful attention to the language used in these choices. The third paragraph ascribes a possible pain reduction role to laughter via endorphins, but this does not mean that laughter is essential. The body probably has other ways to reduce pain. Eliminate choice E. Cross off choice D, which directly contradicts a point made in the third paragraph: Laughter *increases*, not decreases, the CO_2 levels. Choice C may have trapped you. The word *directly* should have made you eliminate this answer; the GRE plays down dramatic or emphatic words (GRE answers often hedge their bets, using lame language such as *may* or *probably* or *suggest*). First, no association between laughter and sed rate has been established. In addition, even if there were such an association, you can't get away with saying that laughter *directly* lowers the sed rate. Laughter very well could lower inflammation, which, in turn, lowers the sed rate. Choice B is not mentioned in the passage. Laughter is associated with increased pulse rate, but the passage says nothing about blood pressure. This leaves only choice A, which is mentioned throughout the first paragraph.

21. **B.** Locate where in the passage the placebo effect is mentioned (the beginning of the last paragraph) and then look at what the author says after this. The author is not fazed by the placebo effect possibility. In the same sentence that mentions placebo effect, the author says that the effect does not minimize the therapeutic potential. The sentences that follow emphasize how laughter is good for health, making choice B a good answer. Eliminate choices A, C, and E, which contradict what the author does in the last paragraph. The author basically says that, even if laughter's main benefit starts out in the mind (which is what a placebo effect is), the body has a positive reaction. Choice D refers to the previous paragraph, which claims that laughter is innate. The author does nothing to dispel this notion, allowing you to eliminate choice D.

22. **D.** You know that the best title has to incorporate the main idea of the passage, which is laughter. Eliminate choices A and C, which don't feature that word. Choice B is beyond the scope of this passage; it describes only how we laugh and what laughter does for us, not why we laugh. Choice E is the trap. The passage says that laughter may have a curative effect, but that is not the main point of the passage. The main idea usually is quite broad and general.

    The main idea or best title often appears in the first sentence or the first paragraph. In Question 17, you decided that the purpose of the first paragraph is to describe the physical features of laughter; develop that answer a little further to come up with the best title.

23. **B.** This question is unusual in that answering the question is rather easy but figuring out what the question is asking is difficult. In other words, it's the wording of the question that is confusing. (Students whose first language is not English shouldn't waste a lot of time on this sort of question. Just make a quick guess.) This question has a double negative: disagree . . . except. If you're asked the exception to what the author would disagree with, you are really being asked what he would agree with. Reword the question before you try to answer it: With which of the following does the author agree? Now the question is a breeze. The author would not agree with statement I, as he thinks the effects of laughter are both mental and physical. Cross off I, eliminating answer choices A, C, D, and E. (I told you the question was a breeze, didn't I?)

    Let's finish the question to make assurance doubly sure. Statement II is not true; the author states in line 25 that laughter is an innate (inborn) response. In fact, you even answered a question (number 18) on this same subject. Statement III is true. Lines 49 – 50 state that ". . . a possible increase in brain and pituitary endorphins . . . ."

24. **C.** The passage mentions that gifts given specifically to one spouse (line 15), property owned by a spouse before marriage (line 10), and property willed to one spouse (line 16) are separate property. It also states that property is separate if it can be willed away by one spouse (line 22). By process of elimination, choice C is the answer.

    You can also use your overall sense of the passage to answer this question. The passage states that community property is something acquired during the marriage. A family business would gain property during the marriage.

25. **E.** The primary focus of the passage was on defining community property and distinguishing it from separate or specific property. While the other answer choices cover things mentioned in the passage (except for choice C; real versus personal property was not covered), they were not the main idea of the passage. ***Remember:*** Just because a statement is true doesn't make it the main focus of the passage.

26. **C.** The author mentions early in the passage that there used to be just a few community property states but that the number has been steadily increasing. From this, you may infer that this increase will continue.

    Choice A is definitely a judgment call. Who is to say whether the community property concept is fair, not fair, the fairest, or the least fair? Passages (unless they are editorial or opinion types, which are very infrequent) rarely give personal opinions or push one person's theories or philosophies.

Choice B is well outside the scope of this passage; nothing was mentioned about homemakers. Choice D goes overboard. Just because the author believes there will be more community property states does not mean states will turn *all* possessions to community property.

You learned in the reading lecture to be wishy-washy, not dramatic. Eliminate answers with "strong" words, such as *all, every, never,* and *none.* Choice E has the same problem: it features the excessive word *all.*

27. **A.** The passage states in lines 17 – 20 that a court may deem a gift community property if the donor's intent was to give it to both parties, even if the donor did not state so specifically. Because statement I is correct, eliminate answers B and D. Statement II is wrong; it brings in the distinction between real and personal property, which was not covered in the passage. (For those of you who have gone through *acrimonious* — bitter — divorces and are all too familiar with the concept of community property, shelf your knowledge while answering these questions. Answer them based only on information stated or implied by the passage.) Statement III is also wrong but very tricky. Nothing in the passage stated that the time of the intent to make the gift was important, only the intent of the donor. If you chose C, you read too much into the question.

28. **D.** The opposite of amusing is *exasperating,* which means annoying. Choice B, *stalwart,* means strong, sturdy, resolute.

29. **E.** *Frenetic* means frantic, or frenzied. The opposite is *placid,* meaning calm, tranquil, peaceful. (*Plac* means calm or peace. Think of Lake Placid, home of the Winter Olympics. Think of Placido Domingo, "peaceful Sunday" whose singing calms you down, soothes the savage breast.) *Toxic* means poisonous. The last time I had a huge fight with my beau, it ended when I collapsed in laughter as he yelled at me, "The only reason I don't throw you in a landfill in the middle of the night is that there are laws against dumping toxic waste!"

30. **A.** *Docile* means easily trained. The opposite is rebellious (*belli* means fight). *Tactless* means imprudent, indiscriminate. *Tawdry* means tacky, gaudy, or cheap. A tactless person may call her friend's new sweater tawdry. *Vulnerable* means open to attack or damage.

31. **B.** *Antediluvian* means old, or outdated. (*Ante* means before, as in 5:00 a.m. is five ante meridian, or before the middle of the day. Literally antediluvian means "before the flood.") The opposite is *contemporary,* meaning modern or current. Choice A, *intrepid,* means brave, not fearful (*in-* means not; *trep* means fear). Choice C, *capricious,* means whimsical, unpredictable, changing suddenly (a *caprice* or a *whim* is a sudden urge, as in going to Capri on a caprice).

32. **C.** *Illicit* means illegal. The opposite is legal. *Affable* means friendly (I like to think of *affable* as "af-friend-able").

33. **C.** The *nadir* is the lowest point (taking the GRE might be your emotional nadir). The opposite is the zenith or the highest point. Getting the good score that will result from your plodding through this book is the zenith of your GRE career. Choice D, *rancor,* is ill will or malice. Please, bear this book no rancor. In choice A, a *euphemism* is a milder, pleasanter way of saying something. My all-time favorite euphemism came from a student of mine who was talking about someone who died: "He's taking a dirt nap."

34. **A.** *Quixotic* means idealistic, impractical (think of Don Quixote tilting at windmills). The opposite is *pragmatic,* which means practical or realistic. Choice E, *lackadaisical,* means mellow, phlegmatic. Choice D, *oleaginous,* means greasy, slick (like oleomargarine). *Question:* What country is the slickest, slipperiest? *Answer:* Greece, of course!

35. **E.** To *garner* is to gather or collect. The opposite is to *disperse,* meaning to hand out, to give out, to distribute. Choice B, *efface,* is to erase or wear away. Think of someone *self-effacing* (modest, not presumptuous) as "erasing his face," making himself inconspicuous.

36. **A.** *Perfidious* means treacherous or disloyal. The opposite is loyal. Choice C, *esteemed,* means respected. The term *self-esteem* is a big buzz word these days, yet most people don't know that self-esteem is actually self-respect. Choice D, *dogmatic,* means opinionated. (I have a plaque on my computer that shows just how dogmatic I am. It reads: Be reasonable — do it my way!)

37. **D.** *Progenitors* are ancestors, those who go before (*pro-* means before; *gen* means people). This is an interesting word, because *progeny* means offspring, people who come after, not before. No one said the language had to make sense. Choice E, *skinflint,* is a miser, a cheapskate, a penny pincher (here is another chance to put several words on one flashcard). Choice C, *fop,* is a *dandy,* a person preoccupied with his grooming and appearance, a clotheshorse. Choice B, *oracle,* is a soothsayer, a prognosticator. (*pro-* means before; *gnos* means knowledge; *-ate* means to make. A *prognosticator* is a person who "makes knowledge before," a fortuneteller. When a doctor gives a prognosis, she prognosticates.)

38. **B.** *Noxious* means poisonous (*nox* means poison; *-ous* means full of). Choice B, *salubrious,* means healthy or healthful (*sal* means health; *-ous* means full of). Many hard vocabulary words are based on Latin roots. Spanish and French languages are also based on Latin roots. If you don't know a word in English, try pronouncing it with a Spanish or French accent and see whether a lightbulb goes on. *Salud* is Spanish for health.

Choice A, *froward:* If you took Practice Exam one, you should certainly know this word by now. It means stubborn, obstinate, obdurate, recalcitrant, refractory, adamant, intractable. Choice C, *inane,* means ludicrous or ridiculous. It would be inane for you not to know *froward* by now. You are too *erudite* (Choice D), too scholarly and well-educated, not to remember that word. Choice E, *vapid,* means dull, tasteless, or uninteresting.

Section 2

1. **B.** The key to a Sentence Completion question is usually the second blank; focus on it first. Predict that if no one would be penalized for not showing up, they didn't have to show up, meaning that their commitment was *voluntary.* You probably predicted the exact word. Put the rest of choice B into the sentence to make sure it fits: yes, if the principal got jeered at, he probably *hastened* or rushed to make the rest of his statement.

The second words in answers A and E are exactly the opposite of what you want to say; eliminate them quickly. If something is *illegal*, the principal wouldn't suggest it, so eliminate choice D. Choice C is possible but doesn't make as much sense in the sentence as choice B.

Sometimes more than one answer "sorta" fits. Your job is to find the answer that fits the best, the one that seems to flow in the sentence. If this seems too subjective (and I've had students get truly upset, sincerely believing their answer just "sounded better" than the correct answer), make a quick guess and go.

2. **A.** If the supervisor was afraid to hire a worker who *bungled* (messed up) so badly on her first day, it appears the supervisor's fears were well-founded or *justified*.

In choice C, *objective* means neutral, unbiased . . . just the opposite of what the supervisor was. Choice D, *vituperative*, means violently abusive. And *innovative* means new, original. A vituperative person may come up with some innovative *epithets* (names, titles) to call the object of his *wrath* (anger).

3. **B.** Predict the second blank first. If the athlete is furious, he is upset over what he considers to be an unimportant or small offense. Eliminate choices A (something *immoral* would not be a small offense) and C, *egregious* (terrible, flagrant); and E, *heinous* (highly criminal or wicked).

Before immediately choosing D (you may even have predicted that the word *minor* would fit into the second blank), plug the answer in and reread the whole sentence. A *lucid* (clear) explanation would not lead us to say that we "understood *enough*."

Sentence Completion is not a place to save time. Because the Sentence Completion questions often come at the very beginning of the section, your adrenaline may be pumping and you'll be zipping through there with only half your brain cylinders firing. Knowing this, make a habit of going back and checking these questions when you've finished the section, or at least when you've finished the analogies and antonyms, before you go on to the Reading Comprehension.

4. **B.** Predict that the blank is something related to quiet, like shy or withdrawn. Choice D is just the opposite of what you want. Choice E, *honorable*, has nothing to do with being shy. You can be extremely honorable and still be shy. Unpredictable is closer to the antonym, not the synonym, of *shy*. That narrows the answers down to two somewhat difficult words. If you don't know either word, make a quick guess (the GRE has no penalty for guessing; you should never leave an answer blank) and move on. *Exuberant* means excited or happy, the opposite of what the sentence requires. *Reticent* means shy, holding back.

5. **A.** The "although" alerts you to the fact that you want a word the opposite of "proceeding slowly." Because someone unenthusiastic probably *would* proceed slowly (how fast do *you* go when you approach a task unenthusiastically?), eliminate it. Scratch off *pensive*, meaning thoughtful, meditative. A pensive person would naturally slow down and examine all aspects of a situation. Eliminate *dilatory*, or slow. A slow person would not have to *force* himself to slow down. You have the answers narrowed down to two. *Uncouth* means unsophisticated or ill-mannered, and has no connection to the sentence. *Impetuous* means hasty, rash, precipitate. An impetuous person would usually rush into things and would have to force himself to slow down and examine the situation more carefully.

6. **D.** Now here's a question that depends entirely on vocabulary and has no roots to help you to define the hard answer choices. Sure, you can predict what types of words go in the blanks, but if you don't know what the words mean, you may as well guess and go. Staring at the question and growing progressively more frustrated won't get you any closer to a correct answer. All you'll do is eventually make a wild guess anyway, so you may as well get it over with sooner than later.

   Here are the definitions: *jejune* means puerile, childish, naive. *Reactionary* means conservative. A reactionary person reacts to trends, rather than setting them himself. *Froward* is not a typo (you thought you had me, didn't you?). It is not a sloppy "forward" but a word entire of itself. It means ungovernable, refractory. I once had a froward copy editor who insisted on changing the word in my text to forward even though I told her a dozen times to leave it alone. *Callow* is the same as jejune, immature. It was callow of me, but I copied the page out of the dictionary with froward, had it blown up to poster size, and mailed it to my froward copy editor.

   Bourgeois means middle class, everyday. *Pulchritudinous* means beautiful. *Reticent* means shy, withdrawn, holding back. *Heretical* means at variance with the orthodox or standard holdings. The student, therefore, was not holding back but was blasting into the professor for his unusual views. In choice E, withdrawn may work in the first blank but a *skinflint* is a miser, a cheapskate, a parsimonious person. That wouldn't make sense for the second blank.

7. **A.** Start with the second blank. If Ken is basking in something, he is enjoying it immensely; it must be good. You could deduce the same thing by knowing that *kudos* means praise, glory, fame. The second word that goes with *kudos and . . .* must be positive as well. *Plaudits* are praises. An *apogee* is the zenith, the highest point. Winning one night on *Jeopardy!* was the apogee of my television career (don't ask what happened the next night; it was my career *nadir* or low point).

   Choice B, a *lapse,* is a pause or break. I had a brain cell lapse the second night on *Jeopardy!* and was full of self-reproof. *Reproofs* are criticisms or condemnations. (To *reprove* does not mean to prove again; it means to criticize or condemn. People often misdefine this word.) In choice C, an *apex* is the top point, the zenith, the apogee, such that it would work for the first blank. But the second blank lets you down. *Fecklessness* is feebleness, irresponsibility. In choice D, the *genesis* of something is the beginning. *Effrontery* is audacity, shameless boldness. And finally, choice E, *nascency,* is birth, the process of being brought into existence. *Perjury* is false testimony, lying under oath.

8. **C.** Well, here's a word that every student knows. A *truant* is absent from school. A *deserter* is absent from the army (*de* = down or away from). In choice E, an *ogre* is a monster. (Notice how *ogre* is really o-GRE? Coincidence or cosmic reality? You be the judge.)

9. **B.** *Iron* is the raw material with which a blacksmith works. *Wood* is the raw material with which a carpenter works. Choice D is a pathetic attempt at humor; brides are really not the "raw material" with which a matchmaker works. Answers that are funny — or that are supposed to be funny — are never right. The GRE is about as funny as a zit on your butt.

10. **A.** *Layers* are the tiers (layers) of a cake; *strata* are the tiers (layers) of an atmosphere. (Think of the stratosphere.) Even if you don't know what strata are, you can get the right answer by process of elimination.

11. **D.** *Credulous* means full of trust (*cred* = trust; *–ous* = full of). Someone who is credulous is naive and gullible. *Dubious* means full of doubt (*dub* = doubt; *-ous* = full of). Someone who is dubious is *not* credulous and therefore won't go on a blind date with your out-of-town cousin, who has a "nice personality." (Yeah, right.) Choice E, *bibulous,* does not mean "full of the Bible"; it means full of drink, having imbibed too much, drunk.

12. **C.** To *instigate* is to bring about or create a rebellion. To *spawn* is to bring about or create offspring. One joins a club, but to *join* does not mean to "create" a club. To *initiate* is to begin and creates a start, not a conclusion. To *arraign* is to make a formal accusation in court. An arraignment does not "create" guilt (the person charged may just as easily end up being found innocent). To *challenge* is not necessarily to bring about victory (the challenger could lose). Choices are often wrong if the first word is not *necessarily* connected to the second word. For a choice to be correct, there must be a *necessary* connection.

13. **B.** *Euphonious* means full of good sound (*eu* means good; *phon* means sound; *–ous* means full of). *Savory* means full of good taste, or tasty. *Pusillanimous* does not mean full of pus. (Did you really think that the GRE would feature a word that means full of pus?) Pusillanimous means fearful or timid. *Dissonant* means not harmonious, such as dissonant sounds. (No, it does not mean dis- sun, or without sun, shady. That trap was too obvious, even for me.) *Expired* means dead, brought to an end, concluded (to *expire* is to die). *Hapless* means luckless (*hap* = luck). A hapless driver returns to his car to find an expired meter and a meter maid who is very much alive.

14. **B.** Something that is weak is not impregnable (*im* means not; you can make a good sentence without knowing the word, just the root). *Impregnable* means invulnerable and able to withstand attack. *Quixotic* means idealistic or impractical. *Rambunctious* means rowdy, unruly. *Slovenly* means sloppy. *Fastidious* means careful. *Senescent* means old. On a day when your senescence is depressing, you can comfort yourself with the old joke: After the Middle Ages comes the Renaissance!

15. **A.** You can get a good idea of the meanings of the difficult words in the questions by using two tips you've been given. First, use your roots. *Eu* means good. If you are euphoric, you are extremely happy because life is so good (you will be euphoric when you receive your GRE score). Second, try connecting English words with their equivalents in other languages. In Spanish, *lágrimas* means tears; you learned in Biology class that lachrymal glands produce tears. *Lachrymose* means tearful, sad. The words are antonyms. In choice A, the words are opposites as well: an affluent, or rich, person, is not destitute, or broke.

Okay, what if you can't figure out the meanings of the words in the question? The vocabulary in the answer choices isn't too bad. Work backwards. In choices B, C, and D, the words are similar in meaning. *Dexterous* means skillful, as in a dexterous magician. *Lax* means casual, such as a lax professor who doesn't bother to collect homework. *Weary* means fatigued. Because you can't have three right answers, they must all be wrong choices. The words in choice E appear to be unconnected. Someone jovial, or cheerful, may or may not be intelligent; there is no automatic connection between being cheerful and being intelligent. You have now eliminated all the answers but the correct one, A.

16. **E.** *Putrid* means foul-smelling (when you were a child, you probably yelled, " P.U!" at your friends; had you been truly precocious, you would have yelled, " Putrid!") Even if you weren't quite sure of the precise meaning, you probably had an idea that the word "just sounded negative." Don't be afraid to go with those feelings; your gut reaction is often correct because your subconscious knows things your conscious can't quite grasp. You reason that "perfume is not putrid" — to most people, that is.

In choice A, a *dotard* is a doting person, someone who is foolishly fond. (Think of a first-time parent as a dotard, someone who just can't get enough of that baby.) *Beneficent* means good, or kind, and may or may not describe a leader. Choice C is the trap. Flowers don't necessarily have to be sweet-smelling; leave them out too long and you'll find out how putrid they can become. If you chose this answer, you probably got caught up in the meanings of the words (they all have to do with smell) rather than the relationship between the words. Choice D has synonyms: A sponge is absorbent. Only choice E remains. Slime is *not* immaculate, meaning perfect or pure.

17. **D.** The marks along the edge of the maps are the ticks. You can deduce this from the second sentence, which says that ticks are printed in blue. Of the answer choices, only marks can be printed. You can't print a beat or print an insect, for example.

    If you chose A, B, or C, you probably didn't go back to the passage to see how the word was used but merely went on instinct. Always go back, back, back to check how the *author* uses the word; often he uses it differently than you'd expect.

18. **B.** In line 12, you learned that computers are necessary for this translation. Use this statement to infer (the passage doesn't come right out and say this) that such translation is not always convenient (where's a computer when you need one?).

    Choice A is the trap, but it is illogical. A computer most likely would give better or more precise readings than a human would.

19. **A.** The assumptions do not compromise, or lessen, the accuracy of the measurements.

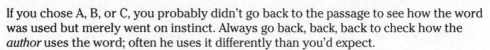

    If you chose B, you probably didn't go back to see how the word was used in the passage. A question that tests vocabulary in context can be one of the easiest questions to answer correctly but only if you invest a few seconds to go back to the passage and check the context. The question wants to know how the author uses the word, not how you would use it.

20. **A.** Lines 31 - 33 tell you that the zone numbers increase as they go east. Because Florida is east of California, it's a safe bet that Florida's zone number is higher than California's. Because statement I is correct, eliminate choices B and C. Because the United States goes farther east than Mexico, the two countries probably don't have the same zone numbers. Because statement II is wrong, eliminate choices D and E. Only A is left.

    For those of you who like to finish what you start: Statement III is wrong because the zones measure only from west to east, not north to south. This is a little tricky because you read about northing (measuring the distance in meters from the equator) near the spot where you read about zone numbers. You can avoid this trap by eliminating answers as you go, as I did above.

21. **E.** The last sentence reassures readers that the grid system becomes "extremely clear and straightforward to use" with a map. Even if you don't know the meaning of *feasibility* (probability or possibility), you could get the correct answer from the word *reassure*.

    If you chose B, you forgot one tip you learned in the reading lecture: The GRE rarely says anything mean and nasty about anyone. Your answers should be sweet and kind, no matter how grumpy *you* are over having to read all this dull material.

22. **C.** Going back to the passage to look for the answer to this question is a waste of time. This is an inference question, one you can answer only by "reading between the lines" and getting a general idea of the tone and purpose of the passage. Often, the best way to answer this sort of question is by the process of elimination. The passage is not specifically about the U.S. Geographical Survey; the USGS is mentioned only as an example of one type of organization that uses the UTM system. The focus is on the UTM grid location system, not on the USGS, eliminating choice A.

    Although hikers need to know how to read maps, the focus of the maps discussed in this passage is on a global scale. If a backpacker or hiker is so lost she doesn't know what zone of the earth she is in, she has bigger problems than understanding the UTM grid system! Dump choice B. Choice D is tempting because computers are mentioned in the passage. However, the focus of the passage is not on using computers, which are mentioned only as being desirable for their accuracy, but on *understanding* how to use the UTM grid system. Eliminate choice D. Choice E can also be superficially tempting. The passage is about reading maps; however, if this were an advertisement for a map-reading course, it went into way too much detail. The student may not need to take the course at all but could make do with just the info gleaned from the passage! Only choice C remains. This is an informational, narrative passage, just giving information on how to read a particular type of map. Such information is likely to be presented in a geography textbook.

23. **E.** This question may seem somewhat subjective. You are asked to use your common sense, your reasoning skills, rather than to go back to the passage and locate a specific sentence or topic. A good way to approach this question is to eliminate wrong answers. Choice A is too comprehensive for this passage. Instructions on using a computer system would be outside the scope of the passage; besides, several different systems may be available. Choice B sounds plausible. However, while it may be somewhat useful to know when the UTM grid system in general doesn't work, the readers probably don't need to know such specific information as why the basic assumption upon which the whole premise rests — that the earth can be mapped on a flat surface — may be flawed. Keep in mind why the passage was written: to acquaint readers with the UTM grid system and how to use it. Choice C would be adding too much information, going outside the scope of the passage. The focus is on the UTM grid system; getting into a discussion of other systems would not enhance the passage but would change it. Choice D is completely extraneous. The passage is not giving a controversial theory, something arguable in which the qualifications of the writer may influence your perception of what is said. Here, the passage gives just the facts. Choice E is the best answer. The passage is about how to use the UTM grid location system. Giving a specific example of that use would clarify the topic in the readers' minds. In general, giving a specific example to supplement the main idea of the passage makes the passage more understandable and relevant to its readers.

24. **D.** Paragraph three states that healthy lungs are gray and blotchy and that smoking and disease discolor the lungs. The safest thing to say is that a smoker is likely to have a lung that is not gray and blotchy in appearance because the lung has changed from its normal state. Choice A is a distortion of the paragraph. The author points out that healthy lungs are not pink, contrary to popular belief, but this does not imply that unhealthy lungs are pink. Choices B, C, and E all represent departures from a normal lung, but the passage gives no indication that these circumstances occur as a result of smoking. Don't get so carried away that you extend your reasoning too far.

25. **D.** This question requires you to put together different parts of the passage. The first paragraph states that the lungs are separated by the large blood vessels, the esophagus, and the heart. The last paragraph identifies the two lobes as left and right. (Without this information, the lungs could be separated into top and bottom halves or quarters, for all you know.) This makes choice D correct. Choice A is wrong because the diaphragm separates the chest, the location of the lungs, from the abdominal cavity. The passage explicitly states that the two halves of the lung differ in the number of lobes and implies that they differ in the number of alveoli (since lobes are large clusters of alveoli, it stands to reason that the right lung, with three lobes, has more alveoli), but these factors don't physically separate the two halves of the lungs. This eliminates choices B and C. The bronchial tubes (choice E) lead to the alveoli, but there is no hint about whether these structures separate the lungs into right and left halves.

26. **D.** This question requires you to apply some information in the passage to information introduced in the question stem. Paragraph two states that oxygen permeates (goes through) the air sacs, which are identified in paragraph four as alveoli, and is absorbed into the bloodstream. This implies that the blood vessel leaving the lungs has just picked up oxygen from them and has a relatively high concentration of oxygen. This makes option I true. (At this point, you can eliminate choices B and C.) Option II is also true. The bloodstream and lungs interact at the air sacs, or alveoli, so that the blood vessel traveling towards the lung is doing so to get to the alveoli. Paragraph two indicates that blood vessels that travel from the tissues receive carbon dioxide. These vessels have given off a

lot of oxygen to the tissues, so they must pick up more oxygen. The blood vessel that makes the final trip towards the lungs will not have much oxygen but will have a high concentration of carbon dioxide. This is the opposite of what option III says, so it is false. Only options I and II are true.

27. **D.** Look for a choice that covers the entire passage without being overly broad. Choice D fits well for this factual passage, in which every paragraph contributes information regarding the structure and/or function of lungs. Choice A was not done. The passage mentions that smoking changes the appearance of the lungs, which implies a change in lung function (common knowledge tells you this, too), but the passage provides no demonstration. In addition, choice A is too narrow in focus; eliminate it. Choice B was not done and is not comprehensive enough to answer a main purpose question. The passage provides bits and pieces by discussing bronchial tubes, alveoli, and the bloodstream, but that's about it. Choice C is a detail covered only in paragraph two. It is not broad enough to be a main purpose. Choice E is also too detailed and was not really done. You know that oxygen is absorbed into the bloodstream, but you don't know much about how it is done.

28. **B.** A *dandy* is a fop, a well-kempt person, a clotheshorse concerned with appearances. The opposite is a slob. Choice A, *philistine,* is an uncultivated, unrefined person. Anyone who rips out a page of this book and blows his nose in it is a philistine. Choice C, *curmudgeon,* is a grump, a grouch, a person who grouses. (Make another flashcard with the heading "Grump" — you can put on this card *cantankerous, curmudgeon, grouse , peckish, irascible,* and *choleric.*) Choice D, *slattern,* is a woman of loose morals, an unclean woman. Choice E, *visionary,* is an impractical, quixotic person.

29. **B.** *Wily* means sneaky, tricky, cunning. The opposite is straightforward. *Sporadic* means irregular, intermittent (my wily witticisms are inserted sporadically throughout this text). *Fallacious* means false. *Somber* means serious or grave. *Urbane* means sophisticated, of the city (you probably know the word *urban*, meaning pertaining to the city).

30. **E.** *Ingenuous* means naive, unsophisticated. Choice C, *rash,* means overly hasty or precipitate. Choice A is a trap to get people who mistake ingenuous with *indigenous*, which means native to. Choice B is a trap (just about now, I wouldn't blame you if you had the urge to yell at me, "Shut your trap!") to get people who confuse ingenuous with *ingenious*, meaning intelligent. Choice D, *earthy,* means coarse, unrefined. (The last time I told an earthy joke, my friend asked me, "Do you kiss your mother with that mouth?")

31. **C.** *Extroverted* means outgoing. The opposite is shy. *Bombastic* means big-talking or grandiloquent. *Ubiquitous* means everywhere at once. After you learn these words, you'll be surprised how ubiquitous they are. You will start to see these words in advertisements, editorials, even love letters — well, maybe not every love letter (only those from your more bombastic types!).

Fun Fact: You won't see the word on the GRE, but *ubiety* is a great word to use on your friends, especially the bombastic ones who think their vocabularies are superior to yours. While *ubiquitous* means everywhere at once, *ubiety* means having the property of being in one particular place at one particular time. For example, the planets have ubiety. If you're so wedded to routine your friends can set their clocks by you, you have ubiety.

32. **B.** *Prodigious* means huge (one of the meanings of *pro* is big or much). The opposite is *minuscule* (small). *Agile* means limber, flexible.

Don't confuse *prodigious*, huge, with *prodigy*. A *prodigy* is a highly talented person, especially a child. A ten year old who goes to college is a prodigy. His intelligence may be prodigious, but the child himself most likely is not.

33. **E.** *Querulous* means fault-finding, complaining, peevish. Choice A, *brash,* means rash, impetuous, rudely self-assertive. Choice B, *pristine,* means pure and uncontaminated. Choice D, *unconscionable,* means shocking to the conscience. A judge will often say that while an act may not be illegal, it is unconscionable, "shocking the Court's conscience." Choice C, *dormant,* means inactive. If your sense of ethics is temporarily dormant, you might do something unconscionable.

34. **C.** To *extirpate* means to destroy or remove completely, to abolish. The opposite is to introduce. Words have more than one meaning; one of the nastier things the GRE does is to use familiar words in unfamiliar senses. To *introduce,* you probably thought, meant to bring together, as in introducing two friends. To *introduce* can also mean add or incorporate. Choice B, to *exacerbate*, is to make worse. Eating ice cream can exacerbate a toothache. To *adulate*, choice D, is to idolize, to hero-worship.

35. **D.** To *revere* is to respect (think of a minister called Reverend King). The title is an honorific for someone who is respected, or admired, or venerated. The opposite is *disdain*, which means to have a feeling of contempt, or scorn. To *prattle* is to babble, to talk nonsense. Choice B, *buttress,* means to support, or to strengthen. Choice E, *saunter,* is to stroll, to move leisurely. Choice C, *waft,* is to float or glide; think of perfume wafting on the wind.

Words that are relatively simple can look impossible out of context. If you just keep saying "waft . . . waft . . . waft" to yourself enough times, the word will lose all meaning and sound like nonsense. Try to think of the word in context. Ever hear of the Luftwaffe, the German air force during WW II? Even though the German translates literally as "air weapon," you can visualize the planes wafting or gliding through the air.

36. **D.** To *desiccate* is to dehydrate, to dry out (some people take desiccated liver tablets to get their vitamins). The opposite is to *hydrate*, to add water to. To *beatify* is to make blessed or extremely happy. To *plummet* is to drop, fall, or plunge rapidly.

37. **E.** *Pontificating* means speaking arrogantly, or bragging. The opposite, *self-effacing,* means being modest, withdrawn, reticent. Choice A, *scintillating,* means sparkling, shining, giving off light. Choice B, *fawning,* means groveling, acting docilely. Choice C, *burnishing,* means polishing. Choice D, *desiccating,* means drying out.

38. **D.** *Sanguine* means cheerful, optimistic, confident. Do not confuse sanguine with *sanguinary,* meaning blood-thirsty. The opposite is *morose*, which means gloomy, or sullen. Choice A, *supple,* means flexible, lithe. Choice E, *voracious,* means greedy, ravenous. Are you *voracious* for yet more vocabulary, or has this section sated you?

Section 3

Questions 1–5

First, write down the pool of men, using the initial of their names to make life easier: J, A, E, K, B. Draw six dashes to represent the six seats. Keep in mind that one seat will be empty. You can drive yourself crazy if you forget this.

Next, go through each statement and see how it helps you to fill in the seats. Statement I gives you the information that Anthony cannot sit next to Kato, so write A ≠ K or K ≠ A. Do nothing to your diagram so far.

Statement II gives pretty solid information. Bob is either in seat one or seat six. Put a B in parentheses in both seats for now.

Statement III tells you that the order is E (seat) (seat) B. Aha! Now you deduce that Bob must be in seat six. Statement II told you that Bob was either in seat one — which is not possible because someone is to his left — or seat six. Go back to your diagram. Erase the B from seat one; fill it in without parentheses in seat six. You have a solid piece of information at last.

Statement IV tells you that Jared must be in seat two or seat one, such that there are two spaces between him and the empty seat. The empty seat cannot be seat six (Bob is there) or seat three (Eric is there). It could be seat five or seat four. On your diagram, put a J in parentheses in seats one and two.

Statement V tells you that Kato is in seat five. That type of solid information is an out-and-out gift to you. It often comes as the last statement, after you've sweated through the earlier ones. For that reason, I usually preview the statements, reading them all before I start making a diagram. A solid piece of information like this lets you work backwards. Using this info, you find that seat four must be the empty seat (you knew earlier it was either seat four or seat five). Now, with the information given by statement IV, you know that seat one is filled by Jared.

Anthony must have persons on either side of him, according to statement I. This means that he must be in seat two, surrounded by Jared and Eric. (You already knew that by the process of elimination, as discussed earlier.)

Here's your final diagram: Jared, Anthony, Eric, (empty seat), Kato, Bob. With this completed diagram, answering the questions is easy.

1. **C.** Look at your diagram. Statements IV and V helped you to determine that seat four is empty.

2. **D.** Set up six spaces:

    —   —   —   —   —   —

    Put Kato in seat five:

    —   —   —   —   K   —

    For Eric to be three spaces to the right of Bob, Bob must be in seat one and Eric in seat four:

    B   —   —   E   K   —

    At this point, it looks as if Anthony can occupy seat two or seat three because he may not sit next to Kato. Draw these possibilities:

    B   A   —   E   K   —

    B   —   A   E   K   —

    When you have two possible options, be sure to write down *both* of them. I suggest that you make two separate drawings; don't try to fit both possibilities on one drawing; your work can get sloppy and confusing.

    The only one of these two options that will accommodate Jared, who must be two spaces from the empty seat, is the former option:

    B   A   J   E   K   —

3. **C.** Statement II narrows Bob's seats down to one or six. Statement III lets you deduce that Bob sits at the end of the row, in the sixth seat, because no one could be to Bob's left if he were sitting in seat one.

4. **E.** The author's conclusion about feeling pain follows from evidence about the use of a drill. This logically follows only if there is a connection between the drill and pain, which is what choice E provides. If choice E isn't true, you cannot be certain that pain will result.

    Choice A is too specific. Earache does not have to be assumed because the drill can produce pain in a variety of ways. Choice B is way off because it provides a reason to think that pain *won't* result from the drill. Choice C assumes more than what needs to be assumed. The patient may be getting an inlay today and may assume that the experience will be similar to her past experiences because the drill will be used. In this argument, she is using the evidence of the drill to conclude that she will feel pain. The author does not need to assume choice D. She may actually *know* (not just assume) that other factors caused her pain, but she is focusing on the drill here.

5. **B.** The argument uses the increase in percentage to conclude that cancer is more deadly. To weaken the argument, find a choice that says that the increased percentage reflects something other than an increase in the virulence of cancer.

Choice B is not obvious at first, but what it is saying is that fewer people are dying from diseases other than cancer. Because everyone has to die, if fewer die from something other than cancer, more will have to die from cancer, even if it is not more deadly.

You do not need outside knowledge to answer a question, but what you do know can be helpful. The test makers will not put in a question that is contrary to common sense, history, or general knowledge. One hundred years ago, many children died of such diseases as diphtheria, long before cancer could develop in their bodies. The longer one lives, the better one's chances are of developing cancer. More people die of cancer now, not because it's more deadly but because they live long enough to get the disease.

You may have been tempted to go with choice A because it sounds so direct, but it actually doesn't do the job. Scientists may have developed many cures, but according to the numbers, the cures haven't kept pace with the disease. More cures do not mean that the disease is more curable if the disease increases in virulence. Choice C does not negate that cancer is more deadly. Heart disease may also be more deadly, but that doesn't affect cancer. Choice D *strengthens* the argument by giving a reason why we must be more concerned about cancer today. Choice E would be a candidate if the medicine cured cancer, but all that's discussed is pain relief.

Questions 6–12

First, list your pool, using the first letters of the names. Break the pools up into newcomers and veterans:

Newcomers: R, S, T, V, Y

Veterans: H, I, J

Now, go through each of the statements, making notes on its content. Notice that this sort of game does not require you to make a diagram. You are not trying to find the positions or order of the people.

For statement I, jot down H ≠ I because Hank will not serve with Ingrid. This statement also allows you to deduce that, because two veterans are needed, they will be either H + J or J + I. This means that J definitely will be on the board. When you deduce a solid piece of information like this, write it in big letters and circle it. It usually affects the rest of the problem.

For statement II, write two separate comments: T ≠ J, and V ≠ J. Because you deduced just a moment ago that J must be on the board, neither T nor V can be on the board. Because R, S, and Y are the only newcomers left, and because three newcomers must be on the board, they get the job.

Statement III gives you that Y ≠ H. That means that H cannot be on the board because Y must be on the board. Earlier you deduced that the veterans are going to be either H and J or J and I. Eliminating H gives you J and I. Your final grouping, therefore, is Newcomers: R, S, Y, and Veterans J and I. Now you're ready to answer any question dumped in your lap.

6. **A.** You just figured out that the only possible group is J, I, R, S, Y.

7. **B.** In this case, H can serve. The only thing holding him back was Y's reluctance to serve with him. Putting H back into the game gives you two possible groups: H + J + R + S + Z and I + J + R + S + Z.

When a question introduces a new player or a new member of the pool, it often is very time-consuming. You in effect have to redo the entire game, going through each statement as if you were reading it for the first time with a new group. If you're rushed for time, this is a good question to "guess and go" on. Fill in something (because wrong answers are not counted against you on the GRE), but don't waste much time on the question.

8. **C.** Take one rule at a time and note the violators. These violators must be included in the answer because the question asks for the options that are *not* possible. There must be three newcomers and two veterans. Option I has only one veteran, so it must be part of the answer, eliminating choice B. The rule that states that neither Tawny nor Virginia will serve with Jack makes option IV impossible, eliminating choice A. Options II and III do not violate any of the rules and are possible, leaving C as the correct answer.

9. **A.** With I on the board, the combination must be I + J + R + S + Y. Did you recognize the stupidity of this question? Ingrid must always be on the board in our game. That means that the question doesn't add any new information but is really just asking you to read your original diagram.

10. **A.** This is an easy question if you see the trick. Because Hank will not serve with Ingrid, the Board cannot have three veterans. If you wasted time on this question figuring out the possible groupings of newcomers—well, take *solace* (comfort) in the fact that you earned some anonymous test maker (okay, me) brownie points with her boss.

11. **A.** The first sentence of the stimulus (the paragraph giving the information) makes a conclusion (passbook accounts are great investments) that follows from some evidence (allows one to accumulate a fortune). The real problem with the argument comes from the next sentence, which backs up the first sentence with some correlational data (wealthy investors have invested in passbooks). What is needed to make this argument convincing is some evidence that shows that it actually was the passbook investments that made these investors wealthy. The second sentence does not accomplish this. It's probable that the investors became wealthy through some other investments. They may have invested in passbooks at one time (perhaps as children), but their wealth arose from something else. Furthermore, it's probable that the majority of passbook investors do not become wealthy, further weakening the connection between passbook accounts and wealth. It could be an underlying cause, such as the realization that money doesn't do good just sitting around or the desire to maintain a balance of safe and risky investments, that leads one to invest in both passbooks and very profitable investments.

    In choice A, the second sentence fails to establish that calculus causes high GRE math scores. (Don't panic, don't panic — calculus is *not* required for the GRE; calculus is *not* tested on the GRE. This is just a question.) All you know is that calculus and high GRE math scores go together, but it could very well be that there is an underlying factor, such as a high math aptitude, that causes someone to take calculus *and* to do well on the GRE math. This is the same weakness found in the reasoning of the original statement.

    Choice B is incorrect because the second sentence explains how penicillin cures diseases. It explains cause and effect and is therefore more persuasive than the original statement. Choices C, D, and E are weak because the first sentence is not as absolute as what's seen in the last sentence of the original statement. Furthermore, unlike the original statement, the arguments in these choices are pretty logical.

12. **D.** Because students lose five points for each class they miss, a student absent for three classes will lose at least 15 points, making it impossible to have more than 85 points. Because such a student cannot earn an A, it can be inferred that 85 points is not enough for an A.

    Choice E is possible, and its truth would cast some doubt on choice D as the answer. However, the stimulus states the impossibility of an A right after it mentions the five point deduction for each absence. This makes choice D a much more parsimonious and likely explanation than choice E, which requires more outside knowledge about Professor Garcia and her grading policy than does choice D.

    Nothing in the stimulus discusses point values for other factors, the importance of the final, or what it takes to earn a B. This lack of info eliminates choices A, B, and C.

Questions 13–20

Your task is to determine which three characteristics belong on each plant. A good way to represent the plants is with a circle divided into three parts. Fill in the information for each plant according to the following scheme:

Start out with four such circles and put L in number two and Y in number four.

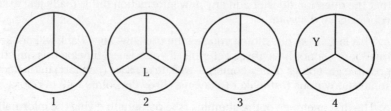

The rule prohibiting round yellow peas means that if a pea is yellow, it must be wrinkled, and if a pea is round, it must be green. This may be symbolized as Y → W; R → G. Because of this, fill in number four with a W.

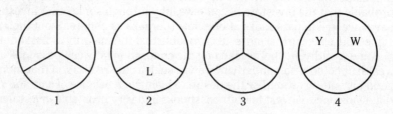

Do not assume that W → Y. A green wrinkled pea does not violate the rule. In other words, W → Y or G. Similarly, don't assume G → R.

The *penultimate* (next to last) rule can be summarized as R → L. This does not mean L → R (round guarantees large, but a pea can be large without being round). What you do know is S → W because if S → R, there would be a round pea that was not large. Combine R → L with R → G and write R → L + G. Round peas are both large and green.

Put an asterisk (*) by the sentence, "Each characteristic is found on at least one of the plants." Doing so helps you to keep this statement in mind all the time.

The first rule can be summarized as Y ≠ G.

13. **D.** Use the process of elimination to dump some answers quickly. Begin with the rule that states that plant number four is yellow. Can you find any choice that violates this rule? Choice C is such a violator. Choice A is out because it includes round yellow peas. In choice B, there are two yellow and two green peas, which is incompatible with Y ≠ G. Choice E has no round peas, but the rules require at least one to be round. This leaves choice D as the answer.

14. **A.** Draw a quick diagram and utilize your deduction that R → L + G.

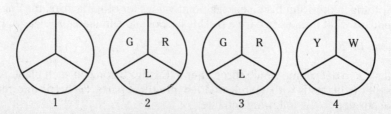

With two green peas and one yellow pea, the remaining pea must be green, or else there would be two green and two yellow. This can't be because Y ≠ G.

15. **B.** This problem may be a good one to skip for the time being. Little work can be done before looking at the choices. In other words, this turkey is a real time-gobbler.

What you are looking for is the choice that will lead to only one possibility for the size of number four (you already know the color and the shape). If you are really on top of things, you will realize that number four must be small if number one and number three are large (number two is large, so if numbers one, two, and three are all large, number four must be small because the rules tell you that each characteristic is found on at least one of the plants).

Choice A makes number one small and number three large but doesn't restrict the size of number four.

Choice B is what you want. If number one is R, it is also L. Number three is obviously L. This makes number four S because there must be at least one S.

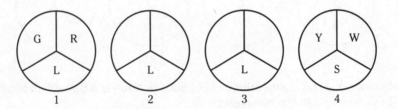

Choice C misses the mark because number three could be small or large. The same is true of choice D. Choice E provides the color for number two, a plant whose size was already known. Being told that number four is wrinkled is redundant; you already knew that.

16. **D.** Draw a quick diagram, remembering that S → W (number one) and R → L + G (number three).

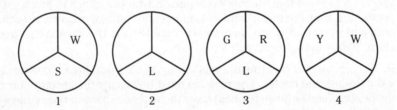

If number one is Y, number two must also be Y (and W, because Y → W) because Y ≠ G. This will give three Y and one G. Number four may be either S or L, so there are two possibilities when number one is Y.

If number one is G, number two is G, but it may be W or R. Number four may still be S or L. In summary, here are the four possibilities when number one is G:

1	2	4
G	G W	S
G	G W	L
G	G R	S
G	G R	L

Add these four to the two possibilities when number one is Y, and you get six.

17. **B.** If number two has the only large pea, numbers one, three, and four must have small peas. Remember that S → W and draw:

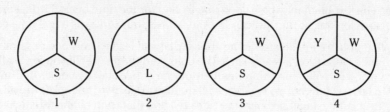

A quick look shows that number two must be R (and also G because R → G) as there must be one R.

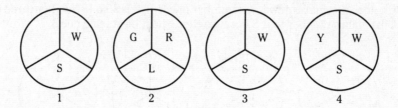

Number one and number three could both be Y to yield three Y and one G. Neither must be G, so only number two must be G.

18. **D.** The argument is that diamonds are a better investment than yachts. The evidence used to support this conclusion deals with the ratio of diamond purchases to yacht purchases (by those who can afford both). To justify the conclusion, you must assume that this ratio is the key statistic, and that there isn't some other factor that would supersede this supposed 10,000:1 ratio in favor of diamonds.

Choice D annihilates this supposed advantage. One out of every ten thousand people can afford to buy a diamond, but only one out of every million people can afford to buy a yacht. This means that for every one person who can afford to buy a yacht, one hundred people can afford to buy a diamond, and yet the ratio of people who can afford to buy both and who actually buy diamonds is only 10 to 1. This means that people who can afford to buy both prefer yachts.

19. **D.** The argument is that the music is recognizable from three characteristics: chords, voice timbre, and banter. The rock fan must be making the assumption, therefore, that the Beatles (and *only* the Beatles) have those three characteristics the way they appear on this tape. If other groups had the same chords, voice timbre, and banter, they would be indistinguishable from the Beatles.

Choice A is too specific. Chords are not necessarily the most distinctive feature of a song; this fan also thinks about voice timbre, for example. Choice B is probably true but is irrelevant to the conclusion that this tape probably comes from the Beatles. If anything, the very rarity of such bootleg tapes argues against this particular tape's being such a Beatles' session. Choice C is way too broad. Nothing is said about any other forms of art. It also flies in the face of common sense. You probably know that people can identify paintings, for example, from characteristics used by the artist (brush strokes, perspective, use of color, and so on).

Choice E is very tempting. However, the rock fan doesn't assume that the Beatles are the most distinctive group, just that there are means of identifying their distinct characteristics on a tape.

20. **A.** The inane conclusion is that skateboarding is more dangerous than performing without a net on a trapeze or high wire in the circus. This conclusion is based on the fact that, in one year, more skateboarders died than trapeze and high wire performers died. You could show this conclusion to be flawed by showing the number of deaths among those performers as a percentage of all performers versus the number of deaths of skateboarders as a percentage of all skateboarders. If there are, for example, 100 trapeze artists and 3 died, that's a much larger percentage than if there are 10 million skateboarders and 3,000 died.

Choice B addresses the problem of a longer time span, but it still does not deal with the deaths as a percentage of all involved in the activity. That would be like saying that because more people have died in traffic accidents in the past decade than from jumping out of planes without a parachute, riding in a car is more dangerous than jumping out of a plane without wearing a parachute. Choice C does not change the conclusion. The causes for the death rate do not show that it is illogical to conclude that skateboarding is more dangerous than working the trapeze. Choice D is tempting; however, unless it compares the injuries as a percent of those people involved in the activity, you're right back to the original problem. Choice E talks about a percentage but then goes overboard and brings in the age group question. The original conclusion dealt with everyone in the activity as a whole, not people in various age groups.

Questions 21–25

Is the room suddenly spinning around? Take heart. A game like this looks harder than it really is. An overview of the stimulus and questions reveals that this is a grouping game in which you must select from various subgroups. In grouping games, be aware that not all of the entities have to be chosen.

A good way to keep track of the information is to list a roster, using a different style of letter (for example, uppercase print, uppercase script, lowercase print, lowercase script) to separate the subgroups. This can be done as follows:

A	B	C	math
d	e		humanities
f	g	h	social sciences
J			

Next, go to the rules. Work first with the rules that are the most concrete and/or easiest to incorporate into the diagram. Start by circling "e" (because Elaine is chosen no matter what). Note how many of the subgroups must be chosen.

A	B	C	2 or more
d	e		1 or more
f	g	h	1 or more
J			0 (doesn't *have* to be chosen)

Work with the remaining rules, using some notations that will help you to remember the rules. Because the team may *not* include two or more social science players, change the notation on *f g h* to read = 1.

Whenever possible, try to combine rules. The Carlos/Fahid relationship may be represented as follows. If C, then *f*. This does *not* mean if F, then C. Instead, think of it as "if not Fahid, then not Carlos." If *f* is not present, it's impossible for C to be present because C guarantees the presence of *f*.

Still with me, or packing your bags to be ready when the men in the shiny white coats come? Hang in there. Remember, the hardest part of these games is getting the grouping clear in your mind. After you've done that, you can zip right through the questions. Conversely, if you don't have the groupings clear from the start, you probably won't be able to do any of the questions.

To continue: "If *J*, then no *f*; if f then no *J*." You may combine this information with the previous statement that "if C, then *f*" to come up with the conclusion that "if C, then *f* but no *J*" and "if *J*, then no *f* and no C."

In summary:

If C, then *f*

If no *f*, no C

If C, then *f* but no *J*

If *J*, then no *f*

If *f*, no *J*

If *J*, then no *f*, no C

Finally, you're ready to go to the questions. Loosen up! Don't get hung up on having to do the first question first. If you get stuck, move to a question you *can* do and then come back to the previous question. Within one logic game, it's not necessarily true that the first question is the easiest and the last is the hardest. I mention this so that you don't draw a blank on the first question and give up, muttering to yourself, "Well, good grief; if I can't get even the first one, what chance do I have on the later problems? I may as well drop the whole game."

21. **C.** Choose one rule at a time and check the choices for violations. Choice E violates the rule that Elaine must be chosen. A grouping game often has one solid piece of information, that someone must be chosen or must not be chosen. That's a great piece of information to keep uppermost in your mind, as it eliminates answer choices quickly. Choice B is wrong because if Carlos is selected, Fahid must be selected as well. Choice A is wrong because it has two social science players (you can't have more than one); choice D is wrong because it does not include two math players. By the process of elimination, choice C is correct.

22. **B.** Draw a roster:

A	B	C	
d	e		Ⓔ
f	g	h	
J			

If J is chosen, f is out, which also means that C is out.

A	B	~~C~~	
d	e		Ⓔ
f	g	h	~~F~~
J			Ⓙ

Because the coach must select two math players, A and B must be chosen, making B the correct answer.

23. **D.** Draw a roster, incorporating the conditions of this question:

A	B	C	
d	e		Ⓔ
f	g	h	G̶
J			

Remember that the coach must select two from the top row, so try A and B.

A	B	C	Ⓐ Ⓑ C̶
d	e		Ⓓ Ⓔ
f	g	h	G̶
J			

The coach must select one from the *f g h* row, so she has two options; she can select either *f* or *h*.

If the coach selects A and C, she must also select *f*, because you learned earlier that "if C, then *f*."

A	B	C	Ⓐ Ⓒ B̶
d	e		Ⓓ Ⓔ
f	g	h	Ⓕ G̶
J			

A similar result occurs for B and C, the final way to select two math players.

A	B	C	Ⓑ Ⓒ , A̶
d	e		Ⓓ Ⓔ
f	g	h	Ⓕ G̶
J			

In conclusion, there are four possibilities, choice D.

24. **A.** If you combined the rules as suggested in order to get "if Carlos, then Fahid but not James," you have seen that choice A is impossible. If you are not sure of your choice, check the remaining choices. All you need to do is to show that each choice is possible; if it's possible, eliminate it because the question asks which is *im*possible.

Choice B is possible:

A	B	C	Ⓑ Ⓒ
d	e		Ⓓ Ⓔ
f	g	h	Ⓖ
J			

Keep an eye open for information you already deduced or used in previous problems. You know that answer choice C here was the answer to question 21. This indicates that choice C is possible (C and h need not be together). You may also look at your last diagram for question number 23 to verify this possibility.

Choice D is good:

A	B	C	Ⓐ , B, C
d	e		Ⓔ
f	g	h	Ⓕ
J			

And choice E is also a winner:

A	B	C	Ⓐ Ⓑ
d	e		Ⓓ Ⓔ
f	g	h	Ⓗ
J			

25. **D.** James will be selected if there are only two math players and one humanities player. This means Damien must be rejected, narrowing the field to choices B and D. If you are in a big hurry, take a guess. If you've got time, try one answer. Let's do B:

A	B	C	
d	e	Đ	Ⓔ
f	g	h	G̶
J			

This still allows A, B, and C to be selected:

A	B	C	Ⓐ Ⓑ Ⓒ
d	e		Đ Ⓔ
f	g	h	Ⓕ G̶
J			

Note that *J* is not selected. But with answer choice D, there is no way to keep *J* out:

A	B	C	Ⓐ Ⓑ Є̶
d	e		Đ Ⓔ
f	g	h	F̶
J			Ⓙ

Note: "If no *f*, then no *C*." There is only one social science player; choose *g* or *h* and then choose *J*.

Section 4

1. **A.** You didn't actually work this out, did you? One of the things the QC questions test is your knowledge of when to pick up your pencil and when just to guesstimate. This problem is a definite guesstimate. With 365 days per year (366 in a leap year), Column A would be $365 \times 3 + 366$. Don't actually work it out. Column is 40×10, because a decade has ten years. You can see at a glance that Column A is much larger.

Although it's not a trap in this particular problem (the first problem in the batch is too easy to have a big trap), often a question can getcha if you forget about leap year. For example, if a question asks you how much money Mark makes if he earns $200 a day every single day for four years, your answer will be $200 off unless you remember that one of those years has 366, not 365, days.

If you didn't grow up in the United States, you may be accustomed to different units of measurement, such as metric rather than standard. It's important that you take a few minutes to go back to the Units of Measurement portion of Chapter 12 and make sure that you know, for example, how many inches are in a foot, how many pounds are in a ton.

2. **D.** If you chose A, you fell right for my cunningly devised trap (okay, so it was a cheap trick). Don't forget that a negative squared is a positive. If a were –2, for example, then $-2^2 = 4$, and Column A is larger. And what if a is a fraction? If $a = \frac{1}{2}$, then $\frac{1}{2}^2 = \frac{1}{4}$, and B is bigger. If the answer could be A or could be B, it depends on what you plug in, choice D.

Remember the Sacred Six I asked you to get into the habit of plugging in? They are 1, 2, 0, –1, –2, $\frac{1}{2}$. You don't need to plug in 0 or 1 this time, but you do need to plug in the fraction. You should chant to yourself as if it were a mantra: "positive, negative, zero, fraction."

3. **C.** Please tell me you didn't actually work out this problem. You know that the word *of* means times, or to multiply. If you were to do this problem as a decimal, you'd have $.20 \times 120$ and 1.20×20. Because the number of decimal places is the same, the solution is the same as well.

This problem is very common. However, don't get complacent, see this sort of thing, and immediately choose C. What if Column A said .20 percent rather than 20 percent? That would make the multiplication $.0020 \times 120$, a very different answer indeed. Keep a wary eye on the decimal point.

4. **D.** When a geometry problem is all talk and no action, all words and no picture, it is often choice D. The answer depends on how the picture is drawn. Take just Column B, for example. If the perimeter is 20, the sides could be 1, 9, 1, 9 for an area of 9. Or the sides could be 6, 4, 6, 4 for an area of 24. Or the sides could be $\frac{1}{2}$, $9\frac{1}{2}$, $\frac{1}{2}$, $9\frac{1}{2}$, for an area of 4.75. And there are even more possibilities for the sides of the pentagon!

Even though officially the D answer means "there is not enough information," I prefer to think of it as "there is too much information, too many possibilities." If you could get a *superfluity* (abundance) of different answers, select D.

5. **C.** Line the equations up vertically and either add or subtract them to get the same numerical coefficients (the numbers before the variables). In this case, you add:

$$3a + 5b = 12$$
$$5a + 3b = 28$$
$$8a + 8b = 40$$

Now divide both sides of the equation by 8, to get $a + b = 5$. Finally, $3 \times 5 = 15$.

6. **B.** When a negative is cubed, it remains a negative. For example, $-2^3 = -2 \times -2 \times -2 = -8$. Therefore, whatever Column A is, it's negative. Stop right there and don't strain the brain any more.

As you go through the QC questions, keep reminding yourself that the name of the game is Quantitative Comparisons, not Problem Solving. You don't have to solve the problem, more times than not. You work until you see which column is going to be greater, and then you stop. The actual solution is irrelevant and unnecessary. And remember: Every second you save by not working on the QCs is another second you can use on the regular multiple-choice problems where you *do* need to do all that drudge work.

7. **A.** The volume of any figure is (*area of the base × height*). Because the base of a cylinder is a circle, the volume of a cylinder is π radius^2 × height. Divide the volume, 200π, by the height, 8, to find that the area of the base is 25π. Because the base is a circle of area = π radius^2, the radius is 5. But don't choose B; you're not done yet.

The circumference of a circle is 2π radius, which here is 10π. If you chose C, you fell for the trap. You forgot your π! The circumference of 10π is actually $10 \times$ approximately 3.14, which is more than 10 (don't bother to figure it out exactly). The moral of the story: Keep your eye on the π.

If your first thought when you look at a problem is that the columns are equal, think again. Usually — not always — you have to do actual calculations to get a C.

Usually when a geometry problem is all words and no pictures, it's choice D, because the comparison will depend on what the picture looks like. This is an exception to the tip, put in just to keep you from using the tips automatically rather than actually thinking the problem through.

8. **B.** If you chose D, you fell for the trap. You probably looked at the question, saw that only one side was given, and figured you didn't have enough info to answer the question. Wrong. You should have reminded yourself of the tip that when a figure is given, the answer is rarely D. (This is the flip of the tip that when a geometry problem gives words but no pictures, it is usually D.)

Do you remember your Pythagorean Triples? They were discussed in Chapter 10. For many right triangles, the sides have a special ratio. For a 30:60:90 triangle, that ratio is *side*: *side*$\sqrt{3}$: 2 *side*. The side opposite the 30 is the shortest side. Here that's the 5. The side opposite the 60 is the next shortest side, the "*side*$\sqrt{3}$" side. Here that would be $5\sqrt{3}$. Although you don't need to know this to find the area of the triangle, the hypotenuse (the side opposite the 90-degree angle) is the longest side, the "2-side" side. Here it is 10.

The area of a triangle is $\frac{1}{2}$ *base* × *height*. The base is $5\sqrt{3}$; the height is 5. Therefore, the area is $\frac{1}{2}$ $25\sqrt{3}$. Don't bother finding it exactly; it certainly is less than $25\sqrt{3}$. If you chose C, you did *alllllll* that work and, because you forgot the very last step, missed the stupid question anyway.

How can you prevent making a careless mistake like forgetting to multiply by $\frac{1}{2}$ in this problem? Simple. Write down the formula for the problem immediately. It may seem childish and extra work, but it takes only a gigasecond and can prevent careless errors. When you see the formula, you plug the numbers into it and work it through.

9. **A.** Do what's in the parentheses first: $1 - \frac{1}{6} = \frac{5}{6}$. Square that to get $\frac{25}{36}$. (To multiply fractions, just multiply horizontally: numerator times numerator, denominator times denominator.) To divide by a fraction, *invert* (turn upside down) and multiply: $1 \times \frac{36}{25}$. That's greater than one; you don't need to be any more precise than that.

If you chose B, you made a careless mistake. You forgot that dividing by a fraction means flipping it upside down and multiplying. Yes, $\frac{25}{36}$ is less than 1, but $\frac{36}{25}$ is more than 1.

10. **C.** This is a symbolism problem. It looks more intimidating and difficult than it actually is. Substitute the numbers for the variables in the "explanation." Use the numbers in the same order as the variables. That is, 3 is in the first position, and *a* is in the first position, so substitute a 3 for an *a*. 6 is in the second position and *b* is in the second position, so substitute a 6 for a *b*. 12 is in the third position, and *c* is in the third position, so substitute a 12 for a *c*. That gives you $3(3) + 4(6) - \frac{1}{2}(12) = 9 + 24 - 6 = 27$.

The more calculations you do, the less surprised you should be when the answer comes out to be choice C. This does not mean that, as soon as you find yourself doing a lot of pencil pushing, you should give up and choose C, hoping for the best. It does mean that if you do no work, and you just think the columns are equal, you've probably fallen for a trap, because you frequently have to perform the actual calculations and prove that the columns are equal.

11. **B.** This problem is rather lengthy *unless* you see the shortcut. Here's the long way first: An arc is a fraction of the circumference of the circle. The circumference is 2π *radius*. Because the area of a circle is π *radius*^{2}, the radius here is 6. The circumference, therefore, is 12π. The arc is the same fraction of the circle that the central angle is of 360. Here, put $\frac{45}{360}$ and reduce it to $\frac{1}{8}$. That means the arc is $\frac{1}{8}$ of the circumference of the circle. $\frac{1}{8}$ of 36π is certainly less than 36π.

Ready for the shortcut? You can cut off the last step entirely. You still have to break down the area to find the radius and then work back up to find the circumference. (You should be so comfortable with formulas that you can do this step without even breathing hard.)

You can see by looking at the figure that the arc is not the entire circumference, but only a part of it. That means that the arc is less than 36π, and B is larger. You don't need to — and certainly don't want to — find the exact measure of the arc.

If you're getting brain cramps, go back to the Circles section of Chapter 10 and look under Arcs.

12. **A.** If you chose C, you fell for the trap. $\sqrt{10} \times \sqrt{10} = 10$. Column A therefore is simply 10^3, not $\sqrt{10}^3$.

Don't even think about trying to work this out. You do not need to know how to do square roots for this test. (You should, however, have memorized the perfect squares and square roots up to 20, just to make your life easier. There's a table of these in Chapter 11.) Just write out what you need to work out — then quit. As soon as you see that Column A would be $10 \times 10 \times 10$ and Column B would be $\sqrt{10} \times \sqrt{10} \times \sqrt{10}$, you're done.

13. **A.** You didn't fall for the trap and put C, did you? I keep warning you: If your first reaction is that the columns are equal, you need to think again. The average of Column A is approximately 11^2, not 11.

Suppose that Column A said a^2, b^2, and c^2, and Column B said b. What would your answer be then? It would be D, because everything would depend on the value of the variables. Sure, Column A may still be b^2, and Column B may be b. But what if $b = 0$? The columns are the same. What if $b = 2$? Then A is bigger. What if $b = \frac{1}{2}$? Then B is bigger. Be very wary of these "obvious" questions, especially when they are so near the end.

14. **C.** This problem is basic algebra, turning words into equations. Do it one step at a time. "Five less than" means minus five. Six times one-third is the same as 2 because $6 \times \frac{1}{3} = \frac{6}{3} = 2$. Combine the terms: $2x - 5$.

If English is not your first language, this type of wording problem can be extremely difficult for you. If you find yourself reading and rereading and rereading the question, just make a random guess at it and go on. You're wasting too much time on a problem that you may not get right anyway, given the confusing way it is set up. Don't let your ego get in the way, telling you that surely this is a simple algebra problem. Yes, the algebraic equation is easy; but getting to that equation is rather difficult.

15. **B.** Because m is less than 5, subtracting 6 from m gives you a negative. Any number to the negative power is the reciprocal of that number to the positive power. For example, $2^{-3} = \frac{1}{2}^3$. Or $10^{-7} = \frac{1}{10}^7$. Because the number is going to be a fraction, it is going to be less than 1. You don't know how much less than one, but it's not important to know that. You only have to compare the quantities, not find the exact solution.

If you got confused on the negative powers, return to the Bases and Exponent section of Chapter 11.

16. **A.** When the question gives you the formula, how can you miss? The diameter is 8, which means the radius is 4. Next $4^2 = 16$, and $16 \times 1.5 \times \frac{1}{3} = 8$. Just leave the π in the answer; don't multiply it out unless you are told to do so.

17. **C.** You can find the probability by using this formula:

$$\frac{\text{\# of possible desired outcomes}}{\text{\# of total possible outcomes}}$$

The first thing to do is find the denominator. How many candies will be left after LaVonne has chomped into the others? She starts with 47 candies (20 + 15 + 12). You know that she throws some of them away. You can eliminate choice A immediately because the denominator must be less than 47.

She throws away a creme (down to 46), a nut (down to 45), a chew (down to 44), a nut (down to 43), a creme (down to 42), and a chew (down to 41). The denominator for the probability of the next candy that she pulls out will be 41 because she'll have some chance out of 41 of pulling out a nut. That narrows the answers down to B and C.

As a shortcut, subtract 6 (the number of candies that she already pulled out) from 47, the number of candies that originally were in the box. I solved the problem the long way to show you where the 41 really comes from.

Now find the numerator. She starts out with 12 nuts, pulls out one (down to 11), and then pulls out another (down to 10). The probability that her next candy will be a nut is $^{10}/_{41}$. (This type of problem is discussed in the probability section of Chapter 11.)

18. **D.** Let x be the number of books they check out and make $x + 20$ represent the number of books that they put back. The equation now is $x + (x + 20) = 84$. Next, $2x + 20 = 84$. Then $2x = 64$. Finally, $x = 32$.

If you chose B, you forgot to answer the question, which wants to know how many books were put back, not how many were checked out. $84 - 32 = 52$.

You can use a great shortcut to narrow down the answers. You know that more books were put back than were checked out. That means that more than half the books were put back and fewer than half the books were checked out. Half of 84 is 42; more than that must have been put back. Only answers D and E could fit. Instead of working through all the garbage algebra, use those two answers. If 52 books were put back, then 20 less than 52, or 32, were checked out. Does $52 + 32 = 84$? Yup, it does, and you've finished the problem. If you want to check, try choice E. If 64 books were put back, 20 fewer than 64, or 44 books were checked out. Does $64 + 44 = 84$? Nope. Choice D was right all along.

19. **B.** The area of a parallelogram is simply *base × height*. The base goes from -4 to -13, a distance of 9 units. The height goes from 1 to 5, a distance of 4 units, and $8 \times 4 = 32$.

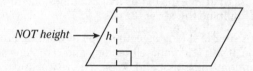

The height is not the side of the parallelogram, *CD*. If you solved for that answer, you did unnecessary work. The height is a straight line, going from the tallest point down to the base (a height is always perpendicular to the base), as shown in the preceding figure.

20. **B.** Plug in numbers. Because you're dealing with dollars (and with percentages), make the cost be $100. Then the profit is $320 (320% of 100 = 320). The selling price, which is *cost + profit*, equals $420. If the cost, $100, goes up 25%, it is now $125. The selling price remains constant at $420. That means the new profit is $(420 - 125 =) 295$. The percent that profit is of selling price is $^{is}/_{of} = {}^{295}/_{420} =$ about 70%.

You could have eliminated answers D and E immediately by using common sense. The profit can never be more than the selling price because the selling price is a combination of cost plus profit.

If you chose A, you found the percentage that the cost was of the selling price ($^{125}/_{420}$). It's a good idea to circle what the question is asking for so that you keep it in mind. The mere fact that the answer you got is one of the multiple choices does not in the least indicate that you got the right answer — only that you may have given the test-makers the satisfaction of seeing another fish go for the bait.

21. **A.** Simply add up the numbers on the graph: January = 20, February = 30, March = 30, April = 10, May = 50, and June = 40.

The first question after a graph is usually ridiculously simple. It checks that you know how to read the chart. Do not look for tricks or traps built into the first question. Those will come later.

22. **E.** Did I getcha on this problem? You know from your previous calculations on the preceding problem that the new employees hired from January through June of 1994 sum up to 180. However, that does not mean there are only 180 employees in the entire company. Looking at the second graph gives you the idea that there probably were other employees to begin with. Be careful of assuming too much on a graph.

23. **E.** If you chose A, congratulations — you're normal! Most people do not read graph questions carefully enough to find the cunningly laid trap. The title of the second graph is "Number of New Employees Laid Off by Company X." Yes, if you waste your time adding up all the numbers, you will find that there were 280 *new* employees laid off during those years. You don't, however, have any idea how many old employees were laid off as well.

24. **E.** This relatively simple problem takes two steps. In May there were 50 new employees hired. 50 = 20% or $\frac{1}{5}$ of the total (250) employees. If there were 250 employees and 50 of them were laid off, then $\frac{1}{5}$ (back to that same number!) were laid off.

    Did you see the shortcut in this problem? The 50 in the top graph is the same as the 50 in the bottom graph. Therefore, whatever percent you have for the top graph is the same as the percent for the bottom graph. You did not need to go through all of that work.

25. **E.** First, figure out the percent increase in new hires between January and February. Twenty new employees were hired in January while 30 were hired in February. To find a percent increase or decrease, you use the formula: *Number increase or decrease divided by original whole* (the number you began with). Here, that's $\frac{10}{20} = \frac{1}{2} = 50\%$.

    The number of employees laid off in 1994, according to the bottom graph, was 50. The number laid off in 1995 was 50 percent greater than this. Fifty percent of 50 is $\frac{1}{2}$ of 50, or 25. Add 50 + 25 = 75.

    Did you fall for choice D? The increase in new hires between January and February was 10, but this does not mean that the number of layoffs in 1995 was 10 higher than the number in 1994. You must figure the *percentage*.

26. **D.** This is your basic butt-ugly question. It isn't hard; it just is a pain in the posterior, taking a lot of time and busy work. It's a time-rate-distance problem (you should remember the DIRT formula from the math review: Distance Is Rate × Time).

    Make a chart.

Person	Time	Rate	Distance
Michelle	9 hours	($33\frac{1}{3}$ kph)	300 kilometers
Devrae	(54 hours)	($11\frac{1}{9}$ kph)	(600 kilometers)

    The values in parentheses are things you have to find for yourself.

    First, you know that Michelle leaves home at noon and travels until 9 p.m., a time of 9 hours. If she goes 300 kilometers in those 9 hours, her rate of speed is 300 ÷ 9 = $33\frac{1}{3}$ kph.

    Devrae travels twice as far, for a total of 600 kilometers. She goes a third as fast as Michelle: $11\frac{1}{9}$ kph. (Divide $33\frac{1}{3}$ by 3.) That means that she goes 600 kilometers at $11\frac{1}{9}$ kph, for a total of 54 hours. The trap is that Devrae doesn't leave until 3 hours after Michelle, or at 3 p.m. Monday. When you add 54 hours to 3 p.m. Monday, you get 9 p.m. Wednesday.

    From 3 p.m. Mon. to 3 p.m. Tues. = 24 hours

    From 3 p.m. Tues. to 3 p.m. Wed. = 24 hours

    From 3 p.m. Wed. to 9 p.m. Wed. = <u>6 hours</u>

    54 hours

    If you forgot that Devrae didn't leave the same time as Michelle and said she left at noon on Monday, your calculations would have her arriving at 6 p.m. Wednesday, answer C. Wouldn't you just hate to do all this work and then make that stupid mistake? Circle things in the problem that smell fishy so you don't *carp* (complain) later about missing them.

27. **C.** This problem is much easier than it looks. The number of degrees in the interior angles of *any* triangle is 180, regardless of that triangle's size or shape. Therefore, $\frac{180}{180} = 1$, which is 100 percent.

If you chose D, you thought that because the big triangle looks to be twice the size, or area, of the little one, the big triangle's angles must be twice as large as the little triangle's. When it comes to what's inside, all triangles are created equal. Regardless of the size or shape of the triangle, its interior angles sum up to 180 degrees.

28. **C.** The key to this problem is knowing that Gigi and Neville work at the same rate. If they finish the lawn in 12 hours, each did $1/2$ of the job in 12 hours, meaning it would have taken Gigi working alone 24 hours to finish the lawn. Because 3 hours is $1/8$ of 24 hours, she could have done $1/8$ of the job in that time.

29. **E.** Does this problem make you think of Egyptian hieroglyphics? Join the crowd. Instead of just saying, "That's History, babe!" and guessing at this problem, make it easy to work through by *plugging in numbers*. Choose a number that has an easy square root. Make $x = 9$ (because $\sqrt{9} = 3$). Now solve the question: $(\sqrt{9} + 2) \div (\sqrt{9} - 2) = (3 + 2) \div (3 - 2) = 5/1 = 5$. Keep in mind that 5 is the answer to the problem. It is not the value of x. Jot the 5 down to the side, draw a circle around it, put arrows pointing to it, do whatever it takes to remind yourself that the answer you want is 5. Now go through each answer choice, seeing which one comes out to be 5. Only choice E works:

$$(9 + 4\sqrt{9} + 4) \div 9 - 4 = (9 + 4 \times 3 + 4) \div 5 = (9 + 12 + 4) \div 5 = 25/5 = 5.$$

Be very, very careful not to put 3 in for x in the problem. The $x = 9$; the square root of $x = 3$. I suggest you make a chart to the side, simply writing down $x = 9$ and ANSWER = 5.

When you plug in numbers, go through every single answer choice, *soporific* (sleep-inducing) though that may be. If you started with choice E, for example, and made a careless mistake, you would find that choices D, C, and B didn't work either . . . and probably choose A by process of elimination. If you take just a second to work out A, you'll see that it too is wrong, alerting you to the fact that you made a careless mistake somewhere.

For you algebra addicts who can't live without your fix: Simplify the denominator by multiplying each side through by $(\sqrt{x} + 2)$:

$[(\sqrt{x} + 2) \div (\sqrt{x} - 2)] \times [(\sqrt{x} + 2)(\sqrt{x} + 2)]$. The numerator is $(\sqrt{x} + 2) \times (\sqrt{x} + 2)$. Use FOIL (First, Outer, Inner, Last) to multiply these: $\sqrt{x} \times \sqrt{x} = x$. Then $\sqrt{x} \times 2 = 2\sqrt{x}$. Next, $2 \times \sqrt{x} = 2\sqrt{x}$. Finally, $2 \times 2 = 4$. Add: $x + 4\sqrt{x} + 4$.

The denominator is $(\sqrt{x} - 2) \times (\sqrt{x} + 2)$. Use FOIL again to multiply these: $\sqrt{x} \times \sqrt{x} = x$. Then $\sqrt{x} \times 2 = 2\sqrt{x}$. Next, $\sqrt{x} \times -2 = -2\sqrt{x}$. Next, $-2 \times +2 = -4$. The $2\sqrt{x}$ and $-2\sqrt{x}$ cancel each other out, leaving you with $x - 4$.

If you took my advice in Chapter 11 and memorized some basic FOIL problems, you knew immediately that $(a + b)(a + b) = a^2 + 2ab + b^2$ (just substitute x for the a, and 2 for the b). You knew that $(a + b)(a - b) = a^2 - b^2$ (substitute the x for the a and the 2 for the b). If you haven't memorized these, go back to Chapter 11 and do so now.

30. **A.** If 10 plums cost a cents, then each plum costs $1/10 \, a$ and 2 plums cost $2/10$ or $1/5 \, a$. If 6 apples cost b cents, then each apple costs $1/6 \, b$ cents, and 2 apples cost $2/6 \, b$ or $1/3 \, b$ cents. Now use 15 as a common denominator for 5 and 3. Convert: $1/5 \, a = 3/15 \, a$, and $1/3 \, b = 5/15 \, b$.

This pretty confusing problem assumes you have some sort of sick fetish for fractions. You can work out the problem without stooping so low as to deal with those nasty little things at all. The easy way to do this problem is to substitute numbers for the variables. Let $a = 10$, such that each plum costs 1 cent and two plums cost 2 cents. Let $b = 6$ such that each apple costs 1 cent and 2 apples cost 2 cents. Then the total is 4 cents. Plug the same values into the answer choices to see which one comes out to be 4. In a, you have $3(10) + 5(6) = 60$ divided by $15 = 4$.

You must check all the answer choices when you plug in your own numbers. Did you get as far as choice E? If you did, you got 4 there as well ($1/15 \times 10 \times 6 = 1/15 \times 60 = 4$). What now? If you get more than one correct answer based on the terms you plug in, plug in different terms and try again.

Suppose that this time $a = 20$ and $b = 6$. Now the cost of each plum is 2 cents, making the cost of two of them 4 cents. The cost of the apples remains the same. Two plums (4 cents) plus 2 apples (2 cents) = 6 cents. The new answer you're looking for is 6.

Don't bother going through all of the answer choices again. You've already narrowed the field down to A or E; try just those two.

Now choice A is $(60 + 30) \div 15 = 90 \div 15 = 6$. It works. Choice E is $^1/_{15} \times 20 \times 6 = ^1/_5 \times 120$, which does not equal 6. Throw away E; A is correct.

I was incredibly kind on this problem in making A the correct answer. A less magnificent human being would have switched answers A and E. Then, if you didn't bother plugging in the answers for every single answer choice and stopped at A, you would fall for the trap. And wouldn't that be a horrible way to finish this section?

Section 5

1. **D.** If you chose A, you fell for the trap. What if $a = 1$ and $b = 1$? Then $c = 1$ and the columns are equal. What if $a = 2$ and $b = 2$? Then $c = 4$ and A is the answer. If the answer DEEEE-pends on what you plug in, choose D.

2. **B.** If you chose C, you fell for the trap. Think of this one logically: 16 is a smaller number than 32, and $^1/_{32}$ is a smaller number than $^1/_{16}$. You're taking a smaller part of a smaller number in Column A. You're taking a bigger part of a bigger number in Column B. If you actually worked it out, you got .5 for Column A and 2 for Column B. *If the columns look equal, there's a trap.* If you immediately choose C without doing any calculations, you are playing the test maker's game.

3. **B.** 50% more than $^1/_2$ is not 100 percent. *If the columns look equal, there's a trap.* If you chose C, you fell for the trap. Prove this to yourself by plugging in numbers. Say that $x = 2$. $^1/_2$ of 2 = 1. 50% more than 1 = 1.5. Prove it again by plugging in a bigger number like 100. $^1/_2$ of 100 = 50. 50% more than 50 = 75.

4. **C.** Do you remember your Pythagorean Triples? (These were covered in detail in Chapter 10.) One very useful triple applies to a 30: 60: 90 triangle like this one. The ratio is: *side: side* $\sqrt{3}$: 2 *side*. The *side* portion is opposite the 30-degree angle, which here is side a. The 2 side portion is opposite the 90-degree angle, which here is side c. You could plug in numbers to prove this to yourself. Let $a = 1$. Then $b = 1\sqrt{3}$, and $c = 2$. Plug in 100. $a = 100$, $b = 100\sqrt{3}$, and $c = 200$.

5. **A.** Plug in numbers. $a = 4$, $b = 3$, $c = 2$, $d = 1$.

$$\frac{b+c}{d} = \frac{3+2}{1} = 5$$

In Column B $\quad \dfrac{d+c}{b} = \dfrac{1+2}{3} = \dfrac{3}{3} = 1$

Remember when you plug in numbers in a series, *plug in consecutive terms first and then nonconsecutive terms.* Let's try 100, 80, 50, and 1.

$$\frac{b+c}{d} = \frac{80+50}{1} = 130$$

Column B $\quad \dfrac{1+50}{80} = \dfrac{51}{80}$

6. **D.** If you chose C, you fell for the trap. Let $a, b, c = 1, 2, 3$. The average equals $1 + 2 + 3$ divided by 3 = 6 divided by 3 = 2. Column A: $3 - 1 = 2$. Column B = 2. So far the answer is C. The key words here are *so far*. Plug in more than once. Let's say that a is 3, b is 2, and c is 1. The average is still 2. However, Column A now comes out to be: $1 - 3$, which is -2. That is smaller than Column B because b is $+2$. The answer therefore DEEEE-pends on the terms.

7. **B.** If you chose C, you fell for the trap (how totally sick and tired are you by now of hearing that?) 252 – 226 = 26. If a problem is this easy, think about it twice. There is a great math saying: "To get from here to there, subtract, then add back one." Try this with small numbers. Say that 3 people are waiting in line and hold ticket numbers 3, 4, and 5. If you simply subtract 5 – 3, you're saying that only two people get in. However, you know that Mr. 3, Mr. 4, and Mr. 5 all get in. Subtract 5 – 3 = 2, and add back 1: 2 + 1 = 3. For this problem: Subtract 252 – 226 = 26 and then add back one: 26 + 1 = 27. Twenty-seven people were seated.

8. **B.** Drop an altitude from point B to the base. Let's label that line BX. It is parallel and equal to line AD, making it 6. Triangle BXC is a 30:60:90 triangle. The ratio of sides in a 30:60:90 triangle is: $side:side \sqrt{3}: 2\ side$. BX = 6. XC = $6\sqrt{3}$. BC = 12. To find a perimeter add all the sides. $6 + 8 + 12 + 6\sqrt{3} + 8$ (DX = AB). The sum is $34 + 6\sqrt{3}$. Estimate now; don't actually try working out a square root. You know that $\sqrt{3}$ is more than 1, such that $6 \times$ "more than 1" is more than 6. Then 34 + "more than 6" is more than 40.

9. **A.** Along the 6-foot side of the patio there are $(6 \times 12 = 72; 72 \div 3 = 24)$ 24 tiles. Along the 8-foot side $(8 \times 12 = 96; 96 \div 3 = 32)$ 32 tiles. $24 \times 32 =$ more than 600. Do *not* bother doing the exact calculations. The question does not ask you for an ultimate solution, only to compare the quantities.

10. **C.** To multiply like bases, add the exponents. 6 + 5 + 1 (did you forget that any number is the same as itself to the first power?) + –3 = 9. If you chose D, you forgot the purpose of the question. True, you do not know what x^9 equals. But you don't care. You are only to compare the quantities, not solve the problem. $x^9 = x^9$ no matter what x equals.

11. **D.** This should have been a ridiculously easy problem if you know your *number sets,* including prime and composite numbers. (I once got a call from a seriously irate mother of one of my students. She had heard her son talking about our tutorial and was convinced I was teaching the kid about "number sex." I told her that as far as I know, there's no sex you can count on!) Prime numbers are those numbers that can be factored down only into 1 and themselves. Prime numbers greater than 5 include 7, 11, 13, 17, and so on to infinity. Composite numbers can be factored down into more than 1 and themselves. Composite numbers less than 9 include 8, 6, and 4. If x is 7 and y is 8, then column B is bigger. If x is 11 and y is 8, then column A is greater. Because the answer DEEE-pends on what you plug in, choose D.

12. **D.** For the average of $x + y$ to equal 90, $x + y$ must equal 180. That tells you that $a + b = 180$ because the interior angles in any quadrilateral sum up to 360. However, you do not know how much of that 180 is a and how much of that 180 is b. If you chose C, you fell for the trap. Angle a could be 179 and angle b could be 1 or vice versa. *If the columns look equal, there is a trap. In addition, a problem that is not drawn to scale is often choice D, because you cannot rely on anything given in the picture.*

13. **A.** If you chose C, you fell for the trap. If the columns look equal . . . well, you know this trick by now. In Column B, $(a + 5)(a – 5)$ is $a^2 + 5a – 5a – 25 = a^2 – 25$.

Cancel quantities that are identical on both sides. Dump the a^2 to get 0 in Column A versus –25 in Column B. Because a negative is less than 0, Column A is greater.

Could you think of a short way to do this problem? How about . . . Plug In Numbers??! Let $a = 1$. Column A is 1. Column B is $6 \times –4$ which is –24. Column A is bigger. Let $a = 2$ (remember you always, always, always plug in more than once; otherwise, you would never know whether the answer DEEE-pends on what you plug in.) If $a = 2$, Column A = 4. Column B = $7 \times –3 = –21$.

Have you noticed that every answer comes out to be $a^2 – 25$ in Column B? This just goes to prove to you that plugging in numbers gives you the same thing as doing the problem algebraically. For those of you who have been out of school for a while and are terrified by the mere thought of algebra, take heart in knowing that plugging in numbers not only almost always gives you the right answer, but probably gives it to you more quickly than does the algebra.

14. **C.** To multiply like bases, add the exponents. One over a^3 is the same as a to the negative third power. Add: $a^{10} \times a^5 \times a^{-3} = a$ to the $(10 + 5 – 3) = a^{12}$.

Did you choose D because you don't know what a is? The value of a here, although unknown and unknowable given the information you have, is irrelevant. $a^{12} = a^{12}$, no matter what the value of a. This question is very similar to number ten. If both questions *befuddled* (confused) you, return to Chapter 11.

15. **C.** Use the Pythagorean theorem to find BC. $AC = 2$ (it goes from –2 to –4, a distance of 2 units). $AB = 4$ (it goes from 2 to 6, a distance of 4 units). The Pythagorean theorem says $a^2 + b^2 = c^2$. Here $2^2 + 4^2 = c^2$. Then $4 + 16 = c^2$ so $20 = c^2$. Next, $c = \sqrt{20}$. Take out a perfect square of 4. $\sqrt{20} = \sqrt{4} \times \sqrt{5} = 2\sqrt{5}$.

16. **B.** The pattern is a set of 4. Divide 4 into 38, and you get 9 with a remainder of 2. That means that the 36th student ($4 \times 9 = 36$) finishes a set of four. The 37th student starts a new set with math. The 38th student has his English homework checked.

17. **B.** If you chose C, my work here has been in vain. Do you really think a problem this close to the end would be that simple? True, to find an average, you add up the terms and then divide by the number of terms. But this is a Time-Rate-Distance problem and the terms here aren't simply 600 and 400. You have to find the length of time spent flying at 600 mph and the length of time spent flying at 400 mph, and then add *those* and divide.

If you think logically about this problem, know the answer can't be C, but don't want to spend time working it out, you can eliminate a few more answers. You know that the plane must go more time at the slower rate and less time at the faster rate. That means the average is going to be less than half of the "average" 500 mph. Immediately narrow your answers down to A and B. If you're in a hurry, guess and go.

You probably wanted to make a simple Time-Rate-Distance chart for this problem, right? Good thinking . . . but it won't work here. To make a chart of that sort, you have to have at least two of the three variables. For example, if you know rate and distance, you can find time. But here, you have only one variable, rate. You cannot solve for time and distance. What do you do now? Find a ratio.

Use a common multiple of 12 (actually, 1200) miles. In 2 hours, the plane traveling at 600 mph will go 1200 miles. In 3 hours, the plane traveling at 400 miles will go 1200 miles. To find the average, add 600 twice and 400 three times . . . and then divide by 5, not by 2. $600 + 600 + 400 + 400 + 400 = 2400$. $^{2400}/_5 = 480$.

Did the words "arithmetic mean" confuse you? They're put there to prevent any lawsuits over confusion of terms. The "average" can mean different things to different people; the "arithmetic mean" is the precise term. Don't worry about it. The info in parentheses is usually there to cover fundamental anatomical regions in case of litigation. You can ignore it.

18. **C.** If you're like me, your first response to the question "What's the difference between the mode and the median?" was "Median has more letters." But seriously, folks . . . A mode is the most common number, the one that repeats the most times. In this case, the number 8 is found three times. The median is the number in the middle.

The median is not the same as the mean. The mean is the average; add all the terms, and divide by the number of terms. The median is the number in the middle *when the terms are arranged in order* (you can't just look at the problem the way it is and choose the middle term). Just think of the median strip in the middle of the highway. In order, these numbers are $5\frac{1}{2}$, 6, 6, $6\frac{1}{2}$, $6\frac{1}{2}$, 7, $7\frac{1}{2}$, 8, 8, 8, $8\frac{1}{2}$. The middle or median term is 7. Mode – median = $8 - 7 = 1$.

19. **A.** This problem is easier than it looks. If two circles have the same area, they have the same radius because the area of a circle = π radius^2. The radius of circle Y is 5 as well. The diameters of the two circles are 10 each because the diameter of a circle is twice its radius. The length of the rectangle is 20, therefore, and the width is 10.

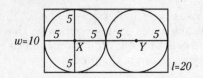

The area of a rectangle is *length* × *width*: $20 \times 10 = 200$.

20. **E.** Did I trick you, or did you remember this type of problem from the math review? When a question asks you to put items in a line, the answer often depends on the order in which the items are arranged — that is, the figure could be like this:

or like this:

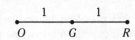

or even like this:

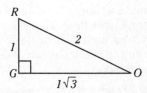

Because you don't know the layout of the flags, you can't answer the question.

21. **A.** The first question after a graph usually is very simple, requiring you only to glean some basic information. Add the numbers: $60 + 70 + 50 + 20 = 200$. Because the left-hand axis tells you these numbers are in hundreds of thousands of dollars, you have 200 00 (hundred) 000 (thousand), or 20,000,000. You'll notice that all the answer choices have the same digits. The test makers assume you can add the numbers on the graph. They are testing your carelessness, trying to trap students who don't take the time to read the axes of the graph.

22. **B.** To find a percentage, put *is* over *of*: what percentage is publicity (900,000) of total (7,000,000). Dump all the zeros. (In problem 21, you didn't care about the digits, but about the number of zeros. A quick look at the answer choices here will tell you the digits are important, the number of zeros is not.) You have $^9/_{70}$. You know that's more than 10 percent but less than 20 percent. The only possible answer is B. You don't have to do a lot of division.

Any time you catch yourself doing long division or multiplying a long problem, stop and see whether you've missed a shortcut somewhere. The point of the problem is not to test your calculating skills but your analytical reasoning skills.

Were you able to read the second axis, the one on the right-hand side? Don't make the mistake of assuming it's the same as the one on the left. It begins at 20 and goes from there.

23. **C.** In 1980, publicity expenses were $700,000; double that to $1,400,000. To find the percentage, put the part ($1,400,000) over the whole ($5,000,000). Get rid of the zeros and look at this as 28%.

Always glance at the answer choices first, to see how precise your answers have to be. In this case, the choices were so far apart you could guesstimate wildly.

24. **E.** Look at the title of the right-hand axis. It tells you how much money was spent on publicity. It does not break that publicity down. You can't assume all the money was spent on television; maybe some of it went to radio, newspapers, men walking around in sandwich signs, whatever.

25. **D.** In 1970, publicity expenses were "90." (Don't bother figuring out all the zeros; make life easy.) In 1990, they were "40." If you put choice A, for the 500, you probably subtracted 90 – 40, got 50, and figured the digits were right. Wrong. To find a percent greater than, put *the number greater than* over the original whole. In this case, the number greater than is 50 (90 – 40). Put that over the original whole (what something is greater than) to get $^{50}/_{40} = 1.25 = 125$ percent.

   If you got confused on the percent part of the problem, go back to the percentages section of the math review. This concept is covered as "percent increase/decrease."

26. **B.** Understand what the explanation means. (The explanation is made up for this particular problem. There is no such thing as a "circle" operation in the real world — only in the little universe of the GRE. Lucky you.) The explanation says that you have a number in the circle. If that number in the circle is a prime number (meaning that it can be divided only by itself and 1), you add the number in the circle to the square of the number in the circle.

   If the number in the circle is a composite number (one that can be divided by something other than just 1 and itself), you square that number and subtract the number in the circle from the square.

   Ugh. You may have to repeat those instructions to yourself a few times. You're really just substituting the number in the circle for the x in the appropriate equation.

   Because 4 is composite, you use the second line of the explanation. Square 4: $4^2 = 16$. Subtract from that the number in the circle. $16 – 4 = 12$.

   Because 5 is prime, you add it to its square: $5 + 25 = 30$.

   Add the two results: $12 + 30 = 42$.

   This problem has all sorts of trap answers. If you used the first line ($x + x^2$) for both terms, you got 50. If you used the second line ($x^2 – x$) for both terms, you got 32. If you confused prime and composite numbers, using the composite rule for 5 and the prime rule for 4, you got 40.

27. **D.** A triangle perfectly inscribed in a rectangle has an area exactly half the area of the rectangle. This blessed event happens because the base of the triangle is the same as the length of the rectangle. The height of the triangle is the same as the width of the rectangle.

   The height of triangle *EBC* is not *BE*; it is a straight line dropped from point *B* to the base. Remember that a height is always perpendicular to the base.

   Because the area of a triangle is half the area of the rectangle, the shaded or leftover area must be the other half. The halves are equal.

28. **B.** The formula for the interior angles of a polygon is $(n - 2)180$ degrees, where n stands for the number of sides. To find out one particular angle in a regular polygon (regular means that all sides are equal and that all angles are equal), divide by n. Your equation, therefore, is as follows:

$$\frac{(n - 2)\, 180}{n} = 135$$

Cross-multiply: $135n = (n - 2)180$. Distribute the terms in the parentheses: $135n = 180n - 360$.

Now the problem is a regular algebra problem:

$$360 = 180n - 135n$$

$$360 = 45n$$

$$8 = n$$

The figure has eight sides — trap answer D. If each side is 3, the perimeter (the sum of all the sides) is 24.

29. **C.** If the area of the hubcap is 16π, its radius is 4 (because the area of a circle is πr^2). That means that the radius of the wheel is twice that figure, or 8. The circumference of the wheel would be 16π (because circumference $= 2\pi r$, or πd). A wheel rolls the length of its circumference in one revolution. Multiply 16 by 3.14 (3.14 is an approximation for π); you get 50.24. Divide that figure into 400 to get 7.96, or approximately 8 revolutions.

The important point to remember here is that a wheel travels the length of its circumference in one revolution. Finding the circumference isn't the hard part; the hard part is knowing that finding the circumference is what you're supposed to do.

30. **E.** If you chose A, you fell for a trap. (Are you getting totally sick and tired of hearing that expression? Don't fall for so many traps, and you won't have to hear it.) Dividing like bases means subtracting the exponents. For a^{10} divided by a^5, subtract: $10 - 5 = 5$. Divide 6 by 3 and get 2. You know that the first term is $2(a^5)$, so you can narrow the answers down to C, D, and E.

b^5 divided by b^9 is b^{-4}, or $1/b^4$. That result eliminates answers C and D; you can stop now.

Just for fun, though, I'll finish this calculation. c^7 divided by c^7 is 1. Any number divided by itself is 1. (Or you could think of it as being $7 - 7 = 0$; any number to the 0 power is 1.) The answer 1 doesn't change in the multiplication; ignore it.

Answers A and B were traps for people who tried $10 \div 5 = 2$ instead of subtracting exponents.

Answers C and D were traps for people who forgot that a negative exponent is in the denominator, not the numerator. ***Remember:*** 2^{-3} really is $1/2^3$. If you forgot this, return to the thrilling math review.

Section 6

Questions 1–5

This is an ordering game in which you are to determine the order of wealth of the parties. Whenever you encounter an ordering game, be sure to note whether the question wants the answer "forwards" or "backwards" (for example, from richer to poorer or poorer to richer). This sort of question often has a trap answer.

First, make a pool of the players: *E, R, J, G, L.* Put the pool neatly to the side of the game and refer to it often. Now use the statements to determine the relative wealth of the parties.

Do not begin by making lines or spaces to fill in. Instead, make a freehand diagram and leave plenty of space between the parties. Be especially careful to put in all the possibilities, even if doing so seems a lot of tedious work.

From statement I, you know to put *E* above *R* and *E* below *J.*

From statement II, you put *G* below *L.* For the moment, place that information to the side as you do not have any relationship yet between *J E R* and *L G.*

Statement III gives you *R* above *G* and *R* below *J.*

Your final order is as shown below. Notice that you do not have any idea where *L* goes, except that it is above *G*.

→ L ?

J

→ L ?

E

→ L ?

R

 → L?

G

1. **D.** Just look at the chart and see that Julie is above Glenn.

2. **A.** Place Lauren at the top of the list. Now read the list from the bottom to the top because the question called for a listing from poorest to richest. If you put answer B, you fell into the trap of putting the answer backwards. And didn't I warn you about that?

3. **D.** If Edgar is above Roxanne and below Julie, then Roxanne must be below (less rich than) Julie. Statement I gave you that information such that its repetition in statement III was superfluous.

4. **C.** The UCLA fan criticizes basketball without a shot clock because he feels that such a rule allows for a game that does not capture the essence of basketball. There is nothing in his statement that criticizes a team's decision to employ a certain strategy. In fact, he implies that a team with inferior talent should play a keep-away game if it is permitted to do so by the rules. He simply says that a team should not be allowed such an option. Nevertheless, the North Carolina fan, by defending the use of a keep-away game, acts as if the UCLA fan said teams shouldn't play such a game. This is what choice C says. For the North Carolina fan to dispute what the UCLA fan said, he should defend the lack of a shot clock, saying something on the order of how such a lack adds intrigue, and so on. Choice A does not really capture the scope of the argument. Neither fan discussed excitement or boredom. The UCLA fan seems to imply that the lack of a shot clock produces a not-so-satisfying game, so if the North Carolina fan thinks choice A, he hasn't misunderstood too much.

   A casual reader might be tempted by choice E because the North Carolina fan defends deployment of a keep-away strategy. In addition, this is not what the UCLA fan said. All he said was that a keep-away game could allow a team with inferior ability to win. This does not mean that teams with superior ability could not perfect a keep-away strategy and win many games by using such a strategy. Therefore, choice E qualifies on the criterion of the North Carolina fan's misunderstanding. What makes this choice incorrect is that the response does not address the issue of superior teams. The North Carolina fan would have to say something along the lines of, "The shot clock produced a fair game. Teams with superior talent played superb games of keep-away and won many basketball games."

   Choices B and D are implied by the UCLA fan. The North Carolina fan should have picked up on these points. If he had, there would have been less misunderstanding.

5. **C.** The author leaps to his conclusion that Angelica will attend Harvard after saying that Angelica has been accepted to Harvard. This follows only if it is true that acceptance definitely leads to attendance, which is what choice C says. If choice C is not true, it is easy to see how Angelica could attend elsewhere or nowhere at all.

Choice A is very tempting in that it seems to force Angelica to attend Harvard. However, Angelica could decide to stay out of school next year. Choice C is matter of fact and says that students such as Angelica will attend Harvard. Because choice A does not guarantee Angelica's attendance, it is eliminated.

Choices B and E both miss the mark in that they focus on what it takes to qualify for Harvard. Angelica has already been accepted, so she presumably has met Harvard's standards. She may choose, even after fighting so hard to get where she is, not to attend Harvard.

Choice D expresses a reason why many students desire to attend Harvard, but this does not force Angelica to attend. She may decide that, for other reasons, she will attend a different school; prestige may not be important to her.

Questions 6–12

This game requires you to make a calendar. This is one of the most straightforward, simple games you are likely to encounter. First, put the pool of events to the side: ride, cash, and day off from work. Next, draw a calendar.

Statement I tells you that all three events must be present for Valerie to get the tickets: a ride from her neighbor, cash from the bank, and a day off from work.

Statement II doesn't help you for the moment; leave it alone and come back to it later.

Statement III tells you that you can eliminate Sunday, Thursday, and Friday because Valerie could not get a ride from her neighbor on those days because Valerie's husband can't take the kids to the park.

From Statement III you learn that *bank open in the afternoon* and *a day off* amount to the same thing. That's good news because you can virtually eliminate one variable. That is, you don't have to treat going to the bank and getting off from work as two separate contingencies. Either both happen or neither happens. Because the bank is open in the afternoon only on Wednesday and Thursday, those are the only days Valerie can get off work. From statement III you eliminated Thursday, meaning Wednesday is the only day Valerie can get tickets.

6. **C.** Just look at the calendar. Wednesday is the only day that all three qualifying events happen in order for Valerie to get a ticket: she can get a ride from her neighbor (because Valerie's husband is available to take the neighbor's kids to the park), the bank is open in the afternoon, and Valerie can get off work to get cash.

7. **D.** If the bank is open in the afternoon, Valerie can get off work and go there any weekday. However, she can't get the ride on Thursday or Friday because her husband isn't free to take the neighbor's kids to the park. That means that Valerie can get tickets only on Monday, Tuesday, and Wednesday, two *additional* days. Did you choose C? You didn't read the question carefully. It doesn't ask how many days Valerie can get the tickets, but how many *additional* days she can get the tickets given the bank's new hours. Because Valerie already had one day to get the tickets, having three days now means that she has only two additional days.

8. **E.** This question is trickier than it looks. Even though Valerie doesn't have to go to the bank anymore to get money, she still can get off work only on the days when the bank is open in the afternoon. That means she can get off work only on Wednesday and Thursday. But she can't get a ride from her neighbor on Thursday because Valerie's husband isn't free to take the kids to the park on Thursday. In other words, nothing changes with this question. Valerie still has only Wednesday to get the tickets.

Have you noticed that you've used the information about when Valerie's husband can take the kids to the park for every single question so far? An exclusionary statement, one that tells you when something cannot happen, is a good solid piece of information that often narrows the answer choices down significantly.

9. **E.** Now this question is actually easier than it looks. (I must be slipping in my *dotage*, or old age.) Because Valerie can get a ride on the bus, she no longer cares about her neighbor, meaning she doesn't care when her own husband is free to take the neighbor's kids to the park. That whole consideration is wiped out. She still cares when the bank is open in the afternoons, because that's the only time she can get off from work. If the bank is open every afternoon except Tuesday, she can get off work to get the tickets every weekday except Tuesday.

10. **B.** Valerie no longer has to go to the bank, but she still can get off work to see the concert only when the bank is open in the afternoons: Wednesday and Thursday. Thursday is still excluded. Valerie's husband couldn't sit for the neighbor's kids then, so he can't go to the bank instead.

11. **B.** Because of the word *except*, you need to find the one choice that does *not* provide a reason for why those who live in high-achieving districts are likely to complain.

    Choice A is very explicit in presenting a factor that accounts for complaints from high-achieving districts.

    Choices C and D are especially good at explaining why parents in high-achieving districts are more likely to complain than those in low-achieving districts.

    Choice E doesn't focus on how high scores lead to complaints in the way that choices C and D do, but is it still provides an explanation. For all we know, the activists are complaining about low scores in other districts, but the fact remains that they live in a high-achieving district. The complaints are coming from such a district, even though they're not about that district.

    Choice B is the credited response for a similar reason that choice E is not the answer. Choice B describes complaints about high-achieving districts, but the complaints are coming from parents who live outside the districts. As such, choice B does not explain so many who live in high-achieving districts complain.

12. **D.** The ad claims that Apogee test prep is effective in raising scores. To determine whether this is true, you need to see some data regarding score increases. The problem is that the data indicate scores after the students took the course but do not say by how many points (if any) these scores are higher than what the students were scoring before they took the course. Choice D would allow you to subtract pre-scores from post-scores and see whether the scores went up.

    Choice A is very close in that the before-or-after issue does address the heart of the matter about whether scores went up. The problem with choice A is that it isn't of much use when it comes to evaluating the ad's claim. If these scores were achieved before Apogee students took the course, what were they after? Maybe these scores are very impressive, but perhaps the scores were even higher after. (It does seem incongruous that the company would not list the higher, after-course course scores, but the possibility mentioned does exist.) If these scores were achieved after the course, what were they before? Simply knowing whether the scores were from before or after is not enough information.

    From one perspective, choice B is useful in that the numbers cited in the ad wouldn't be impressive if the national averages were much higher. However, even if the scores are low, it's still possible that Apogee raised scores. It could be that Apogee students had very low pre-scores.

    The argument to rule out choice C is similar to that used to rule out choice A. Consumers may not enroll in the course if they find out that the course doesn't last long; but even if this were the case, the course could still raise scores.

    Choice E is out. A GRE student would certainly like to earn scores that will get him/her into graduate school, but the ad makes no claim about this. Even scores that are not good enough for graduate school may still be substantially higher than they were earlier.

Questions 13–19

First, make life much easier by changing the professors' names to initials: *E, F, G, H, I, J, K, L*. Map out the connections. *E* is a key figure, so place her near the center and go from there. You don't have to go in order. It's easier to get a chain going by working with common elements. For example, $E \rightarrow F$ links up with $F \rightarrow K$, which links with $K \rightarrow E$. This is shown in the following figure:

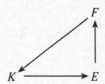

The completed map is as follows:

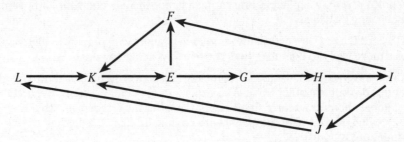

13. **B.** Try the shortest route for both $E \rightarrow F$ and $E \rightarrow G$. For $E \rightarrow F$, it's $E \rightarrow F \rightarrow K \rightarrow E \rightarrow G \rightarrow H \rightarrow I \rightarrow J \rightarrow L$. That's nine days. For $E \rightarrow G$, it's $E \rightarrow G \rightarrow H \rightarrow I \rightarrow J \rightarrow L \rightarrow K \rightarrow E \rightarrow F$. It's still nine days, so the answer is *B*.

    Note that it's crucial to go from $H \rightarrow I \rightarrow J$. Going from $H \rightarrow I \rightarrow F$ forces a lot of extra circulating to pick up *J*. Similarly, $H \rightarrow J \rightarrow L$ forces a lot of extra connections to pick up *I*.

14. **B.** *G* must see the journal if it is to reach *H* (nobody else connects to *H*). The others can be avoided.

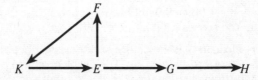

15. **A.** Look at the original diagram. Choice A will work because $F \rightarrow K \rightarrow E \rightarrow G \rightarrow H \rightarrow I \rightarrow J \rightarrow L$.

    Choices B and C are similar in that *G* and *H* will get the journal twice as one tries to hit all the professors on the periphery of the figure. *K* will receive the journal twice in an effort to get to both *L* and *F*, so choice D is out. *L* (choice E) looks tempting as it's on the periphery, but *K* will have to receive the journal twice as it circulates to both *F* and *J*.

16. **C.** Work backwards. To get the journal back to *G*, it must get to *E*. To get to *E*, it must get to *K*. The shortest route from *G* to *K* is through *H* and *J*. This produces the following route:

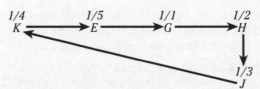

    If *E* receives the journal on 1/5, *G* will receive it on 1/6.

17. **D.** Trace out the routes.

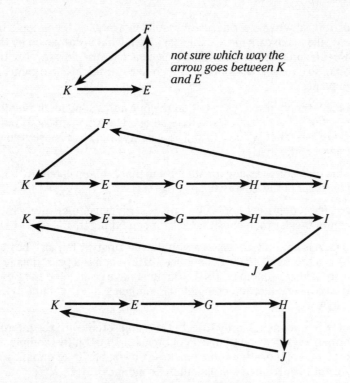

not sure which way the arrow goes between K and E

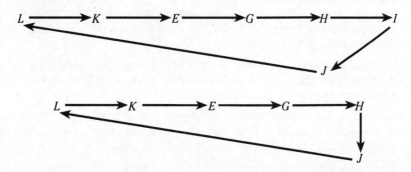

If you stopped here, you fell for the trap and chose B. Yes, there are four routes, but the last two routes may be modified by having *J* go to *L* before *K*.

18. **B.** The argument concludes that cars are safer than planes. The evidence used to support this conclusion deals with the percentages of accidents that result in fatalities. To justify the conclusion, one must assume that these percentages are the key statistic, that there isn't some other factor that would overcome the supposed 50 to 1 advantage in favor of cars.

Choice B wipes out the 50 to 1 advantage. One out of every two plane accidents results in fatalities, but for every two plane accidents, there are approximately one million car accidents. One percent of one million is ten thousand. This means that for every one fatal plane accident, there are about ten thousand fatal car accidents. Suddenly, cars don't seem so safe.

Choices A and C simply indicate that humans make efforts to ensure that planes and flying are as safe as possible. They do not weaken the argument, though, because it still could be the case that many people die in plane accidents.

Choice D apparently indicates that cars are more dangerous than the one percent figure suggests, but it doesn't affect the picture enough to make this the correct answer. The one percent figure takes everything into account, so even with this information, the fact remains that only one percent of car accidents result in fatalities. The information does indicate that when a car accident results in a fatality, there could be multiple deaths, and this would make cars more dangerous than what is conveyed by the one percent figure. However, consider that the typical plane accident involves more than one hundered people, so choice D doesn't do enough to contradict that argument that cars are safer than planes.

Choice E simply provides detail on the one percent figure. It is still the case that only one percent of car accidents result in fatalities. The argument does not make the claim that cars are safer than planes no matter what type of road is used, so choice E does not get to the heart of the matter.

19. **E.** This question is asking for something that is inconsistent with the information, meaning that four of the items will be consistent.

These four consistent items don't necessarily have to be *true*, which makes this type of question trickier than ones that ask for something that is true or false.

Choice A is not only consistent with the information but also has to be true. Economics 101A is a prerequisite for Economics 101B, which is a prerequisite for Economics 101C. If you are taking Economics 101C, you must have completed the prerequisite Economics 101B. To have taken and completed Economics 101B, you must have completed Economics 101A.

Choice B is not necessarily true, but it is consistent with the information. Nothing in the information forces you to take Economics 101B upon the completion of Economics 101A. Completion of the latter course makes you eligible for Economics 101B, but it is not sufficient to guarantee enrollment in Economics 101B.

This necessary/sufficient distinction is very important on the GRE. Economics 101A is necessary for Economics 101B, but it is not sufficient. The connection between Economics 101A and 102A is an example of a sufficient condition. Completion of Economics 101A forces you to take Economics 102A, so 101A is sufficient for 102A. It is not, however, necessary in that you might be eligible for 102A even without taking 101A. The stimulus does not shut off this possibility.

Choice C is tough to eliminate, but it is consistent. Economics 101A is certainly a requirement for Economics 101B, but there may be several other requirements. If you did not fulfill these prerequisites, you are ineligible.

Choice D is not necessarily true because Economics 101A and 101B are necessary, but not sufficient, for Economics 101C, but the choice still presents a situation that is entirely possible. Choice D is consistent, so it is not the answer.

Choice E is impossible. If you will not take Economics 102A, you could not have completed Economics 101A because 101A guarantees 102A. Without taking Economics 101A, you are ineligible for Economics 101B, in direct contradiction to choice E.

Questions 20–25

A good way to keep track of this matching game is to use circles to represent the first-, second-, and third-place finishers. Divide each circle into three parts so that you can "match up" the horse, jockey, and trainer for each position. Here is the basic plan:

Here is the initial diagram.

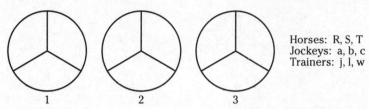

Fill in the diagram as much as you can, starting with the most concrete information. The last rule can readily be incorporated into the diagram.

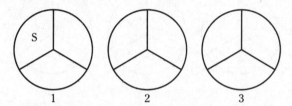

Next, work with the second and third rules as they contain a common element, Lukas, which may allow for additional deductions. If Lukas and Jolley are not consecutive, they must be first and third, or vice versa. This also means that Whittingham must be second. Draw both possibilities:

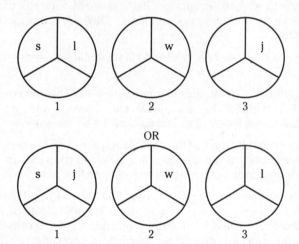

The second rule states that l and b go together, so insert this information into both of the above possibilities. Here is the result:

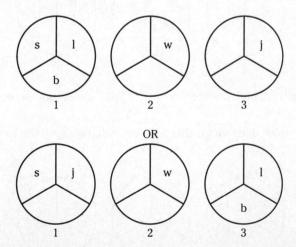

The first rule can now be incorporated into the diagram. (It would not have been so easy had you started with this rule.)

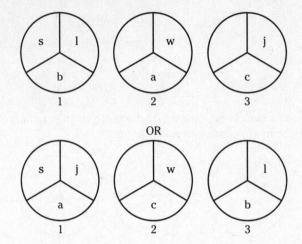

20. **E.** What you are trying to do is to determine which choice would force you to go with the bottom options of your two diagrams. Note that it is only this bottom option in which Cordero's horse finished second.

    Choice A works with either option. Choice B works only with the top option. Choice C works with either option, as does choice D. Choice E is the answer because it fits only the bottom option.

21. **A.** Check each rule, one at a time, and eliminate inconsistent choices until only one choice is left.

    The straightforward, final rule eliminates choice E. The first rule makes choice B impossible. Choice D violates the second rule, and choice C would make it impossible to separate Lukas and Jolley. This leaves choice A as the answer.

22. **D.** The hypothetical nature of the choices requires you to spend some time checking whether each choice is a possibility. It is usually a good idea to skip such a question temporarily and do the other, shorter questions first.

    Choice A is out because Rive Ridge could finish second or third with Cordero (see the diagrams). Choice B is false: The Jolley-trained horse would be first. Choice C is similar to A. Here, Rive Ridge could finish second or third. Choice D is the answer because only the bottom option can accommodate it. The following results:

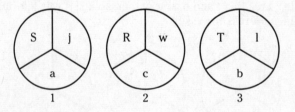

    Rive Ridge is second. Choice E is false. If Tim Tam is trained by Whittingham, Tim Tam is second.

23. **C.** Make a quick diagram for this problem. You must use the top option from the master diagram.

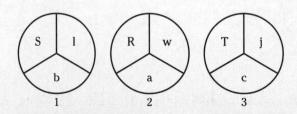

Choice C is the only one consistent with this diagram.

24. **B.** Consult the bottom diagram. Choice B is the only option that fits. A little thinking about the nature of a multiple-choice test would enable you to eliminate choices D and E right off the bat. If either one were an answer, the test maker would have to accept two choices, which won't happen. If, say, choice D were an answer, one of A, B, or C would also be correct because one of these three has to train Rive Ridge.

25. **B.** Only the top diagram allows Whittingham to finish ahead of Jolley. Choice E is definitely out because it has to be true. Choices A, C, and D are all possible. Choice B is the answer because Lukas trains Baeza's horse.

Part VII
The Part of Tens

Andy felt almost certain that this was the experimental section of the GRE.

In this part . . .

This unit is your reward for surviving the previous 22 chapters. No brain power is required for these next few chapters. You don't have to work through math problems, don't have to memorize new vocabulary, and don't have to stimulate the synapses at all. These chapters are just for fun, but they do provide invaluable information, such as relaxation techniques to help you get through the GRE. Read on.

Chapter 23

Ten Wrong Rumors about the GRE

In This Chapter (Remember: These statements are WRONG!)

▶ Filling in all A's is better than jumping around, filling in A, B, C, D, or E

▶ You can't have three A's in a row

▶ "Lesser-taken" tests are easier

▶ Tests in different parts of the country are different

▶ You can't study for the GRE

▶ Your GRE score will be about the same as your SAT score from high school

▶ The GRE tests IQ

▶ You must pass certain classes to take the GRE

▶ Your score won't improve if you keep retaking the GRE

▶ The GRE has a passing score

Sure, you've heard them: the horror stories about the GRE. Rumors abound, growing more wild with each telling: "You have to know calculus!" (Absolutely not.) "It's an open book test this year!" (You *wish!*)

As a test preparation tutor, I get calls all the time from students trying to check out the latest scuttlebutt. Here are ten of the most common stories that make the rounds every year— as dependable as oversleeping the morning of your most important final.

Filling in all A's is better than jumping around, filling in A, B, C, D, or E

You have a one-in-five chance of getting a random guess correct (one-in-four in QCs, because the answers there are only A, B, C, and D, without an E). Each new problem starts over again with that same chance. Whether you fill in all A's or alternate letters makes no difference; your chances are still one-in-five. Remember: The GRE does not penalize you for wrong answers. The GRE is one of a very few exams that reward you for random guessing. Never leave an answer bubble blank on this test.

You can't have three A's in a row

You *can* have three A's or B's or whatever in a row. It's highly unlikely, but not absolutely impossible, that you may even have *four* in a row. But counting how many of the same answers in a row you have is the last thing you should worry about. Suppose that you check your answer grid and discover that you have three A's in a row: Which one are you going to change? You may change the *wrong* one— who knows? You waste time and gray matter when you try to outsmart the test makers with thoughts such as "Well, I put a C last time, and I haven't had a D in a while, so I'd better put down a D."

"Lesser-taken" tests are easier

Many students take the GRE in October or June. These seem to be the most popular times to take the test. Tests given in December, for example, often are taken by fewer students. Some students have heard a rumor that the test makers are trying to encourage more people to take the December exam by making that exam easier. Wrong. The exams are all designed to have the same basic level of difficulty. They often test the same concepts "forwards and backwards." A test in October, for example, may give you a ratio and ask you to find a total; a test in December may give you a total and ask you to find a ratio. That's why looking over your old test before retaking the exam is a good idea. (Yes, you can get a copy of your old tests. Currently, the charge is $10. This Test Disclosure service, however, is not available for all administrations. For example, the April 1995 test was disclosed, but the June 1994 test was not.)

Tests in different parts of the country are different

No way. You can't fly out to Snakes Navel, Kansas, to take the test, thinking that the students there get to take easier exams than do the students in big cities like Detroit or New York City. Everyone suffers the same indignities. All exams are the same — or at least at the same level of difficulty.

You can't study for the GRE

Why would I be writing this book if that were so? Studying can be done in two ways, each advantageous in its own right. First is the last-minute cram, a review in a few weeks of the types of questions, the approach to each question, the tricks and traps involved in the questions. (Sound familiar? This method is what you've been working on throughout this book.) Second is the long-range study program, in which you learn vocabulary and work on math questions from your freshman year in college on. Obviously, if you've got a year or two to put into this, you should get a dynamite score. Most people, however, benefit greatly from even a few weeks or months of intense study.

Your GRE score will be about the same as your SAT score from high school

Are you the same person you were in high school? You have matured, learned better study habits, and suddenly come to the shocking realization that no one is going to spoon-feed you anymore. You may not have studied much for the SAT, figuring that you could always get into *some* college, somewhere, no matter what your score. You were probably right. But getting into graduate school is not as easy. There aren't as many graduate programs as undergraduate programs, making the competition more cutthroat. Because you realize this, you study harder and study smarter. Besides, your vocabulary almost certainly has improved significantly after four years of college, and vocabulary is usually the most difficult portion of the exam for students.

The GRE tests IQ

Nope. The GRE supposedly tests your ability to do well in graduate school. Some cynics say that all the GRE tests is your ability to take the GRE. Getting into a debate over that point is rather futile because you're stuck with taking the GRE, and worrying about it just wastes brain power you can use for other things. But be reassured that the GRE is not an IQ test. You can learn to improve your GRE score with all sorts of tricks, traps, and techniques; that's *much* harder to do on IQ tests.

Have you ever heard of Mensa, the national high-IQ society? Although the GRE is not a measure of IQ per se, if you do well on the GRE, you can sometimes get automatic membership in Mensa (something that looks great on résumés and impresses the socks off dates' parents). Call the local Mensa chapter to find out what the qualifying score is. Hey, you put the effort into getting the score; scarf up all the benefits from the score that you can get.

You must pass certain classes to take the GRE

Although taking classes such as advanced logic or linguistics is useful, let's get real here: Not many people take those courses today. If you are reading this book as a freshman or sopho-more and have the option of taking logic classes, excellent. Doing so will help you with the analytical ability portion of the GRE. But you certainly don't *have* to have a class like that to do well on the GRE. (That's a relief; who has room for that class in an already overcrowded curriculum?) As far as math goes, the GRE tests basic algebra, geometry, and arithmetic. A year of algebra and a year of geometry are sufficient. In short, the GRE has no "required courses" or "prerequisites."

Your score won't improve if you keep retaking the GRE

Although having your score jump hundreds of points is uncommon, it has happened. Your improvement depends on the reason your score was low in the first place and on how much you study before retaking the exam. If your score was low because you didn't understand the format of the exam (for example, you looked at a QC question and wondered where the answer choices were!), you can certainly improve that score by taking a few practice exams and becoming more comfortable with the question styles. If your score was low because you fell for all the traps set in the GRE, you can improve your score by going through these materials, learning to recognize those traps, and studying the tips and tricks for avoiding those traps. But it is unrealistic for a slow reader to think that a few weeks of study is going to double her reading speed or for someone who doesn't understand algebra at all to think she can get a year's worth of algebra instruction in an afternoon. You do need *some* basics under your belt.

The study time you put into preparing for the second exam is also important. If you take the exam, get back your scores, register for another exam, and then just a few days before the second exam begin studying again, you may as well forget it. Although experience helps, your score won't soar simply because you've done this before. You have to study for the second test, or you'll repeat the mistakes of the first.

The GRE has a passing score

You can't pass or fail the GRE, but a particular graduate school may have a cutoff score that you must get to be considered for admission. This score is often based on your GPA. A school may decree, for example, that if your GPA is in the 3.0 to 3.5 range, you can get an 1100 (com-bined verbal and math), but if your GPA is in the 2.5 to 3.0 range, your GRE must be at least a 1200. You will want to find out the GRE ranges considered acceptable by the schools you are considering.

Chapter 24

Ten Dumb Things You Can Do to Mess Up Your GRE

. . . .

In This Chapter

▶ Losing concentration

▶ Panicking over time

▶ Messing up numbering on the answer grid

▶ Rubbernecking

▶ Cheating

▶ Worrying about the previous sections

▶ Worrying about the hard problems

▶ Transferring information from problem to problem or section to section

▶ Forgetting to double-check

▶ Looking back and playing "coulda-shoulda"

. . . .

*T*hroughout this book, you've learned techniques for doing your best on the GRE. I'm sorry to say, however, that there are just as many techniques for messing up big time on this test. Take a few minutes to read through them now, to see what dumb things people do to blow the exam totally. By being aware of these catastrophes, you may prevent their happening to you.

And no — no Booby Prize is awarded to the student who makes the greatest number of these mistakes.

Losing concentration

When you're in the middle of an excruciatingly boring Reading Comprehension passage, the worst thing you can do is let your mind drift off to a more pleasant time (last night's date, last weekend's soccer game, the time you stole your rival school's mascot and set it on the john in the dean's private bathroom). Although visualization (picturing yourself doing something relaxing or fun) is a good stress-reduction technique, it stinks when it comes to helping your GRE score. Even if you have to pinch yourself to keep from falling asleep or flaking out, stay focused. The GRE is less than five hours of your life. You've had horrible blind dates that lasted longer than that, and you managed to survive them. This too shall pass.

Panicking over time

Every section on the GRE is 30 minutes long. You know going into the test exactly how many questions are in each section and therefore how many minutes you have per question. It's not as if this is some big mystery. You can waste a lot of time and drive yourself crazy if you keep flipping pages ahead, counting up how many more questions you have to do. Because questions go from easier to harder and you're probably going to guess wildly at some of the super-hard ones at the end anyway, why fuss? You can do what you can do; that's all. Looking ahead and panicking only wastes time and is counterproductive.

Messing up numbering on the answer grid

Suppose that you decide to postpone doing question number 11, hoping that inspiration will strike. Then you accidentally put the answer to question 12 in question 11's blank . . . and mess up all the numbers from that point on. After you answer question 30 and suddenly realize that you just filled in bubble number 29 and have one bubble left— *aaargh!* Stroke City! It's easy for me to say, "Don't panic," but the chances are that your blood pressure will go sky-high, especially when you eyeball the clock and see that only one minute is left.

If you have a good eraser with you (which is one of the things I suggested in Chapter 2 that you bring with you), the wrong answers on the answer grid should take only a few seconds to erase. But how on earth are you going to resolve all those problems and reread and reanswer all the questions? You're not; you're going to thank your lucky stars you bought this book and took the following advice: When you choose an answer, *circle that answer in your test booklet first* and *then* bubble in the answer on the answer grid. Doing so takes you a mere gigasecond and helps you not only in this panic situation, but also as you go back and double-check your work.

Throughout this book, I've reminded you that random guesses can't hurt you on the GRE, as there is no penalty for wrong answers (except on the CAT, the Computer Adaptive Test, discussed in Chapter 1). Never leave a bubble blank. Make a random guess. Fill in the bubble; then put an arrow in the margin of the test booklet (*not* on the answer grid) to remind yourself to review that question. Because you have all the bubbles filled in, you won't make a numbering error like the one described in the preceding paragraph.

Rubbernecking

Rubbernecking is craning your neck around to see how everyone else is doing. Forget those bozos. You have too much to do on your own to waste precious seconds checking out anyone else. You don't want to psyche yourself out by noticing that the guy in front of you is done with his section and is leaning back whistling while you're still sweating away. Maybe the guy in front of you is a complete moron and didn't notice that the booklet has yet another page of problems— so he did only half the section. After the exam booklet is in front of you, don't look at anything but it and your watch until time is called.

Try not to sit by the clock in the classroom. Because everyone looks at the clock constantly, you may become self-conscious, thinking that *you're* being checked out. People staring at you every few seconds can be quite distracting. You need to keep your mind entirely on what you're doing, not continually looking up and catching someone's eye.

Cheating

Dumb, dumb, *dumb!* Cheating on the GRE is a loser's game — it's just plain stupid. Apart from the legal, moral, and ethical questions, let's talk practicality: You can't predict what types of vocabulary words will show up in the questions; what are you going to do, copy a dictionary on the palm of your hand? All the math formulas you need can't fit onto the bottom of your shoe. Copying everything that you *think* you may need would take more time than just learning it. Besides, the GRE tries very hard to test critical reasoning skills, not just rote memorization. The test never asks a question as straightforward as, "How many degrees in a triangle?" The questions require thinking and reasoning, not just copying down a formula. Short of having a brain transplant, cheating is impractical.

Worrying about the previous sections

Think of the GRE as seven separate lifetimes. You are reborn six times and so get six more chances to "do it right." Every time the proctor says, "Your time is up. Please turn to the next section and begin," you get a fresh start. The GRE rules are very strict: You cannot go back to a previous section and finish work there or change some of your answers. If you try to do so, the proctor will catch you, and you'll be in a world of hurt. But suppose that you're too ethical even to consider going back to earlier material. There's still the problem of *worrying* about the previous section. If you're now in section five working on math, you shouldn't be racking your brain trying desperately to remember what that frustrating, "it's-on-the-tip-of-my-tongue" vocabulary word in section four was. Forget one section as soon as you enter the next. Think of it as you would a new boyfriend or girlfriend in your life: Out with the old, in with the new.

Worrying about the hard problems

As you've learned throughout this book, the GRE contains some incredibly hard problems and questions. Forget about 'em. Almost no one gets them right, anyway. A ridiculously few total 1600s (remember, many schools use only the verbal and math scores, ignoring the analytical score) are scored every year, and if you get into the 1500s or even the 1400s, you are in a super-elite club of only a few percentage of the thousands and thousands of students who take the GRE annually. Just accept the fact that you either won't get to or can't answer a few of the final questions, and learn to live with your imperfection. If you do go fast enough to get to the hard questions, don't waste too much time on them. Scan them; if you can't think of how to begin, choose an answer at random. Then go back and double-check your easy questions. Keep reminding yourself that every question counts the same in a section, whether that question is a simple $1 + 1 = 2$ or some deadly word problem that may as well be written in Lithuanian.

Transferring information from problem to problem or section to section

Each question exists in its own little world. If $x = 17$ in question number 15, it does not necessarily equal that in question number 16 (unless a note says something like, "Questions 15 and 16 refer to the following information"). Now, that sounds incredibly simplistic, but it's surprising how many people transfer information from problem to problem. This practice is especially prevalent in dealing with symbolism questions. If you learn in a symbolism question in section one that $\triangle{x} = 25$, it is highly unlikely to equal 25 in another triangle problem in section five.

Here's something that can make your life totally miserable: Even vocabulary can change! Remember that words can have more than one meaning. *Check*, for example, can be used in section two to mean reviewing for mistakes (as in, "Dominic decided to *check* his project before turning it in, knowing that he often made careless mistakes"). But in section four, *check* may mean to stop or to hold back (as in, "Frances wanted to tell her daughter off, but *checked* herself, deciding not to make a scene in public"). Erase everything from your mind as you move from one question to another.

Forgetting to double-check

If you finish a section early, go back and double-check the *easy* and *medium* questions. Don't spend more time trying to do the hard questions. If a question was too hard for you five minutes ago, it's probably still too hard for you. Your brain capacity probably hasn't doubled in the last few minutes. If you made a totally careless or dumb mistake on an easy question, however, going back over the problem gives you a chance to catch and correct your error. You're more likely to gain points by double-checking easy questions than by staring openmouthed at the hard ones. *Remember:* Every question counts the same. A point you save by catching a careless mistake is just as valuable as a point you earn, grunting and sweating, by solving a mondo-hard problem.

Looking back and doing "coulda-shoulda"

Don't discuss the questions with your friends in the bathroom during break. They don't really know any more than you do. All your friends may tell you that they got answer A for question five — but maybe answer A was the trap answer and they all fell for it. If you get depressed because you chose answer B, you're only hurting yourself. Maybe B was right all along, and you alone brilliantly recognized and circumnavigated the trap. Why put yourself through this grief? The same is true after the exam. Forget the postmortem. You did what you did; no sense fretting about it until you get back your scores.

Chapter 25

Ten Relaxation Techniques You Can Try Before and During the GRE

Most people are tense before the test, with butterflies dancing in their stomachs. The key is to use relaxation techniques that keep your mind on your test and not on your tummy.

Breathe deeply

Breathing is grossly underrated. Breathing is good. Take a deep breath until your belly expands, hold your breath for a few counts, and then expel the air through your nose. (Be careful not to blow anything but air, especially if your boyfriend/girlfriend is sitting next to you.) Try not to take short, shallow breaths, which could cause you to become even more anxious, as your body is deprived of oxygen. Try breathing in and out deeply while reciting something in your mind, such as your favorite line from a movie, or a totally stupid, mindless rhyme.

Rotate your head

Try to see behind your head. Move your head as far as possible to the right until you feel a tug on the skin on the left side of your neck. Then reverse it and move your head all the way to the left until you feel a tug on the skin on the right. Move your head back, as if you're looking at the ceiling, and then down, as if looking at your feet. You'll be surprised how much tension drains out of you as you do this a few times.

Be careful that you perform this exercise with your eyes closed and make what you're doing obvious. You don't want a suspicious proctor to think you're craning your neck to look at someone else's answer grid.

Hunch and roll your shoulders

While breathing in, scrunch up your shoulders as if you're trying to touch them to your ears. Then roll them back and down, breathing out. Arch your back, sitting up super-straight, as if a string is attached to the top of your head and is being pulled toward the ceiling. Then slump and round out your lower back, pushing it out toward the back of your chair. These exercises relax your upper and lower back. They are especially useful if you develop a kink in your spine.

Cross and roll your eyes

Look down at your desk as you're doing this so that people won't think you're even stranger than they already know you are. Cross your eyes and then look down as far as you can into your lower eyelids. Look to the right and then up into your eyelids and then look to the left. After you repeat this sequence a few times, your eyes should be refreshed.

Shake out your hands

You probably do this automatically to try to get rid of writer's cramp. Do it more consciously and more frequently. Put your hands down at your sides, hanging them below your chair seat, and shake them vigorously. Imagine all the tension and stress going out through your fingers and dropping onto the floor.

Extend and push out your legs

While you're sitting at your desk, straighten your legs out in front of you; think of pushing something away with your heels. Point your toes back toward your knees. You feel a stretch on the backs of your legs. Hold for a count of three and then relax.

Cup your eyes

Cup your hands, fingers together. Put them over your closed eyes, blocking out all the light. You're now in a world of velvety-smooth darkness which is very soothing. Try not to let your hands actually touch your eyes. (If you see stars or flashes of light, your hands are pushing down on your eyes.)

Rotate your scalp

Put your open hand palm-down on your scalp. Move your hand in small circles. Feel your scalp rotate. Lift your hand and put it down somewhere else on your scalp. Repeat the circular motions. You're giving yourself a very relaxing scalp massage.

Curtail negative thoughts

Any time you feel yourself starting to panic or thinking negative thoughts, make a conscious effort to say to yourself, "*Stop!*" Don't dwell on anything negative; switch over to a positive track. Suppose that you catch yourself thinking, "Why didn't I study this math more? I saw that formula a hundred times but can't remember it now!" Change the script to, "I got most of this math right; if I let my subconscious work on that formula, maybe I'll get it, too. No sense worrying now. Overall, I think I'm doing great."

Before the test or during a break, visualize

Don't do this *during* the test; you just waste time and lose concentration. Before the exam, however, or at the break, practice visualization. Close your eyes and imagine yourself in the exam room, seeing questions you know the answers to, cheerfully filling in the answer grids, happily finishing early and double-checking your work. Picture yourself leaving the exam room all uplifted, and then five weeks later, getting your scores and rejoicing. Think of how proud your parents are of you. Imagine the acceptance letter you get from the graduate school of your dreams. Picture yourself driving a fire-engine-red Ferrari ten years from now, telling the *Time* magazine reporter in the passenger seat that your success started with your excellent GRE scores. The goal is to associate the GRE with good feelings.

Index

Here's a complete listing of IDG Books' ...For Dummies® titles

Title	Author	ISBN	Price
DATABASE			
Access 2 For Dummies®	by Scott Palmer	ISBN: 1-56884-090-X	$19.95 USA/$26.95 Canada
Access Programming For Dummies®	by Rob Krumm	ISBN: 1-56884-091-8	$19.95 USA/$26.95 Canada
Approach 3 For Windows® For Dummies®	by Doug Lowe	ISBN: 1-56884-233-3	$19.99 USA/$26.99 Canada
dBASE For DOS For Dummies®	by Scott Palmer & Michael Stabler	ISBN: 1-56884-188-4	$19.95 USA/$26.95 Canada
dBASE For Windows® For Dummies®	by Scott Palmer	ISBN: 1-56884-179-5	$19.95 USA/$26.95 Canada
dBASE 5 For Windows® Programming For Dummies®	by Ted Coombs & Jason Coombs	ISBN: 1-56884-215-5	$19.99 USA/$26.99 Canada
FoxPro 2.6 For Windows® For Dummies®	by John Kaufeld	ISBN: 1-56884-187-6	$19.95 USA/$26.95 Canada
Paradox 5 For Windows® For Dummies®	by John Kaufeld	ISBN: 1-56884-185-X	$19.95 USA/$26.95 Canada
DESKTOP PUBLISHING/ILLUSTRATION/GRAPHICS			
CorelDRAW! 5 For Dummies®	by Deke McClelland	ISBN: 1-56884-157-4	$19.95 USA/$26.95 Canada
CorelDRAW! For Dummies®	by Deke McClelland	ISBN: 1-56884-042-X	$19.95 USA/$26.95 Canada
Desktop Publishing & Design For Dummies®	by Roger C. Parker	ISBN: 1-56884-234-1	$19.99 USA/$26.99 Canada
Harvard Graphics 2 For Windows® For Dummies®	by Roger C. Parker	ISBN: 1-56884-092-6	$19.95 USA/$26.95 Canada
PageMaker 5 For Macs® For Dummies®	by Galen Gruman & Deke McClelland	ISBN: 1-56884-178-7	$19.95 USA/$26.95 Canada
PageMaker 5 For Windows® For Dummies®	by Deke McClelland & Galen Gruman	ISBN: 1-56884-160-4	$19.95 USA/$26.95 Canada
Photoshop 3 For Macs® For Dummies®	by Deke McClelland	ISBN: 1-56884-208-2	$19.99 USA/$26.99 Canada
QuarkXPress 3.3 For Dummies®	by Galen Gruman & Barbara Assadi	ISBN: 1-56884-217-1	$19.99 USA/$26.99 Canada
FINANCE/PERSONAL FINANCE/TEST TAKING REFERENCE			
Everyday Math For Dummies™	by Charles Seiter	ISBN: 1-56884-248-1	$14.99 USA/$22.99 Canada
Personal Finance For Dummies™ For Canadians	by Eric Tyson & Tony Martin	ISBN: 1-56884-378-X	$18.99 USA/$24.99 Canada
QuickBooks 3 For Dummies®	by Stephen L. Nelson	ISBN: 1-56884-227-9	$19.99 USA/$26.99 Canada
Quicken 8 For DOS For Dummies,® 2nd Edition	by Stephen L. Nelson	ISBN: 1-56884-210-4	$19.95 USA/$26.95 Canada
Quicken 5 For Macs® For Dummies®	by Stephen L. Nelson	ISBN: 1-56884-211-2	$19.95 USA/$26.95 Canada
Quicken 4 For Windows® For Dummies,® 2nd Edition	by Stephen L. Nelson	ISBN: 1-56884-209-0	$19.95 USA/$26.95 Canada
Taxes For Dummies,™ 1995 Edition	by Eric Tyson & David J. Silverman	ISBN: 1-56884-220-1	$14.99 USA/$20.99 Canada
The GMAT® For Dummies™	by Suzee Vlk, Series Editor	ISBN: 1-56884-376-3	$14.99 USA/$20.99 Canada
The GRE® For Dummies™	by Suzee Vlk, Series Editor	ISBN: 1-56884-375-5	$14.99 USA/$20.99 Canada
Time Management For Dummies™	by Jeffrey J. Mayer	ISBN: 1-56884-360-7	$16.99 USA/$22.99 Canada
TurboTax For Windows® For Dummies®	by Gail A. Helsel, CPA	ISBN: 1-56884-228-7	$19.99 USA/$26.99 Canada
GROUPWARE/INTEGRATED			
ClarisWorks For Macs® For Dummies®	by Frank Higgins	ISBN: 1-56884-363-1	$19.99 USA/$26.99 Canada
Lotus Notes For Dummies®	by Pat Freeland & Stephen Londergan	ISBN: 1-56884-212-0	$19.95 USA/$26.95 Canada
Microsoft® Office 4 For Windows® For Dummies®	by Roger C. Parker	ISBN: 1-56884-183-3	$19.95 USA/$26.95 Canada
Microsoft® Works 3 For Windows® For Dummies®	by David C. Kay	ISBN: 1-56884-214-7	$19.99 USA/$26.99 Canada
SmartSuite 3 For Dummies®	by Jan Weingarten & John Weingarten	ISBN: 1-56884-367-4	$19.99 USA/$26.99 Canada
INTERNET/COMMUNICATIONS/NETWORKING			
America Online® For Dummies,® 2nd Edition	by John Kaufeld	ISBN: 1-56884-933-8	$19.99 USA/$26.99 Canada
CompuServe For Dummies,® 2nd Edition	by Wallace Wang	ISBN: 1-56884-937-0	$19.99 USA/$26.99 Canada
Modems For Dummies,® 2nd Edition	by Tina Rathbone	ISBN: 1-56884-223-6	$19.99 USA/$26.99 Canada
MORE Internet For Dummies®	by John R. Levine & Margaret Levine Young	ISBN: 1-56884-164-7	$19.95 USA/$26.95 Canada
MORE Modems & On-line Services For Dummies®	by Tina Rathbone	ISBN: 1-56884-365-8	$19.99 USA/$26.99 Canada
Mosaic For Dummies,® Windows Edition	by David Angell & Brent Heslop	ISBN: 1-56884-242-2	$19.99 USA/$26.99 Canada
NetWare For Dummies,® 2nd Edition	by Ed Tittel, Deni Connor & Earl Follis	ISBN: 1-56884-369-0	$19.99 USA/$26.99 Canada
Networking For Dummies®	by Doug Lowe	ISBN: 1-56884-079-9	$19.95 USA/$26.95 Canada
PROCOMM PLUS 2 For Windows® For Dummies®	by Wallace Wang	ISBN: 1-56884-219-8	$19.99 USA/$26.99 Canada
TCP/IP For Dummies®	by Marshall Wilensky & Candace Leiden	ISBN: 1-56884-241-4	$19.99 USA/$26.99 Canada

DUMMIES PRESS™

10/31/95

The Internet For Macs® For Dummies® 2nd Edition	by Charles Seiter	ISBN: 1-56884-371-2	$19.99 USA/$26.99 Canada
The Internet For Macs® For Dummies® Starter Kit	by Charles Seiter	ISBN: 1-56884-244-9	$29.99 USA/$39.99 Canada
The Internet For Macs® For Dummies® Starter Kit Bestseller Edition	by Charles Seiter	ISBN: 1-56884-245-7	$39.99 USA/$54.99 Canada
The Internet For Windows® For Dummies® Starter Kit	by John R. Levine & Margaret Levine Young	ISBN: 1-56884-237-6	$34.99 USA/$44.99 Canada
The Internet For Windows® For Dummies® Starter Kit, Bestseller Edition	by John R. Levine & Margaret Levine Young	ISBN: 1-56884-246-5	$39.99 USA/$54.99 Canada

MACINTOSH

Mac® Programming For Dummies®	by Dan Parks Sydow	ISBN: 1-56884-173-6	$19.95 USA/$26.95 Canada
Macintosh® System 7.5 For Dummies®	by Bob LeVitus	ISBN: 1-56884-197-3	$19.95 USA/$26.95 Canada
MORE Macs® For Dummies®	by David Pogue	ISBN: 1-56884-087-X	$19.95 USA/$26.95 Canada
PageMaker 5 For Macs® For Dummies®	by Galen Gruman & Deke McClelland	ISBN: 1-56884-178-7	$19.95 USA/$26.95 Canada
QuarkXPress 3.3 For Dummies®	by Galen Gruman & Barbara Assadi	ISBN: 1-56884-217-1	$19.95 USA/$26.95 Canada
Upgrading and Fixing Macs® For Dummies®	by Kearney Rietmann & Frank Higgins	ISBN: 1-56884-189-2	$19.95 USA/$26.95 Canada

MULTIMEDIA

Multimedia & CD-ROMs For Dummies® 2nd Edition	by Andy Rathbone	ISBN: 1-56884-907-9	$19.99 USA/$26.99 Canada
Multimedia & CD-ROMs For Dummies® Interactive Multimedia Value Pack, 2nd Edition	by Andy Rathbone	ISBN: 1-56884-909-5	$29.99 USA/$39.99 Canada

OPERATING SYSTEMS:

DOS

MORE DOS For Dummies®	by Dan Gookin	ISBN: 1-56884-046-2	$19.95 USA/$26.95 Canada
OS/2® Warp For Dummies® 2nd Edition	by Andy Rathbone	ISBN: 1-56884-205-8	$19.99 USA/$26.99 Canada

UNIX

MORE UNIX® For Dummies®	by John R. Levine & Margaret Levine Young	ISBN: 1-56884-361-5	$19.99 USA/$26.99 Canada
UNIX® For Dummies®	by John R. Levine & Margaret Levine Young	ISBN: 1-878058-58-4	$19.95 USA/$26.95 Canada

WINDOWS

MORE Windows® For Dummies® 2nd Edition	by Andy Rathbone	ISBN: 1-56884-048-9	$19.95 USA/$26.95 Canada
Windows® 95 For Dummies®	by Andy Rathbone	ISBN: 1-56884-240-6	$19.99 USA/$26.99 Canada

PCS/HARDWARE

Illustrated Computer Dictionary For Dummies® 2nd Edition	by Dan Gookin & Wallace Wang	ISBN: 1-56884-218-X	$12.95 USA/$16.95 Canada
Upgrading and Fixing PCs For Dummies® 2nd Edition	by Andy Rathbone	ISBN: 1-56884-903-6	$19.99 USA/$26.99 Canada

PRESENTATION/AUTOCAD

AutoCAD For Dummies®	by Bud Smith	ISBN: 1-56884-191-4	$19.95 USA/$26.95 Canada
PowerPoint 4 For Windows® For Dummies®	by Doug Lowe	ISBN: 1-56884-161-2	$16.99 USA/$22.99 Canada

PROGRAMMING

Borland C++ For Dummies®	by Michael Hyman	ISBN: 1-56884-162-0	$19.95 USA/$26.95 Canada
C For Dummies® Volume 1	by Dan Gookin	ISBN: 1-878058-78-9	$19.95 USA/$26.95 Canada
C++ For Dummies®	by Stephen R. Davis	ISBN: 1-56884-163-9	$19.95 USA/$26.95 Canada
Delphi Programming For Dummies®	by Neil Rubenking	ISBN: 1-56884-200-7	$19.99 USA/$26.99 Canada
Mac® Programming For Dummies®	by Dan Parks Sydow	ISBN: 1-56884-173-6	$19.95 USA/$26.95 Canada
PowerBuilder 4 Programming For Dummies®	by Ted Coombs & Jason Coombs	ISBN: 1-56884-325-9	$19.99 USA/$26.99 Canada
QBasic Programming For Dummies®	by Douglas Hergert	ISBN: 1-56884-093-4	$19.95 USA/$26.95 Canada
Visual Basic 3 For Dummies®	by Wallace Wang	ISBN: 1-56884-076-4	$19.95 USA/$26.95 Canada
Visual Basic "X" For Dummies®	by Wallace Wang	ISBN: 1-56884-230-9	$19.99 USA/$26.99 Canada
Visual C++ 2 For Dummies®	by Michael Hyman & Bob Arnson	ISBN: 1-56884-328-3	$19.99 USA/$26.99 Canada
Windows® 95 Programming For Dummies®	by S. Randy Davis	ISBN: 1-56884-327-5	$19.99 USA/$26.99 Canada

SPREADSHEET

1-2-3 For Dummies®	by Greg Harvey	ISBN: 1-878058-60-6	$16.95 USA/$22.95 Canada
1-2-3 For Windows® 5 For Dummies® 2nd Edition	by John Walkenbach	ISBN: 1-56884-216-3	$16.95 USA/$22.95 Canada
Excel 5 For Macs® For Dummies®	by Greg Harvey	ISBN: 1-56884-186-8	$19.95 USA/$26.95 Canada
Excel For Dummies® 2nd Edition	by Greg Harvey	ISBN: 1-56884-050-0	$16.95 USA/$22.95 Canada
MORE 1-2-3 For DOS For Dummies®	by John Weingarten	ISBN: 1-56884-224-4	$19.99 USA/$26.99 Canada
MORE Excel 5 For Windows® For Dummies®	by Greg Harvey	ISBN: 1-56884-207-4	$19.95 USA/$26.95 Canada
Quattro Pro 6 For Windows® For Dummies®	by John Walkenbach	ISBN: 1-56884-174-4	$19.95 USA/$26.95 Canada
Quattro Pro For DOS For Dummies®	by John Walkenbach	ISBN: 1-56884-023-3	$16.95 USA/$22.95 Canada

UTILITIES

Norton Utilities 8 For Dummies®	by Beth Slick	ISBN: 1-56884-166-3	$19.95 USA/$26.95 Canada

VCRS/CAMCORDERS

VCRs & Camcorders For Dummies™	by Gordon McComb & Andy Rathbone	ISBN: 1-56884-229-5	$14.95 USA/$20.99 Canada

WORD PROCESSING

Ami Pro For Dummies®	by Jim Meade	ISBN: 1-56884-049-7	$19.95 USA/$26.95 Canada
MORE Word For Windows® 6 For Dummies®	by Doug Lowe	ISBN: 1-56884-165-5	$19.95 USA/$26.95 Canada
MORE WordPerfect® 6 For Windows® For Dummies®	by Margaret Levine Young & David C. Kay	ISBN: 1-56884-206-6	$19.95 USA/$26.95 Canada
MORE WordPerfect® 6 For DOS For Dummies®	by Wallace Wang, edited by Dan Gookin	ISBN: 1-56884-047-0	$19.95 USA/$26.95 Canada
Word 6 For Macs® For Dummies®	by Dan Gookin	ISBN: 1-56884-190-6	$19.95 USA/$26.95 Canada
Word For Windows® 6 For Dummies®	by Dan Gookin	ISBN: 1-56884-075-6	$16.95 USA/$22.95 Canada
Word For Windows® For Dummies®	by Dan Gookin & Ray Werner	ISBN: 1-878058-86-X	$16.95 USA/$22.95 Canada
WordPerfect® 6 For DOS For Dummies®	by Dan Gookin	ISBN: 1-878058-77-0	$16.95 USA/$22.95 Canada
WordPerfect® 6.1 For Windows® For Dummies® 2nd Edition	by Margaret Levine Young & David Kay	ISBN: 1-56884-243-0	$16.95 USA/$22.95 Canada
WordPerfect® For Dummies®	by Dan Gookin	ISBN: 1-878058-52-5	$16.95 USA/$22.95 Canada

ORDER FORM

IDG BOOKS WORLDWIDE

Order Center: **(800) 762-2974** *(8 a.m.–6 p.m., EST, weekdays)*

Quantity	ISBN	Title	Price	Total

Shipping & Handling Charges

	Description	First book	Each additional book	Total
Domestic	Normal	$4.50	$1.50	$
	Two Day Air	$8.50	$2.50	$
	Overnight	$18.00	$3.00	$
International	Surface	$8.00	$8.00	$
	Airmail	$16.00	$16.00	$
	DHL Air	$17.00	$17.00	$

*For large quantities call for shipping & handling charges.
**Prices are subject to change without notice.

Ship to:

Name _____

Company _____

Address _____

City/State/Zip _____

Daytime Phone _____

Payment: ☐ Check to IDG Books Worldwide (US Funds Only)

☐ VISA   ☐ MasterCard   ☐ American Express

Card # _____ Expires _____

Signature _____

Subtotal _____

CA residents add applicable sales tax _____

IN, MA, and MD residents add 5% sales tax _____

IL residents add 6.25% sales tax _____

RI residents add 7% sales tax _____

TX residents add 8.25% sales tax _____

Shipping _____

Total _____

Please send this order form to:
IDG Books Worldwide, Inc.
7260 Shadeland Station, Suite 100
Indianapolis, IN 46256

*Allow up to 3 weeks for delivery.
Thank you!*

IDG BOOKS WORLDWIDE REGISTRATION CARD

RETURN THIS REGISTRATION CARD FOR FREE CATALOG

Title of this book: **The GRE® For Dummies®, 2E**

My overall rating of this book: ❑ Very good [1] ❑ Good [2] ❑ Satisfactory [3] ❑ Fair [4] ❑ Poor [5]

How I first heard about this book:

❑ Found in bookstore; name: [6]

❑ Advertisement: [8]

❑ Word of mouth; heard about book from friend, co-worker, etc.: [10]

❑ Book review: [7]

❑ Catalog: [9]

❑ Other: [11]

What I liked most about this book:

What I would change, add, delete, etc., in future editions of this book:

Other comments:

Number of computer books I purchase in a year: ❑ 1 [12] ❑ 2-5 [13] ❑ 6-10 [14] ❑ More than 10 [15]

I would characterize my computer skills as: ❑ Beginner [16] ❑ Intermediate [17] ❑ Advanced [18] ❑ Professional [19]

I use ❑ DOS [20] ❑ Windows [21] ❑ OS/2 [22] ❑ Unix [23] ❑ Macintosh [24] ❑ Other: [25]_____
(please specify)

I would be interested in new books on the following subjects:
(please check all that apply, and use the spaces provided to identify specific software)

❑ Word processing: [26]

❑ Data bases: [28]

❑ File Utilities: [30]

❑ Networking: [32]

❑ Other: [34]

❑ Spreadsheets: [27]

❑ Desktop publishing: [29]

❑ Money management: [31]

❑ Programming languages: [33]

I use a PC at (please check all that apply): ❑ home [35] ❑ work [36] ❑ school [37] ❑ other: [38] _____

The disks I prefer to use are ❑ 5.25 [39] ❑ 3.5 [40] ❑ other: [41]_____

I have a CD ROM: ❑ yes [42]   ❑ no [43]

I plan to buy or upgrade computer hardware this year: ❑ yes [44]   ❑ no [45]

I plan to buy or upgrade computer software this year: ❑ yes [46]   ❑ no [47]

Name: _____   Business title: [48] _____   Type of Business: [49] _____

Address (❑ home [50] ❑ work [51]/Company name: _____)

Street/Suite# _____

City [52]/State [53]/Zipcode [54]: _____   Country [55] _____

❑ **I liked this book!** You may quote me by name in future
  IDG Books Worldwide promotional materials.

My daytime phone number is _____

IDG BOOKS

THE WORLD OF
COMPUTER
KNOWLEDGE

❑ **YES!**
Please keep me informed about IDG's World of Computer Knowledge.
Send me the latest IDG Books catalog.

COMPUTER
BOOK SERIES
FROM IDG

NO POSTAGE
NECESSARY
IF MAILED
IN THE
UNITED STATES

BUSINESS REPLY MAIL
FIRST CLASS MAIL   PERMIT NO. 2605   FOSTER CITY, CALIFORNIA

IDG Books Worldwide
919 E Hillsdale Blvd, STE 400
Foster City, CA 94404-9691